The Principles of
Monetary Economics

The Irwin Series in Economics

Consulting Editor
Lloyd G. Reynolds *Yale University*

The Principles of
Monetary Economics

JAMES M. BOUGHTON
Associate Professor of Economics
Indiana University

ELMUS R. WICKER
Professor of Economics
Indiana University

 1975

RICHARD D. IRWIN, INC. Homewood, Illinois 60430
Irwin-Dorsey International London, England WC2H 9NJ
Irwin-Dorsey Limited Georgetown, Ontario L7G 4B3

© RICHARD D. IRWIN, INC., 1975

First Printing, February 1975

ISBN 0-256-01667-4
Library of Congress Catalog Card No. 74–24444
Printed in the United States of America

To our parents
and to the spirit of
Allison Krause, Jeffrey G. Miller,
Sandra L. Scheuer, and William K. Schroeder

Preface

This book is an introduction to the economics of money. As the title suggests, the focus is on money rather than banking, on economics rather than business. Nevertheless, we hope that readers will gain an appreciation for the richly varied structure of the financial institutions—the central and commercial banks, the savings institutions, the specialized lenders —through which money is supplied and from which money is demanded. But our motivation for writing this book is a conviction that the best approach to the study of money is to treat it as a market phenomenon. We have tried, therefore, to concentrate on the structure of the monetary system while minimizing the amount of extraneous institutional and historical detail.

Changes in the cost and quantity of money have played a powerful role throughout history in generating economic instability as well as in promoting stabilization. Traditional treatments of the subject, however, have often failed to confront the causal processes by which monetary policy works. Perhaps because governments implement these policies through highly regulated institutions, the topic has long been treated as if it could be described by a few formulas suggestive of mechanical rather than behavioral analogies.

It is our belief that human and corporate behavior are as important in the study of money as they are in the study of history. There exists here an interaction between individuals and institutions, between personal and national interests, that creates a kind of energy that makes monetary policy work. Our goal is to explicate, to criticize, and to implant a lively and lasting interest in that process. We hope that we have provided the reader with a simple but adequate basis for describing and interpreting Federal Reserve actions.

During the four years in which this work evolved, we incurred a great many intellectual debts to colleagues and students who read mimeographed or photocopied versions of preliminary chapters. We hope that these friends will sense a kind of repayment rather than remorse when they see what we have made or failed to make of their suggestions in the pages that follow and will feel either pleased or placated rather than implicated at finding their names therein. Edward Kane, Lloyd Reynolds, and Ronald Tiegen provided wisdom to which both the structure and the detail of our final work owe much. Susan Allen edited our early drafts and forced us to write acceptable English prose. The students at Indiana University served, often amiably, as our test market; we are especially grateful to the participants in the Money Seminar for filtering out a number of impurities. James Fackler, Ernestine Grogg, Raouf Hanna, and Mark Wasserman also provided particularly generous doses of criticism and support. And we are perhaps even more indebted than most authors to our publishers who gave us a lot of rein over a long period of time to enable us to develop the book we wanted to write.

This book in a very real sense is the product of our students and of their insights and inspirations, an acknowledgement to which James Boughton wishes to add a personal explanation. He wishes this book to commemorate the spirit of the students in his money and banking class at Duke University in the spring of 1970 who responded with a remarkable expansion of consciousness in sympathy with the lost students at Kent State University and the protest for which they died.

Not just one but both of us have been sustained by the vitality of the family presided over by Carolyn Wicker, around whose hearth so many irreconcilable differences became mutual beliefs. But what we are most grateful for are all the little ways—the offer of a quiet chair in the sun in Camden, an atelier in Nice, a plate of oysters in New Orleans—that our friends have made it fun for us to write this book.

January 1975
Paris, France   JAMES M. BOUGHTON
Bloomington, Indiana   ELMUS R. WICKER

Contents

part one

Introduction

chapter 1

Money, Banking, and Economics

1.1 INTRODUCTION

Money has the enviable reputation of being the most popular economic good in existence. Have you ever heard of anyone who hated money? Not a day passes when each of us does not enjoy some of the services of money, either as a payments medium or as a desired form of holding our wealth. It makes no difference whether we are 4 or 40; employed or not; male or female; Asian, African, or European.

But knowing how to use money carries no understanding of who produces it, how it is produced, or what powerful effects it may exert on the overall level of economic activity in the country. It may, for example, come as a surprise to the student that commercial banks create money. We tend to associate banking with lending and with money *changing* activity but not with money *creating* activity. But that is because we focus our attention on the narrow role that banks play in our own daily lives rather than on the important functions they perform for the economy as a whole. It is the latter role that we spotlight in this book.

Our central purpose is to describe the role of money in a modern economy: its uses in trade, the way it has evolved and has been supplied over the centuries, the nature of the demand for it, its relationship to general economic activity, and its role in governmental control of the economy. Some of the

3

early chapters, which describe the origins and evolution of money, are necessarily rather general. The later discussions concentrate on the economic system of the United States, though the principles they illustrate are applicable to most developed countries today.[1]

In the course of our analysis of money, we describe the institutional structure in which money is handled in the United States. But we caution the reader at the outset that we are little interested in these institutions—commercial banks, central banks, and savings depositories such as savings and loan associations—for their own sake. We do not offer a complete description of them, of their behavior, or of their history. What we do wish to offer is an understanding of how these institutions affect the performance of our economy.

The method of analysis is economic theory. We anticipate that the reader has been introduced to the concepts of supply and demand and to the economic "laws" that govern them. For the principles of monetary economics are applications of the principles of economic theory. Money and banks do not exist by accident; they exist because they are able to serve us, to satisfy certain economic demands better than the systems that preceded them. Neither do they form a closed or static system; they evolve in order better to supply the services we desire.

Before we begin to analyze the principles of money, we must pause in this first chapter to examine the monetary environment in which we live: money, banking, and economics.

1.2 MONEY

The word *money* serves a variety of purposes in everyday language. Some examples of its semantic versatility are readily recognized in the following expressions:

---

[1] The major exceptions are the economies of the Soviet Union and of other countries patterned after it. There the role of money is quite different from that described here, and it requires a separate analysis. See Nicolas Spulber, *The Soviet Economy*, rev. ed. (New York: Norton, 1969).

1. The president makes a lot of money.
2. The Rockefellers have a lot of money.
3. Please count your money.
4. The dollar serves as money in the United States.

In the first example, the word *money* is being used mal-apropos for *income.* The president makes, or earns, a salary of $200,000 per year. If he is honest, he does not make money. So we must discard this first usage completely if we wish to clarify our thinking about money.

In the second example, money stands in place of wealth. The Rockefellers, for all we know, may have no money at all, though they certainly have an unusually large accumulation of assets of various kinds. If, to suggest the extreme, all of their wealth is in the form of land and oil, we clearly do not wish to identify that wealth with money. People will continue to use this expression as well as the first, in spite of all entreaties from us. But it does confuse, and we urge the reader to join us in helping to bury it.

The third example suggests a definition of money with which we can work. It usually refers only to those financial assets which can be used in payment for goods and services. Most commonly, it refers to currency: paper money and coin. But there is a second means of making payment which has long since replaced currency as the dominant asset for this purpose: checking accounts at commercial banks. And other assets increasingly are being used, including lines of credit (credit cards and the like). Unlike income (which is a flow of payment over time, such as $200,000 per year), these are stocks of assets which may be measured at any specified point in time. Unlike wealth (which is also a stock but is a general collection of assets), these are specific assets used for a specific purpose.

The final example provides yet another meaning: money as an abstract unit of measurement. Prices of goods in the United States are expressed in terms of dollars, and this measurement would not need to be altered if we completely changed the types of assets we used for making payments. Prices in France are quoted in francs; in Italy, the lira is the unit of account. For lack of a separate word, the general term for a country's unit of account is money.

These examples by no means exhaust the possibilities for the word, either in popular usage or in technical discussions of monetary theory. No real purpose other than confusion would be served by a complete catalog. We do suggest that we settle on a single definition at the outset, one that will help to focus the discussion as we go along:

> **Money is any asset which is widely used in an economy as the means of payment.**

A shorthand expression for this concept is that money is the "medium of exchange" in an economy. It is a definition which we shall stretch a bit as we go along, since there is no really clear line dividing the assets which meet this definition from those which do not.[2] In reference to the unit of measurement, it is preferable to use the expression "unit of account." Keep in mind only that money is a flexible concept which we must define so as to make it serve us, so as to be specific enough to distinguish money from other familiar concepts but general enough to reflect the complexities of the real world.

In practice, the assets which most nearly meet our definition are, in the United States and most other Western countries, currency and demand deposits. And in the United States, as we indicated above, demand deposits are the dominant means of payment (Figure 1–1). And this leads us to the second element in our monetary environment.

1.3 BANKING

There is a dizzying variety of financial institutions in the American economy. There are savings and loan associations

---

[2] For a more detailed description of these problems, see Chapter 17, section 17.4.2.

FIGURE 1–1

The Stock of Money in the United States, 1947–73

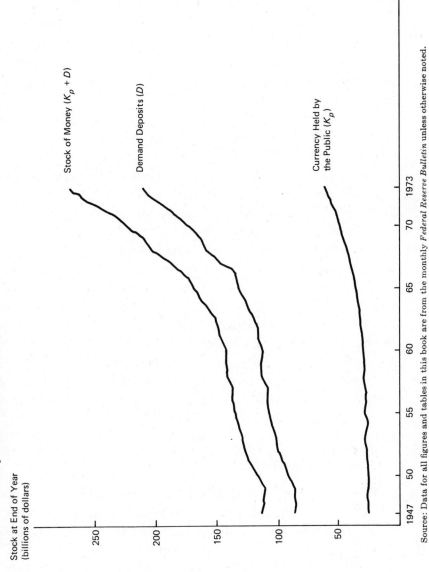

Source: Data for all figures and tables in this book are from the monthly *Federal Reserve Bulletin* unless otherwise noted.

and mutual savings banks, both of which specialize in the *intermediation* of funds between savers and home buyers. They receive deposits mostly from individuals,[3] and they make loans to individuals and businesses, mostly for the purpose of building or buying residential housing. These loans are secured by the value of the homes and are known as *mortgage* loans. There also exist credit unions, pension funds, life insurance companies, and a host of similar specialized financial intermediaries.

It is important to distinguish these intermediaries from commercial banks. When we use the term *bank*, we refer to an institution which is legally empowered to accept *demand* deposits, a type of account against which the owner may write checks which are freely negotiable and which are payable at the bank on demand. Now for the same reasons that it is impossible to delineate precisely money from similar assets, it is impossible to draw a firm line between the activities of banks and those of "thrift institutions" such as savings and loan associations. The latter may permit (in some states) the use of "negotiable orders of withdrawal" against their savings accounts, instruments which differ little from checks. But at the moment, there is a wide gulf between the acceptability of bank checks (or of cash) in payment and the acceptability of the liabilities of any other type of institution. On this empirical basis, we draw the line between banks and other financial intermediaries.

1.3.1 Commercial Banks

There are more than 14,000 commercial banks in the United States, ranging in size from one-room rural offices with well under $1 million in assets, to the mammoth New

---

[3] In the case of savings and loan associations, the deposits are legally ownership shares in the association, and the income on them is a dividend rather than interest. In practice, the distinction is of minor significance.

York and California banks with billions of dollars of assets. Each of these banks is a private business corporation in business to earn profits, but the degree of competition faced by the various banks varies as much as the banks themselves. The smallest banks are likely to monopolize the local markets in which they operate; the largest banks may be part of an oligopoly in their home cities while competing vigorously in national and international lending markets. In terms of sheer size, the industry is heavily concentrated; about one third of the dollar volume of bank loans to businesses in the United States is made by the six largest banks in New York City.

Given this concentration of assets and the importance of a sound banking system to the community, close governmental control is an essential part of the game. Entry into the banking business is carefully regulated both by the federal and state governments. Federal legislation prohibits banks from establishing offices (known as "branches") outside of the state in which the head office is located; and the states may further limit branching within their boundaries. All banks must submit to periodic inspections of their records by federal or state examiners, and most of them are required to publish summaries of their assets and liabilities in local newspapers at least twice each year.

The major purpose of these regulations is to prevent fraud or mismanagement from leading to bank failures as well as to insure that bank services will be fairly provided to all communities, in a competitive environment if possible. The government examiners check both the *liquidity* of each bank's assets (i.e., the ability of a bank to meet withdrawals of deposits out of cash or readily marketable assets, without having to wait until loans are repaid) and its *solvency* (i.e., the net worth of the bank). So the net effect of government control is to establish rather strict limitations on the composition of assets and liabilities held by each bank. The objective of the banker is to maximize his profits within these limitations, though individual banks may place even stricter limits on themselves than do the regulatory authorities.

The nature of the banking business can be grasped more firmly within the context of a *balance sheet*. Abstracting from the great mass of detail shown in such a list of assets and liabilities, the appearance of a typical bank balance sheet is as follows:

Assets	*Liabilities*
Cash assets	Deposits
Currency	Demand deposits
Claims on other banks	Time deposits
Earning assets	Borrowings
Loans	Miscellaneous liabilities
Securities	Net worth
Miscellaneous assets	

TABLE 1–1

An Aggregate Balance Sheet
For all U.S. Commercial Banks
As of December 31, 1973
(in billions)

Assets			*Liabilities*		
Cash assets..........		$118	Deposits............		$682
Currency...........	$ 11		Demand deposits....	$310	
Claims on banks....	107		Time deposits.......	372	
Earning assets.......		684	Borrowings..........		59
Loans..............	495		Miscellaneous........		36
Securities..........	189		Net worth...........		58
Miscellaneous........		33			
Total Assets....		$835	Total Liabilities.		$835

The heart of the bank's portfolio of assets is the part we have labeled "earning assets" (see Table 1–1). The operating income of banks is derived by making loans and purchasing securities. One could further divide loans into a wide variety of types: loans to business customers (the original staple fare for the banking industry and the reason these firms are called "commercial" banks); loans to individuals, usually for specific purposes such as to purchase durable consumer goods (particularly automobiles), homes (mortgage loans), or financial assets (particularly corporate stocks); loans to farmers; even loans to other banks. Thus one feature that distinguishes banks from other intermediaries is that they are far less specialized in their lending activity; any change in the ability of the banking system to make loans or in the cost of these loans could have a pervasive effect throughout the economy.

The other part of the portfolio of earning assets is securities, primarily debt obligations of the federal, state, and local governments. Banks normally hold substantial quantities of such securities, even though the yields may be quite a bit lower than the yields on loans. One reason for this behavior may be insufficient loan demand; but if that were the only reason, the banks could improve their profitability by charging lower rates on loans, inducing customers to borrow more, and thereby shifting assets out of securities into loans. Interest rates on loans and on securities would thereby tend to equalize. A more substantive reason is that securities are more liquid than loans. If a banker wishes to make new loans, or if he faces a sudden increase in withdrawals from deposit accounts, he can sell some of his securities to raise funds.

Cash assets include currency and a variety of demand deposit accounts at other banks or at the "central" bank (about which we have more to say later in this section). These assets are noninterest-earning, but they still are desired members of the portfolio. First, banks use them for ordinary business purposes, primarily for making payments. Second, a cushion of cash provides an even greater degree of liquidity than do securities. And third, each bank is *required* by law to hold a certain minimum amount of cash and deposits, the minimum being specified as a ratio to the bank's deposits. In subsequent chapters, we discover that this regulatory practice is used by central banks mainly to control the total volume of deposits accepted by the banking system.

The principal liabilities of any bank are its deposits (Table 1–1). *Demand deposits* are simply the accounts we know

familiarly as "checking accounts" and which constitute the
bulk of the U.S. money supply. One should note that demand
deposits differ from ordinary liabilities in an important way:
they are not, in a true economic sense, the debt of the bank.
When a bank accepts demand deposits, it incurs an obligation to provide checking services to the customers. But
neither the value of these services to the depositor nor their
cost to the bank is systematically related to the amount of
deposits; it is determined more by the amount of activity on
each account, the number of checks and deposits. Thus when
a bank's demand deposit liabilities rise or fall, we cannot infer
that its indebtedness (its obligation to its customers) is necessarily changing. This property implies that increases in the
total amount of demand deposits in the economy may bring a
real increase in wealth for the whole economy. (Contrast that
result with an increase in debt such as corporate bonds, where
the newly created assets are exactly matched by an increase
in the debt of the corporation.)

The other type of bank deposits, known as *time deposits,*
includes ordinary savings accounts, Christmas clubs, and similar devices, and "certificates of deposit." These certificates
are issued by banks for specified maturities, usually for 90
days or more but sometimes for as little as 30 days. Because
the bank can count on keeping the deposit for a known length
of time, it can afford to pay higher rates of interest than on
"passbook" savings accounts. The largest certificates (those
issued for $100,000 or more) may legally be negotiated by
the owner; but time deposits do not circulate in payment,
and by our preliminary definition of money we must exclude
them from that term.

Banks also borrow by issuing debt obligations not legally
classed as deposits. In some states, banks are permitted to
issue bonds directly to the public; this practice, however, is
not widespread. Banks do quite often borrow from one another; there exists a large market for such loans—known as

the "Federal funds market"—which we shall see again later in this book, for it plays an important role in the conduct of monetary policy. Interbank loans, of course, show up as assets for the lending banks and liabilities for the borrowers. Finally, banks borrow from the central bank. This last method of borrowing also has a role in monetary policy.

The net worth of a bank is the difference between the value of its assets and the value of its liabilities. If this net worth were to drop to zero, the bank would be insolvent and eventually would have to close its doors. Now obviously any responsible banker has a self-interest in maintaining capital solvency. But to protect depositors against both dishonesty and incompetence, the laws under which banks are chartered require the initial shareholders to pay in specified minimum amounts of capital.

Profitability, liquidity, solvency—these are the goals in the management of the bank balance sheet; goals which could be reached by individual banks in a normal competitive environment but which can be guaranteed for the whole system only through careful supervision and regulation by the government. If a zest for high short-run profits were to dominate the behavior of a banker, it would be not only the owners of the bank (the shareholders) who would ultimately suffer, but the depositors as well. If one bank failure were to occur without adequate protection for its depositors, there could occur a general loss of confidence in the banking system. And confidence is the keystone that supports all bank profits, because it enables the bank to keep a small amount of cash assets on hand and to hold most of its portfolio in the form of earning assets.

When large numbers of banks fail, a portion of the outstanding stock of demand deposits and therefore of our economy's money are destroyed. Trade is impaired; output falls; unemployment increases. It is the fear of widespread insolvency, of the sort of financial panic that recurred fre-

quently in this country from the 1830s until the 1930s, that
has motivated the increasing degree of government regulation
of banking since 1933.

Protection for bank depositors has three elements in the
U.S. economy. First, deposits of all but about 300 backwater
banks are insured by the Federal Deposit Insurance Corporation (FDIC) up to $40,000 per account;[4] so, in the event
of a bank failure, most depositors will receive full payment
from their accounts. Second, both the federal and state governments regulate the banks which they charter, in the manner described above.[5] These regulations provide a second line
of defense by reducing the danger that poorly managed banks
will become insolvent.

1.3.2 The Federal Reserve System

The third defense is also the best offense, in that it actively
promotes a sound environment in which the banking industry
can operate. We refer now to the country's *central bank*, the
Federal Reserve System. The Fed, as it is commonly called,
consists of 12 regional Federal Reserve banks supervised and
controlled by a seven-member Board of Governors headquartered in Washington, D.C. and appointed by the president of the United States with the approval of the Senate.
The regional banks are owned by the commercial banks that
elect to "join" the system, these banks being known as "member banks." Ownership, however, does not carry with it the
same degree of control as in the case of a regular business
firm; the Fed exists primarily to serve the public and only in a
very narrow way to serve the interests of the banks. Member-

---

[4] As of the end of 1973, about $4.5 billion out of $681.8 billion of total deposits were held in uninsured banks.

[5] Banks in the United States may elect to be chartered either by the state
in which they are located (9,600 state banks) or by the federal government
(4,600 national banks). For a history of this and other perversions, see the
American Bankers Association, *The Commercial Banking Industry* (Englewood
Cliffs, N.J.: Prentice-Hall, 1962).

ship is mandatory for all national banks and optional for state banks; only about 40 percent of all commercial banks, holding just over three quarters of total deposits, are members of the system. The advantage of Fed membership to the individual banker is that he obtains services (and perhaps prestige) from it. Each regional reserve bank acts as a banker to its member banks. It is in that sense a "bankers' bank" and has a very similar balance sheet (Table 1–2).

TABLE 1–2

An Aggregate Balance Sheet
For the 12 Federal Reserve Banks
As of December 31, 1973
(in billions)

Assets			*Liabilities*		
Cash assets..........		$ 20	Federal Reserve Notes..		$ 64
Currency..........	$ 0.3		Demand deposits......		31
Claims*...........	20.0		Of member banks....	$27	
Earning assets........		82	Other.............	4	
Loans.............	1.0		Miscellaneous........		6
Securities..........	81.0		Net worth...........		2
Miscellaneous........		1			
Total Assets....		$103	Total Liabilities.		$103

* These are highly specialized claims—gold certificates, special drawing rights, and cash items in process of collection—described more fully in Chapters 5 (section 5.3) and 12 (section 12.4.2).

As with commercial banks, the heart of the Federal Reserve's asset portfolio is its earning assets, which constitute over 80 percent of the total. But there are two major differences. First, almost all of the earning assets held by Federal Reserve banks are securities rather than loans, and almost all of their securities are debt obligations of the U.S. Treasury.[6] The only loans made by Federal Reserve banks in normal circumstances are to the member commercial banks. These loans are made only upon the request of the member bank, and the

[6] The Department of the Treasury is part of the executive branch of the federal government, and it has a number of monetary and fiscal functions; see Chapter 5.

regulations and overall administration over the lending process are tight enough to restrict this lending to very small
proportions most of the time.[7]

The second major difference is that the Federal Reserve
banks are not profit-seeking enterprises, and they do not manage their portfolios of earning assets so as to maximize or
even to generate profits. The Fed is a quasi-governmental
agency: owned by the commercial banks, it is controlled more
by the Congress and the president through their powers of
review, legislation, and appointment of officials. Actual policy
decisions are made by Federal Reserve officials independently
of any direct control by either of these constituencies,[8] but in
this regard public control clearly dominates. The Board of
Governors in Washington, D.C., themselves appointed by
the president, in turn appoint three of the nine directors of
each Federal Reserve bank. The member banks elect the
other six directors, but the chairman must be a board ap-
pointee. The president of each bank is chosen by the nine
directors subject to the approval of the board in Washington.

This mixture of bank and public control over the system
belies the true governmental function of the Federal Reserve
System. Its role as a bank for banks is definitely secondary to
its role as an agency for the federal government. It acts as a
banker for the U.S. Treasury; it supplies currency to the
economy; it regulates the member banks; and its mandate
from Congress, though legally rather vague in this context,
gives it the responsibility to use its powers to regulate the
course of economic activity—to try to stabilize prices, employment, and international payments.[9] These are public
goals and social responsibilities. One of the most important
functions of the Federal Reserve System is to manage its
holdings of securities so as to further these broad objectives.

---

[7] See Chapter 14, section 14.3.1.

[8] This point is discussed more fully in Chapter 13, section 13.2.

[9] See Chapter 13.

Exactly how it performs this function occupies much of our attention throughout this book.

The largest item on the liability side of the Fed's balance sheet is one that has no counterpart on commercial banks' ledgers at all: Federal Reserve notes.[10] These notes are the paper currency in your billfold. Like demand deposits but even more so, they are an accounting liability but not an economic debt. In fact, Federal Reserve notes are not redeemable at the Fed for anything but new notes! So the reader need not think that the small value of the actual capital of the Federal Reserve, shown in Table 1–2 as net worth, indicates that the system is on the verge of bankruptcy. The Federal Reserve has few real debts.

Completing this balance sheet are the deposit liabilities of the Federal Reserve banks. There are no time deposits and no demand deposits held by the general public. The bulk of these accounts are the cash assets of member commercial banks. The rest are held by other commercial banks, the U.S. Treasury, and foreign central banks. The deposits of member banks at the Federal Reserve banks are the most important linkage between the Fed's portfolio of securities and its control over the supply of money to the economy; that linkage is examined in detail in Chapters 4 and 14.

1.4 ECONOMICS

The popular title for textbooks about money and for the college course in which they are used is "Money and Banking." This twin billing emphasizes the close relationship between the production of money and the institutions of commercial and central banking. But it may lead the reader and even the author astray by omitting any reference to the subject's environment. One of the motivations behind the writing

---

[10] Since 1935, commercial banks in the United States have been prohibited from issuing their own bank notes. In the 19th century, however, private bank notes were a major part of the U.S. money supply.

of the present book is our desire to elevate that environment —the economy—to an equal billing with money and with banking.

The way money is produced and supplied to the economy and the way money is demanded and used by the individuals and businesses which form the economy are *market* phenomena. Banks are institutions which supply money to the public in response to demands for it. Once we cease to regard this process as mechanical and begin to look for the determinants of changes in either the demand for or the supply of money, then we are setting forth on a path that leads to an understanding of how we can make money work for us. We can see that the demand for money is derived from its *utility* for various functions, and that its value in exchange is governed by its *scarcity* relative to demand. We then begin to see money as an evolutionary phenomenon, the nature of which responds to the availability of resources, to advances in technology, to changes in life styles, to our understanding of economics. Money as a static institution would be a dull subject; money as a living force for the improved functioning of the economy is a topic about which we are eager to share our own enthusiasm.

The study of money as a market phenomenon is an application of economic theory and in particular of the laws of supply and demand. The basic elements of these laws are that the quantity of any good or service which is demanded normally will vary inversely with the price charged for it; that the quantity supplied normally will vary directly with the price which people are willing to pay; and that in any market for a good or service the price and the quantity exchanged normally will tend toward equilibrium values which equate supply with demand.[11] In making such statements, however,

---

[11] Our purpose here is not to review these laws but merely to note that they form the basis for our discussion. The reader who finds them unfamiliar may wish to refer to a textbook on principles of economic theory, such as Lloyd Reynolds, *Economics* (Homewood, Ill.: Richard D. Irwin, Inc., 1973).

one must always assume that none of the other factors which may influence demand or supply—real incomes, prices of other goods, tastes, weather, expectations, ad infinitum—is changing at the same time. To clarify the analysis, we shall frequently note that we are assuming ceteris paribus (that other things are given and unchanged).

Most of our analysis of money is a simple enough application of these elementary principles that no special analytical tools are required to follow it other than an awareness of basic plane geometry. Graphs of supply curves and demand curves enable one to reduce most of the relevant concepts to a single dimension. The only major exception is the process by which demand deposits are supplied (the subject of Chapter 4), a multidimensional process which makes necessary a little linear algebra.

The algebraic technique used in this book doubtless is familiar to most readers. It may be illustrated by a simplified concept of money demand. Suppose that we hypothesize that the quantity of money demanded by individuals and businesses is determined by the amount of income they earn each year. Denoting these concepts by the symbols M^d and Y, respectively, and assuming that the relationship between the two is linear (i.e., could be expressed graphically as a straight line), we may write

$$M^d = a + bY.$$

In this formula, M^d and Y are *variables*, economic magnitudes which we can observe and measure over time or can compare for different individuals or countries. The symbols a and b are coefficients or *parameters*, constants which measure the impact of a change in one variable on the value of another. A specific estimate of this function might be $M^d = \$50$ billion $+ .2Y$, which implies that a is $50 billion and b is 0.2. This hypothetical money demand function is shown graphically in Figure 1–2.

FIGURE 1–2

A Hypothetical Money Demand Function

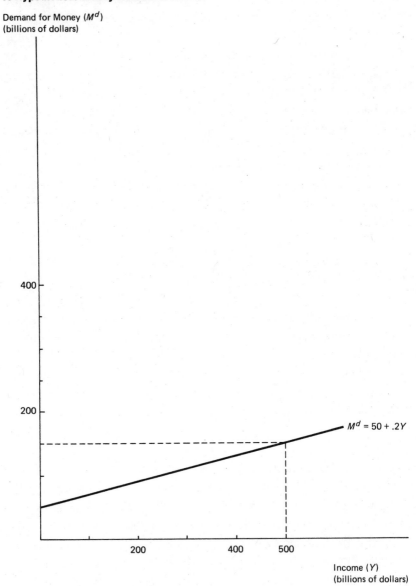

One use for functions of this type is to determine the effect of a change in one variable which is assumed to be *exogenous* (i.e., determined by forces not explained in the function or group of functions being examined) on another variable the behavior of which we are interested in explaining and which we are treating as *endogenous* (determined at least partly by the function). In this example, income is exogenous; whatever determines income in the economy we assume here to be independent of the demand for money. It is the latter which is determined by income. Hence, according to this hypothetical equation, if income is $500 billion, the demand for money will be $150 billion. Furthermore, the value of $b = 0.2$ implies that a $10 billion rise in income will produce a $2 billion rise in the demand for money.

1.5 CONCLUSIONS: MONEY AND PUBLIC POLICY

The study of money is much more than a study of the market for money balances. This market interacts with the real economy: the aggregate demand for and supply of goods and services. Because of that interaction and because of the ability of the Federal Reserve System to exert control over the behavior of the money stock, the policies adopted by the Fed may play an important role in governmental control over the economy.

The nature of the relationship between the market for money balances and the market for goods and services is complex enough to occupy much of the second half of this book. Essentially, the linkage arises because there is a stable relationship between the amount of income which people receive and the quantity of money they desire to hold (i.e., the quantity they demand); it is not as simple or as stable as the example of the previous section might suggest, but it is one of the more predictable relationships in our economy. The Federal Reserve, by making it more or less expensive for people to obtain additional money balances, can thereby restrict or encourage growth in spending and in income.

Money, of course, is not the only important factor in our economy; it is simply one economic good amongst many. Why, then, should we concentrate our attention on money in preference to steel, for example, or automobiles or petroleum? The importance of petroleum was clearly demonstrated during the Arab oil embargo in late 1973 and early 1974. The reduction in the supply of foreign oil created serious shortages in many sectors of the economy, and the decline in incomes in the first half of 1974 can be attributed partly to the oil shortage. If a supply-induced disturbance in the petroleum industry can create such devastating effects on the economy as a whole, perhaps we ought to study, instead of money, the determinants of the demand and supply of petroleum. Is not the supply of petroleum as significant as the supply of money? Furthermore, is not the demand for money determined by precisely the same economic factors that determine the demand for petroleum? In short, is there anything unique about money that warrants special treatment?

We shan't steal all our thunder by revealing prematurely the answers to these questions. Nevertheless, we hesitate to monopolize the reader's valuable time without providing a tentative and plausible explanation for the importance the authors assign to money.

We believe that money can and does exercise a powerful destabilizing role in generating both unemployment and inflation. It is not mere coincidence that there is a close relationship between the behavior of the stock of money and the general level of prices in all of the major wartime inflations in the United States since 1900, including that of the Vietnamese war and its aftermath. It is equally clear that errors of omission and commission by the Federal Reserve contributed to the severity of the depressions of 1920–21, 1929–33, and 1937–38. Historically, money has played in numerous episodes an independent role in generating serious economic disturbances. At times, to be sure, many other forces—such as the availability of oil—dominate the role of money. But few other single forces play such a strong and continuing role.

We also believe that money has a positive role to play in guaranteeing economic stability. By simply avoiding the worst errors of the past, the Federal Reserve should contribute to greater relative stability. But we ought to expect more from monetary policy than the avoidance of error. The final section of this book (Part Four) provides a detailed analysis of the prospects and problems for a truly stabilizing monetary policy.

One man who had a vision of a strong economy as a source of well-being for its citizens and who set out to build that kind of strength was Woodrow Wilson. As president of the United States, he successfully fought for congressional approval of the act which in 1913 provided for the establishment of the Federal Reserve System. He did not see it as a panacea for the economic ills of that day, much less for those of the 1970s. But he did hope that it might gradually grow into a beneficial force for the economy. Wilson's vision is summarized in a quotation from his first inaugural address which forms an unofficial motto for the Federal Reserve System and in the spirit of which we now approach the topic of monetary policy:

> We shall deal with our economic system as it is and as it may be modified, not as it might be if we had a clean sheet of paper to write upon; and step by step we shall make it what it should be. . . .

REVIEW QUESTIONS

1. Dictionaries tend to define "money" imprecisely. Look up the word and criticize the entry. How useful is that definition in determining whether a particular asset (say, demand deposits) should be classified as money?

2. What assets do banks hold that yield no interest or other monetary income? Why do they hold these assets? Does this practice differ essentially from individual behavior? In what ways?

3. Draw a demand curve for bank loans. Who are the "demanders?" What variables determine the quantity (dollar volume) of loans demanded? What is meant by the "price" of loans?

SUGGESTED FURTHER READING

American Bankers Association. *The Commercial Banking Industry.* Englewood Cliffs, N.J.: Prentice-Hall, 1962.

Board of Governors of the Federal Reserve System. *The Federal Reserve System: Purposes and Functions.* Washington, D.C., 1963.

Report from the President's Commission. *Financial Structure and Regulation.* Washington, D.C., December 1971.

Reynolds, Lloyd. *Economics: A General Introduction,* 4th ed. Homewood, Ill.: Richard D. Irwin, 1973.

chapter 2
The Uses of Money

2.1 INTRODUCTION

Have you ever asked yourself what would happen if we were all suddenly to stop using money? How would wages be paid? How would you obtain groceries or gasoline? How would people make payments on their home mortgages and discharge other debts? You don't have to think very long about these questions before concluding that the thought of doing without money is rather uncomfortable. The loss of money would affect immediately, directly, and pervasively the way we conduct our daily lives. Yet money is so familiar that we simply take its existence for granted.

In this second chapter of our study of money, we are going to provide some economic answers to the question: Why was money invented and what role does it play in the economy? We shall take a close look here at the differences between economies which use money and those which do not. Then after we see why money is useful, we can set about trying to discover in subsequent chapters how money is created and used in modern economic systems. First an example.

2.1.1 A Hypothetical Barter System

Suppose that you are planning to buy a bicycle and that you already have decided what type and model you want.

Buying the bike is then no problem, assuming you can afford
it. You find a store which sells your model, and you ask the
price: say, $120. Being broke, you then get a summer job as
a bank teller and earn $100 per week. You put aside $10 each
pay day, and after 12 weeks you take your earnings to the
store and make your purchase. The ease and convenience of
making such transactions is a luxury we normally accept
without question.

Now let us call on your imagination for a moment. How
would this process have to change if we lived in an economy
without money? Suppose then that there is no concept such
as a dollar and no physical unit like our paper and other currency. Now you go to the bike shop and the sales person tells
you that you can buy a ten-speed Honcho for 100 good-sized,
cleaned frying chickens. So you get a summer job. You go to
work for the local brick factory and discover to your chagrin
that you are paid each week in bricks. Then for each item
you want to buy, you have to barter, or trade, your bricks,
either directly or indirectly. Perhaps you find a builder who
will trade you a cubic yard of firewood for each pile of 80
bricks. You save part of this firewood each week, and at the
end of the summer you barter it for whatever you can get:
perhaps 50 gallons of premium gasoline, 6 pairs of work
pants, and 14 pork roasts. Finally you find chicken farmers
who will trade you fryers for the pork, pants, and fuel. Ex-
hausted by now, you haul the chickens into the store and
pick up your bike.

This barter system—an economy without money—is less
efficient than the same economy would be with money. We
can identify the costs. First, unless the seller of a good wants
whatever the potential buyer has to offer in exchange, one
party or the other will have to go through at least one and
perhaps a whole series of intermediate transactions. Our example shows how complicated it can be to trade a pile of
bricks for a bicycle. The necessity under barter for a *double*

coincidence of wants—the necessity for both traders to want whatever the other is offering at a price agreeable to both— was probably the biggest single reason for the invention of money in primitive economies.

A second cost in our hypothetical barter system is that for every single good being traded one has to establish a price in terms of each other good. In the example there was a price for your labor services in terms of bricks, for bricks in exchange for firewood, for firewood in trade with gasoline, work pants, and pork roasts, and for each of those goods against chickens, as well as the price of the bicycle expressed in a number of chickens. That adds up to nine prices which have to be determined just to buy one ten-speed Honcho. By introducing a money standard, we can reduce the required number of price ratios to two: our labor and the bicycle, both in terms of dollars.

The nonpecuniary cost of doing without money, a cost which is implied by the above description, is that the exchange of goods and services might become so time-consuming, troublesome, and even unproductive, that we will simply do a lot less trading than we would with money. We therefore would be able to buy fewer desired goods. And that leads us to some basic principles about money.

How to Buy a Bicycle with 48 Hours of Labor

A. Under a hypothetical barter system

    Step 1:   1 hour of labor buys 100 bricks

    Step 2:   80 bricks buy 1 cubic yard of cut wood (25 logs)

    Step 3:   5 logs buy 1 gallon of gasoline, or
               60 logs buy 1 pair of work pants, or
               10 logs buy 1 pork roast

    Step 4:   3 gallons of gasoline buy 1 chicken, or
               1 pair of work pants buys 4 chickens, or
               3 pork roasts buy 2 chickens

    Step 5:   100 chickens buy 1 bicycle

B. In a money economy

    Step 1:   48 hours of labor = $120

    Step 2: $120 = 1 bicycle

2.2 TRADING ACTIVITY: SHOPPING AND EXCHANGE

The use of money always presupposes some form of organized *trading activity*. Money would not exist if households were self-sufficient or if trade were limited to an occasional and isolated exchange. To understand the emergence of money we must therefore understand the nature of trading activity which essentially has three components. First, one might conduct a search for information about the availability, quality, and prices of goods being offered for sale. Second, some amount of bargaining or haggling over the terms of the sale may occur. This activity of searching and bargaining is referred to in familiar terms as *shopping*. Finally, when the shopping is completed, the trading process then culminates in an act of exchange. But while the use of money is most obvious and most visible during the actual exchange, its true usefulness derives from its role in reducing the costs of shopping. To see why this is so, let us take a closer look at those costs.

2.2.1 Costs of Shopping

Whenever we set out to locate, price, and perhaps to buy goods, we necessarily incur a number of costs, many of which are subtle and indirect. Perhaps the least obvious of these costs is the value of our time expended in shopping. Normally of course we do not take off from work to go shopping. But that does not imply that our leisure time is without value. Most of us would rather be doing something more enjoyable, and even those who thoroughly enjoy expeditions to suburban groundscrapers are likely to find their enthusiasm waning as the hours stretch out. The displeasure associated with increasing amounts of shopping is a personal cost as real, if not as tangible, as a direct outlay of cash.

There are other costs, especially in a nonmoney economy of the type encountered by our budding bicyclist of the preceding section. The shopper has to store inventories of goods awaiting disposal through trade: in our example, chickens, pork roasts, bricks, and firewood. Even the modern suburbanite runs the risk of losing all or part of his inventory of pocket currency, and we should include that risk as a cost of shopping.

Both types of costs—the value of the shopper's time and the cost of handling whatever he is offering in exchange for the goods he plans to buy—will be greater the more shopping one does. Whether we choose to measure "amount of shopping" by the time one spends or the quantity of goods he buys (and for convenience we shall use the latter), we may expect our trader's expenses to increase correspondingly. Furthermore, his displeasure is sure to increase (or his enjoyment to decrease) more and more as the input of time and effort rises. His total costs—both pecuniary and nonpecuniary—will rise, probably at an increasing rate. We could plot these increasing costs for a hypothetical shopper in a diagram like Figure 2–1.

An important point to remember about this cost curve (C) is that it is at least partially subjective, as it concludes both direct expenses and the displeasure or disutility of shopping trips. It is mainly the latter that gives the curve its convex shape.

2.2.2 Benefits of Shopping

If one incurs all those costs whenever he goes shopping, why bother? The question is basic but is readily answered: because shopping leads to trading, to the purchase of goods we desire to possess or consume. Generally, the more shopping one does, the greater will be his overall (partly subjective) benefit. But we also expect shopping trips, like most other economic activities, to be subject to *diminishing marginal returns*. If one had an hour available for a Saturday morning shopping expedition, one could concentrate on get-

FIGURE 2–1

Costs of Shopping

Costs

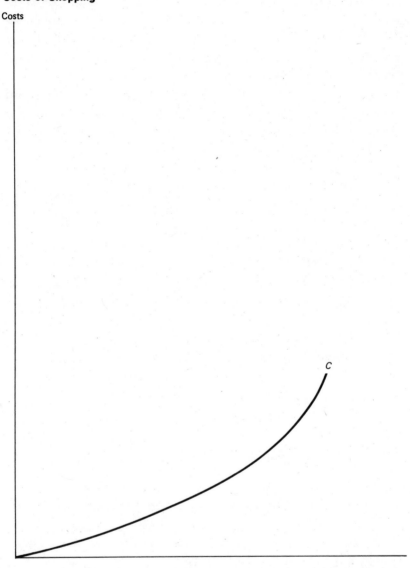

Amount of Shopping

ting those few items which were most important at the moment. If one had another hour to spend, one could get *more* done but probably not twice as much in terms of benefits. So we can plot benefits now along with costs (Figure 2–2).

2.2.3 How Much Shopping?

At first glance, it might appear that the appropriate amount of shopping for an individual would be determined primarily by the amount of money that is available. But that conclusion would be wrong on two counts. First, the limiting factor is not money but wealth. Whatever assets we accumulate over time can be converted into other forms through trading. Money is a most convenient asset for this purpose, but its possession is in no way essential to exchange, as we could see from the barter-economy example which introduced this chapter.[1] Second, the shopper's wealth only *limits* his ability to trade. Once he is broke, his benefit curve will level off in a hurry!

Given that shopping is a resource-using activity (i.e., that one incurs objective or subjective costs in the process), in general it is not worthwhile to keep it up until every possible benefit has been squeezed out of it. But we can be more precise than that. Shopping is a worthwhile activity so long as the costs are not rising more rapidly than the benefits, and the optimum amount of shopping occurs at the point where the excess of the total benefit over the total cost is maximized. At that point the shopper knows that if he just goes to one more store, he might find something he likes better than what he has found so far. But he also knows (or reckons or thinks or feels) that it is not worth the time, trouble, or effort to do so. Maybe next Saturday morning, but right now he would rather go home, have lunch, and watch the Dodgers.

---

[1] We shall examine the qualities of money as an asset more closely in Chapter 7.

FIGURE 2–2

Costs and Benefits of Shopping

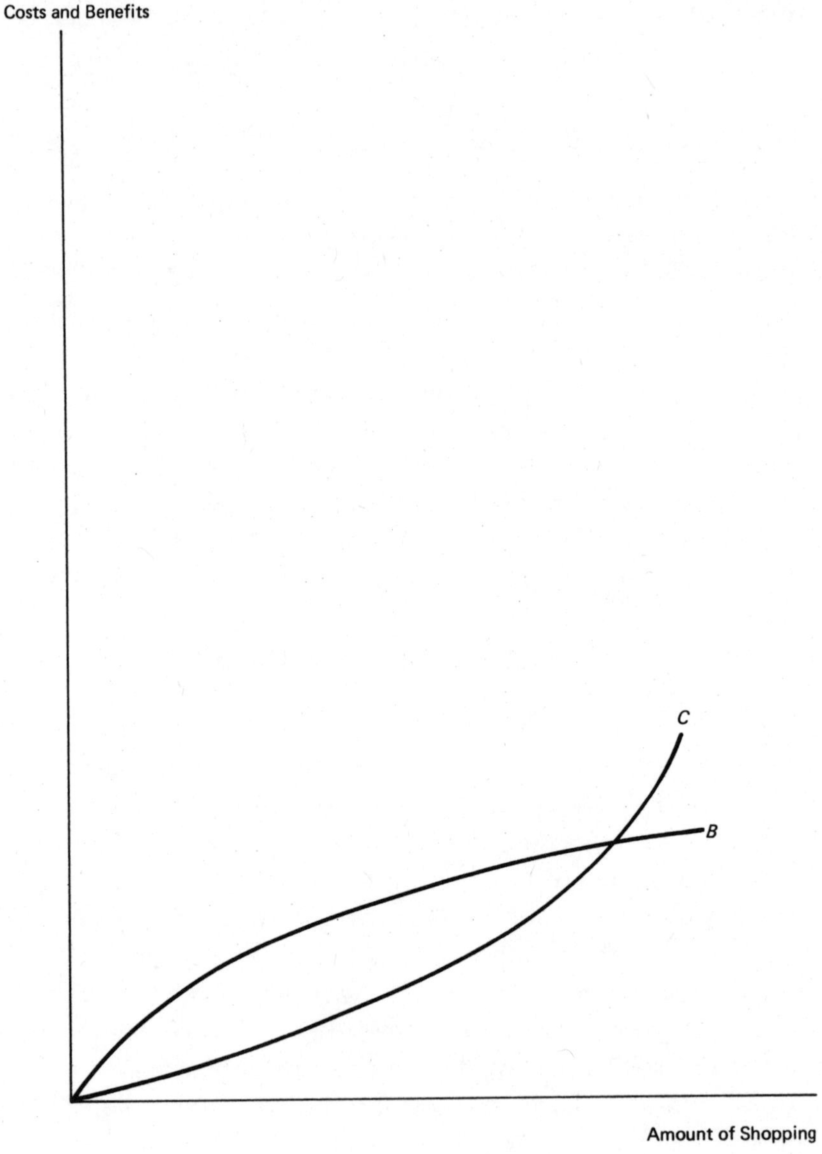

Costs and Benefits

Amount of Shopping

FIGURE 2–3

Optimum Amount of Shopping

Costs and Benefits

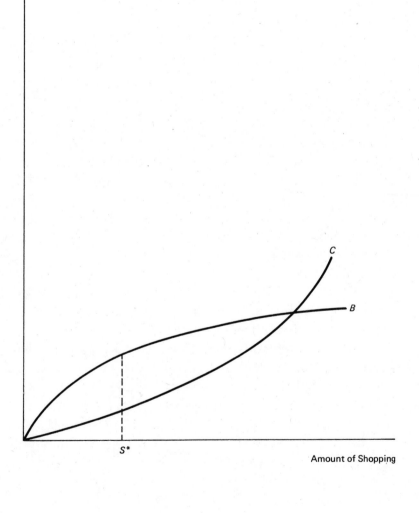

Amount of Shopping

This optimum quitting point, no less real or rational for having been determined by such subjective factors, is shown as S^* in Figure 2–3. Up to that point, the gap between the benefits (B) and the costs (C) is increasing; any additional shopping beyond S^* results in more additional cost than benefit. In technical terms, at S^* the rising marginal cost is just equal to the falling marginal benefit. Any variation away from S^* will necessarily reduce the net benefit from shopping.

2.3 THE INTRODUCTION OF MONEY

We began this discussion by describing a would-be bicyclist on a hypothetical shopping expedition, with and without money. Under the barter system, his biggest problem was to acquire the necessary goods to exchange for the bike. The seller probably would have accepted bricks if the customer insisted, but the seller would have demanded a very high price (a lot of bricks), knowing that it was necessary then to find a way to trade the bricks for wanted goods. The more shopping the cyclist is willing to do, the more likely is the occurrence of obtaining good trades toward the ultimate purchase of the bicycle.

Once we introduce money into the system, the process of acquiring the bike becomes much simpler. The cost of acquiring that item or any quantity of goods will become lower because less time and effort is required to make purchases. The shopper is paid in exchange for his own labor with the same commodity—money—which he intends to use in making his purchases. Money is likely to be easier to carry and, if necessary, to store, than the intermediate commodities used in the barter system. We can quit worrying about broken bricks and spoiled pork. Consequently, as shown in Figure 2–4, we can do more shopping—probably in less time—at

FIGURE 2–4

The Introduction of Money

Costs and Benefits

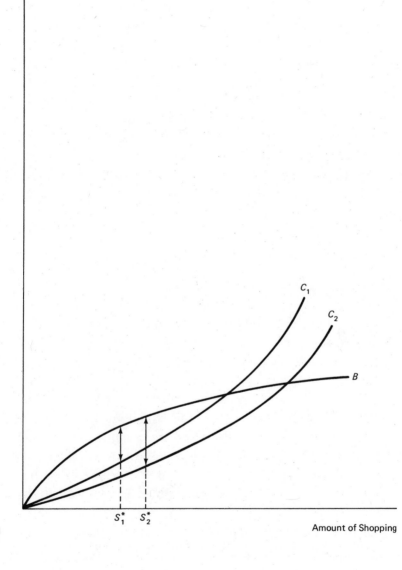

Amount of Shopping

lower costs, once we introduce money into the trading process.[2]

Here, the first cost curve (C_1) represents the sum of the various objective and subjective costs of shopping in a barter economy, while C_2 shows the reductions in costs obtained from the use of money. The diagram clearly indicates an improvement in well-being from the use of money, a result which our intuition should be able to digest comfortably. This improvement really has two components. First, one can obtain a given quantity of goods with a smaller expenditure of time and effort; our friend has more time left for enjoying the bike. Second, the reduction in shopping cost makes it possible to buy more goods than would otherwise be practical; some people who would find the bother of bartering to be a barrier to buying a bicycle will soon be happily peddling.

2.4   SYSTEMS OF EXCHANGE

So far, we have briefly compared two systems for exchanging goods and services: simple barter and the modern money economy. Both theoretically and historically, these systems represent the end points on the spectrum of possibilities for organizing exchange. It should prove useful now to review a few alternatives.

Barter is and has been found primarily in primitive societies. Once the people in an economy begin to specialize in production, they become less self-sufficient and conduct increasing quantities of trade. Then the inconveniences of barter become a spur to the development of *organized markets:* concentrations of traders who meet to engage in exchange. Today, of course, we have specialized economic activity to

---

[2] Benefits, as we have defined them here, should not be affected much in relation to the amount of shopping completed. Recall that the latter term refers to the quantity of goods purchased, rather than the amount of time spent shopping.

Magazine editor Norman Cousins found himself in big trouble. He desperately needed paper to keep publishing his *Saturday Review/World.* Papermakers were turning him down left and right, saying they found it unprofitable to produce high-quality magazine paper.

Finally, one paper-mill owner agreed to co-operate. But first, Mr. Cousins had to find him propane gas for use in the ink-drying process. The editor found the propane (he won't say where) and traded it for "about 50% of our paper needs for the next six months." As a result. "we're no longer in an emergency situation," Mr. Cousins says.

A barter economy is developing again today, possibly on a much broader scale than in the recent past, economists and businessmen say. Such forces as inflation, the energy crisis, wage and price controls and the resulting widespread shortages of raw materials all contribute to the trend. . . . Purchasing managers are offering goods such as gasoline, fuel oil, polyvinyl chloride, . . . and metal bars. In exchange, they want such items as plastic monomers, benzene, . . . steel plate and diesel fuel.

A lack of goods to trade for other products excludes many companies from barter deals, infuriating a few. . . . Even those concerns with the ability to barter goods aren't entirely happy about the primitive way of doing business in a shortage economy. Corporate officials find it difficult to deal in commodities for which they have little expertise or contacts. "None of us like it," says [one]. "We're used to buying for money and selling for money."

But Mr. Cousins of the *Saturday Review/World* liked the way trading helped him. He adds, "We're prepared to go into further bartering or female slavery or anything else to get paper."

Source: Joann S. Lublin, "Wanna Swap?" *Wall Street Journal*, February 13, 1974.

the extent that "trade" is a full-time business and is conducted almost exclusively via the medium of money. But in earlier societies such as medieval Europe, periodic *fairs* were held at which farmers, artisans, and other producers could come together to barter their wares in a central marketplace. And incidentally—or perhaps not so incidentally—a variant of the medieval fair may now be making a comeback in the United States. Once each month recently, the Rose Bowl in Pasadena, California has been opened for a gigantic garage or rummage sale. Thousands of people who make ordinary livings at other activities gather in the open air to try to sell— and often to barter—a seemingly endless variety of new and used merchandise. Perhaps that phenomenon is symptomatic of a quest for a simpler and less established social style, but it may also indicate that apparently inefficient exchange systems are still the best means for conducting some specific kinds of trade.[3]

The advantage of any organized market, regardless of whether money is used in exchange, is that the mere concentration of traders in a single location is bound to reduce the costs of shopping. Opportunities for trade will now be available which with isolated exchange either did not exist or involved prohibitive transactions costs.

An even more major breakthrough in the transition from a barter to a money economy occurs when some traders begin to acquire commodities not because they want them directly but only because the goods can be exchanged easily for whatever the trader does want. Our friend the bicyclist had already discovered the advantages of such *intermediary commodities* when the bicyclist realized one could trade the bricks for various commodities which eventually could be used to acquire the bike. Imagine the shopping cost of having to find not only the right bicycle but also a seller who would be willing to take bricks in exchange! Again the costs of searching and bargaining for goods are reduced. Moreover, the use of intermediary commodities in exchange is probably an essential stage in the evolution of money. It is only a short step from there to the standardization upon a single intermediary good.

---

[3] For an example of how seriously some people still regard barter, see Charles Morrow Wilson, *Let's Try Barter* (New York: Devin Press, 1960).

A final breakthrough in the development of monetary exchange involves the use of a *unit of account*. In nonmoney economies, prices of individual goods must be quoted in terms of whatever other commodity is offered in trade. Suppose that there are 100 goods produced and sold in such an economy. Each of those goods has not one price but 99 prices: one for each other commodity. In total, there will be 4,950 prices for a potential trader to sort out.[4] A bicycle will sell for 100 chickens, or 5 pairs of slacks, or half a side of beef, or . . . . But suppose instead that everybody agrees to quote prices in terms of *one* commodity, perhaps building bricks. The brick then becomes the economy's unit of account, and the number of necessary price ratios drops from 4,950 down to 100.[5] The corresponding reduction in confusion is likely to have a major benefit in reducing the cost of obtaining shopping information.

Please observe carefully that the use of a unit of account and the use of a single intermediary commodity in exchange are quite separate issues. The bike shop might quote its prices in terms of bricks, or even in abstract terms such as dollars, and still insist on taking only chickens in trade. The advantage to the buyer is that he knows immediately how many bricks or dollars it will take to make his purchase, even though he still has to acquire the chickens first.[6]

Figure 2–5 below summarizes the various means available

---

[4] There are, of course, 9,900 prices in all; but half of these are redundant; if a chicken sells for 3 gallons of gasoline, then we know as well that a gallon of gas will sell for one third of a chicken.

[5] More generally, suppose that there is any number of goods being traded, say n. Without a unit of account, the number of price ratios is $n \cdot (n-1)/2$. With the introduction of a unit of account, each good has one price so the number of prices is simply n.

[6] At the risk of belaboring the point beyond boredom, we should observe that the calculation would be as follows. The shop lists a price of 4,000 bricks per bike. The chicken farmer lists a price of 40 bricks per hen. The implied chicken price of the cycle is 100 fryers. If, as in our first example, the farmer also desires commodities other than bricks, a series of similar calculations and trades must be made.

FIGURE 2–5

Systems of Exchange

Costs and Benefits

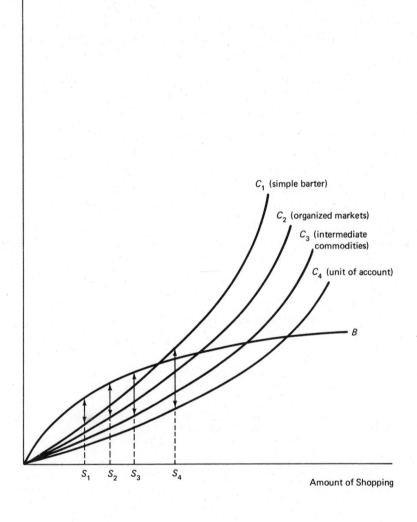

for conducting trade. Each major development in the systems used for the exchange of goods and services has succeeded in reducing either the time required for shopping or the other transactions and handling costs incurred in trade. It should now be clear why money has supplanted barter and why markets have become highly organized. First, the structuring of trade and the use of money in exchange can substantially reduce the costs of shopping for goods. And second, these innovations expand the opportunities for advantageous trade, so that more trade actually occurs.

2.5 MONEY AS AN ASSET

There is more to the usefulness of money than its function in the mediation of exchange of goods and services. You might imagine that our bicyclist, living in a world without money, desires to save part of his summer income to spend in the fall. How does he manage? His only choice is to hold some collection of goods which he hopes to be able to barter for other goods when he is ready. If, as we have supposed, salary is paid in building bricks, he could simply hold onto them through the summer. Or he could buy some other goods that might be cheaper to store or easier to trade. But once the economy begins to standardize trade around a single intermediary commodity and a single unit of account, the chosen commodity will be a convenient *store of value*. That is, it will provide the saver with a convenient form in which to store accumulated wealth.

In a modern economy, money is just one of the many forms in which people can hold *wealth*, which we define as the total stock of economic goods held by a person or group of persons at a particular point in time.[7] There is no reason to expect

---

[7] This definition should be carefully distinguished from that of "net wealth," which consists of total assets ("gross" wealth), less total liabilities owed to others. This latter term we call "net worth" in this book.

people to hold all of their wealth in the form of money. To the contrary, some of the available alternatives are highly desirable in their own right. Included in a typical individual's stock of wealth might be one's ownership of (1) physical goods such as a house, car, and furniture; (2) financial assets that yield income, such as ownership shares in business corporations (e.g., IBM stock), debt securities (bonds) issued by the government or by corporations, and savings accounts in banks or similar institutions, and (3) money, on which interest is not paid in most modern economies.

An important question may have occurred to you by now: Why should a rational person want to hold wealth in a form (money) which earns no interest when assets which do are available? The answer is actually rather complex, and we shall devote most of Chapter 7 to it. But the essence of the argument is that money assets have other desirable properties which compensate to some degree for their lack of income-generating power. First, if all or most transactions are carried out through the exchange of money rather than by direct barter, holding whatever serves as money will make future transactions less cumbersome. Second, suppose that all prices of goods and services are quoted in terms of a single unit of account and that those prices do not fluctuate widely or unexpectedly. Then a money whose own price is firmly fixed in terms of the unit of account will provide a more nearly fixed amount of "purchasing power" than will other assets, the prices of which individually might vary.

Today we seldom give much thought to the convenience or inconvenience of making transactions or storing wealth, unless the monetary system threatens to break down. During periods of rapid price inflation, for instance, more people are likely to be concerned justifiably about whether to hold money or to get rid of it. Nonetheless, barring catastrophes, the money we use seldom prompts many questions about the process of how it evolved. So before we focus closely on the contemporary world, we shall pause in Chapter 3 to examine more fully the evolution of the various types of money.

REVIEW QUESTIONS

1. Explain the existence of barter transactions such as house and automobile "swapping" in the highly organized U.S. economy.
2. Draw up a list showing the amount and timing of all of your larger payments during a period of one month. Explain the payments pattern. What role do you think habit and rational economic calculation play?
3. Cigarettes were widely used as money by Americans in prisoner of war camps during World War II. Why cigarettes instead of shaving lotion?
4. During the American colonial period, bookkeeping accounts were kept in terms of pounds, shillings, and pence, yet the principal medium of exchange was the Spanish dollar. How could such a monetary system work?
5. How many independent price ratios are there in a barter economy with 150 goods? What happens when we introduce a money-of-account?

SUGGESTED FURTHER READING

Clower, R. W. (ed.). *Monetary Theory*. Baltimore, Md.: Penquin Books, 1969; pp. 7–15.

Einzig, Paul. *Primitive Money in Its Ethnological, Historical and Economic Aspects*, 2d ed. Elmsford, N.Y.: Pergamon Press, 1966.

Radford, R. A. "The Economic Organization of a P.O.W. Camp," *Economica*, November 1945.

Wilson, Charles Morrow. *Let's Try Barter*. Old Greenwich, Conn.: The Devin-Adair Co., 1960.

part two

The Market for Money Balances

chapter 3

Currency Production

3.1 INTRODUCTION

Like any other economic good, money draws its value, its power to purchase other goods in exchange, from two fundamental properties: utility and scarcity. This chapter describes the production of currency and the conditions regulating its scarcity.

You probably remember being told as a child that money does not grow on trees—a helpful parental reminder that the basic fact about money is its scarcity! But how many of us were precocious enough to press the question and ask where money does come from? A more pointed question is: who are the producers of money? The answer to that question differs among countries and for different time periods. Perhaps from the bewildering variety of items that have served as money we can obtain a clue about how money production has been organized. Monetary history reveals that barley and silver were used as money in Sumer and Akkad during the first half of the third millennium before Christ. Rock salt was used as money in Asia and Africa around the first century A.D., paper money in ninth century China as well as throughout the world for the past century, red woodpecker scalps by Indians from the West Coast of the United States, tobacco in the Virginia Colony, gold and silver in 18th- and 19th-century Europe, checkbook accounts in 20th century United States, and cigarettes in German prisoner-of-war camps during World War II.

From this far-from-complete list we can identify three general ways of organizing money production:

1. The production of commodity money (rock salt, tobacco, cigarettes, gold).
2. The production of inconvertible paper money by the state or by an agency of the state as a monopoly right (greenbacks during the Civil War, confederate paper money, Federal Reserve notes).
3. The production of bank money, either paper money or checking accounts, by private financial business firms, usually commercial banks.

These three alternative methods of producing money differ with respect to the amount of economic resources absorbed in the money production process (that is, the amount of labor and materials employed in the manufacture of money), and the degree to which the quantity of money produced is controlled by purely automatic (economic) forces or by administrative discretion. Because the third category—bank money —is so different from the first two, in terms of the way it is supplied and in terms of its modern importance, we shall defer our discussion of it until the next chapter. First, some general principles about *currency:* commodity and paper money.

3.2 COMMODITY MONEY

Commodity money is quite simply a good like gold, silver, iron, or tobacco which, in addition to its regular use as a commodity, also functions as the medium of exchange. Any physical good is eligible, though some goods may be better

Store's Trade
Is Penny Ante

Greensboro, N.C., June 14, 1974 (AP).—Kevin McAuley bought $3.72 worth of merchandise in a department store here.

As change from $4, a clerk gave him a quarter and three penny pieces of peppermint candy. The store was short of pennies.

Later that day his wife and her mother decided to find out if the candy was really worth a penny. They went back to the store and made an 80-cent purchase, 84 cents with tax.

They gave the cashier 82 cents in coins and two pieces of peppermint candy.

The cashier didn't know what to do and asked the manager about it. The store had been giving candy in lieu of pennies, but not accepting it.

"The manager sort of threw up his hands," Mrs. McAuley's mother said. "But he approved the transaction."

What happened to the third piece of candy? Mr. McAuley ate it on the way home.

qualified than others. An ideal commodity currency should have a stable and widely recognized value; hence silver was until recently preferable to uranium. It should be reasonably portable; wheat would serve better than the land on which the wheat is grown. It should be divisible into quantities small enough to carry out all transactions; cigarettes work better than cattle. It should be homogeneous and of uniform quality; tobacco works better than marijuana. It should be durable enough to serve as a store of value for people who wish to wait before making all of their purchases; rock salt works better than peaches. But the most important quality for a commodity currency is that it must instill confidence among the people who are asked to accept the commodity in exchange and to hold it, possibly for long periods, before ultimately disposing of it. It is that almost purely psychological quality that seems to adhere most powerfully to gold.

There are two types of commodity money systems. The first type is essentially a private enterprise system. No government action is required except perhaps to certify the quality and quantity of the currency commodity, that is, to vouch for its weight and fineness. The commodity and the commodity currency are indistinguishable, whether it be rock salt, gold dust, or oxen. Commodity money is produced by individual producers in response to the economic forces of supply and demand. The market price of the commodity currency (its purchasing power) is allowed to fluctuate freely. We shall refer to this commodity money system as a *market commodity money*.

Under the second system, the government manufactures commodity currency and operates a price-fixing program for the currency. It fixes the price (the mint price) at which it is prepared to buy and sell the commodity currency and in so doing guarantees that the mint price shall not depart from the market price. The prototype for this *controlled commodity money* is the "gold standard."

3.2.1 Market Commodity Money

The essential properties of a market commodity money system are automaticity and the absence of government intervention. By automaticity we mean that the monetary system is self-guiding, self-regulating, without any external control. As we shall show, the output of commodity money should respond countercyclically to changes in the general level of prices, increasing when the price level falls and decreasing when the price level rises. If there is a close relationship between the stock of money and the price level, countercyclical variations in the money stock will tend to stabilize the price level. The properties of minimum government intervention and automaticity exert a compelling influence on those who desire to organize money production on strict laissez-faire lines. Anarchists as well as disciples of Adam Smith, the great 18th-century Scottish economist and author of *The Wealth of Nations,* might equally be attracted by the lure of a monetary mechanism where the monetary responsibilities of the state are negligible.

To help us understand how a market commodity money system is supposed to work, suppose that we were to use bricks—plain, ordinary building bricks—as money. You probably are ready to protest that bricks are totally unacceptable as money because they are too heavy and too bulky to take on a shopping trip or even to keep around the house, but we shall take care of that objection a little later in this chapter. For although bricks may seem a little strange as a commodity to serve as money, they actually have most of the qualities of an ideal currency.

Bricks are in constant demand for use as a nonmoney commodity, principally as a building material. We expect that the demand for bricks qua commodity should vary inversely with the price of bricks, but if we are to consider using bricks as money, we have to be careful just how we define their "price." We shall suppose that the basic monetary unit, the standard of value, is one brick, that is, the prices of all other goods will normally be quoted in terms of the number of bricks which it takes to buy them. Hence the price of bricks must be measured in terms of the quantity of other goods which one brick will buy. Without getting into the problems of finding an appropriate way to weight all of the diverse goods in the economy, we might simply consider some typical market basket of goods and then measure the number of such units a brick will buy. As the price of bricks (the quantity of goods a brick will buy) goes up, the average price of all other goods (the number of bricks it takes to buy an average good) necessarily goes down. That is to say, the general price level in the economy varies inversely with the price of whatever good we choose to use as the standard of value, in this case the building brick. Figure 3–1 shows a demand curve for bricks, where the price of bricks is measured in this way.

The demand for the commodity as currency should also vary inversely with its price. As the price of bricks falls, the smaller is the quantity of other goods which each brick will buy, and therefore the greater will be the demand for bricks as money. Another way of viewing the same phenomenon is that as the price of bricks falls, the average price (measured in bricks) of other goods is rising. It then takes more bricks to buy the same quantity of goods; ceteris paribus, the demand for currency will rise.

The total demand for bricks (or whatever other commodity we use for currency) is simply the sum of the demand for it as a commodity and the demand for it as currency. This total demand is shown as D_T in Figure 3–2. At a given price, say P_1, the quantity of bricks demanded as a building material is given by the distance OC ($= P_1A$), and the quantity of currency demanded is given by the distance CD ($= AB$).

What makes bricks such an ideal currency commodity is that they are manufactured and supplied in a highly competitive industry characterized by numerous small firms spread throughout the country.[1] Furthermore, there exists a very

---

[1] The production of bricks cannot effectively be centralized, because the value of bricks is so low relative to their bulk and weight. It would not be economical to produce bricks at a central location and then ship them to distant building sites.

FIGURE 3–1

The Commodity Demand for Bricks

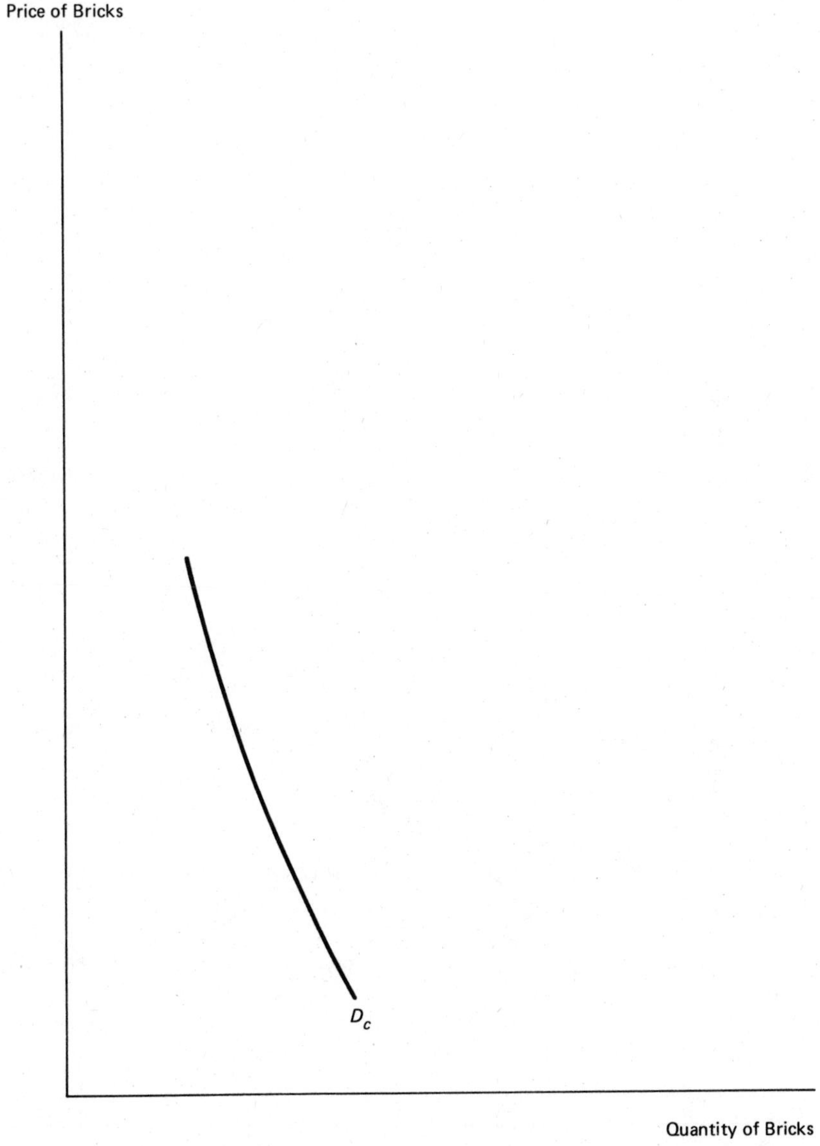

Price of Bricks

D_c

Quantity of Bricks

FIGURE 3–2

The Total Demand for Bricks under a Market Commodity Money (brick standard)

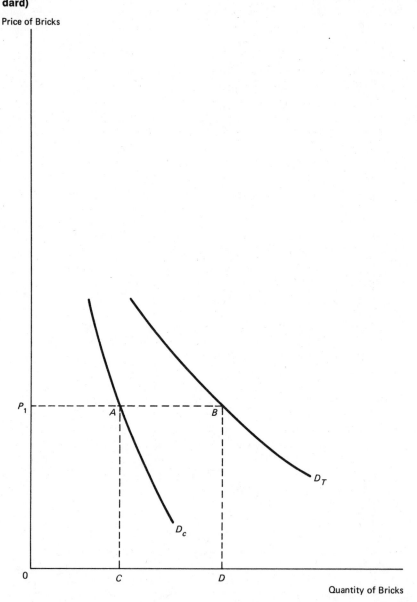

large and durable stock of bricks which can be shifted if necessary between monetary and nonmonetary uses. What does that imply? When the demand for bricks changes (i.e., when either the commodity-demand or the currency-demand curve shifts), the quantity of bricks being supplied will respond easily and quickly. In technical terms, the supply function for bricks should be very highly elastic with respect to changes in the price of bricks. The implication is that the supply curve for bricks will be horizontal, or nearly so (Figure 3–3). If the total demand for bricks rises, the price of bricks will initially tend to rise as brick sellers attempt to ration existing stocks. But the production of bricks will then be more attractive, so brick production will rise until the price is pushed back to its original level. If the demand for bricks as currency should rise, the additional demand can be met initially out of stocks intended for building use. Then as production rises, the new bricks can replace the depleted stocks. In this way, the price of bricks, and therefore the average price level of all other goods, should be highly stable (Figure 3–4).

To summarize: an ideal market commodity currency should have a perfectly elastic supply curve and a large existing stock which can serve either as a commodity or as currency. When the demand for the commodity changes for either reason, the quantity of the commodity supplied will respond quickly, thereby stabilizing the level of prices in the economy. The whole system—at least on paper—works automatically according to the laws of economics and relies very little if at all on the laws and the control of governments.

3.2.2 Controlled Commodity Money

The second type of commodity money originates when the government assumes the sole right and responsibility for producing currency in the form of coins. The government has two responsibilities in this system. First, it defines the unit of

FIGURE 3–3

Equilibrium under a Market Commodity Currency System (brick standard)

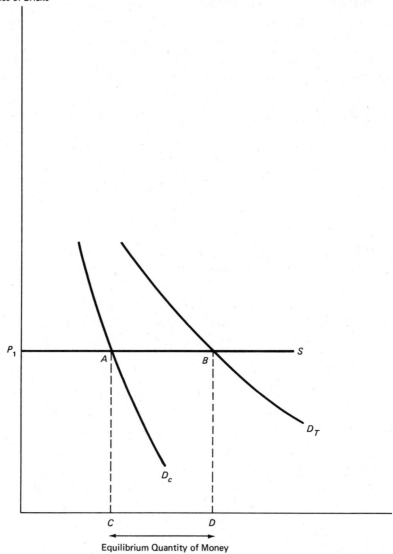

Price of Bricks

Equilibrium Quantity of Money

Quantity of Bricks

FIGURE 3–4

Reaction of a Market Commodity System to a General Increase in Demand

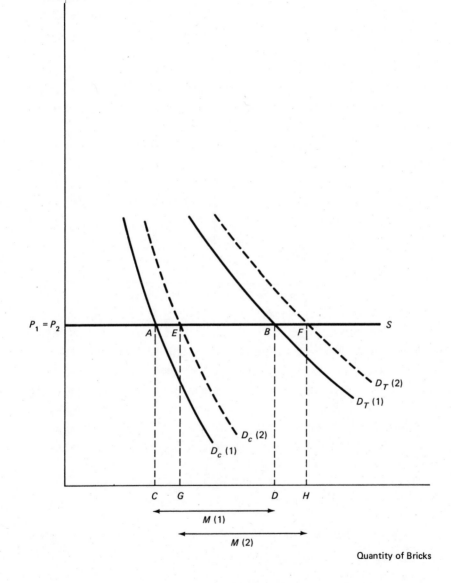

Price of Bricks

$P_1 = P_2$

S

A E B F

D_T (2)

D_T (1)

D_c (2)

D_c (1)

C G D H

M (1)

M (2)

Quantity of Bricks

account (the dollar, the franc, the pound) in terms of the chosen commodity. For example, the government may choose gold as the currency standard and define the dollar as equal to ten grains of gold. Since there are 480 grains in one troy ounce, the *mint price* of gold is $\frac{1}{48}$ ounce per dollar, or $48 per ounce. The second job for government is to operate a minting service. Then anyone may bring raw gold to the mint and exchange it for gold coins stamped with the appropriate denominations in terms of the unit of account. A miner takes an ounce of gold dust to the mint and receives in exchange coinage containing an ounce of gold and stamped with values totaling $48.[2]

The minting service is equivalent to a price-fixing program for the currency commodity. The government in effect is agreeing to buy or sell gold at the fixed price of $48 per ounce. Recall that the ideal market commodity currency would be characterized by a stable price because of a per-fectly elastic supply curve. A controlled—government-oper-ated—commodity currency also has a stable price, but there is a substantial difference. To see how this price-fixing pro-gram works, examine Figure 3–5. The supply curve (S) slopes upward rather steeply. Unlike the highly elastic mar-ket commodity, the supply of a good controlled commodity should be relatively inelastic. There exists a large stock of gold, and additions to the stock are small. The higher the price of gold (in terms of the amounts of other goods it will buy), the more profitable will gold mining be, and the greater will be the new quantity supplied.[3]

The demand for gold as a commodity—for artistic, indus-trial, and dental purposes—is an inverse function of the price

---

[2] In practice, he would go to an assay office, a branch of the mint where the proper weight and fineness of the commodity can be determined.

[3] We ignore for the time being the possibility that gold may be imported from or exported to other countries. See Chapter 12, especially section 12.4. Also note that we treat gold sales by the government as a negative demand, rather than as a true supply.

FIGURE 3–5

Equilibrium under a Controlled Commodity Currency System (gold standard)

Price of Gold

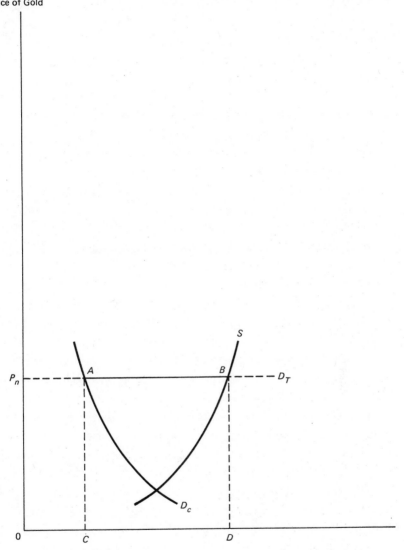

Quantity of Gold

of gold (D_c) in the standard fashion. But the monetary demand for gold is determined by the government and is perfectly elastic at the fixed mint price (P_m). So long as the government stands ready to buy gold at $48 per ounce, no one else will be able to buy gold at a lower price; who would sell it to him? So long as the government stands ready to sell gold to anyone at $48 per ounce, no one else will be able to sell at a higher price; who would buy it from him?[4] Therefore, the total demand for gold is also perfectly elastic at the mint price. A market commodity currency should have a perfectly elastic supply. A controlled commodity currency has a perfectly elastic demand.

Two other points about Figure 3–5 are important to our understanding of the differences between the two commodity systems. First, the horizontal axis no longer measures the quantity of money; it only measures the quantity of the commodity that serves as money. Thus the distance OC is the quantity of gold used as a commodity. CD measures the amount of gold used for money. The value of the money supply, in terms of the unit of account, is the area of the rectangle $ABCD$. For example, if $CD = 1$ billion ounces, and $AC = 48, then the quantity of money is $ABCD = 48 billion. The second point is more substantive. We measured the price of the market commodity in terms of the amount of other goods a unit of the commodity could buy. But in Figure 3–5, the price is the amount of currency that a unit of the commodity will buy. The two are equivalent only if a unit of currency always can buy the same amount of other goods; that is, only if the aggregate price level is fixed over time. That distinction becomes important later (particularly in Chapter 10 and Part Four) when we examine the effects on the economy of changes in the price level. For now we assume prices to be given.

---

[4] Of course, if the government were to set too low a price, it could soon run out of gold to sell. The higher market price would then reassert itself.

In most respects, the two types of commodity money systems are quite similar. They both leave the determination of the optimum quantity of money to economic forces; one by relying on a highly elastic supply of the commodity, the other by imposing a perfectly elastic demand. In neither case is there any scope for the use of discretionary policies to control the quantity of money. The choice between the two systems rests primarily on the nature of the commodity which the community wishes to use for currency. A commodity which is widely and competitively produced will likely have a stable price without any government intervention. A scarce commodity with a largely fixed supply requires government management.

The principal weakness of a pure commodity currency (of whichever type) is the high proportion of the country's resources which must be committed to the production of the money commodity. The absorption of resources in currency production precludes the production of other desirable outputs. Whether we kiln an extra billion bricks or we mine (or purchase from abroad) an extra million ounces of gold, that form of currency production is costly to the community. Economists have estimated that as much as $1\frac{1}{2}$ percent of the national income of the United States might have to be devoted to currency production in order for a strict commodity money system to be compatible with a stable price level.[5] At current levels of national income, more than $15 billion of annual output would be in the form of new currency: the equivalent of 5 million automobiles, hundreds of thousands of homes, or thousands of hospitals, schools, or day care centers.

Would the advantages to society of a pure commodity currency outweigh that cost? The answer depends both on how

---

[5] See Milton Friedman, *Essays in Positive Economics* (Chicago: University of Chicago Press, 1953), p. 210. His analysis dealt with historical data for the first half of this century.

well the commodity money works in practice to stabilize the prices of other goods and on the importance the community attaches to automaticity and to minimizing governmental activity.

3.3 REPRESENTATIVE COMMODITY MONEY

The most serious shortcoming of the brick standard as described above is that bricks are extremely bulky and heavy; they lack portability, one of the desired characteristics of a commodity currency. Bricks also would cease to be durable if they were subjected to the abrasive wear associated with frequent transactions. To a lesser degree, the same problems arise when gold is used as the currency commodity. Therefore, if we are seriously to consider either bricks or gold as currency, we should propose to augment the system with fully convertible paper money. We call such a system a *representative commodity money.*

A representative commodity currency system requires a form of government control or regulation in order to prevent abuse. The state's function is to issue paper money in exchange for the currency commodity in a strict one-for-one ratio. That is, anyone who possesses "hard" currency may sell it to the government in exchange for paper currency. The effect is that the state maintains storage vaults or warehouses, and it issues "warehouse receipts" for the commodities it acquires. Those receipts then circulate as money in place of the bulky commodity. Note carefully that the introduction of representative paper money cannot be used to increase the available quantity of currency. It merely replaces a bulky commodity with a more convenient piece of paper. The advantage is to make the exchange of goods less cumbersome and less expensive. But there are costs: the currency is now much easier to counterfeit, and the public must be willing to believe both that the commodity is being safely stored and that money holders will in fact be able to exchange their paper for the commodity should they desire to do so. In sum, a representative commodity standard requires more faith, a higher order of confidence in the government, than does a simple commodity system.

3.4   FRACTIONAL-RESERVE CURRENCY

Representative commodity money suffers from the same handicap as circulating commodity money: the resource cost is very high. In both cases a large quantity of some good or collection of goods must be allocated to the currency system. So long as the bricks must be stored in warehouses for possible exchange for the circulating paper receipts, they are not available for use in construction of buildings. So long as gold coins circulate as currency, the gold they contain cannot be made into jewelry or teeth. But the use of representative money offers the possibility for substantially reducing that cost without seriously affecting the nature of the monetary system.

Suppose that we have adopted the brick standard, so that our basic currency consists of paper money which is guaranteed by the government to be fully convertible into bricks. Now under most circumstances only a few people are likely to make that conversion. A builder who receives payment (in paper) for a completed house may convert the currency receipts into bricks to use in the next house. Individuals who lack faith in the redeemability of the paper currency may prefer to hold the currency commodity instead. But we might reasonably suppose that over any given length of time no more than, say, 5 percent of the commodity reserve will be needed by the state to make such conversions. The other 95 percent serves no practical function other than to instill confidence among the populace. The state therefore can profit (and thereby the community can profit) by selling the bulk of the commodity reserve and spending the proceeds on real goods and services (hospitals, teachers, bomb craters). So long as the remaining reserve is large enough to insure that anyone who wishes to exchange paper money for "hard currency," no great loss of confidence or other effect on the currency's value should result. Such is the logic behind a *fractional-reserve commodity currency*. The reduction in the size of the currency reserve increases the real wealth of the community.

How does our wealth increase? There is not necessarily any increase in the quantity of currency in circulation; the benefit comes purely from the state's making better use of its assets. For example, suppose the community wishes to build a hospital. The usual procedure would be to raise the funds through taxation. Taxpayers would relinquish part of their purchasing power as consumers and turn it over to the government. Instead of spending our income on automobiles and vacations, we would spend it on the new hospital. But now we suggest an alternative: sell off part of the commodity currency reserve. The quantity of currency outstanding has been determined in the manner shown in Figure 3–3 (or Figure 3–5) above. But we take part of the currency reserve (some fraction of CD) and sell it, perhaps to home builders. The government can then spend the proceeds from the sale on social projects such as our hospital. The sale therefore permits us to divert resources from producing the currency commodity and to use the released workers and capital to help build the hospital. Instead of giving up consumer goods, the community gives up only that part of its commodity reserve which it was not going to use anyway. Everyone is better off, but there is no slight-of-hand involved at all. We simply exchange something we do not want (the excess commodity reserve) for something we want very much (new hospitals). The effect is a one-shot, one-time benefit, but it does bring about a real increase in the wealth and welfare of the community.

The cost that corresponds to this benefit is that our insurance that our paper money will always be convertible into the currency commodity is necessarily reduced. The government must judge the size of the reserve which will preserve convertibility in practice. Will there ever be a "run" on the reserve? Will the citizenry ever demand that more than 5 percent or 25 percent or 50 percent of the outstanding paper money be exchanged for the commodity? Only if we can rely on there being a stable demand for paper money, and only if the government is stable and reliable can we operate on a small fractional reserve. But so long as the minimum fractional reserve is fixed by law—preventing excessive money creation against the given reserve—and so long as the fraction is not set precariously low, a fractional-reserve currency is generally preferable to (i.e., less expensive to operate than) a pure commodity currency system.

The production of convertible paper money need not be confined to the state. Private banks or other business firms may be allowed to produce paper money as well. They would pay out paper money in the process of expanding loans or other assets, subject to a legal limitation that their notes be fully convertible into the reserve commodity. The major problem with such a system, which was in operation in the United States until 1935, is that the costs of using private paper money are bound to exceed the costs of using government-issued paper currency. This higher cost arises primarily from the additional information required, the solvency of the many different currency producers, and the acceptability or redeemability of the paper money which they issue.

3.5 INCONVERTIBLE PAPER MONEY

The next step in the logical evolution of money is the development of *inconvertible paper currency*. Once a representative paper money system is in wide use, and people become accustomed to the idea of accepting paper currency purely as a medium of exchange, as an intermediary step in the exchange process, then the commodity reserve becomes almost completely vestigial. It may still be necessary to hold some kind of commodity reserve in order to provide confidence in the paper currency, but as time passes that vague form of reassurance should become less and less necessary. After all, what we want from the currency which we accept in exchange is the assurance that we shall be able to get rid of it in fair trade at any time in the future. Modern governments usually provide that assurance, not through large holdings of commodities, but through the passage of laws requiring the acceptance of the paper currency for all normal transactions. The paper currency is then said to be *legal tender*.

Regardless of whether the paper money is legal tender or is just widely accepted and trusted, it serves all of the same monetary functions as the old-fashioned commodity currencies. In fact, it is generally even more convenient for us to purchase goods with paper money than it was with most commodities. The major difference in usage is that inconvertible paper has almost no nonmonetary (commodity) uses. What can you do with a $10 Federal Reserve note besides using it as money? The cliché cartoon shows the millionaire lighting his cigar with one. It makes an excellent bookmark and has a good deal of prestige value as wallpaper. Certain specimens have some independent aesthetic or financial value for collectors. We can readily concede that the range of nonmonetary uses is very limited.

The appeal of inconvertible paper is that it is very inexpensive to produce. Compared to the production of commodity money, the resource cost of paper is negligible: instead of several billion dollars per year, we spend only a few million. The marginal cost of producing a dollar bill—whether a $1 or a $100 note—is only a fraction of a penny. Just as a country can cut costs by shifting from a pure commodity currency to a fractional reserve, so can it save expense by eliminating the reserve completely and adopting an inconvertible paper system.

Because the savings from the use of paper currency are so great, governments have long been attracted to it on purely rational economic grounds. In fact, inconvertible paper money was first used more than 900 years ago by the Sung dynasty in China. Not only counterfeiting but even refusal to accept the paper in trade was punishable by death, so two of the usual objections to paper currencies were effectively quieted. Nonetheless, the Chinese experience with paper money has not been an unbroken success; it has rather been a series of experiments, each one of which has eventually ended in abuse and abandonment.[6]

The very persuasiveness of the argument for printing paper money is also its inherent defect. An alternative name for inconvertible paper is *fiat money:* currency which is brought into production by decree, by government fiat. What, then, limits the production of paper money? Who or what determines how much should be produced? Where commodity money is used, the cost of producing additional units provides a natural economic limitation to increases in the quantity of currency. Are there similar safeguards for inconvertible paper? If not, the lure of an easy gain may prove irresistible.

The problem with a paper currency may be illustrated by reference to Figure 3–3. The horizontal line S indicates that the supply of the currency commodity is assumed to be perfectly elastic at the price P_1. That price is determined by the (constant) marginal cost of producing the commodity. Now if the community switches to an inconvertible paper system, it must introduce some new rules. What happens to the supply curve (S)? The cost of producing paper money is negli-

---

[6] For a fascinating account of the early history of paper money in China, see Gordon Tullock, "Paper Money: A Cycle in Cathay," *The Economic History Review* 9 (1957): 393–407.

Even Dollar Bills Cost More These Days

The New York Times/Joyce Dopkeen

Crane & Co., Inc., mill in Dalton, Mass., is protected by a fence and barbed wire. Inside, paper for printing U.S. currency is made to rigid specifications.

This stock is almost the same as the waste cotton and linen used for making currency paper. The picture was taken at another Crane mill close to the first.

By LINDA CHARLTON
Special to The New York Times

WASHINGTON, Aug. 27—If money really does talk, it is probably muttering about inflation just like the rest of us, because the cost of making a dollar bill is going up, too.

It now takes about one cent to produce a dollar—or a thousand dollars for that matter, in a single note—according to Andrew Wilson, chief of the Office of Financial Management at the Bureau of Engraving and Printing.

In 1971, it cost about seven mils, or seven-tenths of a penny, to make a currency note. A thousand notes cost $8.68 two years ago and $10.50 now. And this adds up to a little over $30-million for the 3 billion notes that the Government expects to print this year.

The two major factors in the rising cost of money are the same as in the rising cost of much that money buys—higher prices for raw materials and higher labor costs in particular.

Rising labor costs have been offset to a degree by technological innovations such as more modern presses, Mr. Wilson said, but for the first time in memory the cost of such items as the cotton waste used to make engraving plates have also risen substantially.

The cost of textile wastes affects the cost of paper too. All of that used for currency is manufactured — and has been since 1879—by the Crane Paper Company of Dalton, Mass.

Fred Crane Jr., head of research and development in his family's business, explained that one source of the very special rags that are the raw material of "currency"—their term for this type of paper— has risen from about 14 cents to 24 cents a pound in the last year. Part of the price rise, he said, was due to competition from manufacturers, particularly overseas, who use textile waste to produce more textiles.

Only cotton and linen waste are used in currency because synthetics are "for the birds" in making currency, Mr. Crane said. And, according to Mr. Wilson, about 7 million pounds of textile waste will be needed to supply the demand this year.

The paper is produced in sheets that are roughly 25 inches by 22 inches, large enough for 36 bills. Over the years, the precise composition of the paper has changed in ways that Mr. Crane will not talk about, but it is still rag paper, made of textile wastes and water, made to the bureau's "very rigid specification" in what he describes as "kind of a funny color" and "off-white."

Security High

The building in which the currency is produced is guarded, as are the trucks that transport it, and Crane is "quite fussy about who goes in and out."

The paper is subjected to rigid tests, particularly for strength, but even so, it is short-lived. The usual life expectancy of a $1 bill, according to Mr. Wilson, is 18 months. For the higher denominations," he added, it is—or was a few years ago—three to five years. But in these inflationary days when more money moves out of wallets more quickly, he added, the life expectancy of even a $10 or a $20 bill is not what it used to be.

Source: *New York Times,* August 28, 1973.

gible, so the S curve shifts downward until it is practically on the horizontal axis.[7] There thus exists no equilibrium point at any positive price. Conversely, the pure economics of the case shows that the general price level (the inverse of the price of the currency commodity, in this case paper) would tend to rise toward infinity without ever reaching an equilibrium. Unfortunately, history bears out that gloomy prediction.

The classic example of what is in store for a nation which fails to control the issuance of paper currency is the great German inflation of 1922–23. The German money supply increased astronomically: from 6 billion marks before World War I to over 500 billions of billions of marks (500,000,000,-000,000,000,000 marks) at the end of 1923, a number which does bear a striking resemblance to the mileage to some distant star. During the 16 months of the "hyper-inflation," the quantity of currency in circulation was rising at the rate of 314 percent per month. The response of prices was comparable, but equally incredible. At one point the price of a ham sandwich increased from 14,000 marks one day to 24,000 marks the next! By comparison, the rates of growth which brought about the downfall of at least one ancient Chinese dynasty seem exceptionally mild.[8]

The explanation for the German currency debacle is rooted in the country's defeat in World War I. Government opera-

---

[7] In one sense, the supply curve for paper money may be regarded as horizontal at exactly zero. Suppose we wish to double the supply of paper currency. Instead of printing twice as many bills, we can merely print higher numbers on the same number of units as the old bills wear out. Instead of $1 bills, we print $2 bills, and tens in place of fives. Thus we can in fact make the quantity of currency as high as we wish without incurring any additional cost.

[8] See Fritz K. Ringer, ed., *The German Inflation of 1923* (New York: Oxford University Press, 1969). As impossible as it may seem, the German case is not even the worst on record. Following World War II, Hungary underwent one agonizing year in which the currency supply increased at the rate of 12,200 percent per month while prices rose by almost 20,000 percent per month. By comparison, the worst abuse in China (1260–1330), which is commonly supposed to have brought down the Mongol dynasty, averaged out to about an 11 percent annual rate of growth and never approached the rates of 20th-century Europe.

tions were stifled by the burden of a very heavy debt coupled with the exhorbitant reparations payments imposed by the Allies at Versailles. Financial recovery seemed to depend on the ability of the government to pay its expenses out of its most valuable remaining asset, the printing press. As prices rose, government expenses increased commensurately. The increase in expenses had to be met with a new currency issue. The increase in new currency led to higher prices, higher government expenses, more currency, in a perpetual spiral. By the end of 1923, the economy was rapidly approaching the infinite price level—the zero value for currency—which we described above with the aid of Figure 3–3.

The problem and the promise for inconvertible paper currency is that it requires a stable and responsible government. The laws of the marketplace cannot assure its smooth function. The state must declare a monopoly on currency production and then either elaborate rules to govern its supply or else be willing to exercise restrained discretion. The U.S. government today relies on a mixture of rules and discretion. First, the issuance of paper currency (Federal Reserve notes) is separated from both the executive and the legislative branches which control government spending. That is, control by the government over the Federal Reserve System is kept at a minimum. Second, the United States Treasury is prohibited by law from borrowing more than $5 billion directly from the Federal Reserve System.[9] Thus the government can raise revenues only through taxation or through borrowing from the public and cannot run the printing press to meet its own expenses.[10] Third, the Federal Reserve banks issue currency only at the initiative of the member commercial banks. As we show in the next chapter, that system provides an effective check on the growth of the currency supply

---

[9] The Fed's authorization to lend directly to the Treasury must be renewed annually by Congress.

[10] This point is developed further in Chapter 17, section 17.2.1.

so long as bank deposits are stable. Therefore, the ultimate control over the currency supply in the United States rests with the discretion exercised by the Federal Reserve System in limiting the growth of bank deposits. How well does the system work? Since that question relates to the overall conduct of monetary policy, we defer it until Chapter 17.

3.6 CONCLUSIONS

This chapter has described several different systems for producing currency. Commodity currencies have the advantage of providing an automatic, self-regulating mechanism for bringing the equilibrium quantity of currency into circulation, whether they are decentralized and privately operated (market type) or run as a government monopoly (controlled). They suffer from high resource costs and from the inability of the government to manipulate the quantity of currency for policy purposes. Pure paper systems reduce the resource cost dramatically and provide the possibility for policy control, but only at the expense of opening up the possibility for abuse and ensuing inflation. Fractional-reserve paper systems offer a compromise.

The history of currency production throughout the world has generally witnessed a transition from commodities to paper. Today, paper money has almost completely replaced the use of commodities as a domestic medium of exchange in all industrial countries, and it seems only a matter of time before the transition is complete even for international trade (see Chapter 12). And there is a good reason for this trend. Commodities must be used as a medium of exchange wherever people cannot be highly confident that the value in exchange of paper receipts will be stable over time. In primitive societies and in countries without strong and responsible governments, traders will demand full value in exchange, and the medium of exchange will have to be a highly valued com-

FIGURE 3–6

The Evolution of Currency Standards

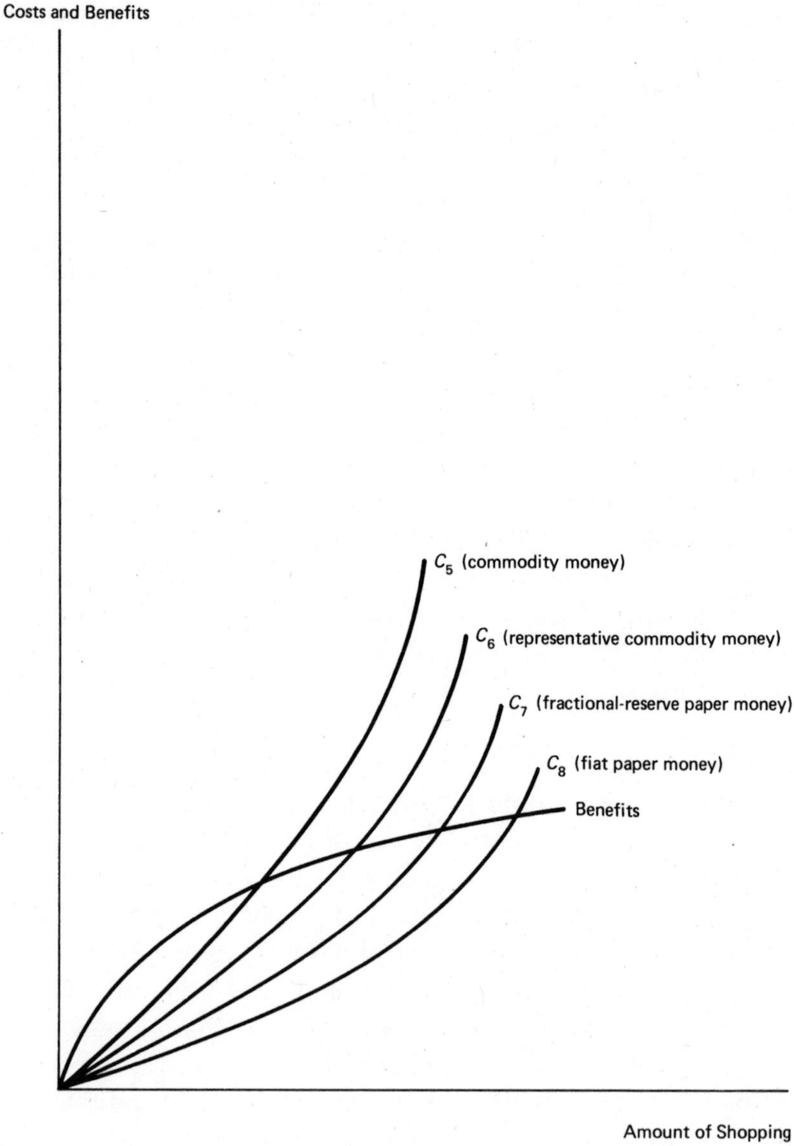

Costs and Benefits

C_5 (commodity money)

C_6 (representative commodity money)

C_7 (fractional-reserve paper money)

C_8 (fiat paper money)

Benefits

Amount of Shopping

modity. But as societies evolve and stabilize, it becomes possible for the community to reduce the real cost of exchanging goods and services by developing more efficient media of exchange. This evolution is illustrated in Figure 3–6, which picks up where we ended Chapter 2 (cf Figure 2–5); the cost curves continue to shift downward with every major development.

Paper currency, especially fiat currency, has proved to be the most efficient form of currency for modern economies. But the payments system of the future will surely be an electronic information system.[11] Instead of using checks to effect deposit transfers, a nationwide computer network will automatically make offsetting debit and credit entrees to the accounts of individual traders, thus eliminating the mountains of paper work (check clearing and bookkeeping chores) entailed by the present system. Business firms and private individuals will have equal access to the system. Retailers will have terminals plugged into a central computer network to effect instant transfer of funds from the buyer to the seller.

When you purchase a typewriter at a Sears store, for example, you will be able to pay by giving the clerk a plastic identification card similar to your present credit card. He will insert the card in a computer terminal which will transmit electronically sales and payment information whereby your bank deposit account will be debited and the Sears account credited.

The monetary implications of an electronic transfer system are far-reaching. For one, the use of currency as a means of payment may be reduced drastically. Second, the level of efficiency with which exchange takes place will be increased, mainly as a result of the substantial reduction in transaction costs due to the decrease in the volume of paper work per-

---

[11] For an interesting description of such a system, see: Mark J. Flannery and Dwight M. Jaffee, *The Economic Implications of an Electronic Monetary Transfer System* (Lexington, Mass.: Lexington Books, 1973).

formed by the banking industry. Of course, the introduction of electronic transfers will necessitate substantial expenditure on computer hardware. According to the best estimates available, however, there should be substantial savings to the private banking industry as well as to the Federal Reserve System from operating the payments mechanism at reduced cost.

Eventually, paper currency may be completely replaced by "electronic money." But the prospects of success for any currency standard rest not only on its theoretical advantages; they depend most importantly on the attitudes, sympathies, and understanding of the public. Electronic money will replace paper currency just as soon as stores, banks, and people are ready to accept it.

REVIEW QUESTIONS

1. How would a society select a market commodity money?
2. Does the replacement of commodity money by paper money necessarily involve a net gain in welfare to society?
3. Is the supply of bricks highly elastic?
4. When the unit of account is designated as one brick, define what is meant by the price of bricks.
5. Explain how the use of brick money could guarantee a stable price level.

SUGGESTED FURTHER READING

Flannery, Mark J., and Dwight M. Jaffee. *The Economic Implications of an Electronic Monetary Transfer System*. Lexington, Mass.: Lexington Books, 1973.

Friedman, Milton. "Commodity Reserve Currency," *Essays in Positive Economics*. Chicago: University of Chicago Press, 1953.

Ringer, Fritz K. (ed.). *The German Inflation of 1923*. New York: Oxford University Press, 1969.

Tullock, Gordon. "Paper Money: A Cycle in Cathay," *The Economic History Review*, 1957, pp. 393–407.

chapter 4
The Supply of Money

4.1 INTRODUCTION

The size and rate of change of the money stock held by the public (M) are important statistics in our economy; changes in M can affect the level of prices, interest rates, income, and employment. Control of the money stock, therefore, is an important tool for stabilizing the economy. Furthermore, by closely monitoring the behavior of M, we may obtain useful clues about the course of the economy in advance of more basic information. Preliminary money supply data are available weekly with only a very short time lag, whereas unemployment and inflation figures are issued monthly, and data on gross national product (GNP) appear quarterly. To begin our study of the relationship between money and the rest of the economy, we examine in the present chapter the factors which determine the supply of money.

Many factors are involved in determining the total supply of money in existence at any moment. Throughout this chapter we present these factors, ultimately arranging them conveniently into a model of the money supply process. It will be useful, however, to begin with a very simplified financial framework in order to demonstrate each element of the supply process in turn.

The most important institution to include in our model is the private commercial bank. The commercial banking industry, in the United States and other industrial countries, plays a vital role in the creation of money. Over 90 percent of the value of all payments made in the United States is made by check, and more than three fourths of the total stock of money is in the form of demand deposits. Thus in our complex economic world, understanding how the supply of money is determined is largely a matter of understanding how commercial banks supply demand deposits.

4.2 COMMERCIAL BANKS AND THE MONEY SUPPLY

Demand deposits are created in either of two ways. The first is the familiar process in which a bank customer exchanges currency for a bank deposit. Everyday language reflects this activity in such expressions as "putting money in the bank" and "depositing money." What is put in the bank can be coin or paper currency, or it could be a check drawn on another bank. When a customer deposits coins and paper money, the bank's balance sheet will show an increase in the asset "currency" (colloquially known in the trade as "vault cash") and a corresponding increase in the liability "demand deposits."[1]

Local Bank

Vault cash + (currency)	Demand deposits +

Since we are interested primarily in the total quantity of demand deposits supplied by commercial banks in the aggregate, we may also notice the effects of the deposit on the aggregate balance sheet for the system:

Commercial Banks

Vault cash +	Demand deposits +

---

[1] See Chapter 1, section 1.3., for a review of the bank balance sheet structure.

Of course, if the customer merely deposits a check drawn on someone else's account (either at the same or a different bank), there will be no effect on the aggregate accounts.

The second way banks supply demand deposits is by acquiring earning assets from the public, that is, by making loans and purchasing securities. When a customer borrows from a commercial bank, he is in effect exchanging his own IOU either for demand deposits or for currency. In some cases the proceeds of a bank loan are held by the borrower in the form of currency. The balance sheet effect then is quite simple: on the asset side of the balance sheet, loans increase at commercial banks, and currency in the vault decreases.

Commercial Banks

Vault cash —	
Loans +	

But a more interesting case arises when customers desire to hold demand deposits preparatory to making payments by check. Since checks are by far the most common medium for making payments in our economy, it is not surprising that most bank loans are transacted in this manner. Furthermore, banks may insist on crediting customers' accounts for the loan proceeds rather than paying cash in order to build up their balance sheets at least temporarily. Therefore, the balance sheet effect of a new bank loan appears as follows:

Commercial Banks

Loans +	Demand deposits +

The expansion of bank loans leads directly and immediately to an increase in the money supply.

Similarly, the repayment of loans at commercial banks will contract the money supply. Borrowers normally write checks against their demand deposit accounts to repay maturing bank loans. The aggregate balance sheet for all commercial banks shows decreases in the asset loans and in the liability demand deposits:

Commercial Banks

Loans −	Demand deposits −

Other banking activities have similar effects on the money supply. Suppose that the banks, instead of making additional loans, purchase government securities from the public. If they pay for the securities with credits to the sellers' demand deposit accounts, we observe the following effects on the balance sheet of the banking system:

Commercial Banks

Government securities +	Demand deposits +

And what if customers buy government securities from their banks? They pay for them by writing checks, and the money supply tends to contract.

Commercial Banks

Government securities −	Demand deposits −

What is clearly revealed by all of these balance sheet effects is the close relationship between the expansion and contraction of demand deposits—the most important component of the money supply—and the lending and investing which comprise the main business activity of the commercial banking system.

4.3   A SIMPLE MONEY SUPPLY MODEL

As a first approximation, let us assume that the only private financial institutions are commercial banks, and that they issue only one type of deposit: there are no time deposits, only demand deposits. We shall assume that the supply of currency is given, determined by an independent "currency authority" (say, the Department of the Treasury). This assumption, which we relax later in the discussion, permits us to concentrate for now on the supply of demand deposits.

4.3.1 The Market for Vault Cash

The key element in determining the *supply* of demand deposits in this simple model is the process of reaching *equilibrium* between the *demand* for currency and its given supply. The demand for currency has three components: demand by individuals or households for "pocket cash," demand by business firms for "register cash," and demand by commercial banks for "vault cash." The first two are related primarily to the volume of consumer spending, particularly on small retail transactions. We may therefore conveniently combine them into a single variable, which we label K_p^d to signify the public's demand for currency.[2] If we assume that the level of retail spending is given, then we may treat the public's holdings of currency as a given exogenous variable[3] and just label it K_p.

The demand by commercial banks for vault cash (K_b^d)—cash kept in reserve by the banks to be used to meet customers' demands for currency—is related primarily to the level of deposits (D) held by each bank. Commercial banks have a legal as well as a business obligation to convert deposits into cash on demand, but that obligation does not imply that they must hold cash equal to their deposit liabilities unless they expect all of their customers to withdraw their deposits at the same time. Under normal conditions a relatively small reserve of vault cash will do the job, just as a government can usually run a fractional-reserve currency system (Chapter 3). For example, a bank with $100 million in demand deposits may be able to operate with as little as $5 million in cash reserves unless it has reason to expect an abnormally large and sudden wave of withdrawals (which probably would signal a collapse in the public's preference for demand deposits). This fractional-reserve policy implies that the banking system's

---

[2] Throughout this book, we use the superscripts d and s to denote the amounts demanded or supplied, respectively.

[3] See Chapter 1, section 1.4.

demand for vault cash, even in the absence of any legal constraints, will be proportional to its total demand deposits:

$$K_b{}^d = v^* \cdot D \tag{4.1}$$

where v^* is the *desired* ratio of vault cash to deposits. It is a fraction determined by bankers' expectations of net withdrawals of deposits.

The amount of currency available to banks to use as vault cash is equal to the difference between the total fixed supply of currency (K) and the amount demanded by the public (K_p). The *supply* of vault cash therefore is

$$K_b{}^s = K - K_p. \tag{4.2}$$

The sum of the amount of reserves held by the banks ($K_b{}^s$ in our simple framework) and the amount of currency held by the public (K_p) is called the *monetary base*. We may define the base generally as a set of assets the value of which the central bank may cause to vary in order to exert control over the supply of money. In this first approximation the only form of base money is currency, and the monetary base is equal to the given supply of currency.

If the market for vault cash is in equilibrium (that is, if the supply of vault cash is equal to the demand for vault cash), then the public's demand for currency also must be satisfied. Indeed, we assume that the market for publicly held currency is always in equilibrium, that the public always can get whatever amount of currency it demands simply by giving up a corresponding value of demand deposits (by writing checks for cash). The market for vault cash is the means for equilibrating the total supply of currency with the total demand for it.

4.3.2   The Supply of Demand Deposits

Now the supply of demand deposits can be determined. At any time there is a given supply of vault cash which is equal to the total supply of currency less the amount held by the public. The supply of demand deposits (D^s) is simply a multiple of the demand for vault cash.

$$v^* \cdot D^s = K_b{}^d \qquad\qquad \text{(from equation 4.1)}$$

or

$$D^s = \frac{1}{v^*} \cdot (K_b{}^d) \qquad\qquad (4.3)$$

If the demand for vault cash equals its supply, then

$$D^s = \frac{1}{v^*} \cdot (K_b{}^s)$$

or (see Figure 4.1)

$$D^s = \frac{1}{v^*} \cdot (K - K_p). \qquad\qquad (4.4)$$

So if, for example, banks desire to hold vault cash equal to 5 percent of their deposits, deposits clearly must be 20 times the supply of vault cash in equilibrium.

We see the reasoning behind this conclusion more readily by asking what happens when the demand for vault cash is *not* equal to the supply. The commercial banks may find themselves holding more vault cash than they desire, perhaps because of an inflow of currency from the public. We then expect them to try to rid themselves of the excess by making additional loans or purchases of securities, which add to the supply of demand deposits. As long as the public's preference for currency remains unchanged, the banks' excess currency must be absorbed eventually as an increase in the quantity of *vault* cash desired when demand deposits rise.

But by how much do total demand deposits increase when a single bank makes a new loan? What happens throughout the system when the individual bank attempts to rid itself of a surplus of vault cash? In other words, what role does the single bank play in the deposit-expansion process which results from an initial inflow of currency to the system? Suppose that our single bank initially is in equilibrium. It has a

FIGURE 4–1

The Supply of Demand Deposits (*D*) in a Simple (first approximation) Model

Supply of Deposits to Public (D^s)

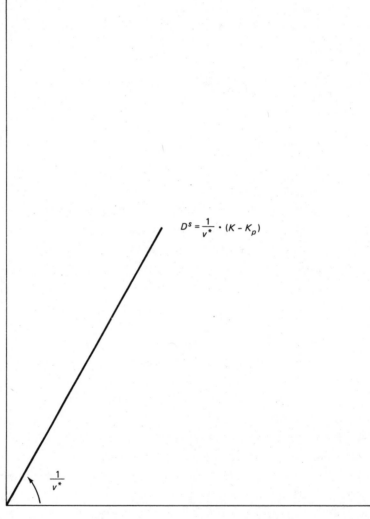

$$D^s = \frac{1}{v^*} \cdot (K - K_p)$$

$\frac{1}{v^*}$

Supply of Currency to Banks ($K - K_p$)

desired relationship (v^*) which it attempts to maintain between its demand deposits and its vault cash; say, $v^* = 5$ percent. We assume that the bank's actual ratio of vault cash to demand deposits (v) is also equal to 5 percent. Because $v = v^*$, the bank's balance sheet is said to be in equilibrium. The banker has no incentive either to increase or to decrease his holdings of vault cash. His balance sheet shows the following figures:

First National Bank

Vault cash	50	Demand deposits	1,000
Loans	950		
	1,000		1,000

Now a customer walks into the bank and disturbs the bank's equilibrium condition by making a cash deposit of $100. Demand deposits and vault cash both rise by $100.

First National Bank

(+100) Vault cash	150	Demand deposits 1,100 (+100)	
Loans	950		
	1,100		1,100

Desired vault cash increases by $5 to $55 (5 percent of $1,100). However, the *actual* ratio (v) has increased from an initial 5 percent to approximately 13.6 percent ($150/$1,100) after the new deposit. The bank is out of equilibrium: v exceeds v^*, and there is surplus vault cash amounting to $95 ($150 − $55).

To reduce surplus vault cash the bank will expand its loans (or acquire additional securities). Suppose that the bank's officers increase loans by $95 and deliver the proceeds of the loans in cash. Vault cash immediately declines to the desired level and the bank is once again in equilibrium:

First National Bank

(−95) Vault cash	55	Demand deposits 1,100	
(+95) Loans	1,045		
	1,100		1,100

What if the bank pays the loan proceeds in the form of an additional demand deposit? Loans will increase by $95, demand deposits will increase by the same amount, and there will be no decrease in vault cash at all.

First National Bank

	Vault cash	150	Demand deposits 1,195 (+95)
(+95)	Loans	1,045	
		1,195	1,195

So how does the bank rid itself of the surplus cash? The borrower obviously did not take out a bank loan in order to increase the balance in his checking account. He borrowed in order to finance some planned expenditure, perhaps to buy a new car or (if he is a business manager) to increase his inventory of goods for sale. Whatever his motives, we are entitled to expect him to spend the funds quite soon after completion of the loan and to write checks which bring his deposit balance back to its former level. The ultimate appearance of First National Bank's balance sheet is the same as if it had paid the loan in currency; the only difference is in the convenience extended to the borrower.

First National Bank

(−95)	Vault cash	55	Demand deposits 1,100 (−95)
	Loans	1,045	
		1,100	1,100

But now we have set in motion the machinery of the monetary system. The First National Bank has done its part, but when our borrower wrote checks on his account, he created new deposits for his creditors. Suppose he wrote a check for $95 to his landlord, who then deposited the check in his own bank, the Second National Bank. If we assume that the SNB is the same size as the FNB and that it was initially in equilibrium, its balance sheet now would appear as follows:[4]

---

[4] As soon as the SNB collects the cash for the check from the FNB. The mechanics of "check clearing" are discussed below, in Chapter 5, section 5.2.4. Note that in this simple example, the banks exchange cash between themselves; actual procedures are less cumbersome.

Second National Bank

(+95) Vault cash 145	Demand deposits 1,095 (+95)
Loans 950	
$\overline{1,095}$	$\overline{1,095}$

Is the Second National in equilibrium? First we calculate v. Vault cash = \$145. Demand deposits = \$1,095. Therefore $v = \dfrac{145}{1,095} \cong 13.2$ percent. Since $v^* = 5$ percent, the bank's balance sheet is out of equilibrium. By how much? Five percent of \$1,095 is \$54.75, so the bank has excess vault cash of \$90.25.

In order to restore equilibrium, the Second National Bank acquires additional earning assets in the same manner as described above for the First National Bank. New loans are made, new deposits are created, and the surplus vault cash is shifted to yet another bank in the system. The immediate effects of the new lending activity by the Second National will be

Second National Bank

(−90.25) Vault cash	54.75	Demand deposits	1,095
(+90.25) Loans	1,040.25		
	$\overline{1,095.00}$		$\overline{1,095}$

and

Third National Bank

(+90.25) Vault cash	140.25	Demand deposits	1,090.25 (+90.25)
Loans	950.00		
	$\overline{1,090.25}$		$\overline{1,090.25}$

Now the Third National has surplus currency of \$85.74 (calculated in the same manner), which provides it with an incentive to increase loans, and the process continues on and on.

The effects of these successive rounds of new lending on total demand deposits may be seen by reintroducing the aggregate balance sheet for the banking system. The initial position might have been as follows:

All Commercial Banks (1)

Vault cash	500	Demand deposits	10,000
Loans	9,500		
	10,000		10,000

The initial activity at the First National produced an increase in vault cash, loans, and deposits.

All Commercial Banks (2)

(+100) Vault cash	600	Demand deposits	10,195 (+195)
(+ 95) Loans	9,595		
	10,195		10,195

Additional increases, each smaller than the one preceding it, were generated by the second and third banks.

All Commercial Banks (3)

Vault cash	600.00	Demand deposits	10,285.25 (+90.25)
(+90.25) Loans	9,685.25		
	10,285.25		10,285.25

All Commercial Banks (4)

Vault cash	600.00	Demand deposits	10,370.99 (+85.74)
(+85.74) Loans	9,770.99		
	10,370.99		10,370.99

Two questions should now come to mind. Why does each new bank have a smaller surplus of vault cash than the one preceding it in the causal chain, and when does the seemingly endless expansion of deposits come to a halt?

The answer to the first question requires a look at the demand deposit accounts. As each bank makes new loans, additional demand deposits are created for the system. As demand deposits rise, desired vault cash rises. As desired vault cash rises, the discrepancy between actual vault cash (which is fixed in amount, except for the initial increase resulting from the outside cash deposit) and desired vault cash is gradually closed. The diminishment of that gap also provides us with the answer to the second question: once demand deposits have risen to the desired multiples of the available vault cash, there will no longer exist any incentive for the banking system to expand loans and deposits.

Our example began with an initial endowment of $500 in vault cash. Suppose that the total fixed supply of currency in the economy is $3,000. The public implicitly has chosen to hold $2,500 in currency. Because the typical banker desires to maintain a ratio of 20-to-1 between his demand deposits and his vault cash ($v^* = 5$ percent), the $500 of currency available to the banking system is capable of supporting $10,000 of demand deposits. When the public voluntarily decreased its holdings of currency, additional vault cash of $100 became available. New lending took place, the public was able to undertake additional spending, and new demand deposits were created in the process. Finally, we reach a new equilibrium. As soon as demand deposits rise by 20 times the increase in vault cash (that is, by $2,000), the equality between v and v^* is restored.[5]

All Commercial Banks (5)

Vault cash	600	Demand deposits	12,000
Loans	11,400		
	12,000		12,000

The result is the same if we use equation (4.4) to discover the new equilibrium position.

$$D^s = \frac{1}{v^*} \cdot (K - K_p) \tag{4.4}$$

---

[5] Mathematically, the expansion process is an infinite summation: $\Delta D = 100 \times (1 + .95 + .95^2 + .95^3 + \ldots)$ where 100 is the initial increase which is repeated at each step and diminished by 5 percent due to the increase in vault cash. The limit to the process is

$$\Delta D = 100 \cdot \left(\frac{1}{1 - .95}\right)$$
$$= 100 \cdot 20.$$

This limit (20) may be thought of as a "demand deposit multiplier." Its operation is analogous to the familiar "spending multiplier" (see Chapter 8, especially section 8.3.1), though the "leakage" here arises from the desire to hold vault cash rather than from the "propensity to save."

Initially, $D^s = \dfrac{1}{.05} \cdot (3{,}000 - 2{,}500) = 20 \cdot 500 = 10{,}000.$

The new equilibrium position is reached when

$$D^s = \frac{1}{.05} \cdot (3{,}000 - 2{,}400) = 20 \cdot 600 = 12.000.$$

4.4 THE ROLE OF THE CENTRAL BANK

Thus far our attention has been focused on the role of private commercial banks in determining the equilibrium supply of demand deposits. Given the total supply of currency and the public's preferences for holding pocket and register cash, the primary factor affecting the supply of demand deposits is the lending and investing activity of commercial banks. This activity arises from the bankers' desires to maintain a small fractional "reserve" in the form of vault cash and to hold the rest of their assets in the form of interest-bearing loans and securities. We now turn our attention to the possibility of variation of the *monetary base* as a cause of changes in the supply of money.

In our first approximation to the money supply model (summarized in equation 4.4), we described a rather primitive monetary system. We had a "currency authority" to issue paper money and coin and a system of private banks to issue demand deposits. Thus in our primitive model the general public had two means of making payments: currency and checks drawn on demand deposits. However, the commercial banks had only one means (currency) of making payments among themselves; there was no *central bank*—a banker's bank—where private banks could maintain deposits to settle claims among themselves. Once we introduce a central bank, the character of our financial system changes.

Let us assume that we have a central bank which the government has endowed with certain legal powers over the private commercial banks. Specifically we assume that the central bank has the power (1) to create a new kind of base money in the form of commercial bank deposits at the central bank (*RD*, for reserve deposits); (2) to determine the supply of *RD* to the banking system; and (3) to require a minimum amount of *reserves* (*R*) which commercial banks must hold as a proportion of demand deposits. Total reserves are defined to include both vault cash and reserve deposits at the central bank. Symbolically,

$$R \equiv K_b{}^s + RD^s. \tag{4.5}$$

In the preceding section of this chapter, we described the manner in which commercial banks supply demand deposits to their customers by making loans. Our central bank supplies reserve deposits to commercial banks in a similar way, either by lending to the commercial banks at the latter's initiative or by purchasing securities from the banks or the public. Suppose, for example, that a private bank experiences an increase in loan demand. It may be profitable for the bank to acquire additional reserves by borrowing from the central bank. If so, the central bank simply credits the bank with an increase in its reserve-deposit account.[6] For example:

Central Bank

Loans to banks (+100)	Reserve deposits (+100)

Commercial Bank

Reserve deposits (+100)	Borrowings from central bank (+100)

The commercial bank now has additional reserves and the means to increase its own lending activity.

A second technique is for the central bank at its initiative to purchase securities from a commercial bank.

---

[6] The practice of borrowing by commercial banks from the U.S. central bank, the Federal Reserve System, plays an important but complex role in our monetary system. See Chapter 15 and 16.

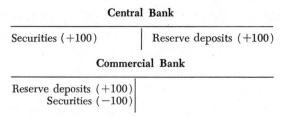

Central Bank

Securities (+100)	Reserve deposits (+100)

Commercial Bank

Reserve deposits (+100) Securities (−100)	

The commercial bank gives up securities and receives in exchange an increase in its reserve account. In this case, as in the first, the commercial bank now has surplus reserves with which to expand loans to its customers.

A variation on this technique is for the central bank to buy securities from the public rather than from a commercial bank. The effect on reserve deposits is the same in each case, as soon as the seller of the securities deposits the proceeds in his checking account. The commercial bank's balance sheet now shows the following changes:

Commercial Bank

Reserve deposits (+100)	Demand deposits (+100)

Both the commercial banks and the central bank can initiate changes in the supply of reserve deposits; the commercial banks by borrowing from the central bank, and the latter through purchases and sales of securities. To the extent that the borrowing volume generates undesired changes in the supply of reserves, the central bank could either offset the effect through security operations or vary the terms on which it is willing to lend. The degree of the central bank's ability to control reserve deposits is in practice likely to be quite high.

This power is indeed crucial for monetary control, because of the role of reserve deposits as part of the cash reserves of the commercial banks and therefore as part of the monetary base. Recall the third power which we gave to our central bank: the right to prescribe a minimum legal ratio of cash reserves to demand deposits. If we denote this minimum ratio as q_D, then we may define the minimum amount of reserves which commercial banks must hold as

$$RR_D \equiv q_D \cdot D, \tag{4.6}$$

where RR_D is the amount of *required reserves* against demand deposits. To repeat: the central bank fixes a *reserve requirement* (q_D) as a ratio of cash reserves to demand deposits. For any given volume of demand deposits (D), this reserve requirement implies a minimum legally required reserve balance (RR_D).

Recall that there are two sources of bank reserves in the present model. The first is vault cash (K_b^s), to which we have now added deposits at the central bank. *Total reserves* (R) are the sum of these two.

$$R \equiv K_b^s + RD^s \tag{4.5}$$

The monetary base can now be extended to include not only currency held by the public and the commercial banks but also commercial bank deposits at the central bank:

$$B = K_b^s + RD^s + K_p \tag{4.7}$$

or

$$B = R + K_p. \tag{4.8}$$

The monetary base (B) is equal to total bank reserves (R) plus currency held by the public (K_p).

Before we introduced the central bank, we discovered that the key elements which determine the supply of money are the total supply of currency (which, in the absence of a central bank, is equivalent to the monetary base), the banks' preferences for holding vault cash relative to deposits, and the public's preferences for holding currency. Having a central bank modifies the picture. First, there is a new component added to the monetary base. Second, the banks' preferences regarding vault cash no longer matter, because the banks are *told* by the central bank what amount of reserves (vault cash plus reserve deposits) they are required to hold. The alert reader, however, will spot an implicit assumption in that last statement: to the extent that commercial bankers demand reserves in excess of what the law requires, their preferences will still matter. For the moment we assume that desired *excess reserves* are equal to zero.

What now determines the supply of money? The factors are essentially the same as detailed in our earlier model: the drive for equilibrium between the given supply of reserve deposits and currency (the monetary base) and the demands for those assets by the banks and the public. The total supply is

$$B = K_b{}^s + RD^s + K_p \tag{4.7}$$

which in equilibrium should be just equal to the sum of the demands on the base, including the banks' demands for vault cash and their (imposed) demands for central bank deposits:

$$K_b{}^s + RD^s + K_p = K_b{}^d + RD^d + K_p \tag{4.9}$$

We can simplify equation 4.9 by cancelling K_p from both sides. This simplification is possible because the public's demands for currency are always satisfied; the banks must pay out currency to their customers at zero cost in exchange for demand deposit balances. For a given monetary base, an increase in the public's demand for currency will reduce the supply of reserves to the commercial banks; but since the market for publicly held currency must be in equilibrium, we can now judge whether the whole system is in equilibrium by seeing if the supply of bank reserves is equal to the banks' demand for reserves. The market-clearing equation reduces to

$$K_b{}^s + RD^s = K_b{}^d + RD^d \tag{4.10}$$

Now the demand-deposit supply model may be simplified and solved. Because excess reserves are assumed to be equal to zero in equilibrium, the total *demand* for bank reserves will be equal to the volume of reserves required against demand deposits.

$$R^d \doteq RR_D$$

or

$$R^d = q_D \cdot D. \tag{4.11}$$

Furthermore, the *supply* of bank reserves is equal to the monetary base (determined by the central bank and the currency authority) less the public's holdings of currency.

$$R^s = B - K_p \tag{4.12}$$

This figure—the monetary base less those portions of it which are used to support assets other than demand deposits —we shall call the *net monetary base, B_n*. In the present model, with only two assets, the net base is equivalent to the supply of bank reserves; however, as we add assets to the model to make it more realistic, the contents of B_n will change.

When the market for bank reserves is in equilibrium, the supply of reserves must be equal to the demand for them. Then required reserves (the amount "demanded") must be just equal to the net monetary base (the amount supplied).

$$R^d = R^s$$

becomes

$$q_D \cdot D = B_n \tag{4.13}$$

and we can readily solve for the equilibrium supply of demand deposits (Figure 4–2):

$$D^s = \frac{1}{q_D} \cdot (B - K_p) = \frac{1}{q_D} \cdot B_n \tag{4.14}$$

Compare equation 4.14 with equation 4.4, the solution for the supply of demand deposits with no central bank.

$$D^s = \frac{1}{v^*} \cdot (K - K_p) \tag{4.4}$$

FIGURE 4–2

The Supply of Demand Deposits (D) in an Economy with a Central Bank (second approximation)

Supply of Deposits to Public (D^s)

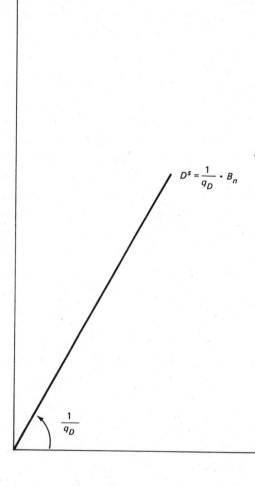

$$D^s = \frac{1}{q_D} \cdot B_n$$

$$\frac{1}{q_D}$$

Net Monetary Base (B_n)

The solutions really are quite similar, except for the expansion of the monetary base to include reserve deposits. The reserve-requirement ratio serves exactly the same function as v^* in the more primitive model. The central bank has increased the banks' demand for cash reserves and thereby has gained a measure of control over the supply of money. Whereas the primitive system relies on the private commercial banks to fix at their own discretion the amount of vault cash (reserves) to be held, we now have an official policy-making body (the central bank) to fix a legal reserve requirement. Any increase in that requirement will, ceteris paribus, cause a decrease in the supply of demand deposits by forcing the commercial banks to cut back on lending in order to meet the higher cash requirements. Any decrease in q_D, so long as it remains above v^*, will tend to induce an increase in loans and in demand deposits.

There is a second method by which the central bank can influence the growth or contraction of the money supply. Whenever the central bank increases the size of the monetary base—by making loans to commercial banks or by buying securities or other assets from the commercial banks—there is a tendency for the supply of demand deposits to rise. Suppose the required reserve ratio on demand deposits is 10 percent, and that the central bank increases the monetary base by $100. What will happen to the supply of demand deposits? The injection of new bank reserves initially creates an excess supply of reserves at the banks which receive them. Those banks can get rid of the excess cash by making new loans, thereby increasing demand deposits. Deposits then continue to rise throughout the system until *required reserves* rise by as much as the initial increase in total reserves. When demand deposits rise by $1,000, or ten times the increase in reserves, then RR_D must rise by 10 percent of the increase in D, or by $100. The system is once again in equilibrium.

4.5 ADDITIONAL USES OF THE MONETARY BASE

From our description so far of the forces determining the supply of money, it appears that the commercial banks play only a residual and passive role. We have assumed that all reserves acquired by commercial banks are absorbed as required reserves against demand deposits; thus the banker is merely the medium through which changes in the monetary base produce changes in the supply of money held by the public. In the present section we introduce a more active role for the banker by recognizing that bank reserves may be absorbed as required reserves against time deposits or as reserves deliberately held in excess of the legal requirements. Both the reserve against time deposits and excess reserves represent competing uses of the monetary base. They reduce the size of the *net* monetary base, therefore reducing the potential supply of money supportable by a given supply of base money.

4.5.1 Time Deposits

Commercial banks issue two general types of deposits: demand and time. Time deposits (including the familiar passbook savings account) are defined as deposits of commercial banks which are not subject to transfer by check, which are not legally payable on demand (that is, deposits on which the banks legally may require the depositor to wait a specified time period before making a withdrawal), and on which interest may by paid.[7] As a matter of fact the banks may choose not to exercise their rights to delay payment; the important distinction is that time deposits generally must be converted into demand deposits or currency in order to be

---

[7] This definition will vary slightly from country to country. Demand deposits could earn interest, and time deposits may be negotiable by transfers similar to checks. The definition given here is for the purest distinction between the two types of accounts.

made negotiable and therefore useful for making payments.[8]

The introduction of time deposits into our money supply model affects the ability of the banking system to supply demand deposits. The central bank may impose a percentage reserve requirement against both demand and time deposits. We assume that the reserve requirement on time deposits is lower than the requirement on demand deposits as it is in many countries today, but in any case demand deposits must compete with time deposits as alternative uses of the monetary base. The total demand for reserves by the banking system is equal to the sum of reserves required against demand deposits (RR_D) and reserves required against time deposits (RR_T):

$$R^d = RR_D + RR_T, \tag{4.15}$$

where RR_T is equal to the value of time deposits (T) times the percentage reserve requirement.

$$RR_T = q_T \cdot T. \tag{4.16}$$

Recalling that the volume of reserves required to support demand deposits is computed in the same manner (equation 4.11), we may write the total imposed demand for reserves as

$$R^d = q_D \cdot D + q_T \cdot T. \tag{4.17}$$

As before, the supply of demand deposits can be solved for by finding the equilibrium solution for the market for bank reserves. The supply of reserves is still equal to that part of the monetary base which is not used by the public as currency:

$$R^s = B - K_p. \tag{4.12}$$

Setting the demand for reserves equal to the supply,

$$q_D \cdot D + q_T \cdot T = B - K_p.$$

---

[8] In the United States, some time deposits—called "negotiable certificates of deposit"—may be sold to third parties. However, they must be sold intact (one cannot write a check for part of the balance), and they must be in amounts of $100,000 or more.

Solving for D, we find again that the supply of demand deposits is equal to the monetary base less the competing uses of the base(for pocket and register cash and now also for time deposits) multiplied by the inverse of the reserve requirement on D.

$$q_D \cdot D = B - K_p - q_T \cdot T$$

$$D^s = \frac{1}{q_D} \cdot (B - K_p - q_T \cdot T) \tag{4.18}$$

Equation 4.18 is identical to our earlier equation for the supply of demand deposits (equation 4.14), excepting one change. Now that there are two classes of bank deposits instead of only one, those reserves which are used to support the "other" class (time deposits) must be subtracted in deriving the net monetary base. Our new equation for the net base is

$$B_n = B - K_p - q_T \cdot T. \tag{4.19}$$

The net base is still defined as that part of the total monetary base which is available to support demand deposits; as additional assets are introduced into our model, we shall have to record carefully the ways in which they absorb reserves. Using this expanded concept of the net monetary base, we observe that equation 4.18 and equation 4.14 are identical:

$$D^s = \frac{1}{q_D} \cdot B_n.$$

To see how our model can be used to help analyze the determinants of the supply of money, suppose that there is a 10 percent reserve requirement on demand deposits ($q_D = .10$) and a 5 percent requirement on time deposits ($q_T = .05$). Suppose also that the central bank supplies \$10 billion in reserve deposits and that the Treasury has issued \$40 billion in coins and paper money. That is, the monetary base equals \$50 billion. Finally, suppose that the public chooses to hold \$30 billion in currency and \$100 billion in time deposits. What is the equilibrium supply of demand deposits? Equation 4.17 can be used to calculate that the net base equals $15 billion, and that those $15 billion of reserves can support $150 billion of demand deposits ($D^s = \$150$ billion).

What happens if the public's preference for time deposits increases because, for instance, the banks begin to offer a higher interest rate on time deposits? The increase in T absorbs bank reserves; as T rises, so does RR_T. For a given supply of reserves there is a smaller quantity left over to support demand deposits. Suppose T rises to $120 billion. Since there is a 5 percent reserve requirement on time deposits, this $20 billion increase in T reduces the net base by $1 billion ($.05 \times \$20$ billion). Hence the supply of demand deposits must fall by $10 billion.

Whenever the public increases its preferences for holding time deposits, banks must reduce the supply of demand deposits (so long as the size of the monetary base is constant). Customers increase their holdings of time deposits at the expense of their demand deposit accounts by drawing down their checking-account balances. *Total deposits* (demand plus time) will rise if the reserve requirement on T is smaller than the requirement on demand deposits ($q_T < q_D$). Nonetheless, the supply of demand deposits and hence the supply of money will fall if the public decides to shift assets in favor of time deposits. Similarly, an increase in the reserve requirement on time deposits (q_T) will reduce the quantity of reserves available to support demand deposits and therefore will reduce the supply of demand deposits.

4.5.2   Excess Reserves

We have assumed so far that no bank will choose in equilibrium to hold cash reserves in excess of legal requirements. We must now relax that partially unrealistic assumption in order to understand why some banks may be expected to desire to hold positive levels of excess reserves (ER). Our central bank pays no interest on reserve deposits; therefore the commercial bank must forego possible interest income when it holds excess reserves in preference to making loans or purchasing other earning assets. Faced with such a choice, why would a rational profit-maximizing banker choose to hold the nonearning asset?

There are at least three reasons why banks may desire to hold excess reserves. First, if bankers have a high expectation of deposits being withdrawn for cash in the near future, they may think that their own cash requirements are higher than those imposed by the central bank. In other words, desired vault cash v^* may be greater than q_D. Second, if bankers expect an imminent increase in loan demand, they may find it convenient temporarily to hold cash in excess of the legal requirement in order to be able to meet that demand. Third, if bankers are experiencing some volatility in demand deposits so that they are unsure as to what the legal reserve requirement is likely to be in the near future, or if they are by nature conservative and want to avoid making any mistakes that might cause them to be short on meeting the legal requirement, then they may desire to hold an extra cushion of reserves to protect their position.

Now we are in a better position to understand why banks demand reserves: as legal requirements against both demand and time deposits and as desired excess reserves.

$$R^d = q_D \cdot D + q_T \cdot T + ER^d \qquad (4.20)$$

Excess reserves are a third competitive use of the monetary base. The public's demands for currency and for time deposits, and the commercial banks' demands for excess reserves all compete with demand deposits for the given supply of reserve dollars. In equilibrium the sum of the demands must be equal to the given supply.

$$q_D \cdot D + q_T \cdot T + ER^d = B - K_p \qquad (4.21)$$

or

$$D^s = \frac{1}{q_D} \cdot B_n \qquad \qquad (4.14)$$

where now

$$B_n = B - K_p - q_T \cdot T - ER^d. \qquad \qquad (4.22)$$

As before, the net monetary base, multiplied by the inverse of the percentage reserve requirement on demand deposits, yields the supply of demand deposits.

It is important for us to recognize that the demand-deposit supply model summarized in equation 4.21 is neither a mechanical nor an automatic process. The central bank determines the size of the monetary base and the level of the percentage reserve requirements. The public decides what amount of currency and time deposits it wishes to hold. And each commercial bank decides on an appropriate desired level of excess reserves. The size of the money supply is affected by each decision.

Suppose that the commercial banks in the aggregate decide to hold $1 billion excess reserves as a cushion against possible changes in deposits and reserve requirements, and that all other conditions are unchanged from the example used in the previous section: $q_D = 10\%$, $q_T = 5\%$, $B = \$50$ billion, $K_p = \$30$ billion, and $T = \$100$ billion. What happens to the supply of demand deposits? With zero excess reserves, the net monetary base was equal to $15 billion, and the equilibrium supply of demand deposits was $150 billion (ten times the net base). The new $1 billion demand for ER reduces the net base by $1 billion; each dollar of excess reserves reduces by $1 the amount of reserves available to support demand deposits. And the billion-dollar drop in the net base must force D^s to fall by $10 billion, to $140 billion. Any further increase in bank demands for excess reserves will induce a further decline in the supply of demand deposits.

4.6 INTEREST RATES AND THE SUPPLY OF MONEY

In the preceding section we described the effects of changes in time deposits and excess reserves on the net monetary base and on the equilibrium supply of demand deposits. We turn now to a brief examination of one important factor influencing the public's preferences for time deposits and the banks' demand for excess reserves: the rate of interest.[9]

Suppose for the moment that the interest rate paid by banks on time deposits is fixed at, say 4 percent. If for any reason the yield on short-term government securities should rise, time deposits would become relatively less attractive to investors who consider the two assets to be close substitutes in their security portfolio. An individual with $10,000 to invest for a few months can buy a riskless, short-term government security through a bank with almost as little inconvenience as in making a deposit in a time deposit account. If both time deposits and government securities are yielding about 4 percent, the individual is likely to be able to minimize total transactions costs by acquiring a time deposit. But if the interest rate on short-term securities rises to 6 percent while the rate paid on time deposits stays at 4 percent, many people probably will shift their preferences in favor of the higher yielding securities. Assuming, then, that banks seldom vary the rate paid on time deposits, we may conclude that any increase in short-term interest rates will reduce the public's demand for time deposits. Conversely, whenever market rates of interest fall, some people who might have been almost undecided before the decline will find it more convenient and less costly simply to acquire time deposits at their commercial bank.

Where we have been using T in the money supply model,

---

[9] The U.S. money supply has been influenced by the interest rate primarily via the banks' demands for borrowed reserves, rather than excess reserves. The present chapter focuses on excess reserves for simplicity; the institutional characteristics of the U.S. system are discussed in Chapter 14.

we may now substitute a demand function for time deposits which depends on the level of short-term interest rates (i). Obviously there are many factors which enter the demand function for time deposits, including the yield on T (which we have assumed fixed), the volume of new saving out of current income, the extent of bank advertising of time deposits, and so on. But a very simple demand function will serve our present purpose. Lumping all the possible arguments other than the interest rate into an exogenous term T_0, the inverse relationship between i and T^d may be expressed by the linear demand function (shown in Figure 4–3),

$$T^d = T_0 - t \cdot i, \tag{4.23}$$

where t is a coefficient (a parameter) measuring the effect of interest rates on the demand for time deposits.

Do we need a supply function? Not as long as the interest rate paid on time deposits is held constant. Banks supply whatever time deposits their customers demand. In other words, as long as changes in the demand for T do not generate changes in the rate offered for time deposits, we have a perfectly elastic supply curve.[10] The demand curve then suffices to determine the actual quantity of deposits outstanding.

Changes in interest rates may also affect the banks' demands for excess reserves. The interest rate on government securities is a very good measure of the *opportunity cost* to the banks of holding excess reserves. It represents the interest income which is foregone by holding a noninterest-earning asset (reserves) instead of a highly liquid earning asset (short-term government securities). When i is low, the opportunity cost of holding cash or reserve deposits is also low. As interest rates rise, the incentive to go to the trouble of converting excess reserves into earning assets increases. We

[10] Time deposit rates in the United States tend to be sticky, partly because of legal regulations. See Chapter 15, section 15.3.

FIGURE 4–3

The Demand by Bank Customers for Time Deposits

Demand for Time Deposits (T)

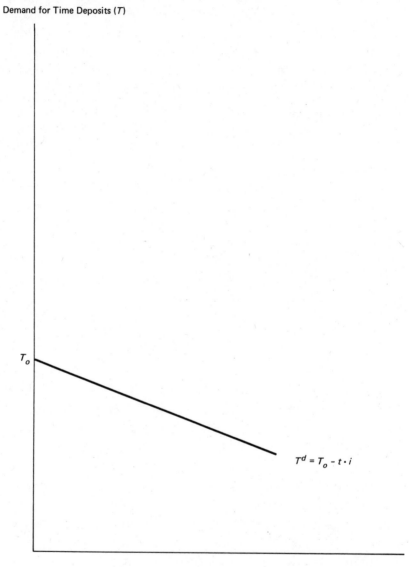

Interest Rates on Securities (i)

can incorporate this effect into our model by adding a simple linear demand function for ER (Figure 4–4).

$$ER^d = ER_0 - e \cdot i, \tag{4.24}$$

where ER_0 summarizes all the other forces which influence the demand for excess reserves (see above, p. 100) and e is a parameter measuring the influence of interest rates. As with the markets for time deposits and for currency held by the public, we do not need to develop a supply function for excess reserves. The central bank merely provides a fixed supply of the monetary base and does not separately supply excess reserves.

An increase in interest rates, then, reduces the public's demand for commercial bank time deposits, and it also reduces the banks' demands for excess reserves. For both of these reasons an increase in interest rates will increase the supply of "base money" available for supporting demand deposits (that is, it will increase the net monetary base) and hence will increase the supply of demand deposits from the banks (see equation 4.21). When the public reduces its holdings of time deposits, new demand deposits are created. Imagine, for example, that a bank customer decides to use his time deposit funds to buy a government bond. He first transfers his savings balance to his checking account, and he then writes a check to pay for the bond. Whoever sells the bond now has an additional demand deposit balance; in this manner the money supply tends to rise.[11]

As a second example, let the commercial banks decide to reduce their holdings of excess reserves. In order to get rid of the surplus reserves, they will buy assets such as short-term government securities, or else they will try to make additional new loans to their customers. As we described earlier in this

---

[11] It is important to notice that we are assuming that the seller of the bond does not simply deposit the proceeds of the sale in a bank time deposit; he either spends the funds or holds the demand deposit. Otherwise, there would be no *net* change in the public's preference for holding time deposits.

FIGURE 4–4

The Demand by Banks for Excess Reserves

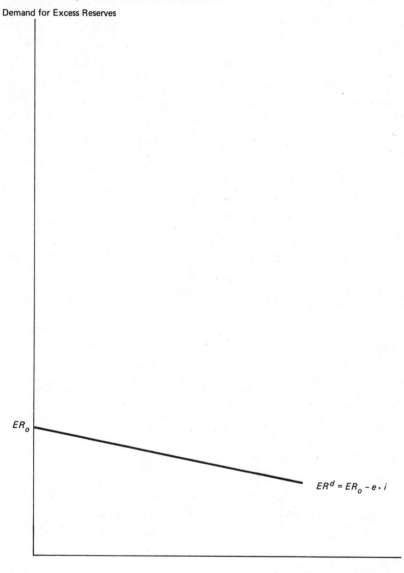

Demand for Excess Reserves

ER_o

$ER^d = ER_o - e \cdot i$

Interest Rates on Securities (i)

chapter, the increase in bank loans (or purchase of securities) leads to an increase in demand deposits as the funds obtained by the borrower (or seller) are disbursed. As a general rule, we may conclude that any decrease in the demand for assets which compete with demand deposits as uses of the monetary base will increase the quantity of demand deposits which will be supplied by the banking system (assuming as we have throughout the chapter that the total size of the base supplied by the central bank is constant). And as a particular consequence of that rule, we may now conclude that an increase in the level of interest rates will tend to reduce those competing demands for reserves and therefore will lead to an increase in the supply of demand deposits.

4.7 THE COMPLETE MONEY SUPPLY MODEL

When we bring together all the factors which influence the supply of money—the size of the monetary base, the exogenous forces determining the competing demands for the base, and the level of interest rates—we can construct a simple model of the money supply. At the heart of the model is the requirement that in equilibrium the total demand for bank reserves must be equal to the supply.

$$(1) \quad R^d = R^s$$

The demand for bank reserves has three components.

$$(2) \quad R^d = q_D \cdot D + q_T \cdot T + ER^d \qquad \text{(from equation 4.20)}$$

The supply of reserves consists of the monetary base less the public's holdings of currency.

$$(3) \quad R^s = B - K_p \qquad \text{(from equation 4.8)}$$

The demands for time deposits and excess reserves are affected by changes in interest rates.

$$(4) \quad T^d = T_0 - t \cdot i \qquad \text{(from equation 4.23)}$$
$$(5) \quad ER^d = ER_0 - e \cdot i \qquad \text{(from equation 4.24)}$$

And, finally, the supply of money is equal to the sum of demand deposits and the amount of currency held by the public.

(6) $M^s = D^s + K_p$

The complete model contains six equations, but there are seven unknowns or endogenous variables (M^s, D, T, ER, R^s, R^d, and i). The other four variables which appear in the equations are exogenous; q_D, q_T, and B are determined by the central bank, and K_p is assumed to be given.[12] We now can solve this system of six equations for M^s, deriving a solution for the supply of money as a function of the exogenous variables and of the rate of interest.

We may write the equation for the supply of money[13] as

$$M^s = \frac{1}{q_D} \cdot B_n + \frac{(q_T \cdot t + e)}{q_D} \cdot i, \qquad (4.25)$$

where the net monetary base (B_n) is

$$B_n = B - q_T \cdot T_0 - ER_0 - (1 - q_D) \cdot K_p. \qquad (4.26)$$

That is, the net monetary base is equal to the total base B (reserve deposits plus total currency in circulation), less that part which is "absorbed" by time deposits, excess reserves, and the public's holdings of currency. Excess reserve holdings, of course, absorb reserves dollar for dollar; hence the full amount of ER must be subtracted from B in deriving the net base. Time deposits absorb reserves only by the fractional-reserve requirement q_T. The public's holdings of currency reduce the base available for demand deposits on a one-for-one ratio, but they also must be added back in to

---

[12] A seventh equation could easily be added to the model, in which the public's demand for currency varies inversely with the level of interest rates in the same manner as time deposits and excess reserves. For example, we might write

$$K_p{}^d = K_{p0} - K \cdot i.$$

However, that complication would not add anything to the character of the model. In the next few chapters we shall take up the determinants of the demands for both currency and demand deposits.

[13] Equation (4.25) is derived in the Appendix to this chapter.

derive the supply of money. We capture both of these effects by subtracting only the fraction $(1 - q_D) \cdot K_p$ from the monetary base.

Finally, note that there are two effects from the interest rate, which operate via the demands for time deposits (t) and for excess reserves (e).

The money supply equation (4.25) summarizes all of the significant influences on the supply of money which we have described throughout the present chapter.

1. An increase in the size of the monetary base will make available additional reserves which can be used indirectly for the creation of additional demand deposits, causing the money supply to rise.

2. An increase in the public's demands for time deposits, or an increase by the central bank of the percentage reserve requirement on time deposits, will reduce the supply of reserves available for supporting demand deposits and cause the supply of money to fall.

3. An increase in the commercial banks' desires to hold reserve balances in excess of the legal requirements will reduce the net base and cause the money supply to fall.

4. An increase in the public's preferences for currency will reduce the availability of reserves for demand deposits and will generate a multiple contraction of deposits which will more than offset the direct increase in the money supply represented by the additional currency holdings. That is, the money supply must fall when the public shifts its preferences in favor of currency.

5. An increase in the level of interest rates will induce the public to reduce its holdings of time deposits and will induce the commercial banks to reduce their holdings of excess reserves. Both shifts bring about increases in the supply of money.

6. An increase in the reserve requirement on demand deposits will reduce the quantity of demand deposits which

can be supported by a given volume of bank reserves. Therefore, any increase in reserve requirements must induce a decrease in the supply of money.

REVIEW QUESTIONS

1. How does the banking system as a whole rid itself of surplus cash? The single bank?
2. Are excess reserves necessarily surplus reserves?
3. What effect will a decrease in the level of short-term interest rates have on (*a*) the demand for time deposits, and (*b*) the demand for excess reserves? How does this effect work?
4. Show how the creation of bank deposits is an example of the application of the principle of supply and demand.
5. How can the public affect the equilibrium level of demand deposits?
6. Who determines the public's supply of currency?

SUGGESTED FURTHER READING

Cagan, Phillip. *Determinants and Effects of Changes in the Stock of Money, 1875–1960.* New York: Columbia University Press, 1965.

Meigs, A. James. *Free Reserves and the Money Supply.* Chicago: University of Chicago Press, 1962; chap. 4.

Smith, Warren L. "Time Deposits, Free Reserves, and Monetary Policy," *Issues in Banking and Monetary Analysis.* Edited by G. Pontecorvo, R. Shay, and A. G. Hart. New York: Holt, Rinehart and Winston, 1967.

Tobin, James. "Commercial Banks as Creators of Money," *Banking and Monetary Studies.* Edited by Deane Carson. Homewood, Ill.: Richard D. Irwin, Inc., 1963.

APPENDIX: DERIVATION OF THE MONEY SUPPLY EQUATION[1]

The model of the money supply process contains the six equations described on pages 97 and 105 of this chapter.

---

[1] For a further derivation using specific equations for the U.S. economy, see the Appendix to Chapter 9.

$$R^d = R^s \tag{1}$$

$$R^d = q_D \cdot D + q_T \cdot T + ER^d \tag{2}$$

$$R^s = B - K_p \tag{3}$$

$$T^d = T_0 - t \cdot i \tag{4}$$

$$ER^d = ER_0 - e \cdot i \tag{5}$$

$$M^s = D^s + K_p \tag{6}$$

To solve the model, we start with the equilibrium condition (equation 1): the demand for reserves must equal the supply. We then substitute in the definitions of R^s and R^d. That is, we replace R^d and R^s with the right-hand sides of equations (2) and (3).

$$q_D \cdot D + q_T \cdot T + ER^d = B - K_p$$

Next, we solve for the supply of demand deposits by making the appropriate subtractions and division.

$$q_D \cdot D = B - K_p - q_T \cdot T - ER^d$$

and

$$D^s = \frac{1}{q_d} \cdot (B - K_p - q_T \cdot T - ER^d).$$

There are still three endogenous variables on the right side of the equation, so we next replace ER and T with their respective demand functions, leaving only i and the exogenous forces.

$$D^s = \frac{1}{q_D} \cdot [B - K_p - q_T \cdot (T_0 - t \cdot i) - (ER_0 - e \cdot i)]$$

We can simplify this result by separating the interest rate from the exogenous influences.

$$D^s = \frac{1}{q_D} \cdot (B - K_p - q_T \cdot T_0 - ER_0) + \frac{(q_T \cdot t + e)}{q_D} \cdot i$$

The final step in deriving a solution for the supply of money is to add the public's holdings of currency to both sides of the equation.

$$D^s + K_p = \frac{1}{q_D} \cdot (B - K_p - q_T \cdot T_0 - ER_0) + K_p + \frac{(q_T \cdot t + e)}{q_D} \cdot i$$

or

$$M^s = \frac{1}{q_D} \cdot (B - q_T \cdot T_0 - ER_0) + K_p - \frac{1}{q_D} \cdot K_p + \frac{(q_T \cdot t + e)}{q_D} \cdot i$$

Combining the terms in which K_p appears,

$$M^s = \frac{1}{q_D} \cdot (B - q_T \cdot T_0 - ER_0) - \frac{(1 - q_D)}{q_D} \cdot K_p + \frac{(q_T \cdot t + e)}{q_D} \cdot i$$

or

$$M^s = \frac{1}{q_D} \cdot [B - q_T \cdot T_0 - ER_0 - (1 - q_D) \cdot K_p] + \frac{(q_T \cdot t + e)}{q_D} \cdot i$$

This last equation is equivalent to equation (4.25) in the text. The long term in the brackets here is simply the net monetary base (see equation 4.26).

chapter 5
The Monetary Base

5.1   INTRODUCTION

One of the key concepts in analyzing the supply of money is the monetary base. We defined the base in Chapter 4 as a set of assets the value of which the central bank may cause to vary in order to exert control over the stock of money. In general, the monetary base is the sum of bank reserves and currency held by the public. It is a key variable because once the size of the base is given, changes in the supply of money can come about only through shifts in the composition of monetary assets held by the banks and the public. For example, the public could cause an increase in the money supply by exchanging currency for demand deposits; commercial banks could cause an increase in the money supply by decreasing their holdings of excess reserves. But for a given desired distribution of assets and set of reserve requirements, changes in the money supply are generated solely by changes in the size of the monetary base. The task of this chapter is to describe the sources of variation in the monetary base in the United States.

The base has three major components: Demand deposit balances of member banks at the Federal Reserve banks, Federal Reserve notes held by member banks and by the public, and coin. The last two components, paper money and coin, are together known as currency. More by historical accident than by logical design, the U.S. Department of the Treasury supplies coins and the Federal Reserve banks supply paper money. However, as we shall see, both forms of currency are channeled to the public through the 12 Federal Reserve banks.

5.2 THE SUPPLY OF CURRENCY

The most important concept to remember about the supply of currency is that it is demand determined. No one in the Treasury attempts to determine the right amount of nickels, dimes, or quarters. No one in the Federal Reserve System attempts to determine the right number of the various denominations of dollar bills. The right amounts are determined solely by the quantities desired by households and business firms. Coins, for example, are typically brought into circulation to accommodate consumer spending on small items. The retail businessman goes to the bank and cashes a check in exchange for rolls of coin. The bank's balance sheet shows a decrease in both vault cash and demand deposits.

Step One:

Member Bank

Vault cash — (coin)	Demand deposits —

The next step comes when the bank replenishes its own supply of coin, which it may do by buying coins from the district Federal Reserve bank. The member bank pays for the coin by a reduction in its reserve deposit balances. The composition of member bank reserves changes, but the total amount is unaffected.

Step Two:

Member Bank

Vault cash + Reserve deposits —	

Federal Reserve Banks

Other cash (treasury coin) —	Member bank reserve deposits —

The third stage in this process occurs when the Federal Reserve bank replenishes its stock of coin. The Reserve bank requests additional coin from the Treasury and makes payment by crediting the Treasury's demand deposit account.

Step Three:

Federal Reserve Banks

Other cash +	U.S. treasury demand deposits +

As a final response, the Treasury orders the mint to produce more coin.

Final effect (all three steps combined):

Member Bank			**Federal Reserve Banks**
Reserve deposits —	Demand deposits —		Member bank reserve deposits — U.S. treasury demand deposits +

The exchange of demand deposits for coin by the public, described in the example above, does not affect the size of the monetary base. The member banks lose reserves equal to the amount of the increase in the public's cash holdings. One component of the base (reserve deposits) goes down and another component (the public's cash holding) goes up. The initial impact of increased holdings of coin by the public falls on coin inventories of the banks. The commercial bank, the Federal Reserve bank, and the Treasury then replenish their inventories in turn.

Paper money in the United States today is issued in the form of Federal Reserve notes. These notes are treated by the Federal Reserve System as accounting liabilities; they represent an obligation to give member banks reserve deposits in exchange. When consumers or businessmen cash checks at the bank, they are exchanging a demand deposit balance for currency.

Step One:

Member Bank

Vault cash —		Demand deposits —
(Federal Reserve		
notes)		

The member bank may now buy additional Federal Reserve notes and pay for them with a debit against its reserve deposit account. The Federal Reserve bank issues new Federal Reserve notes, but there is a corresponding reduction in the System's liabilities for member bank deposits.

Step Two:

Member Bank

Vault cash +	
Reserve deposits —	

Federal Reserve Bank

	Federal Reserve notes +
	Member bank
	reserve deposits —

Two aspects of this example are noteworthy. First, the size of the monetary base does not change when the public exchanges demand deposits for paper money (Federal Reserve notes). Second, the Federal Reserve exercises no control over the amount of Federal Reserve notes issued; it responds passively to the changing currency demands of the banks and the public.

5.3   THE SUPPLY OF RESERVE DEPOSITS

Member bank reserve deposit balances are an asset to the member banks, and they are a liability to the Federal Reserve banks. In addition to their legal function as required reserves, these deposit balances also serve as an active checking account for the member banks. They are to the banks what your own checking account is to you: a means of making payments and discharging debt obligations. However, banks use their reserve accounts mainly for settling official transactions (such as purchases of U.S. government securities from the Treasury or from a Federal Reserve bank) and for settling certain interbank transactions. Banks also maintain conventional demand deposit accounts with other banks, and they settle most ordinary business transactions with "officer's checks" drawn against themselves.[1]

The U.S. Treasury and some foreign central banks and governments also maintain checking accounts at Federal Reserve banks.[2] In general, as we shall show in detail below, increases in Treasury and other deposits imply decreases in member bank reserve deposits, and conversely.

Reserve deposit balances are created and destroyed (i.e., increased and decreased in amount) in a number of ways, only some of which are under the control of the Federal Reserve System. Those factors which tend to create new reserve deposits directly we call "sources of reserves." Factors which when increased tend to reduce the available quantity of reserve deposits are called "uses of reserves." One of the principal "uses" of reserves we have already examined: increases in currency in circulation. An increase in the public's demand for currency directly reduces vault cash at commercial banks. The banks then replenish their supply of vault cash by drawing on their reserve deposit balances.

The other factors which absorb or release reserve deposits differ from changes in currency in circulation in one very important respect: by altering the supply of reserve deposits while leaving the quantity of currency unchanged, they alter

---

[1] An officer's check is sometimes referred to as a "banker's draft." It consists of a check drawn by a bank officer (usually the cashier) against the bank itself.

[2] For convenience in making payments, the U.S. Treasury distributes its deposit accounts among the 12 Federal Reserve banks. Foreign accounts, on the other hand, are all located at the Federal Reserve Bank of New York.

the size of both the stock of reserves *and* the total monetary base. These remaining factors can be classified in three groups: transactions directly controlled or subject to control by Federal Reserve System officials, transactions subject to control by the U.S. Treasury, and market transactions largely outside official control. Let us examine first the role of the Treasury.

5.3.1 Treasury Currency Outstanding

There are three major ways in which Treasury actions affect member bank reserve deposits. The first is an increase in treasury currency outstanding, which consists of all the coins and paper money issued by the Treasury. As can be seen from Table 5–1, the most important component today is

TABLE 5–1

Treasury Currency in Circulation (December 31, 1973)

	Kind of Treasury Currency	Amount in Circulation (millions)
1.	Dollars (coin)........................	$ 733
2.	Fractional coin......................	7,026
3.	U.S. notes...........................	321
4.	Currency no longer issued and in process of retirement.................	288
		$8,368

"fractional coin": pennies, nickels, dimes, quarters, and halves. Still called "silver" by most of us because of their traditional content, coins (except for copper pennies) minted since 1965 are mostly made of cupronickel, an alloy of copper and nickel. True silver coins are no longer minted for general circulation, and the remaining small supply of silver coin still in circulation is believed to be primarily in the hands of collectors and hoarders. But the largest silver hoarder is still the Treasury Department, which holds a strategic stockpile of 140 million ounces plus 3 million old 90 percent silver dollars.

When the Treasury buys copper and nickel for manufacturing the "sandwich" or "clad" cupronickel coins, it pays by checks written on treasury demand deposits at Federal Reserve banks. The mining companies which receive the checks deposit them in commercial banks, and the checks are then forwarded to the district Federal Reserve bank for collection. Member bank reserve deposits increase, and treasury deposits at Federal Reserve banks decrease. The mint eventually transforms the copper and nickel into coins valued in excess of the cost of materials and expenses incurred in the minting process. The resulting profit accruing to the Treasury is called *seigniorage,* a term which was first applied to the revenues exacted from the peasantry by feudal lords. Suppose, for example, that the Treasury buys 1.5 million pounds of copper @ 55¢ (total cost $825,000) and 136,000 pounds of nickel @ $1.28 (total cost approximately $175,000) for a total outlay of $1 million. The direct effect is as follows.

Step One ($ millions):

Member Banks

Reserve deposits +1	Demand deposits of mining companies +1

Federal Reserve Banks

	Member bank reserve deposits +1 U.S. Treasury demand deposits −1

The U.S. mint (a division of the Treasury Department) can convert that amount of copper and nickel into about 430 million dimes with a face value of $43 million. When the Treasury deposits the coins with the Federal Reserve banks, there is a gain to the Treasury (seigniorage) of $42 million.[3]

---

[3] The true net gain is somewhat smaller after the expense of processing the metals and minting the coins is deducted.

Step Two ($ millions):

Federal Reserve Banks

Other cash (dimes) + $43	U.S. Treasury demand deposits + $43

5.3.2 The Monetary Gold Stock

The second treasury influence is through its purchases and sales of gold. The department currently owns (on behalf of the government) close to 300 million ounces of gold, which by an Act of Congress it values at $42.22 per ounce. Whenever the Treasury increases or decreases the size of this stock by buying or selling gold at that fixed price, there is a corresponding effect on member bank reserve deposits. Suppose, for example, that the Treasury were to buy 1 million ounces of gold from domestic mining companies.[4] Payment is made by checks totaling just over $42 million drawn on the treasury's demand deposit balances at one or more of the Federal Reserve banks. The mining companies deposit the checks in local banks, increasing private demand deposits. When the local banks forward the treasury checks to their Federal Reserve bank for collection, the Fed debits the treasury's account and credits the reserve accounts of the member banks.[5]

Step One ($ millions):

Member Banks

Reserve deposits +42	Demand deposits (of mining companies) +42

Federal Reserve Banks

	Member bank reserve deposits +42
	U.S. Treasury demand deposits −42

---

[4] At present the Treasury is unable to make such purchases because the free-market price of gold is well above the official price at which the Treasury must buy. See Chapter 12, section 12.4.

[5] The mechanics of check collection are described below, in section 5.3.4.

The effect of the gold purchase by the Treasury is to increase member bank reserves. Similarly, a sale of gold by the Treasury, say to industrial users, would reduce (use up, absorb) reserve deposits.[6]

What does the Treasury do with the gold it buys? Usually it "monetizes" the gold. The Treasury has the authority to issue a special form of currency known as "gold certificates" and to deposit those certificates in Federal Reserve banks. The certificates must be backed 100 percent by the Treasury's gold stock. Thus when the Treasury purchases additional gold, it may monetize the purchase (i.e., replenish its deposit balance) by issuing new gold certificates.

Step Two ($ millions):

Federal Reserve Banks

Gold certificates +42	U.S. treasury demand deposits +42

One historical note might help to clarify the role of the gold certificates, which in effect are warehouse receipts for an equivalent amount of gold bullion. Prior to 1933, gold certificates circulated alongside Federal Reserve notes as one of the primary forms of paper money in circulation in the United States. Shortly after President Roosevelt assumed office in the spring of 1933, he issued an executive order requiring the American public to surrender to the Treasury most holdings of gold and gold certificates.[7] The Federal Reserve banks, however, continued to hold their gold certificates as a legal fractional reserve against the issuance of Federal

---

[6] The mechanics are somewhat different when the Treasury buys from or sells to a foreign government or central bank. In that case, the Federal Reserve Bank of New York transfers the balance directly from the Treasury's account to the foreign account (or conversely, for a sale of gold by the Treasury). There is no direct effect on member bank reserve deposits. Only when the foreign agency spends or otherwise withdraws those funds will there be an increase in reserves.

[7] In practice the order meant that the public was required to exchange its holdings of gold, gold coins, and gold certificates either for other currency (Federal Reserve notes, silver certificates and coins, U.S. notes) or for bank deposits.

Reserve notes and member bank reserve deposits.[8] Today the certificates are merely bookkeeping entries in the Gold Certificate Accounts of the Federal Reserve banks.[9]

5.3.3 Treasury Deposit Balances

The third form of influence the Treasury has over the volume of member bank reserves is through its demand deposit balances at virtually all commercial banks throughout the country, which are called "Treasury Tax and Loan Accounts." Tax and loan balances arise out of federal tax receipts and the proceeds from sales of U.S. government securities. For example, when a corporation or other business concern withholds personal income tax payments from its employees, it deposits the funds in the treasury tax and loan account at a local bank. Large inflows of tax receipts around April 15 and other tax collection deadlines result in increased treasury balances and decreased deposit balances of the tax-paying public. For administrative reasons, the Treasury does not write checks on its tax and loan accounts; all disbursements are made by checks drawn on treasury accounts at Federal Reserve banks. When the level of those balances falls below what treasury officials consider to be a normal working level, the Treasury makes "calls" on its commercial bank accounts. The commercial bank then is required to transfer treasury funds to the district Federal Reserve bank after a designated short period of time (usually one week). The transfer of treasury balances causes a reduction in member bank reserve deposits.

Member Banks

Reserve deposits —	Treasury tax and loan accounts —

---

[8] The reserve requirement against member bank reserve deposits was repealed by Congress in 1965, and the requirement against Federal Reserve notes was repealed in 1968.

[9] For an example of how the Federal Reserve banks use these gold certificate accounts, see section 5.3.4.

Federal Reserve Banks

	Member bank
	reserve deposits —
	U.S. treasury demand deposits +

The Treasury attempts to time its transfers of funds so as to minimize the effects on member bank reserves. That is, the tax and loan accounts are allowed to absorb most of the fluctuations in treasury operating balances, so that the only direct effect of a large tax collection or sale of bonds is to change the ownership of bank deposits rather than their total volume. During 1973, balances in treasury tax and loan accounts ranged from a low of around $2 billion to a high of close to $10 billion; during the same period treasury deposits at Federal Reserve banks fluctuated only about $3 billion. But the failure to coordinate perfectly government receipts and expenditures still remains a significant source of short-run fluctuations in bank reserves.

The important fact to remember about the influence of the Treasury Department on member bank reserves is that it is not the amount of government receipts and expenditures that matters, and it is not the state of the federal budget (the size of the deficit or surplus) that matters. What does matter is the treasury's decisions as to what to do with its working cash balances: whether to keep them in deposit accounts at commercial or Federal Reserve banks or to hold currency. When the government runs a budget deficit, it is spending more than it is receiving in taxes from the public. The deficit must be financed in one of two ways. The Treasury may borrow by selling securities to the public, or it may temporarily draw down its working cash balances either at Federal Reserve banks or commercial banks. The sale of securities has the same effect on bank deposits as the receipt of tax payments: the proceeds are deposited in the treasury tax and loan accounts at commercial banks. Unless and until the Treasury alters the size of its deposits with the Federal Reserve banks, there is no effect on member bank reserve deposits.

Suppose that the Treasury were to run a deficit by increasing its spending by $100 million (say, on welfare payments) without obtaining an increase in tax revenue. Local offices of the Department of Health, Education, and Welfare (HEW) write checks to the welfare recipients drawn on the Treasury's accounts at the Federal Reserve banks. The direct effect is to increase member bank reserve deposits and decrease treasury deposits.

Step One ($ millions):

Member Banks

Reserve
    deposits   +100
	Demand deposits
	    (of welfare recipients) +100

Federal Reserve Banks

	Member bank
	    reserve deposits +100
	U.S. treasury
	    demand deposits −100

But the Treasury normally tries to minimize fluctuations in its working balances at the Federal Reserve banks. To offset the $100 million withdrawal, it may make calls on its tax and loan accounts at commercial banks.

Step Two ($ millions):

Member Banks

Reserve
    deposits   −100
	Tax and loan
	    accounts −100

Federal Reserve Banks

	Member bank
	    reserve deposits −100
	U.S. treasury
	    demand deposits +100

When the tax and loan accounts get low, the Treasury's next line of defense is to borrow money by selling securities to the public. Individuals, corporations, and banks buy the newly issued bonds and pay for them by making deposits in the tax and loan accounts.

Step Three (*$ millions*):

Member Banks

	Demand deposits
	(of bond buyers) −100
	Tax and loan
	accounts +100

The net effect of the deficit, whether it is financed by with-drawals from tax and loan accounts or by borrowing, is to leave the supply of member bank reserves unchanged.

Final Effect (*$ millions*):

Member Banks

	Demand deposits
	(of bond buyers) −100
	Demand deposits
	(of welfare recipients) +100

Only when the Treasury acts to change the size of its balances in Federal Reserve banks (or allows those balances to be affected by its spending actions) does it alter the supply of member bank reserve deposits.

5.3.4 Federal Reserve Float

Not all of the factors affecting member bank reserves are subject to control from Washington. In particular, the 12 Federal Reserve banks unintentionally inject and withdraw reserves as a by-product of their intermediary role in the process of clearing checks. In order to see this role clearly, we must examine the check-clearing process itself, which constitutes one of the most important operating functions of the district Federal Reserve banks.

Let us suppose that you are a student at a college in California, and that you maintain a checking account in your home town in New York. When you write a check, say for $100, on the Hometown Bank payable to a business near your college, the proprietor promptly deposits it in the account at the Collegetown Bank. Demand deposits in Collegetown rise.[10] The asset which the Collegetown Bank has acquired in exchange for the demand deposit is a claim (your check) on your deposit balance at the Hometown Bank some 3,000 miles away. That claim is not quite as good as cash, so until the check has been processed, the Collegetown Bank will carry it on its books as a "cash item in process of collection."

Step One:

Collegetown Bank

Cash items in process of collection +100	Demand deposits +100

Now the Collegetown Bank will take action to collect the funds from your bank. But it would be an extraordinarily complex and expensive process for them to deal directly with all of the thousands of banks whose checks they receive in the ordinary course of business. To simplify matters, the Federal Reserve System serves as a central bureau for clearing checks electronically. In this case, the Collegetown Bank may send your check in a batch of checks drawn on banks around the country to the Federal Reserve Bank of San Francisco. The Federal Reserve bank then gives the Collegetown Bank *deferred* credit on your check. It will take some time to process your check back to the Hometown Bank. There is no way to know in advance just how long it will take, because the check must be physically processed in San Francisco, flown by jet to New York, processed again, and then mailed to the Hometown Bank. But the Federal Reserve System has established a fixed schedule for deferring credit on cash items, and the maximum deferral is two days. For example, the Federal Reserve Bank of San Francisco would give immediate (same day) credit on checks drawn on banks in

---

[10] At this point, the businessman has an additional $100 in his account, but it will be some time before your Hometown Bank debits your account. This temporary double counting of deposits is called "bank float," and it is not to be confused with the "Federal Reserve float" which we are about to describe.

or very near San Francisco, credit deferred one day on checks from banks in large cities in the vicinity of the Federal Reserve bank or from banks in other Federal Reserve cities, and two-day deferral on all other items.[11] The immediate effect of the transaction on the balance sheet of the San Francisco Fed is shown below.

Step Two:

Federal Reserve Bank of San Francisco

Cash items in process of collection +100	Deferred availability cash items (Collegetown Bank) +100

Two days later, when it is time to credit the reserve account of the Collegetown Bank, your check probably will be in the hands of the Federal Reserve Bank of New York. Now the New York Fed has to pay the San Francisco Fed for the check. So here is where those gold certificates we told you about come in handy: they provide a convenient means for the Federal Reserve banks to settle claims among themselves. Thus at the end of two days, the San Francisco bank credits the reserve account of the Collegetown Bank and at the same time obtains a credit to its gold certificate account.

Collegetown Bank

Cash items in process of collection −100 Reserve deposits +100	

---

[11] The deferral decisions are of course made by computer. Take out your checkbook sometime and notice the strange-looking numbers at the bottom of each check. The first eight digits on the left are a code designating the bank where your account is located. The first two digits designate the district in which the bank is located, the third the office (main or branch) of the Federal Reserve bank to which the check is to be sent for clearing, and the fourth designates the number of days which credit will be deferred to banks receiving your check and processing it through the Federal Reserve System. For example, the code 0720 would indicate a Detroit bank: Seventh (Chicago) District, Detroit branch office, and immediate credit given. The last four digits are the bank's individual number. The same information is given in different form in the upper right corner of your check, for the benefit of those banks which still process checks by hand.

Federal Reserve Bank of San Francisco

Cash items		Deferred availability	
in process of collection	−100	cash items	−100
Gold certificate		Member bank	
account	+100	reserve deposits	+100

Federal Reserve Bank of New York

Cash items		
in process of collection	+100	
Gold certificate		
account	−100	

The failure of the Federal Reserve banks to clear your check within the time limit which they have imposed on themselves has temporarily increased member bank reserves by the amount of the check.[12] The Collegetown Bank has a credit to its account, but there is as yet no corresponding debit at the Hometown Bank. Another view of the same point is that while the $100 asset "cash item in process of collection" is still on the books, the corresponding liability "deferred availability cash item" has been destroyed and replaced by the credit to Collegetown Bank's reserve account. The difference between the two "cash item" figures is known as "Federal Reserve float," and it is a source of member bank reserves.

In another day or two, the check-clearing process will be completed, and the float will be eliminated. The final net effect on the various balance sheets shows no change in the size of member bank reserves.

Final Effect:

Collegetown Bank

Reserve		Demand deposits	+100
deposits	+100		

Federal Reserve Bank of San Francisco

Gold certificate		Member bank	
account	+100	reserve deposits	+100

---

[12] Of course, most of the checks cleared through the Federal Reserve banks are cleared in time. It is the exceptions that are important in this context.

Hometown Bank

Reserve deposits −100	Demand deposits −100

Federal Reserve Bank of New York

Gold certificate
  account −100
	Member bank
	  reserve deposits −100

Federal Reserve float is a major cause of short-run variations in the availability of bank reserve deposits. Bad weather, strikes that delay the delivery of mail, heavy concentrations of check clearings such as normally occur around the first of each month, all tend to generate sharp temporary increases in float.

You may wish to test your understanding of the concept of Federal Reserve float by considering the following data from the consolidated balance sheet of the 12 Federal Reserve banks:

	Week Ending December 13, 1967 (billions)	Week Ending December 20, 1967 (billions)
Assets:		
Cash items in process of collection...............	$8.1	$8.9
Liabilities:		
Deferred availability cash items................	6.4	6.7

What do each of these accounts represent? What is the amount of Federal Reserve float in each of the two weeks? What is the most likely cause of the 30 percent rise ($500 million) in float between December 13 and December 20? What was the effect of that rise on the stock of member bank reserves?

5.3.5 Open Market Operations

The most important determinants of the volume of member bank reserves are those controlled by the Federal Reserve

System in its capacity as our country's central bank. Chapter 4 (section 4.4) described the two major ways in which a central bank may affect the supply of bank reserves: by purchasing securities from (or selling securities to) the banks or the general public and by making loans to commercial banks. The Federal Reserve System actively uses both techniques.

The more effective of these two controls, and the one more widely used by the Federal Reserve System, is the purchase and sale of securities for the account of the Federal Reserve banks. These transactions are known as open market operations, and they are under the control of the System's central policy-making body, the Federal Open Market Committee (FOMC). The FOMC meets every four weeks in Washington to formulate broad policy guidelines for the conduct of open market operations. At the end of each meeting, it issues a "directive" to the manager of the open market account, who is an officer at the Federal Reserve Bank of New York.

The actual buying and selling of securities is conducted at the New York Fed under the direction of the account manager. All of the System's transactions are with a set of 25 approved dealers in government securities, all of whom are located in New York. The Federal Reserve System does not deal directly with member banks in transactions for the Open Market Account, except for the large New York banks which serve as agents for the approved securities dealers.[13] What kinds of securities does the account manager buy? Most commonly, he purchases obligations of the U.S. Treasury: ordinary U.S. government bills, certificates, notes, and bonds.[14] But he also has authority to acquire the obligations

---

[13] Some of the securities dealers are actually departments of large commercial banks. The mechanics of the transaction are unaffected, so we do no harm by treating those dealers as if they were formally separate from the bank itself.

[14] These terms refer to the different forms of debt securities issued by the Treasury. Bills and certificates are issued for maturities of one year or less; notes are issued for maturities of from one to five years; and bonds carry initial maturities of five years or more. They are also differentiated in some of their technical features.

of various credit agencies of the federal government, such as the Federal Housing Administration, the Federal Land Banks, and the Tennessee Valley Authority. We shall have more to say about the role of these agency securities in Chapter 14; however, the quantities purchased by the Federal Reserve System are quite small, so for now we shall assume that all open market operations are in U.S. Treasury securities.

When the manager of the Open Market Account buys securities from a dealer, he pays for them by crediting the reserve account of the commercial bank which serves as the dealer's agent. The bank in turn credits the demand deposit account of the dealer. Member bank reserves rise by the amount of the purchase.

Member Bank

Reserve deposits +	Demand deposits (securities dealers) +

Federal Reserve Bank of New York

U.S. government securities +	Member bank reserve deposits +

A *sale* of securities by the account manager has exactly the reverse effect.

Member Bank

Reserve deposits −	Demand deposits (securities dealers) −

Federal Reserve Bank of New York

U.S. government securities −	Member bank reserve deposits −

By this simple act of changing the ownership of government securities between private corporations (the securities dealers) and the Federal Reserve System, the Fed can quickly and easily engineer whatever changes in the supply of reserves it desires. It is a powerful weapon: the System has the power to acquire whatever volume of assets it wishes (in the form of government securities) simply by *creating* the corresponding liabilities (member bank reserves).

5.3.6 The Discount Window

The second means available to the Federal Reserve System for controlling the supply of reserves is the authority to make loans to member banks. The only reason this device is less effective than open market operations is that its use is at the initiative of the commercial banks which wish to borrow reserve funds. But the System does exert some control over the amount of permissible borrowing.

When a Federal Reserve bank advances a loan to one of its member banks, it credits the reserve deposit balance of the member and enters the loan on its own books under the heading "discounts and advances." The member bank thus obtains additional reserves by incurring a liability for borrowed money.

Member Bank

Reserve deposits +	Liabilities for borrowed money +

Federal Reserve Bank

Discounts and advances +	Member bank reserve deposits +

The total supply of member bank reserves thus rises and falls with the amount of member bank borrowing from Federal Reserve banks. A note on terminology: the department of each Federal Reserve bank which makes loans to member banks is called the "discount department," and bankers commonly refer to it as the "discount window." Borrowing from the Fed is called "going to the discount window," and the rate charged on such loans is called the "discount rate."[15]

---

[15] See Chapter 14, section 14.3.

5.4 CONSOLIDATION OF THE ACCOUNTS

The preceding pages have described most of the major accounts that enter the balance sheets of the Federal Reserve banks. We now can see how they relate to one another and combine to determine the size of the monetary base. A simplified version of the consolidated balance sheet for the 12 Reserve banks, expanding somewhat on the description we gave in Chapter 1 (of Table 1–2) is given in Table 5–2.

TABLE 5–2

Consolidated Balance Sheet of the 12 Federal Reserve Banks
As of December 31, 1973
(in millions)

Assets		Liabilities	
Gold certificates............	$ 11,460	Federal Reserve notes in circulation...............	$ 64,128
Government securities.......	78,516	Federal Reserve notes in the Treasury.............	134
Discounts and advances.....	1,258	Member bank reserve deposits	27,060
Cash items in process of collection...............	8,168	U.S. treasury deposits.......	2,542
Other cash.................	271	Deferred availability cash items...............	4,855
Miscellaneous assets*........	3,599	Foreign and other deposits....	1,884
	$103,272	Miscellaneous liabilities and capital accounts..........	2,669
			$103,272

* Primarily: special drawing rights, acceptances, federal agency obligations, and bank premises.

Increases in the values of any of the asset accounts of the Federal Reserve banks, ceteris paribus, will increase the stock of member bank reserves by the same amount. Increases in the liability accounts are alternative applications of the System's assets and hence absorb funds that could provide reserve deposits.

Although we did not show the effects of some of our individual transactions on the Treasury's balance sheet, we can easily construct such a balance sheet for the Treasury's monetary operations.

5.4.1   Sources and Uses of Reserve Deposits

By rearranging the Federal Reserve accounts, we can obtain a convenient table (Table 5–3) showing the "sources and uses" of member bank reserve deposits.

TABLE 5–3

Sources and Uses of Reserve Deposits (December 31, 1973)

		(millions)
Sources:		
Gold certificates held by Federal Reserve banks..........		$11,460
Federal Reserve Credit:		83,087
Government securities held by Federal Reserve banks...	$78,516	
Discounts and advances............................	1,258	
Federal Reserve float.............................	3,313	
Other cash (treasury currency held by Federal		
Reserve banks)................................		271
		$94,818
Less, alternative uses:		
Treasury deposits at Federal Reserve banks.............		2,542
Foreign and other deposits...........................		1,884
Federal Reserve notes outstanding...................		64,262
Miscellaneous Federal Reserve accounts		
(miscellaneous liabilities less miscellaneous assets)....		−930
		$67,758
Equals: Member Bank Reserve Deposits.................		$27,060

In order to emphasize the major determinants of changes in the availability of reserve deposits, we have netted out the two cash items accounts to get Federal Reserve float, and we have netted out the two miscellaneous accounts and treated the difference (liabilities less assets) as a factor absorbing funds. In addition, we have combined the three items which are either controlled by or at least the responsibility of the Federal Reserve System—the securities portfolio, loans to member banks, and float—into one heading, Federal Reserve Credit.[16]

---

[16] For simplicity, we continue to treat Federal Reserve holdings of earning assets other than treasury securities as "miscellaneous." In practice they are part of Federal Reserve Credit.

5.4.2   Sources and Uses of the Monetary Base

Member bank reserve deposits are one of the three components of the monetary base, the other two being vault cash held by member banks and currency held by the public. Both of these components of currency in circulation include treasury currency as well as Federal Reserve notes. Thus the sources of the monetary base include the sources of reserve deposits, listed above, plus the remaining portion of treasury currency. The factors absorbing funds are as above with the addition of treasury currency in circulation. That is, we can compute the size of the monetary base by including treasury currency as a source and then allocating *total* currency (treasury currency and Federal Reserve notes) among the major holders: the Treasury, Federal Reserve banks, member banks, and the public.

It is important to remember that actions by the Treasury play an important role in determining the monetary base, in addition to those by the Federal Reserve. The monetary accounts of the Treasury include both treasury currency and the stock of gold. So a full statement of sources and uses of the monetary base (Table 5–4) must include a consolidation of both Treasury and Fed accounts.

The gold certificates held by Federal Reserve banks are not a true source of bank reserves. The ultimate source item is the gold stock of the Treasury against which the certificates are issued.

		(millions)
Treasury gold stock		$11,567
Less: Unmonetized gold		107
Equals: Gold certificates		$11,460

As the transactions presented here have shown, increases in the gold stock serve to increase member bank reserves as the sellers of the gold deposit their receipts in commercial bank accounts. We may replace gold certificates with gold stock as a source of reserves so long as we add the difference, un-

TABLE 5–4

Sources and Uses of the Monetary Base (December 31, 1973)

		(millions)
Sources:		
Treasury gold stock........................		$ 11,567
Federal Reserve Credit:....................		83,087
Government securities....................	$78,516	
Discounts and advances..................	1,258	
Float...................................	3,313	
Treasury currency outstanding (held by Federal Reserve banks, commercial banks, and the public).............................		8,716
		$103,370
Less alternative uses of funds:		
Treasury cash............................		318
Unmonetized gold.......................	$ 107	
Treasury currency held by the Treasury.....	77	
Federal Reserve notes held by the Treasury..	134	
Treasury deposits at Federal Reserve banks....		2,542
Foreign and other deposits at Federal Reserve banks........................		1,884
Miscellaneous Federal Reserve accounts.......		−930
		$ 3,814
Equals: Monetary base......................		$ 99,556
Member bank reserve deposits...............	$27,060	
Vault cash at member banks................	6,987	
Currency held by the public.................	65,509	

monetized gold, as an alternative use of funds. The unmonetized gold, which is held by the Treasury, then may be lumped together with the currency held by the Treasury to form an item called "treasury cash" or "treasury cash holdings."

While all of these factors, many of which are not subject to control by the Federal Reserve System, affect the size of the monetary base, the ultimate control of the base is in the hands of the System and in particular in the hands of the Federal Open Market Committee. The task of the committee is to observe movements in the various accounts comprising the sources and uses of the monetary base, to forecast short-run changes as accurately as possible, and to *offset* any undesired changes in the base resulting from the uncontrolled variables. It is perfectly consistent to observe that changes in the size of the monetary base over some period of time resulted from, say, changes in the stock of treasury currency outstanding and yet to argue that the change in the base was ultimately the result of FOMC policy decisions. After all, a decision not to react to an outside influence is just as forceful as an active purchase or sale of government securities. The Federal Reserve System controls the size of the monetary base through its residual control over the volume of open market operations which it chooses to employ.

REVIEW QUESTIONS

1. Using the table labeled "Member Bank Reserves, Federal Reserve Bank Credit, and Related Items" in a recent monthly *Federal Reserve Bulletin*, construct a table of sources and uses of member bank reserves showing what factors account for the change in member bank reserves between the latest month for which data are available and the corresponding month of the preceding year. (Use "End of Month" figures). What can you learn from this table?

2. When the U.S. Treasury revalued the monetary gold stock from $35 an ounce to $38 an ounce in 1972, what effects, if any, did this action have on the sources and uses of reserve deposits?

3. Show the balance sheet effects on member banks and Federal Reserve banks of the following transactions:
   a. The public repays loans at member banks.
   b. The Federal Reserve purchases securities from the non-bank public.
   c. Banks purchase Federal Reserve notes from the Fed by drawing on their reserve deposit accounts.
   d. The Treasury transfers deposits from member banks to Federal Reserve banks.
   e. Foreign governments holding deposits at Federal Reserve banks purchase military planes from the U.S. government, paying by check on their demand deposit balances at the Fed.

4. Explain how the account manager must act if he is instructed by the FOMC to control the monetary base.

SUGGESTED FURTHER READING

Board of Governors of the Federal Reserve System. *Federal Reserve Bulletin.* Washington, D.C.; monthly.

————. *Annual Reports.* Washington, D.C.; annually.

————. *The Federal Reserve System: Purposes and Functions.* Washington, D.C., 1963.

chapter 6

The Transactions Demand
for Money

6.1 INTRODUCTION

A seemingly simple concept like the demand for money can be obscured by careless language and faulty economic reasoning. Intuition tells us that a typical individual's "demand for money" is infinite: How could anyone ever have enough money? At the same time we might also conclude that the demand for money should be zero. Why would anyone choose to hold money when he really desires the goods and services that money can buy? Both of these inferences clutter our thinking only because they are based on a faulty or imprecise concept of the demand for money. We derive services from money, the nature of which we described in Chapter 2. However, in that chapter we were mainly concerned with the choice of the asset to be used as money. Whereas, in this chapter we confine our attention to the determinants of a desired money balance, given the existence of money.

6.2 ECONOMIC TRANSACTIONS AND THE DEMAND FOR MONEY

Most working people receive their income at regular intervals, perhaps once each week or every two weeks, and they make expenditures with irregular frequency. We shall defer for the moment the question of the timing of expenditures and shall assume for simplicity that the typical individual spends the same amount each day. For example, he may receive a paycheck for $100 on Monday. He immediately deposits $30 at his company's credit union. The remaining $70 he deposits in his checking account at the local bank, except for some small amount which he takes in the form of currency or "pocket cash." This $70 constitutes his demand for money as of that particular moment in time.

As the week progresses our typical worker spends $10 each day. Some of his expenditures are financed by checks drawn on his demand deposit, while others are made simply by payment of currency. Still others may be made on credit, perhaps by using a bank credit card or through a revolving credit plan at a department store. In order to keep the story uncomplicated, let us assume that during the week $10 of expenditures are "charged" in this manner but that our friend pays, at some time during the week, a bill for that amount covering earlier charges. Thus his outlays of money (currency and demand deposit balances) equal $10 each day of the week.

Let us now define the demand for money by an individual as the average amount which he chooses to hold over some period of time. Furthermore, the time period—to truly reflect the individual's choices—must be at least as long as the interval between pay days. The worker of the previous paragraph begins each Monday with $70. He then spends $10 during the day and goes to bed with $60 to his credit. We may conclude that his *average* demand for money on Monday is $65. Then he begins Tuesday with $60, he spends $10, and his average money holdings on Tuesday are $55. This process continues each day, and his demand for money on Sunday is just $5. Thus his *average* demand for money over the entire period is

$$M^d = (65 + 55 + \ldots + 15 + 5) \div 7 = \frac{\$245}{7} = \$35. \qquad (6.1)$$

FIGURE 6–1

An Individual's Demand for Money for Transactions: Example 1

Money Balance ($)

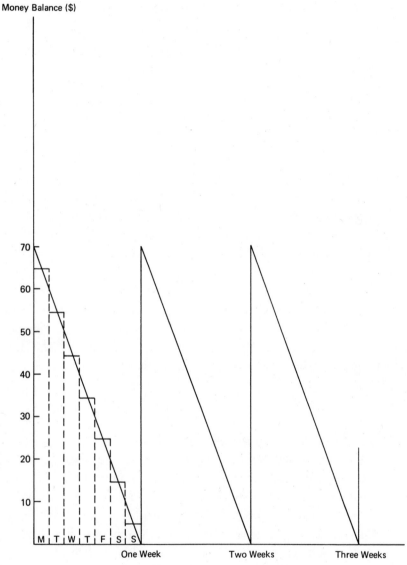

It is this $35, representing the average demand for money over the entire pay period, that is the appropriate concept of the demand for money by the individual. If we were to choose a shorter period we would see only part of the picture. If we were to choose a longer period (say, three weeks) we would learn nothing new.

The most important determinant of the demand for money as we have defined it is the volume of transactions or expenditures made by the individual. If, as in our example, those expenditures are made at a steady rate, the demand for money by the individual will always be just one half of the total money value of transactions ($35 = ½ · $70). Figure 6–1 illustrates this conclusion. We measure the individual's daily average money balances on the vertical axis, and time on the horizontal axis. As long as expenditures occur at a constant rate the size of the remaining money balance will be represented by a straight line between the initial demand ($70) and the terminal demand ($0) each week. Money balances are restored on pay day, and the process repeats. The *average* demand for money, for however many weeks we examine, is equal to the value at the midpoint of the line representing the size of the declining balance.

6.3   THE TIMING OF TRANSACTIONS

But why, you should ask, would anyone desire to hold excess money balances (i.e., more than he requires for transactions between now and next pay day), when he could earn interest on those balances just by going to a little extra trouble to acquire a time deposit or savings and loan account? Some reasons arise from shrewdness and some, perhaps, from laziness. Such reasons constitute the realm of "liquidity preference," a topic which we shall save for the next chapter.

Expenditures, of course, do not always occur at a steady rate. We all know people who spend a major portion of each paycheck immediately upon receiving it. Others spend money irregularly and often wind up a pay period with a substantial amount of pocket cash. The man who spends money quickly may be said to have a lower demand for money than the individual described in our first example. By spending $60 on Monday, $10 on Tuesday, and nothing for the rest of the week, he would have

$$M^d = (40 + 5 + 0 + \ldots) \div 7 = \frac{\$45}{7} = \$6.43, \qquad (6.2)$$

even though he has exactly the same income and transactions value as the first man we described. Figure 6–2 (constructed in the same manner as Figure 6–1) illustrates the demand for money by a quick spender.

Just as plausibly we might suppose that other people regularly leave large minimum balances in their checking accounts. Our first example described a man putting $30 into a credit union account because he did not intend to spend it right away. He might instead have deposited the entire $100 in his checking account and have finished the period with a $30 balance. If he also were slow in making expenditures, his demand for money might then be

$$M^d = (98 + 90 + 82 + 69 + 53 + 46 + 37)$$
$$\div 7 = \frac{\$475}{7} = \$67.86.[1] \qquad (6.3)$$

This pattern of demand is graphed in Figure 6–3.

One more example will complete the picture. What if our worker were paid only every second Monday instead of once each week? Would that alteration in the timing of his income affect his demand for money? At the start of the period he would receive a paycheck for $140, instead of $70. By spending $10 per day, he would end the second week with a zero

---

[1] The implied spending pattern is $4 spent on Monday, $12 on Tuesday, $4 on Wednesday, $22 on Thursday, $10 on Friday, $4 on Saturday, and $14 on Sunday. Thus, for example, he starts Sunday with $44, ends with $30, and has an average balance of $37.

FIGURE 6–2

An Individual's Demand for Money for Transactions: Example 2

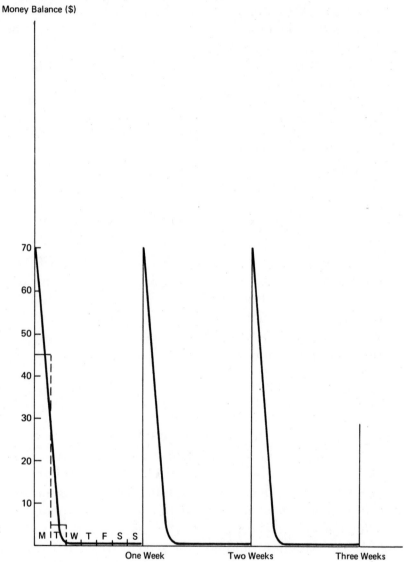

FIGURE 6–3

An Individual's Demand for Money for Transactions: Example 3

Money Balance ($)

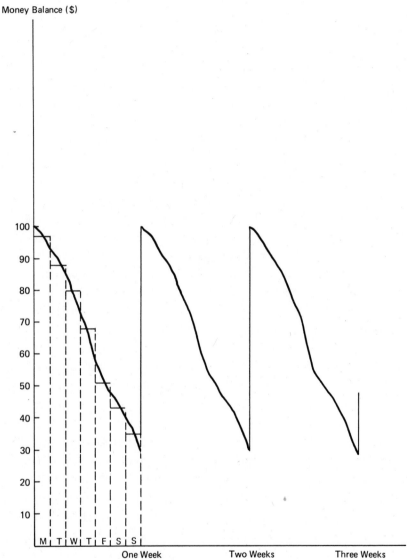

Time

balance, just in time for the next pay day. His average demand for money during the period would be

$$M^d = (135 + 125 + 115 + \ldots + 15 + 5)$$
$$\div 14 = \frac{\$980}{14} = \$70. \qquad (6.4)$$

Doubling the length of the interval between income payments will, ceteris paribus, double the individual's demand
for money.

Clearly the timing both of expenditures and of income is
an important determinant of the demand for money. At any
given level of income, businesses and individuals still have to
make choices about the manner in which they will pay out
their money balances. Those choices are an essential element
in determining the amount of money required to conduct
transactions; as we have seen in the four examples described
above, different individuals with the same incomes and the
same value of transactions may have sharply differing demands for money balances. If the timing is sluggish, a relatively large amount of money will be required. In short, the
more transactions are handled with a given amount of money,
the smaller will be the individual's demand for money at any
given level of income. To understand why the demand for
money is at one level rather than another, we will have to
investigate the major factors which influence these decisions.

Before examining these determinants, we observe that the
aggregate demand for money in our economy is merely the
sum of all individual demands, both consumer and business.
The major difference between the individual demands and
aggregate demand is that while the individual's demand
varies widely over very short periods of time, this variation
vanishes in the aggregate. It disappears both because different people are paid on different days and spend their money
at different rates and because as the individual's money balances decline over the week, those of the typical business
rise correspondingly. The $10 per day spent by the consumer

becomes income to the company, whose bank balance rises throughout the week until its employees are paid on the following Monday.

A second distinction between individual and aggregate demands for money is that individual demands are subject to variation for a large number of reasons which we could not begin to enumerate. Why do two men or women who appear to be very much alike in most of the ways that we can measure have quite different ways of managing their money balances? The answer would tell us more about personal psychology than about the demand for money. But individual differences cancel out in the aggregate and permit us to focus on those factors which are in the area of economic decision making. From this point on we shall be concerned primarily with the aggregate, rather than the individual, demand for money.

So far we have identified two important elements to the demand for money: the volume of transactions or expenditures made by the aggregate of individuals and businesses in the economy, and the timing of income payments and expenditures. Any increase in the volume of transactions is likely to generate an increase in the demand for money. Any increase in the rate at which money is spent will increase the efficiency with which money is being used and therefore will decrease the amount of money demanded at a given level of income. This close correspondence between the demand for money and the value and timing of transactions arises for this reason: one of the most important purposes for which money is demanded is simply for making transactions in goods and services. One type of utility or service which we derive from possessing money is that it renders the exchange of goods and services easier and more efficient than it would be otherwise.[2] There are, of course, other services rendered

---

[2] See Chapter 2. In this context, as elsewhere, we must be quite careful to distinguish money from wealth in general.

by money, and we shall examine them in the next chapter. But certainly the demand for money is in large measure a *transactions demand*.

The quantity of money which will be demanded for carrying out a given volume of transactions will depend, as stated above, on the timing of transactions and on the extent to which money balances not immediately required are transferred into some other form of asset. To state the same point differently, the ratio of transactions volume to the quantity of money demanded depends on the extent to which people are willing to trouble themselves in order to cut down or to economize on their money balances.

6.4 A SIMPLE DEMAND-FOR-MONEY FUNCTION

If the volume of transactions were the only important determinant of the demand for money, then we might expect M^d to be in constant proportion to the *value* of transactions at all times. Designating the average number of transactions taking place in an economy over a given period of time (say, one month) as T; and the average price of each transaction as P, so that the money value of the transactions is $P \cdot T$; we can write the demand function for money as, for example,

$$M^d = k \cdot (P \cdot T), \tag{6.5}$$

where k is merely a constant factor of proportionality.

On the other hand, even if $P \cdot T$ is the only important determinant of money demand, the relationship between $P \cdot T$ and M^d may not be constant if the demand function is nonproportional, such as

$$M^d = a + k' \cdot (P \cdot T), \tag{6.6}$$

or even nonlinear, such as

$$M^d = (P \cdot T)^{k''}. \tag{6.7}$$

But in any case the ratio of money demand to the transactions value should be constant or else varying systematically when the value of transactions $(P \cdot T)$ changes.[3] Still, in order to know how much money will be demanded at any given level of transactions activity, we must know how large a number k is likely to be. The previous section of this chapter has given us some clues to examine.

We have observed that if the typical individual holds only the amount of money which he will require for expenditures before the next pay day, and if he makes those expenditures at a steady rate, then his *average* holdings of (i.e., demand for) money will be exactly half of his actual expenditures. Since the total demand for money in the economy can be derived by summing all of the individual demands, it follows that with this type of behavior $k = \frac{1}{2}$. A more rapid pattern of spending, such as concentrating most cash outlays into the first few days after each pay day, would imply a lower value for k. Either a slower rate of spending or a desire by some persons to hold extra reserves of money beyond what they expect to spend in the near future would lead to a larger value for k. At least in theory we may suppose that k could be very near zero or in some extreme cases could even be greater than one. To judge the likely range of values for k, we shall have to examine the factors which strongly affect it.

6.5 ADDITIONAL DETERMINANTS OF MONEY DEMAND

One important determinant of k is the availability of alternative means of payments. People desire to have money in order to make it easy to buy goods and services and to make various other kinds of economic transactions. If there are other assets besides money which serve the same purpose, then the demand for money will be correspondingly smaller. A good example of a substitute for money is the use of credit

---

[3] For example, if $M^d = (P \cdot T)^{k''}$, where $k'' > 1$, then $M^d/(P \cdot T) = (P \cdot T)^{k''-1}$. Any increase in the value of transactions will increase the demand for money more than proportionally, and $M^d/(P \cdot T)$ will rise.

cards such as BankAmericard, Master Charge, and American Express. These card plans make it possible for large numbers of people to charge a major portion of their regular purchases each month and then to make one cash payment, perhaps on pay day, to clear all their obligations. The widespread use of such cards makes it possible for people to hold much smaller average cash balances while carrying on the same level of economic activity.

There are many other kinds of close substitutes for money as a medium of exchange. Any form of short-term credit which is regularly available will help to lower the demand for money relative to total expenditures. Many businesses regularly extend "trade credit" to other businesses with whom they deal. Retail stores, in turn, often extend credit to individual customers. Some banks are willing to permit overdraft (negative balance) privileges to preferred customers; that is, to permit an individual to write checks to make purchases even though he has no money in his account (but don't try that unless you clear it with your bank first!). Many people use "traveler's checks" instead of money, particularly when they are traveling to places where a check drawn on their local bank would not be readily accepted. And there are many other variations on the theme: money as we have defined it is merely one of a large number of instruments which can be used as a convenient medium of exchange. The availability, convenience, and expense of the various kinds of substitutes of money will be important determinants of the demand for money and therefore of k.

A second major determinant arises because of the fact that money balances in the United States do not earn interest. Commercial banks are forbidden by law from paying interest on demand deposits subject to check, although they may and do pay interest on other types of deposits. Currency, of course, is always redeemable at exactly its face value. Therefore the decision as to whether to go to the trouble to transfer money balances which are not required immediately for transactions purposes into some other form (perhaps a savings deposit at the same bank) will depend on how much interest can be earned by the transfer. If banks and other institutions are paying only 2 percent on short-term time accounts, then only a relatively small number of people will find it to be worth the time and trouble to put their assets in that form. But when interest rates get up around 5 percent or 6 percent and banks begin paying interest on deposits left with them for as little as 20 or 30 days, then many more people will see an incentive to acquire savings deposits. The demand for money will therefore be lower when interest rates are high than when they are low. We explore this point more fully below, for it is one of the important keystones in monetary theory.

A third factor influencing k is the psychology of the so-called business cycle. Historically, national income in the United States has undergone periodic cycles, the expansionary phases of which often have been characterized by a confident optimism on the part of both businessmen and consumers. That optimism has led to increased desires to spend out of a given level of income and to decreased desires to hold cash. People have made greater use of credit and have compressed their cash outlays closer to pay day in order to sustain higher levels of spending. Conversely, the contraction phases of business cycles generally have been characterized by rising balances of idle cash as the desire to spend and therefore the value of market transactions have fallen. Thus, in our terminology k has shown a tendency to fall during business expansions and to rise during recessions.

We may conclude with two general statements about the transactions demand for money. First, money demand is roughly proportional to the value of economic transactions,

$$M^d = k \cdot (P \cdot T).$$

Second, the coefficient k is a function of three factors:

1. The availability of close substitutes for money as a medium of exchange.
2. The level of interest rates on savings accounts and similar assets.
3. Whether the business cycle is in an expansionary or contractionary phase.

6.6 TWO SPECIAL CASES

There are two special cases of the transactions demand for money which have important policy implications. Together these special cases are known as versions of the "classical quantity theory of money." Because of its beguiling simplicity and the strength of the political fabric which can be woven from it, the quantity theory of money has enjoyed a long history of wide acceptance among both economists and politicians. David Hume, the famous British philosopher, historian, and economist, gave one of the earliest and most satisfactory accounts of the relationship between money and prices in his essay entitled "Of Money" written in 1752. Hume's version remained the standard until well into the 19th century. We owe the "transactions version" (our first special case) to a man who is perhaps the most distinguished American economist: Irving Fisher, who taught at Yale during the first quarter of this century. Cambridge University's great economist, Alfred Marshall, contributed the "income version" of the quantity theory (our second special case).

6.6.1 The Exchange Theory

The first special case of the transactions demand for money arises when k is highly stable over long periods of time. Suppose that the pattern of income receipt and of expenditures and methods of payment in our economy is determined not by purely economic considerations as we have hypothesized here and in Chapter 2, but by habit, tradition, and the existence of a particular set of institutions (such as commercial banks) which influence and govern our financial affairs. Some workers are paid each month, while others are paid every two weeks. Some consumers regularly pay by check, others by cash. Some people place part of their paycheck in a savings account each month; others never do so. Surely, say the quantity theorists, the explanation for these behavioral patterns lies as much in the force of habit as in the rational calculation of cost and benefit. The pattern should be slow to alter in the face of changes in the relative scarcity of money or in the level of interest rates. If habit and tradition are strong enough forces, then a given quantity of money will always be required (demanded) to carry out a given value of transactions, and k will be constant.

The theory that the demand for money is always roughly proportional to the value of transactions may be termed the *exchange* theory of the demand for money. It has many aliases; one which is in common usage is the transactions version of the classical quantity theory of money. We choose the former name because it is shorter and because it suggests clearly that the demand for money (in the aggregate) is determined by the fixed and habitual ways in which we go about exchanging goods and services in our economy.

Another way to illustrate the possibility of k being constant over long periods of time is to use the concept of the *velocity* of money. V is defined as the number of times that the average dollar of money "turns over" or changes hands during some specified period of time. V expresses a rate of flow, so it will be larger for longer time periods. For example, if the velocity of money is 2 per month, then it is also 24 per year.

The total flow of money over a year's time is equal to the stock of money (M) multiplied by the number of times the average dollar changes hands during the year. A business which pays its workers with paychecks is causing that

amount of money to change hands one time. When the workers spend the money, it changes hands again. Then when the
recipients of those expenditures spend the money again, it
changes hands a third time. Clearly the pattern of receipt and
expenditure which we have been examining is closely linked
with the velocity of the money stock.

The central fact of the transactions demand for money is
that the total flow of money over any time period must always be exactly equal to the total value of the flow of goods
and services being exchanged during the same period. That
is, every transaction has two elements: the transfer of a good
from seller to buyer, and the transfer of an equal value of
money from buyer to seller. The flow of money in one direction is equal to the flow of goods and services in the other direction, simply because the value of the goods and services is
measured by the amount of money which it will bring on the
market. A diamond ring is said to have a value of $500 only
because someone is willing to exchange that amount of
money for it. Since the total value of the flow of goods and
services is $P \cdot T$ and the total flow of money is $M \cdot V$,

$$M \cdot V \equiv P \cdot T, \tag{6.8}$$

where the third line ($\equiv$) indicates that the equation is an
identity, always true by definition. This identity is known as
the "equation of exchange," and it is one of the fundamental
tools of monetary theory.

The considerable usefulness of the equation of exchange
occurs because of its relationship to the demand function for
money developed in general form earlier in this chapter:

$$M^d = k \cdot (P \cdot T). \tag{6.5}$$

This demand function expresses a behavioral relationship. It
is not an identity; it merely summarizes in a convenient way
the relationship which we suppose to exist between the value
of transactions $P \cdot T$ and the stock of money which people
desire to hold, M^d. However, if we assume that the money

market is in equilibrium—i.e., that the demand for money is equal to the quantity supplied—then we may interchange M (the quantity supplied) and M^d (the quantity demanded) in the equation of exchange.

$$M^d \cdot V = P \cdot T$$

in equilibrium, so

$$M^d = \frac{1}{V} \cdot (P \cdot T). \qquad (6.9)$$

Therefore, unless the market is out of equilibrium,

$$k = \frac{1}{V}.$$

As Chapter 9 will explain, strong forces tend automatically to equate the demand for money with the quantity supplied. Thus for all practical purposes we may simply regard k and V as alternative means of expressing the relationship between the value of transactions and the quantity of money which people wish to hold. The faster the rate of circulation of money (V), the smaller will be the ratio of desired money balances to the value of transactions (k). Conversely, any decrease in desired money balances (given the value of $P \cdot T$) automatically requires an increase in the velocity of money.

To summarize the exchange theory of the demand for money: if the total stock of money circulates at a constant rate, possibly because of the powerful influence of habit and tradition, then the size of the money balances required or demanded for the purpose of carrying out transactions will always be strictly proportional to the value of those transactions.

6.6.2 The Income Theory

The second special case of the transactions demand function is really a branch of the first. Now we assume not only that k is constant but also that only certain kinds of transactions—those which can be characterized as income transactions—are relevant to the demand for money. These assumptions lead to a demand function in which the quantity of money demanded is proportional to total income.

The main reason for making such restrictive assumptions is that *transactions* is too broad a term to be readily measured. All manner of monetary transactions take place in our economy. Not only do we buy newly manufactured goods, we also frequently exchange existing assets, such as houses, cars, and shares of stock in corporations. Such exchanges are known as "secondary" transfers. Many kinds of transactions, known as "intermediate" transfers, take place among firms as one company buys materials and tools from another. Data measuring the total value of secondary and intermediate transactions do not exist. Furthermore, some intermediate transactions do not require a transfer of money. Interfirm transactions often can be settled by bookkeeping entries, particularly where a single parent company owns the individual businesses. Stock and bond sales generally are paid for "on paper," with only net differences being settled by transfers of money. Therefore it may be true that secondary and intermediary transactions involve only minimal demand for money, although we lack the data for making a true test of that hypothesis.

The one type of transaction for which complete data are readily available is the income transaction. The sum of all income transactions during any period may be measured by the gross national product (or national income at market prices), which we may denote Y. If k is stable and if the relationship between $(P \cdot T)$ and Y is stable, then the demand for money may be thought of as a stable function of the level of GNP:

$$M^d = k' \cdot Y, \tag{6.10}$$

where k', like k, is a constant factor of proportionality. This theory (that k' is constant) is the *income* version of the quantity theory of money or, for short, the income theory of the transactions demand for money.

Just as we were able in the preceding section to define the inverse of k as the velocity of money, we now define the inverse of k' as the *income velocity* of money, V_y. But V_y is a somewhat more abstract concept than is V. It is easy to visualize the total velocity of money as a measure of the turnover rate of the stock of money used in making economic transactions. The income velocity of money, by contrast, measures the ratio of total national income to the stock of money, a concept one step removed from measuring the rate of monetary circulation; the income transaction is only one of many kinds of transactions.

To strictly state the income theory of the demand for money, the income velocity of money (or, conversely, k') is hypothesized to be constant over long periods of time. However none of the great quantity theorists—David Hume, Irving Fisher, Alfred Marshall—ever believed that a strict proportion exists between money and income at all times. All have recognized that the theory has qualifications. What these men held in common, according to America's reigning quantity theorist, Milton Friedman of the University of Chicago, is the "belief that these qualifications are of secondary importance for substantial changes in either prices or the quantity of money, so that one will not in fact occur without the other."[4] Thus a milder form of the income theory is that V_y should be highly stable over time with only gradual and predictable changes. If V_y moves in a random or unpredictable way, then clearly the income theory is not a good representation of the demand for money.

---

[4] Milton Friedman, "Money: Quality Theory," *International Encyclopedia of the Social Sciences*, David L. Sills, Ed., Vol. 10 (New York: The Macmillan Company, and the Free Press, 1968).

6.7   The Velocity of Money in the United States

Figure 6–4 describes the path of annual observations of income velocity for nearly a century, from 1869 through 1960.[5] Clearly, now we can dispense with the notion of a strictly constant velocity of money. For the first ten years (the 1870s) covered by the chart, V_y bounced around violently, rising by almost 20 percent between 1875 and 1880. Then it spun into a secular decline which lasted, with several interruptions, until after the end of the Second World War. Since 1946 velocity has been rising steadily.

The most interesting feature of Figure 6–4 is the massive decline from a high of 4.97 in 1880 to a low of 1.16 in 1946. Why should velocity fall so dramatically, or at all? Does it not seem odd that in 1880 a single dollar of money in circulation could sustain income transactions of $4.97, but a similar dollar of money in 1946 could support only $1.16 of income? Two explanations are possible. One is that money may be a "luxury good" (like jewelry), the demand for which tends to rise more than in proportion to any increase in income.[6] Thus as income rose markedly during the past century the demand for money could be expected to rise even more, causing the ratio of income to money demanded (V_y) to fall. The difficulty with this explanation is that income has continued to

---

[5] For the early years covered by Figure 6–4, separate data on demand and time deposits are not available. In order to present a consistent data series over the entire period, the chart plots the ratio of net national product to the money supply plus time deposits in commercial banks; that is, total bank deposits plus currency held by the public. The velocity data are from Milton Friedman and Anna Jacobson Schwartz, *A Monetary History of the United States, 1867–1960* (Princeton, N.J.: Princeton University Press, 1963), p. 774. The Friedman-Schwartz book contains an extensive analysis of the behavior of the money stock and of its velocity over the period.

[6] The view that money is a luxury good was first advanced by Milton Friedman. Money balances yield services such as rendering transactions easier and more convenient, just as jewelry yields services such as increasing one's physical attractiveness. If we view those services as a luxury, then we are likely to devote a larger part of our assets to them when income is high than when it is low. Mathematically we say that the income elasticity of a luxury good is greater than one.

FIGURE 6–4

Annual Velocity of Money Plus Time Deposits, 1860–1960

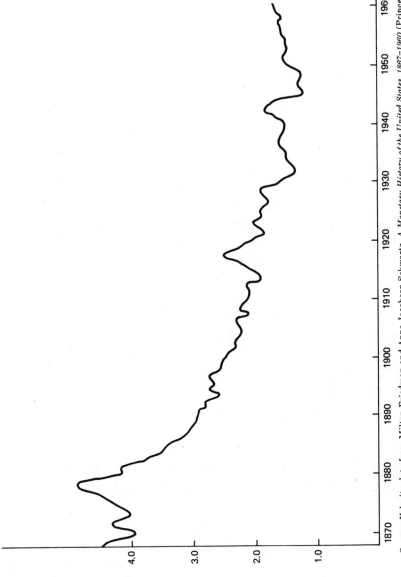

Source: Velocity data from Milton Friedman and Anna Jacobson Schwartz, *A Monetary History of the United States, 1867–1960* (Princeton, N.J.: Princeton University Press, 1963), p. 774.

rise very sharply since 1946 while velocity has not continued to fall. In fact, it has steadily increased. A second explanation is that factors other than income influence the demand for money, and those factors on balance produced a decline in V from 1880 to 1946 and an increase in V since 1946. We shall examine the nature of those other factors shortly.

The recent pattern of velocity is equally interesting (Figure 6–5).[7] At the start of 1947 the stock of money in the United States totaled $110 billion, and gross national product was at $224 billion per year. The income velocity of money therefore was just over 2.0. By the end of 1970 the money stock had almost doubled, to $214 billion. GNP, however, had more than quadrupled to $988 billion per year. The demand for money per dollar of income had dropped sharply, leading to an increase in V_y from 2.0 to just over 4.6. Furthermore the rise was broken by numerous small cycles around the upward trend. In other respects the upward movement was highly regular and stable.

Some of the cyclical variation in V_y is associated with business recessions. The shaded areas in Figure 6–5 represent the five postwar recessions; in each case velocity has declined. Several explanations for this phenomenon have been offered. One is that the demand for money may be related not to current income but to some longer run measure of our living standards, such as wealth or expected income over a span of several years.[8] During recessions income is low relative to what people expect it to be over the next few years. Hence spending and the demand for money both may be high relative to actual present income.

A second explanation of the cyclical behavior of velocity is

---

[7] In Figure 6–5, income velocity is defined in the manner described in the text. It is the ratio of GNP to the stock of money, both seasonally adjusted. Thus the data used for the two figures (6–4 and 6–5) are not comparable.

[8] Milton Friedman has developed the concept of long-run expected income as an important variable: the term which he applies to the concept is "permanent income." See his *A Theory of the Consumption Function* (Princeton, N.J.: Princeton University Press, 1957).

FIGURE 6–5

Income Velocity of Money, Quarterly, 1947–70

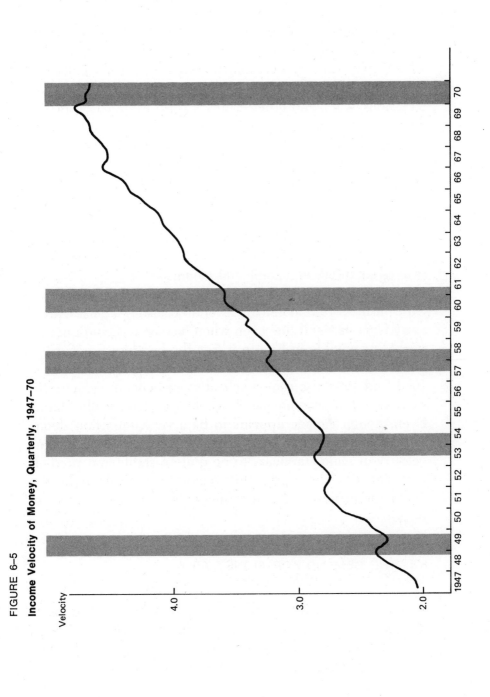

that the demand for money may be sensitive to people's expectations about the stability of the economy. A drop in confidence may lead to increased hoarding of cash balances as reserves against emergencies. Thus velocity would fall during recessions, wars, and other crises. A third explanation is that the demand for money may not be functionally related to income at all. Recall that velocity is defined as the ratio of income to the stock of money. Normally both income and the stock of money tend to rise over time. That common trend could account for the observed stability of velocity. When income falls for any reason while M is continuing to grow, velocity naturally will fall. On the other hand, both economic theory and most of the accumulated evidence do point to a strong link between income and money.

In addition to those cycles in velocity which are associated with business recessions, on several occasions V_y has varied away from its trend line even when income has continued to rise. Most notable in Figure 6–5 is the bumpiness occurring toward the end of the Korean War. But 1956, 1959, 1964, 1966, and 1968 also show cyclical movements in velocity. In each case the economy as a whole was reasonably stable. Even though income appears to be a very important determinant of the demand for money—and therefore the income velocity of money appears to be quite a stable and predictable statistic—there are other factors which affect the demand for money and cause fluctuations in the velocity of money.

6.8 THE DEMAND FOR MONEY AS A TRANSACTIONS INVENTORY

One of the variables which clearly supplements income as a determinant of money demand is the level of interest rates. In fact, one *has* to introduce a measure of the *cost* of holding money balances in order to have a full explanation of the transaction demand; lack of synchronization of receipts and expenditures by itself does not explain why money is held for transaction purposes. The mere fact that we receive our income at the beginning of the week and spend it at a steady rate throughout the week does not mandate the holding of money balances. There is more to it than that, particularly where large sums are involved.

Making a $100 payment on Friday requires $100 on Friday. If we hold $100 out of our receipts on Monday to make a $100 payment on Friday, there must be a compelling reason. Ideally we would like to lend or invest our $100 for five days earning interest income until payment is due on Friday. But there is no guarantee that it is profitable to do so. Is the interest earned worth the extra bother of finding a suitable asset to buy? The options available for getting four days of interest on $100 are not very great. If you have to spend valuable time knocking on your neighbors' doors in search of a suitable borrower, the value of the search time may well exceed your anticipated earnings. If so, then you may be satisfied with holding $100 of cash balances until Friday when payment is due.

This problem—determining whether to hold money until transactions are scheduled—may usefully be thought of as analogous to the problem of determining optimum inventory stocks. We may then ask what determines the size of our holdings of money *inventories*. We shall discover that our old friend transaction costs, which we introduced in Chapter 2, again proves helpful.

A car dealer, to consider a simple example, would like to know how many new automobiles he ought to have on the lot and in the showroom. His options may vary all the way from zero (selling only to order) to as many as he expects ever to sell. Upon what basis can he make a rational decision? The dealer has to find that level of inventory holdings which will minimize his total costs. Therefore, we must examine the relevant costs. Consider the alternatives. If he orders new automobiles from Detroit only once a year, he incurs heavy storage and insurance expenses. Furthermore, he suffers a loss of income by having wealth tied up in the form of automobiles rather than interest-bearing assets. But his transactions costs (cost of reordering) are negligible in this case. He can avoid the loss of income and the heavy storage expense by replenishing his depleted inventory more frequently. By so doing he saves on storage fees but incurs additional expense connected with reordering.

The problem the car dealer faces is analogous to the problem faced by every transactor in our economy. But it is particularly relevant to the behavior of corporate treasurers whose responsibility it is to determine desired cash balances at minimum cost. Corporations that have large enough balances available, even for a few days, may be able to purchase interest-bearing assets for the interim.

Corporate treasurers, like production managers, have the options of holding money balances (inventories) in an amount sufficient to meet anticipated expenditures, or to hold short-term, interest-bearing assets (perhaps treasury securities) until payments are due. Holding large money balances, like holding large stocks of new automobiles, is expensive because of the resulting loss of income. Corporate treasurers (like production managers) can attempt to escape this loss of income by more frequent asset switching; that is, they can swap money for securities and synchronize the maturity date of the security with payments dates. Asset switching, however, involves expenses, including fees to brokers for handling the exchange of money for securities and securities for money.

An important implication of this concept of money as an inventory is that the transactions demand for money by business firms will vary systematically with the level of interest rates available on short-term assets. A rise in interest rates increases the opportunity cost of holding money balances, but it does not affect the cost of making transfers into or out of securities. Therefore, more firms will find it profitable to make very short-term security purchases when interest rates are high than when they are low.

This explanation suggests an alternative explanation for the observed dips in velocity since 1946. Recessions tend to be associated with relatively low levels of interest rates because the demands for bonds and bank loans usually fall along with overall business activity. With the exception of the 1949 recession, short-term rates fell sharply during each of the shaded periods of Figure 6–5.

But the full extent of the impact of interest rates on the demand for money cannot be attributed to business transactions demand alone. In order to develop a complete theory of the demand for money which explains the evidence from the performance of the U.S. economy, one must examine the reasons people and businesses *hold* currency and demand deposits for longer periods of time. We must examine the properties of money as an asset.

REVIEW QUESTIONS

1. How much discretion do households and business firms exercise over the transactions demand for money?
2. What connections are there between the analysis of the uses of money (Chapter 2) and the behavior of the transactions demand for money as set out in this chapter?
3. Does the transactions demand for money vary approximately in proportion with the money value of transactions? What explains this relationship?
4. What determines the amount of currency (coins and paper money) the public desires to hold?
5. Why not analyze the demand for money in the same way we analyze the demand for oranges? Is there any difference?
6. What determines the velocity of money?

SUGGESTED FURTHER READING

Baumol, William J. "The Transactions Demand for Cash: An Inventory Theoretic Approach," *The Quarterly Journal of Economics.* November 1952.

Friedman, Milton. "Money: Quantity Theory," *International Encyclopedia of the Social Sciences.* New York: Macmillan, 1968.

Hume, David. "Of Money," reprinted in Eugene Rotwein (ed.), *David Hume: Writings on Economics.* Madison: University of Wisconsin Press, 1970.

Laidler, David E. W. *The Demand for Money.* Scranton, Pa.: International Textbook, 1969; chaps. 3 and 4.

chapter 7

The Asset Demand for Money

7.1 INTRODUCTION

The primary function of money, as illustrated by the preceding chapter, is as a medium of exchange. The use of money facilitates the exchange of goods and services. But money is also an asset which can be held. Money is one of the very many forms in which people hold their accumulated wealth. And if we are to account fully for the demand for money, we must understand its demand as an asset as well as a medium of exchange.

At first blush, it seems curious that there should be such a thing as an "asset demand" for money. Neither currency nor demand deposits earns interest, while many other assets do: savings deposits at banks and savings and loan associations, securities of all kinds. Unlike automobiles, real estate, or works of art, money does not yield any obvious consumable services that would make it worth holding for its own sake. And yet, in the United States, the average individual holds money balances (about 80 percent in the form of demand deposits) equal in value to more than a month's income! The theory of the transactions demand for money described above in Chapter 6 can explain only a fraction of those balances. Workers are paid, say, every two weeks. Then transactions balances should average less than two weeks' income and probably no more than one week's income. There does seem to exist a significant asset demand for money in addition to the transactions demand.

7.2 WHY HOLD MONEY?

One of the important characteristics by which assets can be compared is their marketability: the ease and cheapness with which they can be generally converted into other assets. The medium of exchange is obviously the most marketable asset in any economy, but almost all assets are marketable to some degree. Two other characteristics we have already mentioned: some assets generate interest or other income, and many assets are intrinsically desirable for the consumable services they provide. If we are willing to oversimplify matters a bit, we can list the typical assets held by individuals and divide them into three principal categories (Table 7–1).

The first group, monetary assets, includes not only money —currency and demand deposits—but also all assets which are convertible into money at face value (dollar-for-dollar), on short notice and with virtually no risk. It is important to note that those assets generally are not *perfect* substitutes for money. Demand deposits (a form of money) can be directly exchanged for almost any other good simply by writing a check. Savings accounts at commercial banks must first be converted into currency or demand deposits. Although that conversion has no explicit cost, it does require extra time, thought, and trouble. To withdraw funds from savings accounts may mean losing previously accumulated time toward interest income. Withdrawals often cannot be made except during the working hours of the bank. So the banks compensate for this loss of convenience by paying interest on savings deposits.

Money and other monetary assets are attractive assets to

TABLE 7–1

Types of Assets

I. Monetary assets, desired mainly for their marketability:

Currency
Demand deposits
Travelers' checks
Savings deposits at commercial banks
Certificates of deposit
Other bank time deposits (e.g., Christmas and vacation club accounts)
Savings and loan accounts
Mutual savings bank deposits
Credit union deposits

II. Other financial assets, desired mainly for their income prospects:

Debt instruments (securities)—
   Government securities
   Corporate securities
Ownership instruments (equities)—
   Corporate stocks

III. Consumer goods, desired mainly for their consumable services:

Clothing and other personal items
Furniture
Automobiles
Real estate

---

hold simply because they are marketable at fixed and known prices and on very short notice. People who hold monetary assets have a great deal of flexibility in reacting to changing circumstances. Suppose an emergency occurs, requiring a sudden expenditure. Suppose a bargain is offered: either a consumer good goes on sale or an issue of stocks or bonds drops to an attractive price. Suppose we decide to chuck everything and head for Europe or Latin America. If we hold money and other monetary assets, we have the flexibility to act without suffering a possible loss in the value of our wealth.

But why hold money when we could hold savings deposits and earn interest? Some people do. Some people hold part of their wealth in the form of demand deposits; some, in savings deposits. But the latter are not perfect substitutes for money, because they are slightly less convenient. The cost of "marketing" a savings deposit—the cost of, say, exchanging a savings deposit for a new car—is higher than the same cost if we hold demand deposits. So long as the interest rates paid by banks on savings accounts are not too high, some of us will use our checking accounts as a depository for our wealth. To summarize: people demand monetary assets in order to have flexibility, in order to have assets that are marketable at fixed and known prices and on short notice. Money is one of the assets that satisfy that demand.

The other financial assets on the list—stocks and bonds—are *not* convertible into money at face value on short notice. They are marketable, but not at a fixed price. For example, suppose that an individual buys a government security with a face value of $10,000 maturing in exactly one year. If the buyer holds the bond for the full year, the bond can be redeemed through a bank for the $10,000 plus interest from the U.S. Treasury. But what if the purchaser wants to sell it before that time? The individual has to find a buyer. Now there is an organized and active market for most government securities, so finding a buyer is not likely to pose much of a problem. But the seller cannot know in advance the price which a buyer will be willing to pay. If the bond's owner wants to sell in a hurry, he may not be able to get more than, say, $9,900 for it. If the owner is willing to wait and perhaps to shop around among securities dealers, he may be able to get a better price. And for corporate stocks, the risk of taking a loss on one's purchase is even greater. Stocks generally carry no maturity date, so the owner of the stocks always must sell at whatever price the market will offer.

The attraction of stocks and bonds is that they offer the possibility of substantial financial gain. If the market price of an asset can fall, then it also can rise. We run the risk of having to sell our government security at $9,900 instead of its $10,000 face value. We have the dream of selling it at $10,100 or more. It is important to note here that the distinction between monetary assets and securities is not in the observed rates of return. Normally, the returns on monetary assets are lower than the returns on other financial assets. As of mid-1974, banks are paying 5 percent to 5½ percent on savings accounts, while government securities are yielding around 7 percent and high-grade corporate bonds, 8 percent. The small investor can readily find mutual funds with a history of yielding 8 percent and more. But the yields on stocks and on bonds fluctuate far more than do the interest rates paid on bank deposits, and there are times when the actual percentage returns on savings deposits are higher than those on many securities. There are many times when the observed returns on stock ownership are negative.

The distinction between monetary and other financial assets is in the types of risk involved. The possibility of fluctuation in the market price of an asset is known as the risk of capital loss (or capital gain, when the price rises). Monetary assets carry no risk of capital loss, while all other financial assets do, to some degree. We shall show momentarily how changes in interest rates affect the tradeoff between the risk of capital loss and the potential for capital gains on bonds and other securities.

Equities—common corporate stocks—are like securities in that investors buy them primarily because they expect them to yield an income and to rise in value over time. While money is held for its marketability, both securities and equities are held for income. But equities differ from securities in that the attractiveness of equities depends largely on whether we expect business profits to rise or fall. When business is poor, stock prices fall. There are many exceptions to that rule, because the stock market is subject to many psychological pressures; no one has yet come up with a suitable theory for predicting stock prices! But as a general rule, people buy stock in corporations because they expect the companies to make profits and either to distribute those profits in the form of stock dividends or to reinvest the earnings in the business (increasing both the total value of the company and the value of each share of stock).

The final group of assets consists of consumer goods: the personal assets which we desire for their own sake rather than for the liquidity or income which we expect to get from them. But that definition does not imply that we scorn any income we might get from consumer goods. A man might buy a painting because it looks beautiful on the living room wall *and* because he expects its value to appreciate over the years. He buys a vacant lot because he expects to build a house on it someday and because he knows that if he changes his mind he can probably sell the land at a profit. In other words, consumer goods may be attractive both because of their intrinsic value and because their owners expect the prices of those consumer goods to rise.

Each of the assets listed in Table 7–1 is unique; each has its own qualities which make it attractive for some people to hold. But we would like to emphasize the major characteristics by which those assets can be grouped and compared. Monetary assets are desired mainly for the quality of being marketable on short notice at fixed and known prices. Securities and equities are desired mainly for the prospect of financial gain. Consumer goods are desired mainly for the services we get from using them. Therefore the asset demand for money is really a preference for liquidity over interest income and the acquisition of consumer goods.

7.3 HOW MUCH MONEY TO HOLD?

Our catalog of assets suggests some of the variables that are most important in determining how much money people will wish to hold. One of the most important is the size of our income: the more income we have, the more assets we are likely to accumulate, and the more funds will we have to allocate to money as well as other assets. Equally important are the returns that we get from holding assets other than money. As interest rates paid on bonds and other securities rise, more people will find those assets to be attractive instead of money. As our expectations about the course of business profits become more favorable, we are more likely to want to hold corporate stocks. If we expect the prices of consumer goods to rise, we may become speculators by buying more goods today. Now let us examine each of these factors in more detail, starting with interest rates.

7.3.1 Interest Rates

We have already seen in Chapter 6 (Section 6.8) how changes in interest rates can influence the quantity of money demanded for transactions purposes, particularly by business firms. Because interest rates are an opportunity cost on the holding of money balances, profit-maximizing firms will attempt to reduce their money balances in response to increases in rates. Asset-holders also are likely to be influenced by interest rates in the following way.

Suppose that some day you may have a large sum, say $10,000, which you will have decided not to spend for the next year or so. You therefore have to decide what to do with this wealth in the meantime. Being cautious by nature, you regard corporate stocks as a little too risky. Nevertheless you would like to earn some interest income, so you look at short-term government securities. You ask your banker what is available, and the banker recommends a treasury note (a form of bond) which the federal government has just issued. It matures in one year and pays 3 percent annual interest. You tell the banker you will think about it and will call him back tomorrow. What should you do?

Your first thought may be that since your $10,000 currently is earning no interest in your checking account, you will be better off by buying the treasury note. It is a riskless asset, and it will pay you $300 interest at the end of the year. The bank will charge a small brokerage fee for handling the transaction, but you will still come out well ahead. But then you stop and think. Three percent does not seem like a very high return. If you check back over recent years, you are likely to find that short-term government securities have often carried much higher yields. Perhaps you can call up a friend who teaches economics; he tells you that interest rates are low right now and are likely to come back up before long. "How long?" you are likely to ask. "No economist can predict that," he says as he hangs up.

But now you are uncertain as to what to do. One alternative would be to go ahead and buy the available security and consider reselling it if better alternatives appear within the next few months. Assume that you do that, and that in fact interest rates rise to 5 percent after three months. That is, after three months new treasury notes become available which yield 5 percent instead of the current 3 percent. You then would like to sell your 3 percent note and buy the new issue. The problem is that no one will be willing to pay $10,000 for your note, because the buyer will have the same alternatives you have. What a buyer should be willing to pay is a price that will yield him a 5 percent return over the remaining life of the bond (nine months). Since he can buy a new bond paying 5 percent, he can be induced to buy from you only if he can buy at a large enough discount. Let V = Redemption value of the bond, including interest (i.e., the price the Treasury must pay when the bond matures) and P = Purchase price (i.e., the price at which you can sell the bond before maturity, in the open market). Then the percentage return on the bond can be calculated from the following formula.[1]

---

[1] This formula assumes that there is only one interest payment on the bond, made at the same time the bond is redeemed.

$$\text{Percentage yield to maturity} = \frac{V - P}{P}$$

For example, when you first purchase the bond, you will pay $10,000. After one year, you may redeem it at the Treasury (through your local bank) for $10,300. Your return is

$$\frac{V - P}{P} = \frac{\$10,300 - \$10,000}{\$10,000} = 3\%$$

If the bond matures in less than one year, the percentage yield to maturity must be converted into an annual rate in order for you to be able to compare alternatives. If someone were to buy your bond for $10,000 after you had held it for three months (with nine months of life left on the bond), his annual rate of return would be

$$3\% \times \frac{12}{9} = 4\%$$

That is, $300 income in nine months from an investment of $10,000 is an annual rate of return of 4 percent.

We now can calculate the price at which you are likely to be able to sell the bond if interest rates rise to 5 percent after three months: we simply plug in a 5 percent return and solve the above formula for P, the purchase price. The formula is

$$\frac{9}{12} \times 5\% = \frac{V - P}{P}$$

so

$$.0375 = \frac{\$10,300}{P} - 1$$

or

$$1.0375 = \frac{\$10,300}{P}$$

Solving for the purchase price,

$$P = \frac{\$10,300}{1.0375} = \$9,928$$

You therefore will lose $72 on your investment if interest rates rise to 5 percent within the first three months. If you then buy a new security paying 5 percent interest, you can pick up $375 ($\frac{9}{12} \times \$500$) by the end of the year. Your *net* return for the year will be just about 3 percent.[2]

But after working through these calculations, you should realize that there is a third alternative available. You can simply put off buying any bonds until the expected rise in interest rates comes through. Then you will have no income (and no loss) for the first three months, after which you can then buy the $10,000 security to earn $375 for the last nine months. Your total return for the year is $375/$10,000 = 3.75 percent. That clearly is the best choice of the three.

There are other choices. If one could be confident about the timing of the rise in interest rates, he could buy a security with a very short maturity or simply put the money in a savings account. In our example, interest rates rose to 5 percent after three months. You could have maximized your return by finding a bank paying 3 percent on savings accounts. But as we pointed out, we can only guess *whether* interest rates will rise, and our ability to guess the *timing* of a rise, should it occur, is not likely to be very precise. Given that uncertainty, we may very well choose to hold our wealth in the form of money.

We now can draw a general principle about the demand for money. Whenever an investor expects interest rates on securities to rise in the near future, he is likely to hold at least part of his assets in the form of money. Then, if he has guessed correctly, he can easily and with virtually no risk or cost take advantage of the rise in interest rates when it occurs. The more investors there are who expect a rise in inter-

---

[2] Your net return is $375 − $72 = $303. But remember that you have to kick in an additional $72 principal to be able to buy the second bond after your initial loss. Your approximate percentage return for the year is $303/$10,072 = 3.01 percent. When you subtract your extra brokerage and other fees (at least $25), you will find that you would do better just to hold the first bond for the full year.

FIGURE 7–1

The Effect of Interest Rates on the Asset Demand for Money

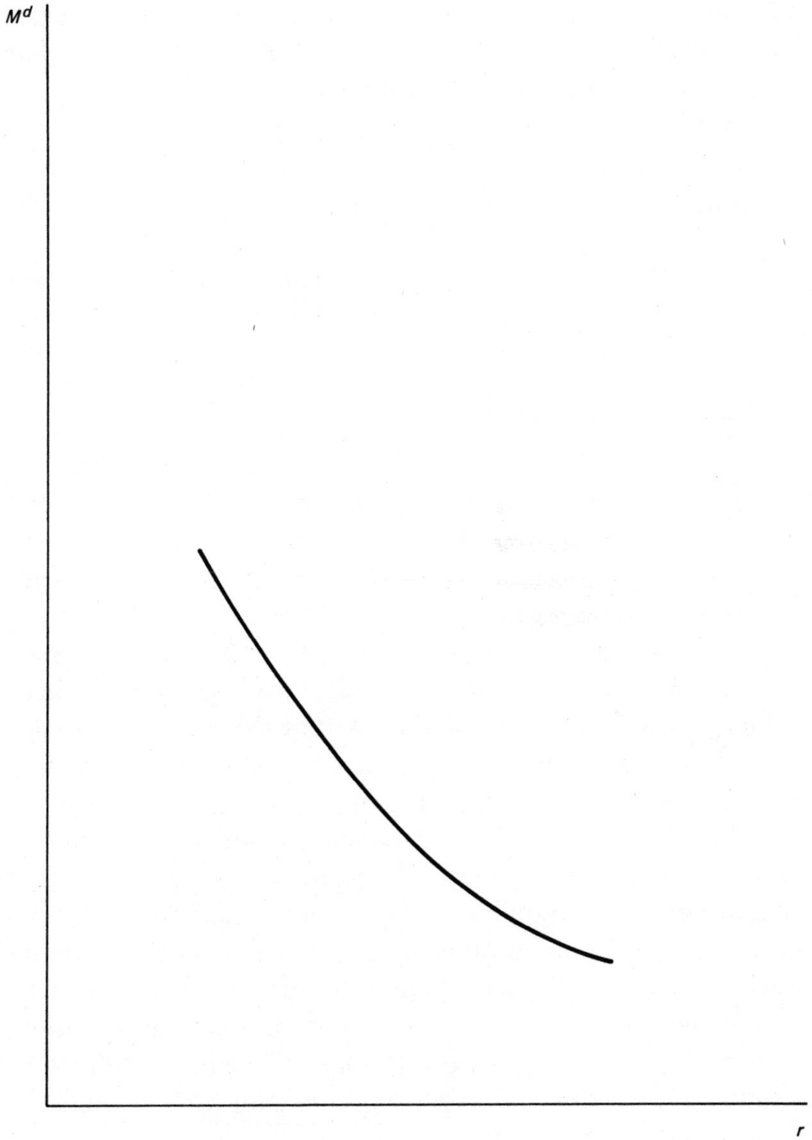

M^d

r

est rates, the greater will be this "speculative demand" for money. And we can go a step further. If investors have a notion of a normal level for interest rates, then whenever interest rates fall below their normal level, the expectation that they will rise again becomes stronger. If interest rates are at historically high levels, investors may expect quite strongly that a drop is imminent. We can conclude from that observation that whenever interest rates fall, some investors will hold money in anticipation of a future increase; when interest rates rise, they will buy securities and draw down their money balances. The asset demand for money will vary inversely with the current level of interest rates (Figure 7–1).

7.3.2 Inflation

Severe and persistent inflation can render money a wholly unsuitable store of value. To see why, just think for a moment about what inflation is. We define inflation as a general increase in the prices of final goods and services. The prices of some goods will be rising rapidly, some slowly, and some likely will be falling. But if, when we weight all of these goods and services by the amounts that the economy spends on them, we find that the price of an average good is rising, we say that we are experiencing inflation.[3]

Inflation decreases the purchasing power of each unit of money, which is why people often refer to inflation as a drop in the "value of the dollar." If the price of a hamburger rises to $.45 from $.30, more money is required to buy each hamburger. Where $.90 would have bought three hamburgers, now it will buy only two. When that happens, what should be the effect on the demand for money? The first effect, since rising prices normally are accompanied by a rising national

---

[3] For a discussion of the various methods of measuring inflation in the United States—the Consumer Price Index, the Wholesale Price Index, and the GNP deflator, among others—see William H. Wallace, "Measuring Price Changes," *Federal Reserve Bank of Richmond Monthly Review,* September 1970.

income, will be a rise in the quantity of money demanded for transaction purposes. That is, to the extent that inflation is offset by a rise in income, people will end up buying approximately the same real quantity of goods and services and will merely use a larger sum of money in the process. That effect is just another manifestation of the principles we discussed in Chapter 6.

The demand for money as a component of wealth, unlike the transactions demand, is likely to *fall* during extended periods of inflation. But what is important is not the fact that prices have been rising, but whether wealth holders expect prices to continue to rise. If you confidently expect the price level to increase, you will avoid holding assets that are fixed in price because their real value will be eroded by inflation. (See Figure 7–2.)

Let us return to our example of the preceding section. You have $10,000 which, for the moment, you do not plan to spend. Now suppose that we have been experiencing substantial inflation: the price level has been rising at an annual rate of, say, 8 percent for the past several months. If you *expect* the inflation to continue, then you will expect the value of money to continue to fall, and you will have a strong incentive not to hold that $10,000 in the form of money or any other monetary asset. The mere fact that inflation has occurred in the past is of no particular relevance; the expectation that it will continue is what matters. You cannot avoid the expected loss of value by putting your assets in a savings account or even by buying a bond. But you can protect yourself by buying goods. (Real estate, for example, is often considered to be a good "hedge" against inflation. There usually is an active market for it, and its value generally rises when overall price levels rise.) Common corporate stocks may be another alternative, but the tendency of stock prices to rise along with other prices is pretty tenuous. The important point to remember is that when you expect prices to rise, you

FIGURE 7–2

The Effect of an Expected Inflation on the Asset Demand for Money

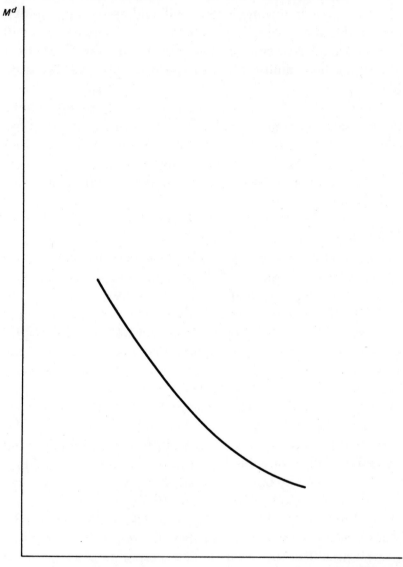

Expected Rate of Inflation

have an incentive to buy the goods whose prices will be rising. When prices of goods rise generally, the price of money must fall correspondingly. The incentive is to switch out of money and into goods.

And what happens when prices fall? Deflation of the general price level happens very rarely—the last year it occurred in the United States was 1949—but we should expect its consequences to be the exact opposite of those from rising prices. When inflation is anticipated, the purchasing power of each unit of money is expected to decline. Deflation of prices will generate an increase in the value of money, and we would expect to see a corresponding increase in its demand.

7.3.3   The Stock Market

One of the assets that people can hold as an alternative to money is common corporate stock. When we buy stocks, we are buying ownership shares in corporations. When the corporation earns net profits, we share in those profits through our ownership of a (small) part of the company. There are two ways in which we might benefit. First, the company might pay dividends on each share of stock; the dividend is a direct distribution of profits to the company's shareholders. Second, the company might retain its earnings and reinvest them in the activities of the corporation. Assuming that those activities continue to generate new profits for the company, the net value of the corporation will thereby be increased, and the market value of each share of stock should rise. To be sure, that market value depends primarily on what prospective stock purchasers *think* the stock is worth; there is no precise linkage between a company's current profits and the price of its stock in the open market. But as a general rule, an increase in profits will push up the price of the stock.

The yield on stocks is therefore the sum of the dividends paid by the company and the rise in the market price of the stock (i.e., the capital gain—or loss). For example, on a given day, you might be able to buy 100 shares of stock in the American Telephone and Telegraph Company (AT&T, or "Ma Bell") for $5,100. It happens that AT&T has a reputation for paying a very regular dividend through good years and bad. On 100 shares, you can strongly expect to be paid an annual dividend of at least $280. Your dividend yield on the stock is therefore 5½ percent (280/5,100). But whether your *total* earnings on the purchase are greater or smaller than 5½ percent depends on the price at which you will be able to sell the stock in the future. If the market price of an AT&T share rises to $54 over the next year, your total yield will be $280 + $300 or more than 11 percent (less brokerage fees). But if the price falls to $48, your net return will be negative, because your capital loss will exceed your dividend income. (See Figure 7–3.)

We have seen above (section 7.3.1) how people who would like to buy bonds can often increase their income by temporarily holding money in anticipation of an expected fall in bond prices (rise in interest rates). The same principle applies here to people who are considering a purchase of corporate stocks. If you expect stock prices to fall in the near future, you might do better simply to hold money, even if that choice means passing up a dividend. Whether you anticipate a fall in bond prices or in stock prices, money offers you a temporary haven for speculating against that drop. We can conclude, therefore, that the asset demand for money is likely to rise whenever asset-holders increase their expectation that stock prices are likely to fall. That speculation might arise because of a current drop in corporate profits, or it might arise because of a general loss of confidence about projected growth in the economy. Whatever the cause, it will discourage stock ownership and increase the desired quantity of money balances.

FIGURE 7–3

The Effect of Stock Yields on the Asset Demand for Money

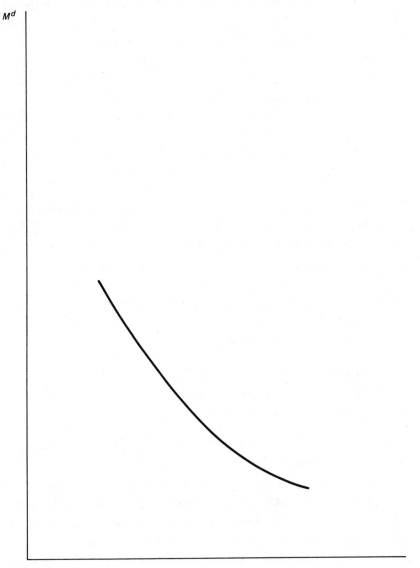

Average Yield on Corporate Stocks

7.3.4   Some General Principles

We now can summarize the past few sections in terms of familiar economic principles. Asset-holders have a number of goods available, each of which is substitutable with the others to some degree. Whenever the price of one good rises relative to the others, the quantity demanded of that good is expected to fall. Whenever the price of a substitute good rises, the demand for the first good will normally rise. The only new wrinkle introduced in this chapter is that the crucial variable for the asset-holder is not the current level of asset prices but the changes which he expects to occur between now and the time he disposes of his holdings. He is not so concerned with whether he has to pay $9,800 or $9,900 for a bond as he is with whether he is likely to be able to sell that bond later at a $100 gain or a $100 loss. So if an asset-holder is choosing among money, bonds, corporate stocks, and durable consumer goods, we expect his demand for money to rise whenever he comes to expect a fall in the prices of any one or all of the three substitute goods. From what we have seen in this chapter, the demand for money will rise when

1. Interest rates on bonds fall.
2. Yields on corporate stocks fall.
3. The rate of inflation falls.

A rise in any one of those variables will cause the demand for money to fall.

Another very important determinant of the asset demand for money is the total value of assets held. It should be clear that no one can hold money as an asset if he has no assets at all, and that the more assets he has, the more money he can hold along with other goods. This rule serves the familiar function of the "budget constraint" in ordinary demand analysis. The asset-holder may be thought of as first sitting down to determine the total value of his assets: what is he worth? Then he makes decisions as to how to allocate wealth among numerous alternatives.[4] The greater his wealth, the more of everything he will hold. But the exact allocation will be determined primarily by relative expected prices, as we have described above.

A final—and perhaps the most important—determinant of the demand for money is what economists usually call "tastes and preferences." In this context, we are talking about the preference of asset-holders for liquidity in their portfolios. Everything else constant, a shift in preferences toward a greater desire for liquidity will increase the demand for money. What would cause such a shift? One factor might be uncertainty about the economy. An example of that kind occurred during the summer of 1970, when the Penn Central Transportation Company declared bankruptcy. Because the Penn Central railroad had been a highly rated borrower of funds from banks and other institutional lenders (more than $70 million just in short-term loans were about to come due when the company went under), its insolvency set off a wave of doubt about the value of other corporate bonds and related securities. Institutions which normally would have been providing funds to corporate borrowers suddenly were reluctant to do so and preferred to hold idle cash until the effects of the Penn Central failure became clear. The result was a temporary but sharp increase in the demand for money. Under more normal circumstances, the aggregate preference for liquidity should be quite stable over time, shifting very gradually if at all. This factor, then, is best regarded as a determinant of the general *level* of the demand for money, rather than as a major determinant of short-run changes in the quantity demanded.

---

[4] By *wealth*, we mean here the value of the gross assets of the individual, other than the earning power of his own labor. But there are many other ways of measuring wealth, any one of which will work reasonably well in explaining the demand for money. For a detailed discussion, see David E. W. Laidler, *The Demand for Money* (Scranton, Pa.: International Textbook Company, 1969).

REVIEW QUESTIONS

1. Why would a rational person hold noninterest-bearing assets (currency and demand deposits) in preference to interest-bearing assets (time deposits, savings and loan accounts, Series E savings bonds)?

2. Why do changes in interest rates affect the demand for a non-interest-bearing asset such as demand deposits?

3. What effects does expected inflation have on the demand for money?

4. Explain how wealth as well as income can affect the demand for money.

5. What effect does the *distribution* of income have on the demand for money?

SUGGESTED FURTHER READING

Duesenberry, James S. "The Portfolio Approach to the Demand for Money and Other Assets," *Review of Economics and Statistics.* Vol. 45, February 1963.

Laidler, David E. W. *The Demand for Money.* Scranton, Pa.: International Textbook, 1969; chaps. 5 and 6.

part three

Money and the Economy

chapter 8
Money and Aggregate Demand: Introduction

8.1 INTRODUCTION

Throughout the first two parts of this book, we have discussed the market for money balances: the determinants of supply and demand in this very important part of the economy. But we have had to postpone until now a detailed answer to the question of why it is so important, of why the concept of money warrants such an extensive review. For the answer lies well beyond the narrow confines of the markets for money balances. Monetary activity—the daily business life that causes the quantity of money, the level of interest rates, the liquidity of assets to change from time to time—in fact has a very real and substantial impact on the rest of the economy. When we read that price inflation is getting worse or better or that the number of unemployed workers went up or down last month, we can be fairly confident that monetary factors were one of the numerous causes of inflation and unemployment, which in turn will inevitably and directly affect our own lives. In this chapter, we first review the concepts of net national product (NNP) and national income in order to provide a simple framework for analyzing some rather complex issues. Then we get back to the monetary side of the economy so that we can answer some of the questions we have raised.

8.2   THE NATIONAL INCOME

One concept which has appeared frequently throughout our analysis of the demand for money is the *income* of those who hold money balances. When we described the individual's behavior, we noted the effect of changes in his or her income on the amount of money he or she desires to hold. When we discussed business decisions, we described the effects of changes in corporate earnings on the amounts of money companies would want to hold. And when we came to the demand for money in the aggregate—the total demand for money in the economy—we introduced but said very little about the concept of national income, the sum of all the incomes of individuals and businesses in the country. We now have to delve a little more deeply into the mysteries of that concept, and we shall soon make an interesting discovery. Not only does the total income of an economy play a major part in determining the quantity of money demanded; it is equally true that the availability and cost of money in the economy play an important role in affecting the nation's income.

If the national income were always constant or always increased at a steady rate, there would be little reason for us to study or worry about it. In practice, it tends to rise very rapidly for periods of one to several years and then to slow down or actually decrease, sometimes dramatically. These erratic movements disrupt the plans and the hopes of millions of people through their effects on prices of goods and on employment opportunities, as well as on individual incomes. Particularly disruptive are the decreases or *recessions*, a recent example of which occurred in the United States in 1970.[1] That was a year characterized by rising unemployment (2

---

[1] The generally accepted definition of a recession is a period of two or more successive calendar quarters (i.e., of six months or more) when the real value of a country's gross national product declines from the previous quarter. Less precisely, recessions which are unusually severe or persistent become known as depressions. Our last depression occurred in 1937–38.

million more people out seeking jobs by the end of the year), increasing poverty (1.5 million more people so classified), and falling output (real net national product off nearly $4 billion from the previous year.) It was not a time of disaster for most Americans, but it was a year of increased hardship. We would like now to take a closer look at that year in order to show how we can summarize the main characteristics of something so complex as the national economy.

A common way to measure the income of a country (though by no means the most obvious) is by the types of output that people produce in the process of earning that income. By the very nature of economic transactions, just as there must be a purchase for there to be a sale so there must be a dollar of output (of goods *or* services) for there to be a dollar of income earned.[2] For example, most output in the United States is produced for individual consumption: cars, washing machines, and tape recorders (called "consumer durable goods" in general); pizzas, blue jeans, and textbooks (called "nondurable goods," even though your blue jeans are likely to last longer than your tape recorder); medical care, concerts, and apartment rentals (called "services"). When we add up all the amounts that people have spent on these items during some period of time, then we also know how much income was earned by the people making and selling them. In 1970, total consumer expenditures and total income from the sale of consumer goods and services came to $618 billion.

The second major category of income in our economy results from the production of goods and the supplying of services by governments. When the federal government, for example, places an order with an aircraft company for military

---

[2] This relationship often is summarized by reference to the circular flow of income from buyers to sellers to producers to wage-earners and back to buyers. If the reader finds it necessary to refresh himself on this principle, he may wish to consult an introductory text such as Lloyd Reynolds, *Economics* (Homewood, Ill.: Richard D. Irwin, Inc., 1973).

transport planes, when the Justice Department hires lawyers to prosecute cases, when the State of California hires a construction firm to build or repair a highway, or when the city of Chicago builds a new hospital, every dollar that is spent becomes income to the persons or companies who receive it. The total of these and other government expenditures in 1970 was $220 billion.

A third category consists of increases in the stock of assets used by business firms to produce goods or services. Increases occur, for example, when General Motors builds an automobile factory, Southern Bell installs new switchboards, or Gene's Grocery adds a frozen-foods counter. Decreases occur simply when these goods wear out, or "depreciate." The difference represents an increase in the country's capacity to produce new goods and services and is therefore to be treated as part of the current output of the economy. This category is known as "net fixed investment expenditure" or simply as "fixed investment,"[3] and expenditures here amounted to $44 billion in 1970.

Total business investment includes, in addition to net fixed investment, any increases in stocks of inventories held by firms. It is important at this stage to notice the distinctions among these various categories of output.

If General Motors builds a new factory, we treat the expenditure as fixed investment. If the company builds an automobile in the factory and sells it in the same year, we treat the sale as consumer expenditure. If it fails to sell the car, then we still include the car as output for the economy by treating it as an increase in the company's stock of inven-

---

[3] In order to avoid needless confusion later on, the reader should take careful note of the difference between this usage of the word *investment* and the more colloquial usage, which includes purchases of corporate stock, bonds, and other financial assets. Throughout this discussion, investment *excludes* all such purely financial transactions which merely transfer the ownership of existing assets without leading directly to current production. On the other hand, investment does include one type of consumer durable good, the construction of residential housing.

tories, or as "inventory investment." The point is that output has been produced and incomes have been paid to the producers of the goods, even though no final sale has been made.[4] Since in any given year, some sales are made from previously produced output (i.e., are sold from inventories) while some current output remains unsold, we simply count the net change in stocks of inventories in addition to total sales. The change in all business inventories in 1970 was an increase of $4 billion; if in any year the stock of inventories actually decreased, we would have to subtract that decline in deriving the total income of the economy.

One final item remains to be included: the net value of exports to other countries. To get this net figure, we first *add* any goods or services produced here but not included in the categories described above because they have been sold abroad or to residents of foreign countries. Examples of these exports include expenditures by foreign tourists in the United States as well as sales of American goods overseas. But if we include these sales as part of our own output, we have to be careful to *subtract* the value of our own expenditures on foreign goods. These imports include, among other things, purchases of goods produced in foreign countries and expenditures abroad by American tourists. In most years in the United States, exports and imports will roughly cancel each other; the net figure (exports minus imports) in 1970 was only $4 billion, and even that figure was unusually large.[5]

When we add up all five types of output described in this section, we obtain a sum known as the *net national product* of the economy over some period of time. By examining both

---

[4] Essentially, there are two kinds of income created here. One consists of the wages paid to the workers who help to build the car. The second is the income to the company and its stockholders. Eventually, this income will take the form of profit when the car is sold; in the meantime, the company, perhaps not always by choice, takes its income in the form of the unsold automobile.

[5] See Chapter 11 for a more complete description of international trade and its relationship to the rest of the economy.

the sum and its parts, we can begin to see what went wrong with the economy in 1970.

8.2.1   The Recession of 1970

The most striking characteristic of Table 8–1 is the strong rise in the real value of consumer spending in 1970.[6] The fact is that in spite of the recession, most people were able to go right ahead with spending plans; if necessary, they cut back on saving plans or even borrowed the funds. But this sterling display of resistance to adversity was more than offset by cut-

TABLE 8–1

Changes in Output in the United States, 1969–70 (in billions of 1970 dollars)

	1969	1970	Change
Consumer expenditure......................	$608	$618	+$10
Government expenditure....................	231	220	− 11
Fixed investment..........................	49	44	− 5
Inventory investment......................	7	4	− 3
Net exports...............................	0	4	+ 4
Total Output (net national product).......	$895	$890	−$ 5

backs elsewhere in the economy. The biggest drop was in government spending, very largely because of the winding down of U.S. direct involvement in the Vietnam War and consequent reductions in the real value of total military expenditures. Fixed investment, both business and residential, fell also, as did the rate of accumulation of inventories. The value of U.S. exports rose by more than imports, so the economy got a slight lift from increased net exports. So overall,

---

[6] By "real" value we mean the value adjusted for price changes: the data are "constant dollar" figures. For example, actual ("current dollar") consumer spending in 1969 was $579 billion. But if all those goods had been sold at 1970 prices, they would have brought in $608 billion, the figure shown in the table. Changes over time in constant dollar (e.g., 1970 dollar) figures measure actual changes in volume or quantity but not in prices.

the reduction in net output for the economy was concentrated mainly in the areas of business and military spending.

A very sensible question to raise at this point would be, "Why should we worry about these little recessions when they seem to affect only the life of concrete and steel, rather than the amounts that real people are able and willing to spend?" And there are two answers to that inquiry. First, we worry because *any* drop in real output, any drop in the value of production of goods and services, implies that some people are making less income and may even be getting laid off from their jobs and unable to find new ones. In fact, a rise in the level of unemployment is both the most inevitable and the most disturbing consequence of a national economic recession. The drop in net output in 1970 was less than 1 percent of the 1969 level, but the number of people unemployed increased by more than 40 percent (from 2.8 to 4.1 million)! Those 1,300,000 people had to bear a much greater share of the burden of the recession than the rest of us. A major part of our revulsion against recessions comes out of a sense of the unfairness and the social danger of that disproportionate weight.

A second reason for concern is that recessions will not disappear unless we take positive measures to cure them. To a certain extent, the economy does contain automatic stabilizers, the most important of which is the dependence of tax revenues on income. To illustrate this principle, suppose that we examine more closely the course of the 1970 recession. The first event of note was the slowdown in government spending that accompanied the change in the course of the Vietnam War and the coming to power of a fiscally conservative national administration. The government began to spend less, and to a certain extent it also taxed less by cutting some tax rates.

But the most striking consequence of the reduction in government spending was that it actually generated such a sizeable drop in tax revenues that the government found itself faced with a large deficit in its own budget. When the government (or anyone else) purchases goods or services, the money it pays out becomes income to workers and to businesses who then must pay taxes on that income. When spending drops off, so do those incomes and those tax payments. Overall, in 1970, we saw a drop of $11 billion in government spending, but a fall of $29 billion in tax revenues. To a degree, this very sharp drop in tax revenues has a favorable effect on the economy: it is one of the main reasons that consumer spending can remain high in the initial stages of a recession. But it is not enough; income is still down, output is still down, and unemployment is up. And gradually but inevitably, this decline is bound to get worse.

Remember the "circular flow" of income. Total spending in the economy is down, and therefore some businesses and individuals have declining incomes. Their spending eventually will have to fall as well. And every dollar not spent by them becomes income not received by someone else. Businesses with falling revenues are forced to lay off more workers, so unemployment rises again. At this point, a psychological effect sets in as workers begin to fear the possibility of losing their own jobs. People become less willing to spend their current incomes when they have increasing doubts about whether their prosperity will continue. And as they spend less, incomes decline still more. Thus the initial drop in output becomes multiplied into a much larger problem. It begins as an annoyance, a minor rash, but it soon spreads through the economy like a cancer.

8.2.2 Uses of Output

To see more clearly how an initial drop in spending can lead to a more general decline in incomes, look at the next table (Table 8–2). The right-hand column is the same set of

TABLE 8–2

Income and Output in the United States, 1970 (in billions of 1970 dollars)

Uses of income:			Uses of output:		
Consumer spending......		$618	Consumer spending.....		$618
Saving.................		61	Investment (net)........		52
By individuals........	$ 54		In buildings and		
By businesses..........	7		equipment.........	$44	
Tax payments (net)......		211	In inventories	4	
By individuals.........	85		In net exports	4	
By businesses.........	126		Government spending...		220
Total Income (NNP).		$890	Total Output (NNP).		$890

numbers shown for 1970 in the first table, except that we have grouped three of the categories of spending together under the general heading of investment. Recall once more that by this term we mean economic rather than financial investment. Thus the first type—investment in buildings (both factories and homes) and productive machinery and other equipment—represents net increases in the stock of real fixed assets used by businesses, plus increases in the stock of residential homes. The second item—inventory investment—measures the increase in business holdings of goods in the process of being produced for sale or else produced but not yet sold. And the third type of investment results from the country's net exports of goods and services to other countries. To the extent that we sell more abroad than we pay out currently for imports, we accumulate currencies and other assets that we can use to buy foreign-made goods in the future. Hence we may regard net exports as a form of investment. As before, we can add total investment to the other uses of current output to get the total value of goods and services produced in the United States during 1970. It is worth noting at this point that the bulk of U.S. output each year, about 70 percent, is produced for and sold to individual consumers. The government (including state and local units) absorbs about a fourth, and we invest only 5 or 6 percent for the future.

How do we know that the output that we produced in 1970 was worth $890 billion, and not $600 or $1,000 billion? Quite simply, we value it by the amounts that people pay for it. If you buy a pair of blue jeans for $10, then that is what they are worth. If a corporation spends $10 million in the construction of a new factory, that is the building's worth, at least for the present. If the Oregon State government pays a filing clerk in the auditing department $10,000 a year, then we presume that the clerk does $10,000 worth of work for (i.e., provides a $10,000 service to) the government.

8.2.3 Spending by Consumers

The spending of $890 billion on output in 1970 created $890 billion of income to the people or the companies that supplied those goods and services, income in the form of wages, salaries, rent and interest income, dividends on corporate stock ownership, and undistributed corporate profits. And what the left-hand half of Table 8–2 shows us is the broad pattern of the ways in which people and business firms disposed of all that income. We already know, by looking at the other column, that we spent most of our income in our capacity as individual consumers. But the rest of our income must be disposed of as well, in one of two general ways. First, we must pay out part of it in the form of taxes. And then whatever is left constitutes saving. It is very important to note here that saving is not necessarily a deliberative act, such as placing funds in a savings account in a bank. Saving is simply the nonact of not spending part of one's current income. The amount of saving during any year is the residual left over from income after we have paid our taxes and bought our various kinds of goods and services.

One of the remarkable facts about the U.S. economy is that the ratio of consumer spending to total saving has been highly stable, year in and year out, for as long as we have been able to measure it. We always spend about ten times as much as we save. Another way of viewing that phenomenon is that once we know how much output is being produced in the economy in a given year, all we need to know is the rate at which the government taxes that income in order to know how much of it will be consumed and how much of it will be saved. For example, suppose we try some rough calculations. Assume that total income (total output) is $890 billion, that 24 percent of that income must be paid out in taxes, and that 91 percent of the rest will be spent on consumer goods and services. If you work that out, you will find that your answers will be very close to the actual figures for 1970. If you then were to start with the value of output in 1974 or 1964, you again would not be far off. Our highly complex economy is not really so complicated as it seems at first.

Since the amount of consumer spending depends largely on the amount of our income left over after taxes are paid, the total amount of income and output in the economy will depend partly on the tax rates imposed by the government, but also on the amounts that the government decides itself to spend on goods and services, and finally, on the amounts that businesses want to spend on investment projects. But what determines the desired amounts of spending by governments and businesses? It is that question, or rather those questions, which we must be able to answer if we wish to know basically how total national income gets determined.

8.2.4 Spending by Governments

The spending decisions of governments, although they may be overall the most important single determinant of national income, we can dispose of fairly quickly here. For the fact is that the federal government can, within limits, spend whatever it chooses in order to achieve its various policies. Though many state and local governments will be constrained by their ability to raise revenues through their tax-ing powers, no such 'effective constraint applies to the federal government in Washington. Hence for practical discussion, we can treat the total amount of government spending as an amount which is determined in large measure by noneco-nomic, primarily political forces. In economic parlance, we say that the amount of government spending is an *exogenous* variable, in the same sense that the Federal Reserve System's holdings of securities acquired through open market opera-tions are an exogenous variable: they help to determine the level of economic activity, but they are not systematically af-fected by it.

8.2.5   Spending on Investment Projects

The investment decisions of businessmen are partly, but only partly, exogenous. When a corporation, for example, undertakes to build a new factory, it must necessarily base its decision largely on its expectations and projections about the course that demands for the products to be produced in this new factory will take over a period of several years. Those ex-pectations may not be influenced very much by changes in income over relatively short periods such as a year or two. Therefore, unlike consumer spending, business investment is not likely to depend very strongly or reliably on the level of income.

Aside from expectations about sales, one important factor which will influence desired investment spending is the level of interest rates in the economy. When a company makes an investment expenditure, it is tying up its assets in that project perhaps for a period of many years. A common way of financ-ing such projects is to sell bonds or other securities to other companies and to wealthy individuals, and then gradually to repay those debts out of the profits the company expects to earn on its investment project. The cost of that form of financing is simply the interest rate which the firm has to pay on its bonds. When interest rates rise, so does the overall cost of the project.

But even if a company has cash on hand to pay all of its costs, it must still view the level of interest rates as a form of "opportunity cost." The corporate treasurer will point out that the company could earn, say, 8 percent on its funds just by buying another company's bonds; if you don't expect to do quite a bit better than that by building your factory, then you should think again about the whole business. No matter how the company plans to finance its investments, a rise in the general level of interest rates will tend to discourage any marginally profitable projects. As a corollary result, the total level of desired investment spending in the economy will tend to be inversely affected by changes in interest rates.

8.3 EQUILIBRIUM IN THE MARKET FOR GOODS AND SERVICES

We now are ready to see what holds the whole system together: what keeps the economy in "equilibrium." Look again at Table 8–2, and this time notice the various interrelationships. We already have noted how income and output must always be the same; they are just two ways of measuring the same flow of money and goods. We also have observed that the value of consumer purchases of goods and services appears on both sides, as the primary use of both income and output. Now the implication of those two facts is that *by definition* the total value of saving and tax payments must be identical to the value of investment plus government spending. But why? There is no law that says that the government must spend exactly what it takes in from taxes, and at first glance the relationship between the amounts that individuals and businesses save and the amounts that they spend on investment projects must appear to be rather tenuous. But what we actually have here is a form of double-entry bookkeeping in which *actual investment* serves as the primary residual or balancing item. As the following example will show, investment has to adjust in order to keep the system intact.

The recession of 1970 was not universally anticipated. The United States was at the end of the longest continuous expansion in its history, and a common view was that our growth would continue at least for some years. Companies, therefore, were generally not prepared for the slowdown. They anticipated a higher level of consumer spending and a higher level of sales, and they formulated investment *plans* accordingly. But then the government cut back on its spending plans. Both government payrolls and government purchases from private business fell, and total income in the economy also fell, by the same amount. If the whole decrease had been matched by tax cuts or reductions in desired saving, the process could have stopped right there. We might have had, say, a $10 billion reduction in government spending on the output side of the table, and a matching $10 billion drop in tax revenues and saving flows on the income side. But in practice, any initial drop in income generates reductions in planned consumer spending, as families are forced to adjust to lower standards of living. Thus spending turns out to be even lower than the reduced level of output.

8.3.1 The Multiplier Process

The basic elements of this process are set out in Table 8–3. The top panel describes a set of hypothetical initial spending plans in which total government spending is at $230 billion ($10 billion higher than actually observed in 1970). On the income side of these accounts, we assume that consumers are just satisfied with the level of saving which they are able to achieve when they spend $630 billion on goods and services. We also assume that total saving (saving by individuals and

TABLE 8–3

The Progressive Worsening of a Recession (in billions of 1970 dollars)

A. Hypothetical initial plans:

Consumption (C)......	630		Consumption (C).....	630
Saving (S)............	70		Investment (I).......	50
Tax payments (T).....	210		Government spending (G).......	230
Income (Y)..........	910		Output (Y).........	910

B. Effects of a reduced level of spending:

Phase I: Cutback in G				Phase II: Reaction by Consumers			
C............	630	C...	630	C....	623	C............	623
S............	62	I....	50	S....	69	I.............	57
Desired:......	69					Desired:........	50
Unplanned:...	−7					Unplanned:.....	7
T............	208	G...	220	T....	208	G.............	220
Y...........	900	Y...	900	Y....	900	Y.............	900

Phase III: Reaction by Business				Phase n: New Equilibrium			
C............	623	C...	623	C.............	610	C...	610
S............	64	I....	50	S.............	67	I....	50
Desired:......	68			T.............	203	G...	220
Unplanned:...	−4			Y.............	880	Y...	880
T............	206	G...	220				
Y...........	893	Y...	893				

businesses) is $70 billion and that governments are able to collect only some $210 billion at the level of income shown. Given these assumptions, the situation shown is an "equilibrium" position which can be maintained so long as it is not exogenously or randomly disturbed; for example, by a change in the level of spending by governments. In this hypothetical world, we would be producing $910 billion of output, and total desired spending (purchases of output) would also be $910 billion.

The lower half of Table 8–3 shows the initial development of a recessionary situation from the hypothetical equilibrium and then shows, in the final panel, the new lower equilibrium position. The first phase of the recession results purely from the reduced level of government spending: income falls by $10 billion. Because tax revenues depend largely on income, they fall also, but by less than the drop in spending. The rest of the decrease in income might be made up initially by an undesired and unplanned reduction in saving. That is, for a short time households might go right ahead with their original plans for consumption and would then have to make up the difference by saving less or, if necessary, by borrowing. But eventually these households will attempt to restore, if not the full amount of their planned saving, at least a comparable portion of their income. At that point total consumer spending falls (Phase II). And here is where the balancing item comes in: when consumption falls without a corresponding drop in output, there automatically occurs an unplanned increase in investment as *inventories* begin to accumulate in stores and warehouses. Businesses had planned on a certain level of consumer spending. Consumers actually spent $7 billion less, and that much undesired investment in stocks of inventories was the inevitable result. Once again the total levels of income and output are identical.

The undesired inventory investment then sets off another chain reaction. Businesses cut back on their orders of goods for sale. Producers cut back on production rates. Profits fall and workers are laid off. We have another drop in national income (Phase III). Again, families see their saving plans disappear along with their heftier paychecks. As their consumption falls accordingly, still more reductions will follow. Eventually, the economy will settle into a lower state of activity with all the characteristics of recession and stagnation.

To illustrate this analysis a little further, we draw your attention to the simple graph shown in Figure 8–1. The upward-sloping line labeled $S + T$ shows how saving plans and tax payments both respond positively to changes in income. But while it is necessary for *actual* investment and government spending levels to correspond to the sum of saving and investment, there is no reason for the *planned* values of these sums to be equal. Thus the second line shows the

FIGURE 8–1

Equilibrium in the Markets for Goods and Services

Planned Uses of Income and Output

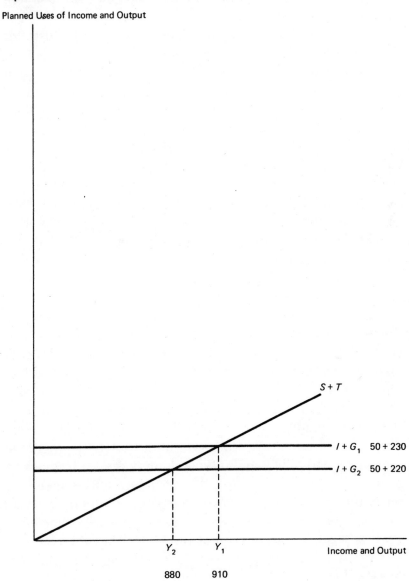

planned level of $I + G$. Since neither category of spending responds systematically to income, we have drawn their sum as a horizontal line.

The central point about this diagram is that it illustrates that there is only one level of income at which planned $S + T$ will equal planned $I + G$. At any other level, we will observe undesired accumulation or decumulation of inventories, and that unplanned investment will trigger reactions by businesses and individuals which will drive the economy toward the equilibrium level. To continue our example, we can see that the equilibrium level of output is $880 billion if the sum of planned investment and government spending is $270 billion. If the economy starts out producing not $880 billion but $910 billion worth of output, then a lot of that output will go unsold because people cannot afford it. Incomes will fall, production of goods will fall, and gradually, perhaps over a period of several years, output will settle toward the lower figure.

The diagram in Figure 8–1 is a static and timeless representation of the dynamic process described in Table 8–3. It shows only the beginning and ending points but not the path taken to get from one to the other. Throughout the rest of our discussion, we shall be using this type of "comparative static" diagram, but we must emphasize the importance of keeping in mind the time lags involved. Though a $10 billion drop in government spending will immediately depress total income by $10 billion and ultimately may reduce incomes by as much as $30 billion or so, the secondary effects take long enough to complete that they may never be fully realized. In practice, our economy is always "tending toward" some equilibrium position, rather than at rest in it. Thus the recession in 1970, which could have been the beginning of a more serious decline in incomes, was actually terminated by the end of that year, primarily by a reversal of the contractionary government policies.

One final note: both Table 8–3 and Figure 8–1 illustrate the fact that a change of $10 billion in the level of government spending can generate a much larger change in total income in the economy; in this case, $30 billion. The ratio of these two changes, 3.0 in our example, is familiarly referred to in economic literature as the *spending multiplier.* This multiplier effect, which comes into play because consumers choose to reduce their own spending in response to the first drop in income, is one of the keystones of macroeconomic theory.

8.3.2 The Role of Interest Rates

We would be quite remiss if we were to leave the reader with too strong an impression of the effect of changes in government spending on the level of income. A simple model such as we have used so far in this chapter implies that the government can easily make total income respond in whatever way it chooses, and that, unfortunately, is not quite the case. Perhaps the most important exception arises because of the nature of business and household investment plans. It is true that those plans are not affected very much or at all systematically by short-term movements in incomes. But they are not entirely exogenous, and they are not always even predictable. Nonetheless, we must and can have a stab at predicting how desired investment will respond to economic variables. And the exercise will later prove extremely valuable, for we shall soon discover that it is in large measure through the effects of interest rates on spending plans that monetary policy plays its role in determining the national income.

The main implication of the fact that investment spending depends on interest rates (as explained above in section 8.2.5) is that there is not one unique level of equilibrium income which corresponds to a given value for government spending; there is a whole schedule of equilibria, one for each rate of interest. Figure 8–2 now expands our earlier diagram to account for this new relationship. Here we see that a *rise* in interest rates has exactly the same type of impact on income as a *fall* in government spending. It produces a decline in income by first causing businesses and home-owners to revise their plans downward. And then a multiplier effect sets in as consumers react to their falling incomes.

There are, at any moment, many interest rates being used for a variety of purposes in our economy. There are rates on corporate bonds, on government bonds, on bank loans, on loans from finance companies, on bank credit cards, and on and on. But over time, most of these rates tend to move at least in the same direction, though they all have different precise values reflecting, among other factors, the risk involved in each transaction. So in order to keep matters reasonably simple, we shall adopt the convention of dealing with "the" interest rate as if it were a homogeneous phenomenon. And unless we specify otherwise, we shall be referring to the average rate on high-grade corporate bonds, both because it is probably the most representative interest rate in the economy and because it is the most important interest rate in the determination of business investment spending.[7]

The interest rate on corporate bonds in the United States in 1970 was at a historically high level, and over the course of the year it averaged about 8 percent. Figure 8–2 thus shows that rate as corresponding to the equilibrium level of income for that year which we calculated above to be on the order of $880 billion. But what if interest rates had been lower? If the bond rate had been, say, 6 percent, it would have been that much cheaper for businesses to acquire the necessary funds for their planned investment projects. The $I + G$ line in the diagram is therefore shown to move upward in response to the drop in interest rates. (Be careful to

---

[7] See Chapter 16, section 16.4.

FIGURE 8–2

Interest Rates and Equilibrium Income

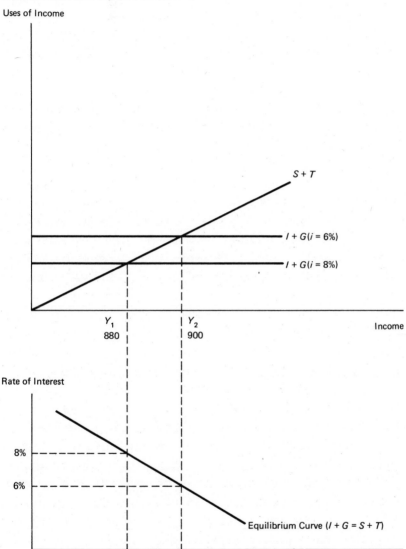

note that the level of government spending is the *same* for the two lines.) Unfortunately, the evidence we have available is not completely clear as to how much of an increase in equilibrium income could have been generated by a 2 percent drop in interest rates that year. The $20 billion shown in our diagram would be toward the middle of estimates which other economists might make. Again, we caution the reader to remember that multiplier effects take time to operate; few would suggest that the whole $20 billion effect could be produced within one year.

The lower half of Figure 8–2 extends the two points calculated above in order to produce an "equilibrium curve." The vertical axis now plots all the possible values for the interest rate on corporate bonds. The horizontal axis still plots levels of income. And at every point on the curve, the economy is in equilibrium in the sense that investment spending is at its desired or planned level; added to the value of government spending, it is just equal to the actual sum of saving and tax payments. We shall call this curve the *EE* curve, as a shorthand expression for what it represents: equilibrium between desired expenditures on goods and services and the current value of output (or expenditure equilibrium).[8]

This new wrinkle in our model forces us to modify somewhat the conclusions drawn about the role of government spending in determining income. Instead of simply changing the equilibrium level of income, a change in *G* will actually shift the whole *IS* equilibrium schedule up or down. The next diagram, Figure 8–3, shows this shift for the two values of *G* examined above ($220 and $230 billion). If a change in government spending were to leave interest rates unaffected, we would not have to alter our conclusions or even the size of the spending multiplier at all. But life is not that simple. The government is a major participant in the bond market.

---

[8] This curve is also commonly known to economists as the *IS curve* as a shorthand expression for its underlying equality: $I + G = S + T$.

FIGURE 8–3

Government Spending and the *IS* Curve

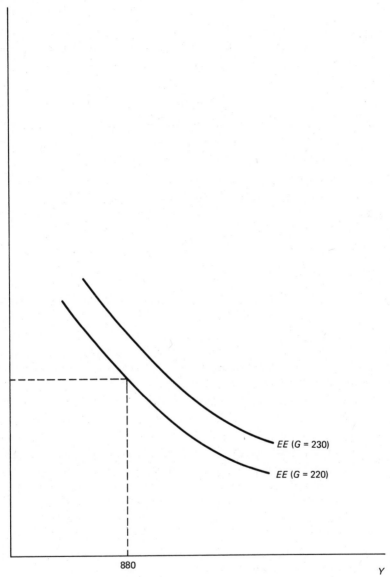

If the government decides to spend an additional $10 billion without increasing tax rates correspondingly, it will have to borrow a major part of that $10 billion by issuing new bonds. And under most circumstances, it will drive up interest rates in the process as it bids funds away from corporations and individuals who are trying to borrow at the same time. As interest rates rise, businesses may be discouraged from undertaking new investment projects. This "crowding-out" effect will reduce the expansionary impact, will reduce the multiplier, for the rise in government spending. As an extreme case, it might nullify the expansion altogether. So before we jump to too many conclusions, we shall take a closer look at the process by which interest rates are determined.

REVIEW QUESTIONS

1. What is the relationship between aggregate income and aggregate output in the economy? Is it meaningful to think of them as having different values?

2. How does a change in the personal income tax rates affect the level of consumer spending? How does a change in the corporate tax rates affect consumer spending? Why?

3. Why is a purchase of common corporate stock by an individual or business not considered "investment" in the sense in which that term is used here?

4. If the economy initially were in equilibrium and business firms collectively increased their planned investment projects, what effects would there be on (a) consumer spending, (b) net national product, and (c) government spending? What major factors have you assumed not to change in answering this question?

SUGGESTED FURTHER READING

Bailey, Martin J. *National Income and the Price Level,* 2d ed. New York: McGraw-Hill, 1971.

Council of Economic Advisers. *Economic Report of the President.* Executive Office of the President. Washington, D.C., Annual.

Dernburg, Thomas F. and Duncan M. McDougall. *Macroeconomics,* 4th ed. New York: McGraw-Hill, 1972.

Reynolds, Lloyd. *Economics: A General Introduction,* 4th ed. Homewood, Ill.: Richard D. Irwin, Inc., 1973.

APPENDIX: A MODEL OF EXPENDITURE EQUILIBRIUM

This chapter has introduced a number of basic macroeconomic relationships describing the behavior of consumers, businesses, and governments in their roles as "demanders" or purchasers of goods and services. These relationships may be combined in various ways, one very useful summary being the *EE* curve presented in the text. An alternative technique for deriving this curve is the algebraic form of expression which we used in Chapter 4 to explain the money supply process.

The relationships described in this chapter comprise five equations, the first two of which are simply definitions:

1. Total net national product in constant dollars (Y) may be divided into three components: consumer purchases (C), investment in plant and equipment, inventories, and net exports (I); and government expenditure (G).

$$Y = C + I + G \tag{1}$$

2. "Disposable" income is the difference between net national product and total tax payments (T).

$$Y_D = Y - T \tag{2}$$

3. Consumer purchases are linearly related to disposable income.

$$C = C_o + c \cdot Y_D \tag{3}$$

where c is the marginal propensity to consume and is a parameter between zero and one, and C_o (the exogenous component of C) is a positive number of dollars.

4. Investment expenditure is inversely related to the level of interest rates (i).

$$I = I_o - v \cdot i \tag{4}$$

where v is a positive parameter expressing the effect of changes in interest rates on desired investment expenditures, and I_o is a positive number of dollars.[1]

5. Tax revenues are proportional to income.

$$T = r \cdot Y \tag{5}$$

where r is the tax rate (a parameter between zero and one). Government spending is assumed to be exogenous to the model.

These five equations now may be solved algebraically for an expression which shows the determinants of total desired expenditure. There actually are quite a few different ways to derive this solution; the important point to keep in mind is that the solution should show desired expenditure (Y) as a function of the variables which are exogenous to this model $(C_o, I_o, G,$ and $i)$. A useful first step is to note that consumption ultimately is determined by total income:

$$C = C_o + c \cdot Y_D \tag{3}$$

$$Y_D = Y - T \tag{2}$$

and

$$T = r \cdot Y \tag{5}$$

Therefore,

$$Y_D = Y - r \cdot Y$$

and

$$C = C_o + cY - c \cdot r \cdot Y \tag{6}$$

Now to find the equilibrium solution, we replace C and I in equation (1) by the determinants of the desired values in each category of expenditure:

---

[1] This equation relates a dollar magnitude (I) to a pure number (i). To be able to add the two components together, v must be measured in dollars.

$$Y = C + I + G = (C_o + c \cdot Y - c \cdot r \cdot Y) + (I_o - v \cdot i) + G$$

Next we collect together all the coefficients on Y:

$$(1 - c + c \cdot r)Y = C_o + I_o + G - v \cdot i$$

and solve for Y:

$$Y = \frac{C_o + I_o}{1 - c + c \cdot r} + \frac{1}{1 - c + c \cdot r} G - \frac{v}{1 - c + c \cdot r} \cdot i \qquad (7)$$

Equation (7) is the *EE* curve derived in the text. The first two terms determine the intercept of the curve (actually a straight line in this model) with the vertical axis. A change in C_o I_o or G will shift the curve, the size of the shift being given by the coefficient $\dfrac{1}{1 - c + c \cdot r}$. The slope of the curve (the change in income associated with a unit change in the level of interest rates) is given by the last coefficient, $\dfrac{v}{1 - c + c \cdot r}$.

The application of this technique may perhaps be clarified by an example. For the conditions prevailing in 1970, we may approximate the expenditure functions of the U.S. economy by the following equation:

(1) $\quad Y \ = C + I + G$
(2) $\quad Y_D = Y - T$
(3) $\quad C \ = \$20$ billion $+ .87 \, Y_D$
(4) $\quad I \ = \$80$ billion $- (\$3\frac{1}{3}$ billion$) \, i$
(5) $\quad T \ = .23Y$

The reader is urged to solve these specific equations by the same process shown above for the general model. He should obtain a result approximating the following *EE* curve:

$$Y = \$300 \text{ billion} + 3G - (\$10 \text{ billion}) \, i \qquad (8)$$

As a final exercise, one should check the results derived throughout this chapter, verifying them as applications of this equilibrium relation.

chapter 9

Money and Aggregate Demand: Conclusion

9.1 INTRODUCTION

One of the central conclusions of the preceding chapter is that income depends in a very important way on the behavior of interest rates in the economy. Business corporations buying new equipment often borrow funds for long periods of time and have to consider the costs of those borrowings. Both corporations and individuals considering making major purchases of goods may reconsider if rates available on savings accounts, bonds, and other assets rise. And when spending falls, income falls along with it. So it was no accident that the recession year 1970 was also a year of extremely high interest rates. The case for low interest rates is often couched in political tones: high rates are said to favor bankers (the enemy) while low rates favor debtors (the people). But an economic case can and must be made as well, for low interest rates are generally favorable to economic growth and development. Before we make that case, we have to examine further the way interest rates are determined and the way they can be altered by policy actions.

216

9.2 INTEREST RATES AND THE MARKET FOR MONEY BALANCES

The determination of interest rates and income are inextricably related. For an interest rate to be an equilibrium rate, it must be just the right value to make businesses want to spend on investment projects the same amount as is being saved throughout the economy; it must be such as to make the supply of bonds and other securities to the marketplace the same as the amount demanded by asset-holders; and it must be such as to make the demand for money balances just equal to the quantity of money being supplied. Ideally, we would not want to overemphasize any of these markets; each is highly important in affecting the general level of interest rates. But our purpose here is to study the role of money in the economy, and we plan therefore to concentrate on the monetary aspects of the problem. We would get to the same results, no matter which path we chose to tread.

The odd aspect of employing the apparatus of the supply and demand for money to illustrate the search for an equilibrium interest rate is that currency and demand deposits do *not* themselves command any explicit interest return. But what seems a drawback is in fact an advantage. It is partly because currency and demand deposits do not yield interest that we tend to use them fairly quickly for transactions purposes or to convert them into some other form of asset on which we can earn income. And, as we saw in earlier chapters and shall summarize again here, both the supply and demand for money can be affected by changes in interest rates on other assets that are closely substitutable, simply because such changes alter the attractiveness of money *relative to* those assets.

9.2.1 Interest Rates and the Demand for Money

One of the key ideas which we would like to emphasize about the demand for money is that there is no necessarily fixed relationship between the amounts of income we have or spending we do over any period, and the amounts of money we hold. Certainly there is a presumption of a strong causal relationship because we do receive our incomes in the form of money and we do use money in making most expenditures. But we can "economize" on money; we can speed up its use or convert it into other kinds of assets. What is needed is an adequate incentive. And that, of course, is where interest rates enter the picture. Corporate treasurers, for example, may use part of their companies' cash balances to buy short-term securities such as treasury bills, bank certificates of deposit, or a variety of similar financial assets on which they can earn some income. But to do so makes their job more difficult. If they have to make unexpected payments or if the inflow of cash from sales is lower than they had anticipated, they may have to sell the financial assets at a loss or else borrow funds in order to make all their payments on schedule. The higher the rate of return on these assets—the higher the rate of interest—the more willing will they be to assume the risk.

Individuals who are well off financially and who have accumulated some assets also will often respond to interest rates in determining the amounts of money they wish to hold. They react in a way similar to corporate treasurers: they normally hold some money balances as a precaution in anticipation of possible necessary or desired expenditures before the next payday. The more interest these individuals could earn by, for example, acquiring a savings account, the less interested (pun intended) would they be in holding extra demand deposits.

The third reason we have noted for the demand for money responding to interest rates is that large corporations, and particularly those such as mutual funds whose primary business is to acquire and hold a variety of income-generating financial assets, may wish to hold money balances in order to be able quickly to buy other assets as soon as their prices fall. These companies are then *speculating* about price movements and in particular about interest rate movements. If they have a notion of a normal level of interest rates, and if interest rates fall significantly below that level, the companies are likely to hold cash until rates become more attractive. Again a rise in interest rates generates a decrease in the quantity of money demanded.

By far the largest part of the money balances we hold is not affected very sensitively by interest rates. The most important determinant of the total amount of money we desire to hold is income. But many individuals and business firms do have "extra" money balances where interest rates are an important determinant of the aggregate demand for money in our economy. How much of an effect interest rates really have is difficult to measure, partly because income and interest rates tend to change together in an interrelated way, and it is far from easy to separate their influences. But it is not impossible. We estimate, as a rough approximation, that a general rise of interest rates of 1 percentage point (say, from 6 percent to 7 percent) would eventually cause about a $10 billion drop in the demand for money (say, from $240 billion to $230 billion).[1]

This effect is shown in Figure 9–1, in which point A is estimated to correspond to what we observed in the United States in 1970: the public altogether apparently desired to hold about $220 billion of currency and deposits at a time when interest rates were at a level of around 8 percent.[2] Had

---

[1] The interest-elasticity of the demand for money implied by this estimate is −0.25. For a detailed but fairly nontechnical review of such estimates, see Ronald L. Teigen, "The Demand for and Supply of Money," in Warren L. Smith and Ronald L. Teigen, eds., *Readings in Money, National Income, and Stabilization Policy*, rev. ed. (Homewood, Ill.: Richard D. Irwin, Inc., 1970).

[2] What we observe or measure is actually the *stock* of money, not the demand for it. We have to estimate the demand.

FIGURE 9–1

Interest Rates and the Demand for Money

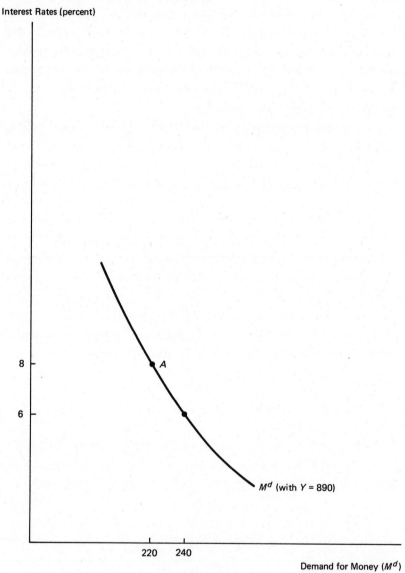

Interest Rates (percent)

interest rates not been at such high levels, the desire to economize on money balances would have been less intense. If our estimate is correct, a 6 percent interest rate—assuming the *same* level of total income for the economy—would have induced individuals and businesses to hold another $20 billion of their assets in the form of money balances.

And what happens when income changes? We know by now that more money will be demanded whenever income rises, because total spending will be that much higher. The curve in Figure 9–1 shows that $220 billion of money would be held, on average, with interest rates at 8 percent and national income at $890 billion. We can also estimate that for every $10 billion more income being paid in any year, another $2 billion of money would be demanded. That is, with interest rates at 8 percent and income at $900 billion, the demand for money would have been about $222 billion. With interest rates at 6 percent and income at $900 billion, the demand for money would have been around $242 billion. So we can draw a whole family or field of money demand curves: one for each level of national income. As shown in Figure 9–2, these curves lie farther to the right as income rises.

9.2.2   Interest Rates and the Supply of Money

The effect of changes in interest rates on the *supply* of money is also important. As we learned in Chapter 4, the most important determinant of the supply of money is the policy adopted by the central bank (in the United States, the Federal Reserve System) with regard to the desired size of the monetary base. If exogenous changes occur in the other factors affecting the size of the *net* monetary base—including excess reserves desired by banks or currency and time deposits desired by the public—the money supply can change, perhaps unpredictably. Changes in reserve requirements also

FIGURE 9–2

Money Demand Curves

Interest Rates (percent)

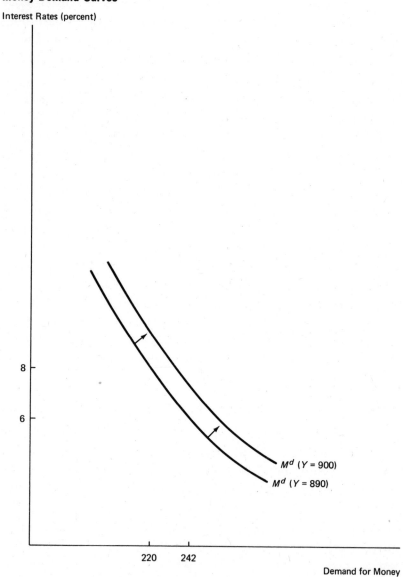

Demand for Money
(billions of dollars)

can alter the amount of money that can be supported by a given value of the net base.[3]

We also have learned that, for a given level of the monetary base, changes in interest rates will alter the supply of money by changing the types of assets desired by banks and, to some extent, by the public. The most important of these effects work through (a) bank demands for excess reserves and (b) public demands for time deposits. A rise in interest rates will encourage banks to be more vigorous in acquiring interest-earning assets and to economize on nominally sterile assets such as excess cash reserves. That shift will tend to increase the supply of money as the banks pay for newly purchased securities or give customers the proceeds of newly made loans. A rise in interest rates paid on securities, savings and loan shares, or other kinds of interest-bearing assets may —since the rates paid on bank time deposits tend to be more stable and to respond sluggishly to changes in other interest rates—induce the public to shift out of bank time deposits. Most of the funds spent on the interest-bearing assets then will be redeposited in bank demand deposits, and the money supply will rise. Thus for a given level of the monetary base, a rise in interest rates will cause an increase in the quantity of money being supplied through the banking system.

In practice, the supply impact of changes in interest rates is usually not very large. Banks do not hold large quantities of excess reserves even when interest rates are very low, so there is not much scope for economizing when rates go up. In recent years, the rates paid on time deposits have become more flexible and responsive, so the volume of asset shifting from time deposits into other assets in response to a rise in interest rates has been reduced. We estimate that a drop in interest rates in 1970 from 8 percent to 6 percent, with no off-

---

[3] See Chapters 14 and 15 for a more detailed description of the various policy instruments available to the Federal Reserve System for bringing about changes in the supply of money.

setting decrease in reserve requirements or increase in the
monetary base, would have caused the supply of money to
fall by about $4 billion.[4] This relationship is illustrated in Fig-
ure 9–3.

The actual size of the monetary base in 1970 was approximately $78 billion: $29 billion in bank reserves and $49 bil-
lion in currency. If the Federal Reserve had desired an increase in the supply of money, it could have initiated purchases of government securities in the open market. Open
market purchases increase bank reserves in the manner described in Chapters 4 and 5. The total monetary base rises; as
the banks convert new reserves into earning assets, demand
deposits and the supply of money increase. By how much?
Again we are in the world of hypothesis, but we can be pretty
sure from past experience that after some passage of time
(perhaps as much as several months)[5] a billion dollars of
open market security purchases would cause the money supply to rise by some $5 billion.

The influence of monetary policy on the supply of money
is represented in Figure 9–4 as a *shift* in the money supply
curve. In general there exists a whole field of supply curves,
one for each value of the monetary base. An increase in the
base shifts the economy to a curve lying farther to the right.

The diagram illustrates (using the 1970 figures as an example) what could happen if the Federal Reserve purchased
$2 billion in securities and drove the monetary base up by
that amount. If there occurred no change in interest rates as
a result of that operation, the money supply would rise by
$10 billion. If interest rates fell to 6 percent, what would hap-
pen? Some of the expansionary impulse would be mitigated
as, for example, banks became less eager to make new loans
at the reduced rates. As illustrated in the diagram, a 6 per-

---

[4] These estimates imply an interest-elasticity of the supply of money of about
0.05.

[5] The reasons for this lag are discussed below in Chapter 17, section 17.3.

FIGURE 9–3

Interest Rates and the Supply of Money

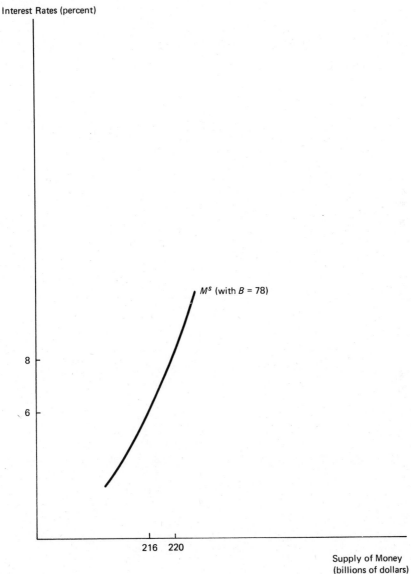

Interest Rates (percent)

FIGURE 9–4

Money Supply Curves

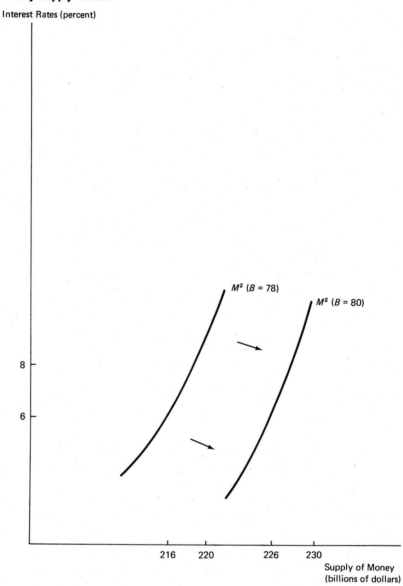

cent interest rate and an $80 billion base would produce a
money supply of $226 billion. So we would get only a $6 billion expansion instead of $10 billion.

9.2.3   Interest Rates and Monetary Equilibrium

This discussion of the effects of interest rates on the supply
of money and especially on the demand for it leads us now to
a central conclusion about money: even though interest is not
paid on money balances, and even though interest rates are
not the most important determinant of either the supply of or
the demand for money, interest rates *are* a key factor in maintaining equilibrium in this market. To understand this point,
examine Figure 9–5, which brings together the information
from the earlier figures in this chapter. The position actually
observed in 1970 is described by point A. There, the money
supply of $220 billion and the interest rate of 8 percent are
assumed to accord nicely with a monetary base amounting to
$78 billion and national income of $890 billion. We can only
infer the precise nature and location of the supply and demand curves, because we can only observe one set of such
values at any given time. But, as the money market tends to
remain close to equilibrium most of the time (i.e., it adjusts
rather quickly when it is knocked out of equilibrium), we
are safe in the assumption that point A is proximate to the intersection of the two curves.

Now we can come back to the hypothetical question of
how the economy might be affected by an open market purchase of $2 billion of securities by the Federal Reserve. To
carry through that operation, the Fed has to induce private
dealers to part with government securities. Normally, the in-
ducement takes the form of slightly higher security prices,
through offers which imply that the yields on securities will
fall somewhat. The security dealers will deposit the proceeds
of the sales in commercial banks. The banks will now have

FIGURE 9–5

Equilibrium in the Money Market

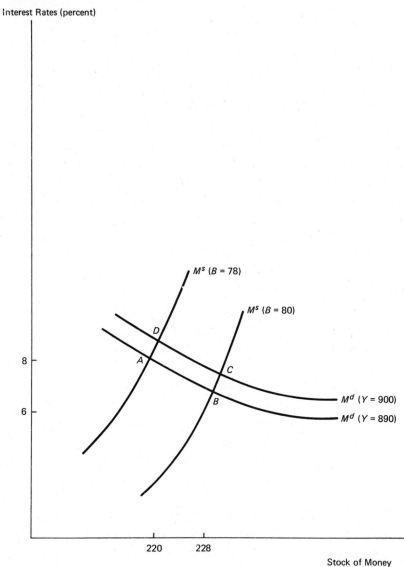

Interest Rates (percent)

M^s $(B = 78)$

M^s $(B = 80)$

M^d $(Y = 900)$

M^d $(Y = 890)$

Stock of Money
(billions of dollars)

excess reserve balances since their required reserve will go up by only a fraction of the rise in deposits and in reserve balances. As explained above, banks now will attempt to reduce their excess reserves by making new loans or by purchasing securities; again interest rates will tend to fall.

This process leads to an increase in the stock of money simply because as new bank loans are made and as the banks purchase securities, the banks' customers are willing to hold additional money balances. For example, by cutting the rates charged for loans, banks can induce customers to finance additional expenditures or purchases of assets. Because the banks are thus able to induce people to use and hold more money, bank deposits rise, required reserves rise, and equilibrium is restored to the banks' reserve positions. But the central point is that the money balances cannot be created until someone becomes willing to hold them, either because interest rates have fallen or because income has risen. In terms of our diagram, there is an initial shift in the money supply curve as a result of the increase in the monetary base through open market operations. The immediate effect of that shift is to generate a movement along the demand curve (from A to B): interest rates fall, and the stock of money which people are willing to hold therefore rises. More gradually, the increased lending produces new spending in the economy, and income rises. Thus the money demand curve shifts upward. The new equilibrium position for the economy is represented by point C.

The supply and demand functions for money cannot *by themselves* indicate exactly where C will fall; that is, exactly *how much* interest rates will fall and how much income will rise when the Federal Reserve disturbs the equilibrium of the market through open market operations or other means (such as by a change in reserve requirements). They do show us how much interest rates will have to fall in the short run, before income has a chance to adjust. But the long-run effect on interest rates will be smaller, perhaps substantially smaller, than the short-run effect. To measure the extent of that offset, we have to combine this information about the money market with what we have already seen (in Chapter 8) about the market for goods and services.

What Figure 9–5 does show unambiguously is the amount that interest rates will have to change in order to sustain a change in national income, given the value of the monetary base and other monetary policy variables. Suppose that income rises for some reason other than a change in monetary policy; for example, because of an increase in government spending. The money demand curve then will shift upward as more money will be desired to handle the higher level of expenditure. With a given money supply curve, what will happen to interest rates? As the diagram shows, they will have to rise (from A to D, or from B to C). The higher interest rates induce banks to increase lending activity (increasing the stock of money) and induce nonbank corporations and individuals to economize on holdings of cash (releasing funds for spending). The higher the level of national income, the higher must be the level of interest rates in order to maintain equilibrium in the market for money balances (so long as we continue to assume that the Fed does not accommodate the increased spending by making more bank reserves available).

This equilibrating relationship between interest rates and income is shown more explicitly in the next diagram, Figure 9–6. The left side of the diagram shows the effect on the money market from an increase in national income; the demand for money increases, and some increase in supply is forthcoming as an effect from increases in interest rates. Thus equilibrium is maintained. Then the right half of the picture summarizes the way interest rates have to move to accommodate a given rise in income, provided that there is no change in the monetary base. Now this relationship is admittedly a

FIGURE 9–6

The Monetary-Equilibrium (*ME*) Relation

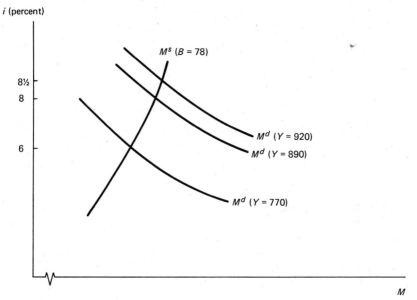

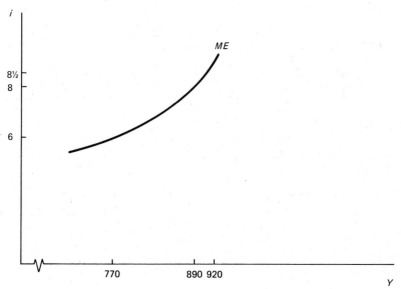

bit abstract, and it might be worth repeating the essential point. The ME curve shows the values that interest rates have to take in order to equilibrate the money market at each level of income, provided that the monetary base is constant. For example, in 1970 we had a total national income of $890 billion and an interest rate of about 8 percent. Could the actual monetary base provided by the Fed have supported, say, another $30 billion of income that year? Yes, it could, but only if interest rates went up even higher, to around 8½ percent. Otherwise, the demand for money would exceed the supply, demands for bank loans would have to remain unsatisfied, and monetary equilibrium would be impossible.

9.3 THE TWO MARKETS COMBINED

The preceding chapter drew a conclusion which at first glance may seem contradictory to the relationships shown in the preceding section. First, we saw that equilibrium between income and desired *expenditures* requires that interest rates *fall* whenever income rises; the decline in interest rates stimulates more desired spending, primarily on business investment projects. And we have just seen that equilibrium between the supply of and the demand for *money* requires that interest rates *rise* whenever income rises; the increase in interest rates mainly discourages the holding of money balances and releases funds for spending purposes. In fact, there is no contradiction between these two conclusions. Taken together, they imply an important fact about our economy: there will be, at any one time, only one unique pair of values for interest rates and income which can equilibrate both the expenditure and money markets. Such an equilibrium, representing again the 1970 scene, is shown in the next diagram, Figure 9–7.[6]

---

[6] We remind the reader that we are still working with real (constant price) values for income. As we shall see in the next chapter, if the price level changes, the equilibrium income level will generally change also.

FIGURE 9–7

Joint Equilibrium in the Two Markets

Interest Rates (percent)

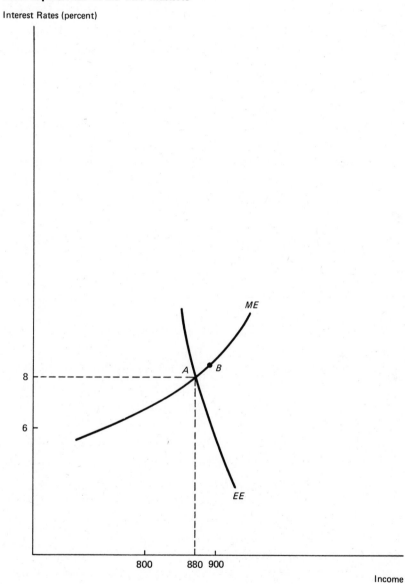

The diagram shows that the equilibrium values for the economy were at an interest rate of just under 8 percent and an income of just over $880 billion (point *A*). But in fact we were not in equilibrium that year. Because of the cutbacks in government spending, we were sliding into a recession and had not quite sunk as far as we would have had the government not acted to correct the problem. With a higher level of government spending, the *EE* curve would have been farther to the right (recall Chapter 8). So it is useful to think of the recession of 1970 as a movement along the *ME* curve from somewhere to the right of point *A* toward the new lower equilibrium. The point reached during the year is shown in the diagram as point *B*. The whole process is shown again in Figure 9–8.

These last two diagrams give us a much clearer picture of the economy than did the earlier figures in which we had only the expenditure (*EE*) curve (as in Chapter 8) or only the monetary (*ME*) curve. We concluded in the last chapter that an increase in government spending would directly and indirectly add to incomes in the economy, but that the amount of the total increase would depend partially on the offsetting impact of rising interest rates; the higher spending by the government would drive up interest rates because part of the increase would have to be financed by additional borrowing. But by how much? That depends on the extent to which people's money balances can be mobilized to buy up the new government securities to help finance the extra spending. In technical language, it depends on the *slope* of the *ME* curve. So by looking at Figure 9–8 above, we can see what would have happened had the government spent $10 billion more in 1970: equilibrium income would have been $26 billion higher ($907 billion instead of $881 billion), and interest rates would have been pushed up by less than half a point (from 7.9 percent to 8.3 percent). So, according to this analysis, the responsiveness of money demands to changes in

FIGURE 9–8

Government Spending and the 1970 Recession

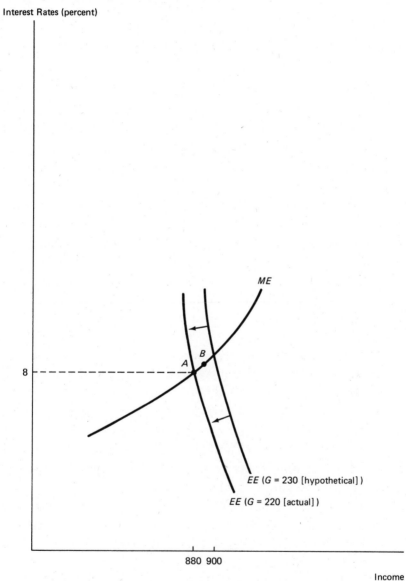

Interest Rates (percent)

interest rates provides a substantial boost to the power of government spending decisions in affecting income.

9.4   MONETARY POLICY AND AGGREGATE DEMAND

For the last several pages, we have been looking at some economic relationships that would prevail if the Fed took a passive role and held the monetary base at some fixed level at a time when the demand for goods and services was changing. Now we can turn the question around and ask about the effects on the economy from an active policy of monetary expansion. Suppose, then, that the Fed had injected an extra $2 billion of reserves into the banking system in 1970 through open market purchases of securities. The immediate impact of such a policy can be readily determined from our study of the money market: the monetary base would rise by $2 billion, the money supply curve would shift to the right, interest rates would fall immediately, and the quantity of money demanded would tend to rise. But what would happen to total income?

In practice, the effect of monetary policy on total income depends in a very important way on the amount of spending that can be induced by a drop in interest rates. Both businesses and consumers will be encouraged to spend when interest rates fall, primarily on projects that require some financing with borrowed funds or that otherwise tie up one's assets. And we now know how much of a response to expect, because we can simply look at the expenditure (*EE*) curve. For example, a 1 percent drop in interest rates should generate about $10 billion more spending per year, assuming that there are no offsetting shifts in other spending plans.

To see the total impact of monetary policy on income, we need only put together the two markets, for money and expenditures (Figure 9–9). As before, points *A* and *B* illustrate, respectively, the equilibrium point and the values actually

FIGURE 9–9

Monetary Policy and the 1970 Recession

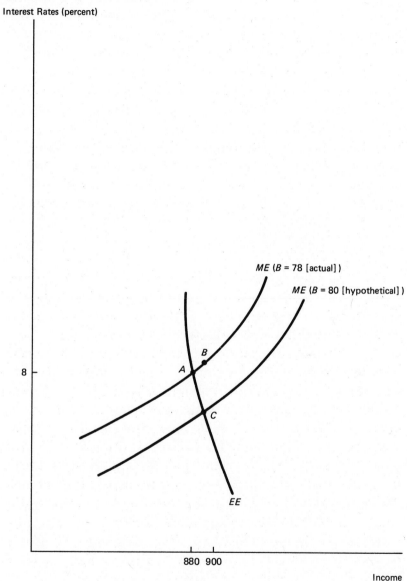

Interest Rates (percent)

ME (B = 78 [actual])

ME (B = 80 [hypothetical])

B

A

8

C

EE

880 900

Income

observed for the economy in 1970. And the new point C is the equilibrium point that would have prevailed if the Federal Reserve System had moved early to counteract the recession through expansionary open market operations. By increasing the monetary base from $78 to $80 billion, they could have driven interest rates down from their high 8 percent level; by the time the economy reached point C, interest rates would have been down to around 6.4 percent. This decline would have substantially stimulated desired spending on business investment projects, consumer purchases of homes and consumer durable goods, and the like. According to this admittedly simplified analysis, we could have experienced an extra $15 billion of income and spending that year.

9.5   CONCLUSIONS

It is apparent now that either fiscal policy (such as increased government spending) or monetary policy (such as increased purchases of bonds by the Federal Reserve) could have been used to combat the recession in the United States in 1970. The fiscal expansion would have operated through an *increase* in interest rates, drawing money balances into circulation to finance additional spending. To the extent that the rise in rates discouraged investment expenditure, the impact of the fiscal policies would have been weakened. In contrast, the monetary policy would have operated through a *decrease* in interest rates, directly stimulating private expenditure. To the extent that the drop in interest rates induced individuals or corporations to hold onto additional money balances, the impact of the monetary expansion would have been mitigated. So we had available two rather different sets of policies which could have been used either separately or in combination to pull us out of the recession.

A number of very troubling questions come to mind at this point. If it would have been so easy to avoid or escape from the recession, why did we lack the will to take appropriate action? Are there hidden difficulties with expansionary fiscal or monetary policies which we might not have discovered yet? And how do we choose which policy to use? Does it make any real difference whether we use monetary or fiscal means to drive up income?

Many of the difficulties in making appropriate use of these policies and appropriate choices between them involve uncertainties about the specific ways in which they affect various parts of the economy. Expansionary fiscal policies might lead to an expansion of government activity beyond what is politically desirable. Or, if expansion is effected through reductions in tax rates, the policy might prove to be relatively ineffective and to lead to ever larger government budget deficits. On the other hand, monetary expansion relies heavily on banks being willing and able to increase lending activity to customers who are prepared to spend the proceeds. Even if such a policy is effective, there is a danger that the resulting distribution of additional income may not be politically desirable. In short, knowing how to use monetary policy properly requires knowing the circumstances in which it is likely to be most effective and knowing how to use it so as at least to avoid adverse effects on the distribution of income. These issues are obviously complex, and we shall discuss them in detail in Part Four of this book.

A more direct difficulty with using either type of policy to combat recessions is that expansionary policies may generate inflation of general price levels. There is no guarantee that increased income will lead to increased output of goods and services; higher output requires a willingness by producers to supply more goods as well as the ability by consumers and investors to buy more. Any gaps between supply and demand will have to be resolved through rising prices. In the case of monetary expansion, the expected drop in interest rates may not occur if banks and other lenders expect the expansion to lead to inflation, and if they accordingly demand higher rates of interest on loans. So in order to see the real impacts of monetary expansion, we have to consider the supply as well as the demand for goods and services. It is to that subject that we now turn our attention.

REVIEW QUESTIONS

1. To what extent would your own personal demand for money balances be affected by a change in interest rates? Which interest rates? If the anticipated effect is small, would you conclude that the aggregate effect on the demand for money also would be small? Explain.

2. Make a list of the various supply and demand relationships in the macroeconomy which are affected by interest rates. Which ones are affected positively and which inversely? Explain.

3. If monetary or fiscal policy were to be used for contractionary purposes (to combat price inflation or to stabilize international payments, objectives which are reviewed in the next three chapters), how would the policy actions affect interest rates and income? In what ways are these effects different from the expansionary processes described in this chapter?

SUGGESTED FURTHER READING

Teigen, Ronald L. "The Demand for and Supply of Money," in Warren L. Smith and Ronald L. Teigen (eds.). *Readings in Money, National Income, and Stabilization Policy,* rev. ed. Homewood, Ill.: Richard D. Irwin, Inc., 1970.
Relevant portions of the books listed at the end of Chapter 8.

APPENDIX: A MODEL OF MONETARY EQUILIBRIUM

The market for money balances can be described by a set of algebraic functions, each one corresponding to one of the graphs introduced in this chapter. The market consists of a demand for money and a supply; it is in equilibrium when the two are equal.

There are a number of complexities in estimating a money-demand function for the U.S. economy, but we need not detain ourselves with them here.[1] A close approximation to empirically tested functions can be expressed by a simple linear relationship showing the demand for money (M^d) as a function of nominal income (real income, Y, inflated by a price index, P, to give income in current dollars)[2] and of interest rates (i):

$$M^d = M_0^d + k(P \cdot Y) - l \cdot i, \tag{1}$$

where k and l are positive parameters (k being between zero and one and l being measured in dollars), and M_0^d a positive number of dollars.[3]

The money supply function is less simple to derive. Recall from Chapter 4 that the supply of money arises out of the process of equilibrating the supply of bank reserves with the demand for them. In the notation of that chapter, we can describe six equations for the reserve market, two of which are identities (definitions) and one, the equilibrium condition; the other three are demand functions.

1. In equilibrium, the demand for bank reserves (R^d) must be equal to the supply (R^s).

$$R^d = R^s \tag{2a}$$

2. The demand for reserves arises because banks are required to hold reserves against demand (D) and time (T) deposits, the requirements being specified as percentages (q_D and q_T, respectively); and because banks may voluntarily wish to hold some excess reserves (ER):

$$R^d = q_D \cdot D + q_T \cdot T + ER^d \tag{2b}$$

---

[1] See David E. W. Laidler, *The Demand for Money: Theories and Evidence* (Scranton, Pa.: International Textbook, 1969).

[2] A more realistic but algebraically more complex specification would show real money demand (M^d/P) as a function of real income (Y).

[3] We are running out of mnemonics by now; the letters k and l are just convenient symbols for parameters.

3. The supply of reserves is the difference between the monetary base (B) and the public's desired holdings of currency (K_p).

$$R^s = B - K_p \tag{2c}$$

4. The public's demand for time deposits is inversely related to the level of interest rates available on alternative assets.

$$T^d = T_0 - t \cdot i \tag{2d}$$

where t is a parameter, t and T_o being measured in dollars.

5. Bank demands for excess reserves also are inversely related to available interest rates.

$$ER^d = ER_0 - e \cdot i \tag{2e}$$

where E is a parameter, e and ER_o being measured in dollars.

6. The money supply is defined as the sum of the supply of demand deposits and the public's holdings of currency.

$$M^s = D^s + K_p$$

In the Appendix to Chapter 4, we solved these six equations (in a similar manner to the solution of the EE curve in the Appendix to Chapter 8) for the money supply function. Rearranging that solution slightly, we find that the supply of money is a function of the monetary base, the various exogenous demands on the base which must be subtracted in deriving the net base, and the level of interest rates.

$$M^s = \frac{1}{q_D} \cdot B - \frac{1}{q_D} [q_T \cdot T_0 + ER_0$$
$$+ (1 - q_D) \cdot K_p] + \frac{(q_T \cdot t + e)}{q_D} \cdot i \tag{2}$$

Finally, we note that the market for money balances is in equilibrium when the demand for money (from equation 1) is equal to the supply (equation 2).

$$M^d = M^s \tag{3}$$

These three equations may be solved together to provide an equilibrium equation for the market: the ME curve. This equation, like the expenditure equilibrium (EE) curve, shows a relationship between income and the rate of interest.

A specific set of equations approximating the position of the U.S. banking system for 1970—the equations underlying the graphs shown in this chapter—are as follows:

I. Demand for money:

$$M^d = \$122 \text{ billion} + .2 \,(P \cdot Y) - (\$10 \text{ billion})\, i$$

Since the price index P is an arbitrarily selected number, we can set it conveniently equal to 1 in 1970 (i.e., we specify income in terms of 1970 dollars; see Chapter 8, section 8.2). So prices drop out of the equation until we encounter some inflation or deflation of the general price level.

$$M^d = \$122 \text{ billion} + .2Y - (\$10 \text{ billion})\, i \tag{1}$$

II. Supply of money:

$$R^d = R^s \tag{2a}$$

$$R^d = .1D + .05T + ER^d \tag{2b}$$

$$R^s = B - \$50 \text{ billion} \tag{2c}$$

$$T^d = \$232 \text{ billion} - (\$2 \text{ billion})\, i \tag{2d}$$

$$ER^d = \$1 \text{ billion} - (\$0.1 \text{ billion})\, i \tag{2e}$$

$$M^s = D^s + \$50 \text{ billion} \tag{2f}$$

Solving as in the Appendix to Chapter 4,

$$.1D^s = B - 50 - .05\, T^d - ER^d. \qquad \text{(from 2a, 2b, and 2c)}$$

Bringing in equations ($2d$) and ($2e$)

$$D^s = 10B - 10[50 + .05\,(232 - 2i) + (1 - .1i)]$$

Collecting terms,

$$D^s = 10B - (500 + 116 + 10) + 2i$$

or

$$D^s = 10B - \$626 \text{ billion} + (\$2 \text{ billion})i.$$

Adding currency to demand deposits (equation 2*f*),

$M^s = D^s + \$50$ billion

or

$M^s = 10B - \$576$ billion $+ (\$2$ billion)i.   (2)

In 1970, as we observed in this chapter, the monetary base was approximately $78 billion (close to $50 billion of currency held by the public, plus more than $28 billion of bank reserves). Interest rates were around 8 percent. The supply of money thereby was put at $220 billion:

$M^s = 10 \times \$78$ billion $- \$576$ billion $+ (\$2$ billion)8
$\quad = \$220$ billion.

III. Equilibrium in the market for money balances:

$M^d = 122 + .2Y - 10i$ (1)

$M^s = 10B - 576 + 2i$ (2)

$M^d = M^s$ (3)

This system of equations may be solved for income, giving us a companion equation for the *EE* curve. Setting (1) and (2) equal to each other,

$122 + .2Y - 10i = 10B - 576 + 2i$.

Collecting terms and solving,

$.2Y = 10B - 698 + 12i$

$Y = 50B - \$3,490$ billion $+ (\$60$ billion)i.   (4)

Equation (4) is the *ME* curve.

Finally, we can combine the *ME* curve with the *EE* relation derived in the Appendix to Chapter 8 in order to determine the equilibrium level of income as a function of both monetary and fiscal policy variables. The *EE* curve (cf. equation 8 in the Appendix to Chapter 8) is

$Y = \$300$ billion $+ 3G - (\$10$ billion)i.   (5)

Combining equations (4) and (5),

$$50B - 3{,}490 + 60i = 300 + 3G - 10i.$$

Solving first for the rate of interest,

$$70i = 3{,}790 + 3G - 50B$$

or

$$i = \frac{379}{7} + \frac{3}{70} G - \frac{5}{7} B. \tag{6}$$

And then for income by plugging equation (6) into equation (5)—or into equation (4), since we have noted that they are equal in equilibrium,

$$Y = 300 + 3G - 10 \left(\frac{379}{7} + \frac{3}{70} G - \frac{5}{7} B \right)$$

$$= 300 + 3G - 541.4 - .43G + 7.14B$$

or

$$Y = 2.57G + 7.14B - \$241.4 \text{ billion} \tag{7}$$

This last equation can be interpreted as an "aggregate demand" equation.[4] It shows the effects of monetary policy (via changes in the size of the monetary base) and of fiscal policy (via changes in the level of government spending) on the total demand for goods and services in the economy. The coefficients of these variables (7.14 and 2.57, respectively) may be regarded as crude estimates of the multiplier effects of these policies.[5]

---

[4] Recall, however, that we have suppressed the role of price changes so far, a simplification we remove in the next chapter.

[5] Some actual empirical estimates are described below. See Chapter 17, section 17.2.2.

chapter 10

Money and Aggregate Supply

10.1 INTRODUCTION

During the soaring sixties, most economists convinced
themselves that the economy could be managed so as to
achieve full employment, and that the way to accomplish
that task was to control the *demand* for goods and services.
The controversy was merely over whether monetary policy or
government fiscal policies were the appropriate tool for the
task. But as the sedentary seventies are developing, it is becoming increasingly clear that the more important job is to
manage the *supply* of goods and services. At present (1974),
the rate of unemployment is rising, real output is declining,
and the rate of price inflation is high and accelerating. Now
are these problems the result of insufficient aggregate demand? Can they be solved by expansionary monetary or
fiscal policies? The answer is partly yes, but only partly. For
a full explanation, we have to take into account the various
determinants of output and employment, and not just the
determinants of demand. The danger is that, even though unemployment is high, an expansionary program might do little
to increase output and a lot to increase the already serious inflation. In this chapter, we shall see the circumstances which
can lead to these gloomy results.

246

In chapters 8 and 9, we assumed that the price level remained unchanged and therefore that the supply of output
would be perfectly elastic with respect to a change in aggregate demand. We were able, within this narrow framework,
to determine equilibrium interest rates and real output. This
assumption may be realistic for certain special states of the
economy: especially those when unemployment is abnormally high and when there is substantial unused capacity
such as during the Great Depression of the 1930s. But it does
not fit the facts of today. Inflation is a major economic problem and the economy has been operating at relatively high
levels of capacity and plant utilization.

A major task which remains is to develop our model of the
economy further with a view to determining the absolute
level of prices. In order to do so we must introduce the no-
tions of a "production function" and of a labor market. The
production function establishes the relationship between the
quantity of labor and output, and the labor market determines real wage rates and the quantity of employment.

10.2 THE AGGREGATE SUPPLY OF GOODS AND SERVICES

The production of goods and services for consumers or
business firms requires the input of various resources: raw
materials (iron ore, wheat), real capital (machinery), financial capital (bank loans), labor and management services,
and land (either owned or rented). These "factors of production" must somehow be combined to transform inputs into
useful and salable outputs. It would be a rather formidable
task to attempt to make any sort of full explanation of all of
the millions of types of production processes in use to produce buttons, automobiles, atomic reactors, medical services,
and the like. But we can simplify the explanation a great deal
by making two assumptions. First, we assume that the econ-

omy produces roughly the same combinations of goods and services over time and continues to use approximately the same techniques of production. The advantage of this assumption is that it implies that there is an "aggregate production function" for the whole economy, a simple description of the way all of the economy's resources are combined to produce the aggregate volume of output each year.

A second useful assumption is that there exists a fixed quantity of all input resources other than labor. There is, at any point in time, a certain amount of land available for business use, a fixed supply of raw materials, and there is a certain real value of capital equipment. The main problem in maximizing the supply of output will then be to insure that wages and salaries are high enough to attract people to work, but not too high to discourage companies from hiring them. That is, we shall need to look closely at the nature of the demand for and the supply of labor.

These two assumptions are not at all unrealistic in the short run. Over a period of years, the operation of the economy can change quite a bit, in terms of the kinds of goods produced, the techniques used in production, and the availability of various resources. And sometimes our gradual evolution can get quite a jolt, such as the sudden shift from excesses to shortages of basic foods in the United States in the early 1970s or the shift in demand from large cars to small. But under most circumstances, there will be a pretty stable relationship between the amount of labor employed and the real value of total output produced.

10.2.1 The Aggregate Production Function

One of the first principles of economic theory to which every student is introduced is that of "diminishing marginal returns." The principle applies virtually to every realm of economic life. For example, we have seen throughout our study of the demand for money that people hold only limited quantities of money relative to their incomes, mainly because there are diminishing marginal returns (in the sense of personal utility) from liquidity which money balances provide. But the original conception of diminishing marginal returns was in the analysis of the production of economic goods.

Within limits, of course, marginal returns are positive: more labor can produce more output. With a fixed supply of capital and natural resources, there normally will be some upper boundary on the process, beyond which the use of more workers could actually decrease output. But we need not greatly concern ourselves with that extremity, because it is unlikely to occur in any real situation. Thus the first principle about the aggregate production function for the economy is that the marginal productivity of labor is normally positive.

Almost as fundamental as this first proposition is the expectation that the marginal productivity of labor will decrease as more of it is applied to the fixed quantities of other resources. A very small firm, or a company making only very small quantities of a particular good, might be able to get even higher productivity out of additional workers than it obtained from its initial few, perhaps by being able to use more efficient methods of production or greater specialization. But beyond that point, limitations on the productivity of additional workers will appear. When we consider all of the production processes of the economy in the aggregate, this proposition implies that increases in the level of employment will increase the level of output, but less than proportionally. One reason for these diminishing marginal returns in the aggregate is that unemployment generally hits the least productive, the most expendable workers. When those workers are rehired, they cannot be expected to be as productive as the rest of the labor force. Hence the second principle about the aggregate production function is that the marginal productivity of labor declines as the quantity of labor employed increases.

These two principles together imply an aggregate production function of the type shown in Figure 10–1. This diagram shows the amounts of labor (N) required to produce various amounts of real output (Y), given the available supplies of other factors of production and given the techniques used in production. But how do we measure these things? What exactly do we mean by N and Y? Well, given the assumptions with which we have simplified matters, measuring N is no real problem: it is just the number of people employed.[1] Real output, however, is a different sort of kettle. It contains all the different kinds of goods and services actually produced in the whole economy. So we cannot add them up directly. Neither can we add their dollar values, unless we assume the absolute price level to be fixed; if prices were to rise, the same real value of output would have a higher nominal value. To avoid these complications, we have to measure Y in exactly the same way we measured it in the preceding two chapters: it is total NNP measured in constant dollars.

10.2.2 The Demand for Labor

The existence of a production function such as we have just described implies a predictable relationship between the amount of labor employed and the amount of output produced. But it cannot tell us by itself just how much employment or output there will be. For that we need to look for some additional information. In 1970, for example, some 79 million workers were hired, and they produced $890 billion worth of output. But there were also another 4 million people seeking work in an average week that year, without success.

---

[1] Measuring employment simply by the number of workers is acceptable only so long as the average quality of labor does not change. Better education, for example, would tend to shift the whole production function to the right unless we changed the units to some sort of "standard worker."

FIGURE 10–1

A Production Function for the U.S. Economy

Labor Input (N)
(millions of employed workers)

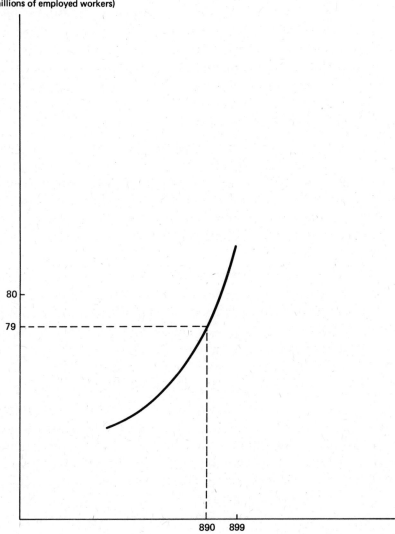

NNP (Y)
(billions of 1970 dollars)

Why were only 79 million people hired, and not 80 or 83 million?

The answer to this most vexing question is simplicity itself. Workers are hired because the managers of companies expect them to contribute at least as much to the company's income as the company pays out to them in wages, salaries, or other compensation. If the expected productivity of a worker is less than the cost of hiring him, he is likely to be pacing the sidewalks instead.

To translate this rather obvious piece of information into a demand for labor, we have only to recall that the marginal productivity of labor is expected to decline as total employment rises, so that the contribution to output of the next million or so workers would be somewhat less than the contributions of those already hired. Therefore, the wages paid to workers will have to decline in order to induce companies to hire more of them.

The relationship between wage rates and the quantity of labor demanded by businesses is shown in Figure 10–2. There are two characteristics of this labor demand curve that are important to us as we analyze the possible effects of monetary policy on the economy. First, the curve is shown to be quite steep; that is, a small drop in wages would be sufficient to generate a fairly large increase in the quantity of labor which firms were willing to hire. Therefore, there might be some advantage in trying to design a policy to drive wages down. Second, the relevant variable determining the demand for labor is not the nominal wage payment but the level of real wages. Firms will not be discouraged from hiring workers if wage increases are fully covered by price increases. Therefore, a policy designed to drive prices up will have the same stimulative effect on employment as one designed to drive wages down, so long as the price increases are not passed back to labor in the form of higher wages. The objective is to get the level of employment up by lowering the real

FIGURE 10–2

The Demand for Labor

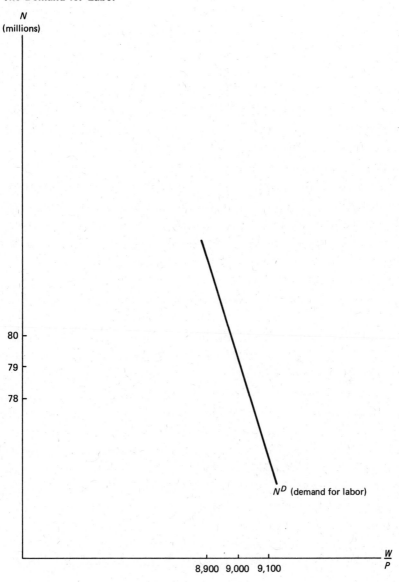

wage, whether it is accomplished through lower money wages or through higher money prices.

10.2.3   The Supply of Labor

The catch in any program to increase the volume of employment is that the workers themselves have to go along with it or it is doomed to fail. So we have to look at the determinants of the supply of labor as well as the demand for it. And, as we shall see, the supply function in this market is more complex than it at first appears.

Basically, the supply of labor services by workers is a function of the level of real wages. An increase in the wages offered to them or a decrease in the prices which they have to pay to buy goods and services should induce additional workers into the labor market. In either case, a given amount of work will enable the worker to buy more goods and services, so the real returns to work are higher. Hence a greater supply of labor.[2]

But this point should not be overemphasized. After all, most of us have to work in order to earn a living. If our real income falls, we are unlikely to go off to sit in a corner. In practice, a fall in real wages affects the supply of labor in two principal ways. It discourages marginal workers, especially second workers in families; for example, men whose wives are already earning a regular income for the family may be induced to stay home and care for the children. And it also may make overtime work less worthwhile, so that the total supply of labor services could fall even if no one actually stopped working completely.

The net result of these various effects is a labor supply curve of the sort shown in Figure 10–3. In contrast to the

---

[2] In extreme cases, this relationship could be reversed. If wages become very high, workers may decide to work fewer hours and obtain more hours of leisure; we could then have what is usually called a "backward-bending" labor supply curve.

FiGURE 10–3

The Supply of Labor

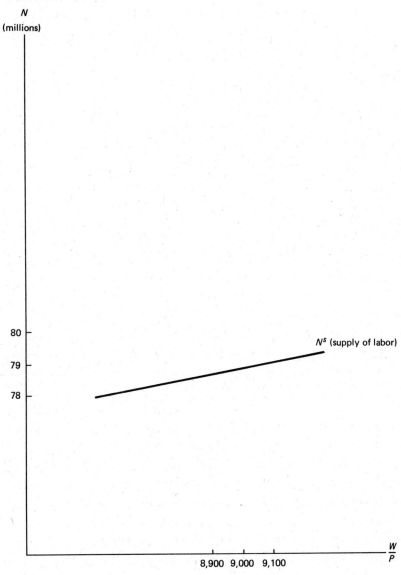

very steep demand curve, the supply curve is quite flat: a large increase in real wages is required to induce additional labor into the market. This insensitivity of labor supply is a direct consequence of the limited choices available to most of us, at least in the short run, as described in the preceding paragraph.

But now comes the complexity. It is reasonable to expect firms to be indifferent between increases in prices and decreases in wages, so that the *demand* for labor will be determined simply by the level of real wages. But workers are less likely to be that fully aware of all the relevant economic information. Certainly they are aware when their wages go up. They also are aware when prices go up, but they may not fully and immediately absorb and relate to that information. Each worker—or each group of workers—has one wage rate, but he has literally thousands of prices on the goods and services he buys. Even if he is sophisticated enough to keep track of government price indexes, he will find that there are a variety of numbers being released and that they reflect past rather than present information. Thus it is natural for workers to react more strongly to wage changes than to price changes. This phenomenon is commonly known as "money illusion." A person who suffers from money illusion thinks he is better off if his wages rise by, say, 10 percent, even if his wages will not buy any more real goods and services. Eventually, he will wake up, but it is the meantime that matters.

The implication of money illusion is that a rise in the general price level will shift the labor supply curve upward, as shown in Figure 10–4. Suppose that prices and wages both rise by 10 percent. The real wage rate is unchanged, but—at least in the short run, which in this context may last for two or three years[3]—workers *think* that wages are higher. There-

---

[3] The length of time required for workers to adjust fully to price increases is difficult to measure empirically, but much of the evidence points to a two- to three-year horizon. One reason for this lag may be that formal labor contracts

FIGURE 10–4

The Effect of Price Inflation on the Labor Supply Curve

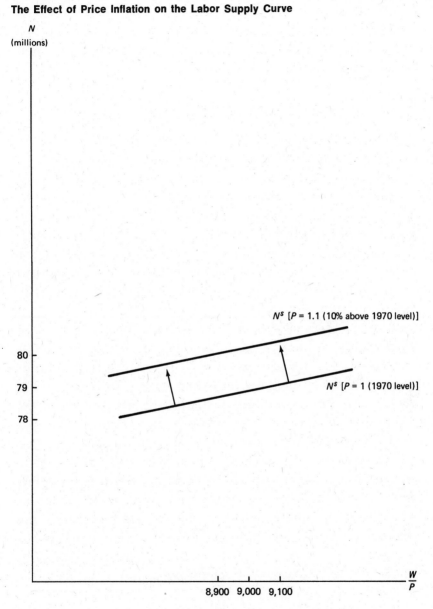

fore, a greater quantity of labor is supplied. This characteristic of the supply of labor is of fundamental importance for monetary policy, because as we shall see, it makes it possible for inflationary policies to increase the level of employment in the economy.

10.2.4   Aggregate Supply and Labor-Market Equilibrium

Since workers and firms have conflicting interests in real wage payments, the former wanting to drive them up and the latter wanting to keep them down, we can only hope that the market will tend toward an equilibrium position. But of course it should. If wages are too high, then the excess supply of labor will cause them to fall (or, more likely in practice, will cause them to grow more slowly than they would otherwise). If wages are too low, firms will have a self-interest in raising them, so long as the higher wages attract workers whose marginal productivity equals or exceeds the cost of employing them. So the labor market will be equilibrated only where the supply and demand curves intersect (see Figure 10–5), and we can expect any divergence from equilibrium to be self-remedying over time.

The equilibrium position of the labor market is one of the anchors to which the aggregate behavior of the economy is tied, along with the equilibrium position of the money market (Chapter 9) and the point at which aggregate saving equals desired investment expenditure (Chapter 8). It is important first because it tells us by itself how much employment we can expect and how much will be earned in real wages. For 1970, the graph shows approximately 79 million workers employed at an average wage of just over $9,000 per year.

We also can learn how much output will be produced. Re-

---

tend to cover three-year periods. The now-increasing use of "escalator" clauses, under which wages adjust automatically to price increases, clearly limits the importance of any money illusion; however, only a minority of workers are covered by that type of contract.

FIGURE 10–5

Equilibrium in the Labor Market

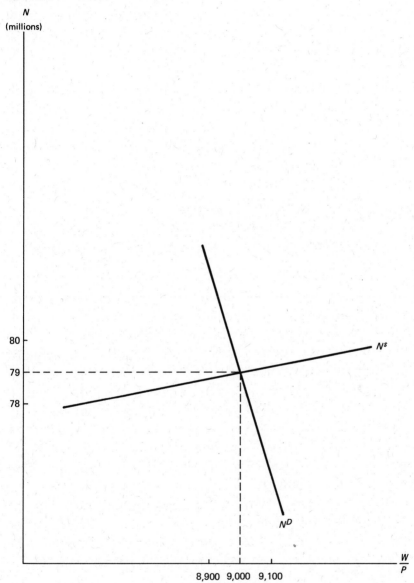

call (from Figure 10–1) that we started with a production function for the whole economy which relates the amount of labor employed to the amount of output produced. That function showed us, for example, that 79 million workers could produce $890 billion of output (at 1970 prices). If prices and wages are such that a real wage of $9,000 just clears the labor market, then $890 billion of output is what we are going to get (Figure 10–6). *And if we want to increase the level of employment and increase total real output, then we have to design a policy that will succeed in shifting one or both of the curves (supply or demand) in the market for labor services.* The remainder of this chapter examines the requirements for such a policy.

10.3 AGGREGATE SUPPLY AND THE LEVEL OF PRICES

So long as workers react differently to income losses through price inflation from the way they would react to income losses through direct wage cuts, it is possible for a policy of general monetary expansion to increase the amount of employment and output. To see the mechanics of a standard inflationary-expansionary policy, suppose that the Federal Reserve had undertaken a more expansionary policy in 1970 and that its actions had succeeded in driving up the price level by, say, 10 percent. Now that is a pretty rapid rate of inflation, and it is a consequence of a policy which we should not accept readily unless we expect some pretty solid positive results to accompany it.

We already have calculated the equilibrium wage rate for the 1970 level of prices to have been just over $9,000. But it surely would have had to be higher if prices had risen by 10 percent, since the same wage would then have enabled the worker to buy only about 90 percent of the goods and services that he could have bought otherwise. A $9,000 wage at the higher price level would be equivalent only to $8,180 at

FIGURE 10-6
Labor-Market Equilibrium and the Supply of Output

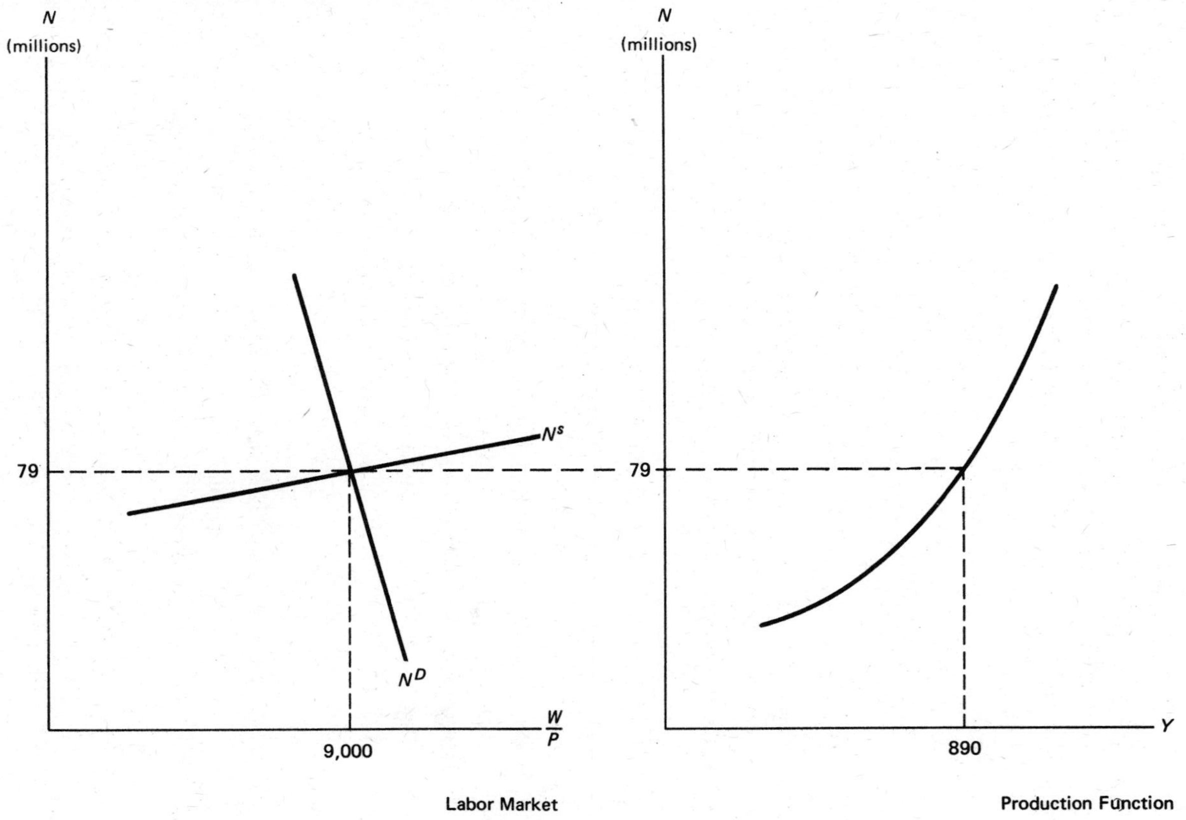

Labor Market

Production Function

the old price level ($9,000 ÷ 1.1), and an annual wage of
$9,900 would be required to generate the same real pur-
chasing power as before. Nonetheless, the equilibrium money
wage is unlikely, at least in the short run, to rise by anything
like $900 per year. As explained in the preceding section, we
do not expect workers to react completely to the inflation,
partly because they may not be fully aware of it and partly
because they may not react immediately to what they are
aware of. So we can suppose that the real wage required by
workers will fall temporarily, which is simply another way of
saying that the nominal wage rises by a smaller percentage
than the price level. This shift in the labor supply curve is
shown in Figure 10–7, where we have assumed that the
nominal wage rises sufficiently to compensate directly for
about a third of the inflation.

At this stage, before anything happens to the volume of
employment, all that the inflationary policy has accomplished
is to transfer real income from labor to corporations. Business
income has risen via the higher prices, as a consequence of
the increased demand for an existing supply of real output.
But here the subtle forces of competition take over, even in a
highly oligopolized and managed economy. The higher prices
make it profitable for businesses to produce more goods than
they did formerly. To produce more goods, they must hire
more labor. And to hire more labor, they must pay higher
wages. In this manner, total output and employment will rise;
the real wage will fall, but hopefully not by very much.

Given the assumption behind the diagram in Figure 10–7,
the supply curve for labor will shift enough that *at the old
level of employment* (79 million), the average worker would
lose about $600 of purchasing power as a result of the infla-
tion. His real wage would fall from around $9,000 to about
$8,400; which is to say, he would demand and get a wage in-
crease only of about $300 per year. But because of the re-

FIGURE 10–7

The Effect of a Rise in Prices on Labor-Market Equilibrium

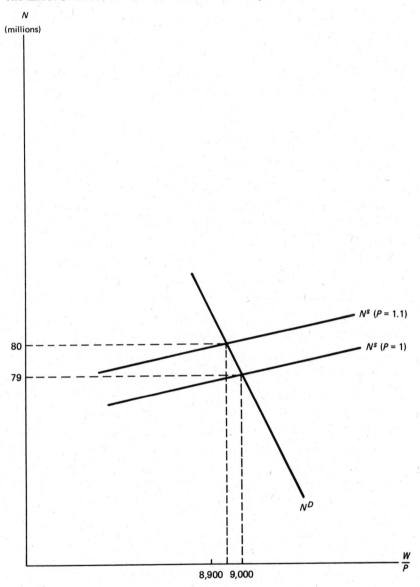

newed desire of businesses to hire more workers, the level of employment actually would rise by well over 1 million workers (representing a fall in the unemployment rate from around 5 percent to around 3½ percent) and the real wage would be off only about $50 per year for the average worker. So these figures, which are rather arbitrary, at least suggest that there can be very definite gains to inflationary policies.

10.3.1 The Aggregate Supply Curve

So long as higher prices will result in higher supplies of output, we can construct an aggregate supply curve based on the labor-market and production-function relationships developed above. All of these elements are brought together in Figure 10–8. For every level of prices, there exists a short-run labor-supply curve. Thus there is a different level of output for every price level, such that higher prices generate higher output. We already have examined two such points; by tracing out all possible values of prices and output supplies, we get the aggregate supply curve shown in the diagram.

It is important not to forget that the upward-sloping aggregate supply curve is a short-run phenomenon. After two or three years of labor negotiations, much of the employment gain may be wiped out. The increasingly obvious inflation, the rising level of corporate profits, the pressures in the labor market associated with very high employment, all will take their toll in the form of greater wage demands. The labor-supply curve will shift back toward its initial position. In the long run, then, the supply of output will depend primarily on the productivity of labor and other factors of production, and on the amount of labor that can be attracted by a given real wage rate. In the long run, the supply of output in the economy is likely to be much more independent of the price level than in the short run (see Figure 10–9).

FIGURE 10–8

A Short-Run Aggregate Supply Curve

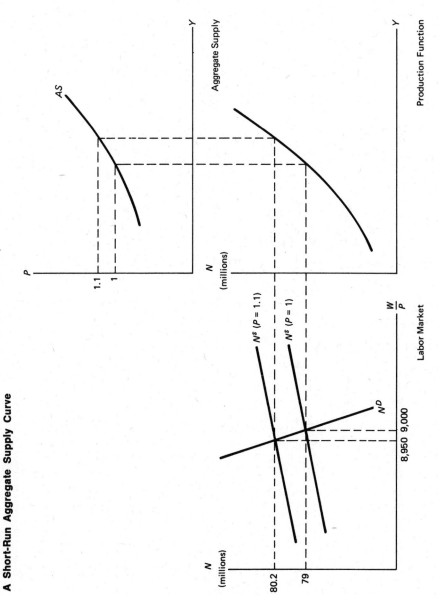

FIGURE 10-9

A Longer-Run Aggregate Supply Curve

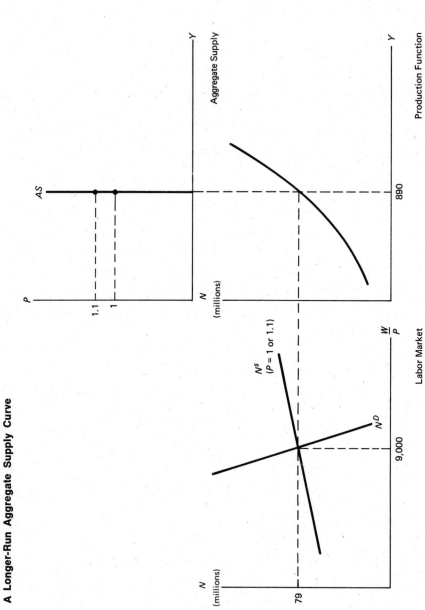

10.4 AGGREGATE DEMAND AND THE LEVEL OF PRICES

We now can begin to see how we might have avoided the recession of 1970 (and how we can help to avoid future recessions). It would be an oversimplification to conclude that prices were too low that year, or that price inflation by itself could have solved all of the country's economic ills. But it would be fair to conclude that a policy designed to create a more favorable business atmosphere could have generated a substantial short-term increase in employment and would have permitted the economy to offset the negative impacts of reduced spending and employment by the federal government. A major part of that more favorable atmosphere should have been a higher aggregate demand for goods and services, and an inevitable side effect of the policy would have been a higher level of prices. To see just how such an expansionary policy would work, we need to add one more theoretical apparatus to our model of the economy: the aggregate demand curve.

In the preceding two chapters, we looked at the two markets which are most important in determining the ability of the public—consumers, business firms, and governments—to purchase goods and services. The first of these, which we have called the market for expenditures, is in real terms essentially independent of the aggregate price level. The real demand for capital goods by businesses is determined primarily by the sales expectations of businesses and by rates of interest or other costs of obtaining funds. A higher price level, so long as relative prices are not altered, would simply mean that firms would pay more for their equipment (and for the labor to run it) and would receive more for the goods they sell. As a general rule, we have no reason to expect business investment plans to be affected systematically (either favorably or unfavorably) by changes in the aggregate price level.

Similarly, consumer behavior is influenced primarily by real income. So long as higher prices are reflected in higher dollar incomes, consumers probably will buy roughly the same real quantities of most things. Finally, government budgets tend to be specified in real terms; when the cost of building a road rises, the government is likely to go ahead and build the road anyway. If real incomes have not fallen, then nominal tax revenues may rise sufficiently to cover the government's higher costs. In practice, of course, none of these relationships is likely to hold precisely in the face of changing prices. But they tend to be accurate enough that we can specify the equilibrium curve for this market (the EE curve) as a function only of real incomes and interest rates and not as a function of the price level.

The market for money balances is a different matter. Monetary policy has to be specified in nominal or dollar terms; the Federal Reserve can alter the supply of reserves to the banking system and thereby can influence the supply of money to the economy. The demand for money, however, will change systematically when the aggregate price level changes. As Chapter 7 demonstrated, a rise in prices generally implies that people will demand more money to buy the same real quantity of goods and services. If monetary policy is not changed, then the price rise will knock the money market out of equilibrium, and interest rates will have to rise to restore order.

These price relationships are illustrated in the next diagram (Figure 10–10), which recalls the description given in Chapter 9 (cf. Figures 9–6 and 9–7). For a given monetary policy stance, there is a fixed money-supply curve (M^s). The ME curve then is derived by calculating the various demands for money (M^d) as real income changes and as the price level (P) is held constant. Thus points A and B are on the ME curve at the original 1970 price level; point A is the equilibrium situation which we derived above in Chapter 9. And

FIGURE 10-10

The Effect of a Rise in Prices on Monetary Equilibrium

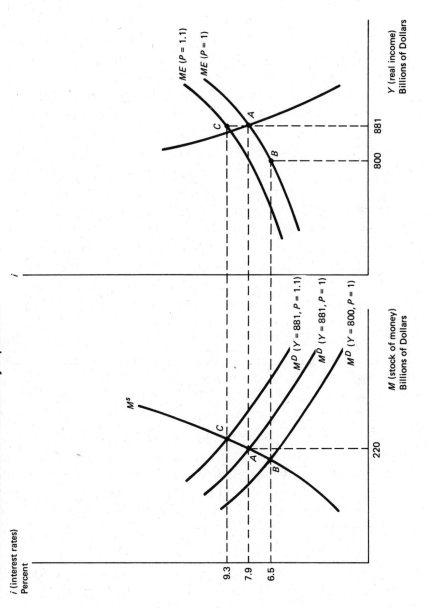

now we also can observe the effects of a rise in prices on the demand for money. The M^d curve shifts to the right in much the same way as if real income had risen.[4] Thus interest rates will have to rise or real income will have to fall in order to maintain monetary equilibrium. Therefore, the monetary equilibrium curve (ME) must shift to the left.

With the EE curve stable and the ME curve shifting as a result of the change in prices, it is evident that in order to maintain equilibrium in *both* markets, real income actually will have to fall; point C preserves monetary but not expenditure equilibrium. Interest rates cannot bear the whole burden of adjustment, because the increase in rates will discourage business investment, inducing a fall in real output. Therefore, with a given monetary policy, we have a classic economic tradeoff: if businesses in general charge higher prices, people will try to obtain more money in order to pay the higher prices; but with no money being made available except at higher interest rates, ultimately real purchases and then the output of goods and services will have to fall.

This effect of prices on the ability of the public to buy gives us an aggregate demand relationship, as shown in Figure 10–11. As we saw earlier, the initial effect of the price rise is to cause the ME curve to shift to the left. But at the original equilibrium level of real income ($881 billion), expenditure equilibrium is no longer achieved (point C). So real incomes and spending have to fall until point B is reached. Once real incomes have declined to $869 billion, we again observe equilibrium in the monetary and expenditure markets. The aggregate demand curve (AD) represents all the points which could be derived in this manner for various levels of prices.

---

[4] *Nominal* income is simply the product of real income and the index of prices; that is, it is income measured in current prices. Thus a 10 percent rise in prices, with real income constant, raises nominal income from $881 billion to $969 billion ($881 \times 1.1$).

FIGURE 10–11

The Aggregate Demand Curve

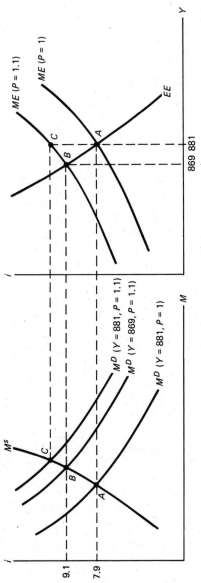

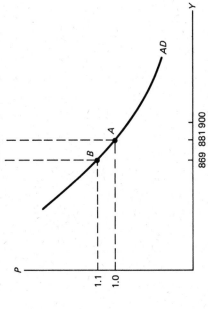

The behavior of the economy in moving from point A to point B can be seen somewhat differently by measuring nominal dollar incomes rather than real incomes. At the initial price index of 1.0, both nominal and real income are at $881 billion. Now we assume that businesses generally try for some reason to charge 10 percent more for goods and services, so that the price index rises to 1.1. The demand for money to buy these things rises, and total dollar spending rises as well. Therefore, total dollar income goes up. But the essential point is that the accompanying rise in interest rates limits the rise in nominal income, so that it goes up by less than 10 percent. Prices rise by more than spending, so real incomes fall.[5]

10.5 AGGREGATE SUPPLY AND DEMAND

Overall, the aggregate economy can be characterized in the same way as the market for a single good, even though it obviously is incredibly more complex. The quantity of output which businesses find profitable to produce will tend to increase when the level of prices is increased: we have an upward-sloping supply curve. And the quantity of output which consumers and businesses are able to buy goes down as the price level rises: we have a downward-sloping demand curve. These curves are different from ordinary market curves in some ways; most notably, the aggregate demand curve expresses *effective* demand, the ability to buy a total quantity of goods as a function of an absolute price level, rather than the desire to buy a specific good or service as a function of its price relative to the prices of other substitutable goods. But otherwise the aggregate concepts are straightforward applications of the basic economic principles of supply and demand.

---

[5] A real income of $869 billion and a price level of 1.1 implies a nominal income of $956 billion (see footnote 4). The increase in nominal incomes thus is only 8½ percent (956 ÷ 881).

These aggregate relationships are brought together in Figure 10–12, where the intersection of the aggregate supply (AS) and the aggregate demand (AD) curves describes a point of *general equilibrium* for the whole economy. At *every* point on the AD curve, both the market for money balances and the market for commodities are in equilibrium; that is, the AD curve summarizes all the points where, at varying price levels but with a fixed monetary policy, the ME and EE curves intersect. Similarly, at every point on the AS curve the labor market is in equilibrium; the AS curve summarizes all the points where, at varying price levels, the N^s and N^d curves intersect. And the one point where the AS and AD curves cross brings all three basic markets into simultaneous equilibrium. Such a point for conditions prevailing in 1970 is shown in the diagram.

10.6 MONETARY POLICY AND GENERAL EQUILIBRIUM

The aggregate supply and demand relationships enable us to examine the effects of monetary policy on the economy much more fully than do the individual market relationships by themselves. We know that when the Federal Reserve takes an expansionary action such as purchasing securities in the open market, we can expect interest rates to fall, and prices and output to rise. We saw the first stages of such a process in Chapter 9, where we examined the increase in output expected to result from a $2 billion open market purchase *assuming constant prices;* there we found a $15 billion impact on income. And now we can see the full process via a diagram such as Figure 10–13. The effects operate as follows:

1. The direct effect of the open market purchase is to expand the monetary base by increasing the supply of bank reserves by $2 billion. Because the supply of reserves is an important argument in determining the supply of money, the M^s schedule shifts to the right.

FIGURE 10–12

General Equilibrium: The Intersection of Aggregate Supply and Demand

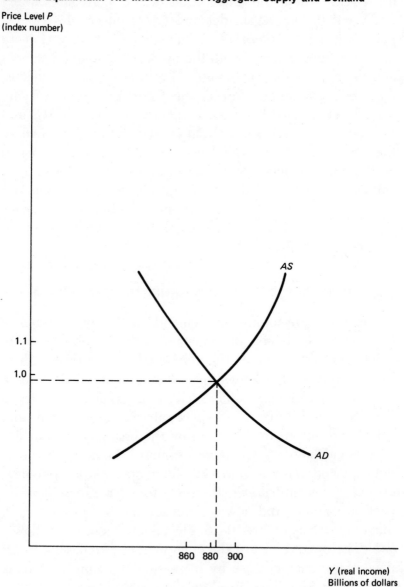

Price Level P
(index number)

1.1

1.0

860 880 900

Y (real income)
Billions of dollars

AS

AD

FIGURE 10–13

Monetary Policy and General Equilibrium

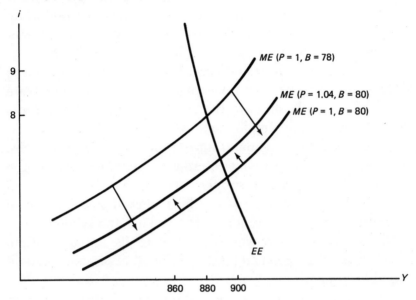

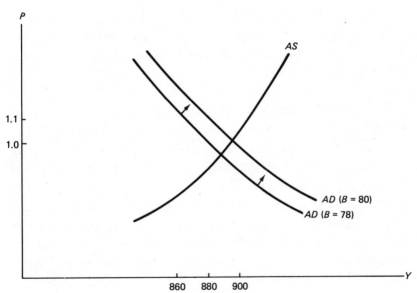

2. The increased availability of money to the public enables banks to make loans at lower interest rates. As rates fall
at given levels of expenditure, the monetary equilibrium
schedule shifts to the right. Additional expenditure is encouraged, and we move to the right along the *EE* curve.

3. As the *ME* curve shifts and the ability of the public to
buy goods *at given prices* is expanded, the whole aggregate
demand schedule shifts to the right. Business activity picks
up, and output and employment rise.

4. The increased demand for output also drives up prices,
the extent of the rise being determined by the steepness (the
slope) of the aggregate supply curve. The combined rise in
output and prices now causes the money demand curve to
shift; more money is required for making transactions. The
ME curve shifts part-way back toward its initial position.
Eventually, the economy settles down at a new general
equilibrium position.

It is now apparent that only about half of the increase in
income described in the last chapter will actually show up in
a rise in output. The effect of monetary expansion on prices
limits the growth of real effective demand. If we had desired
a $15 billion rise in real output as a cure for the 1970 reces-
sion, we still might have been able to achieve it by monetary
policy; but we would have had to use a bigger dose—perhaps
$4 to $5 billion—of open market purchases in order to get it.

When monetary policy is applied in a contractionary direction, a similar chain of events is set in motion but with the
various curves shifting to the left instead of to the right. But
there is a substantive difference between expansionary and
contractionary policies in their effects on output and prices.
Increases in the availability of money, by stimulating the
demand for goods and services, often have their major effects
initially on the prices charged by businesses. Only after a lag
during which orders for goods are gradually translated into
increased rates of production will real economic activity be

generated. In terms of our diagram (Figure 10–13), the economy does not move smoothly up the aggregate supply curve; it traces a steeper path in which prices move first and output later.

To analyze the effects of contractionary policies, we have to note two modifications. First, in practical terms, *contraction* generally takes the form of decreased rates of growth rather than actual declines. Thus aggregate price levels rarely show absolute decreases. A prolonged period of restricted growth in the supply of money would be expected to produce merely a slow rate of growth in the level of prices. Secondly, prices are likely to resist decreases more than increases. Businesses faced with reduced demand for their products often react first by producing smaller quantities. Only if the decline is sufficiently prolonged will they become generally willing to cut prices. It is this dichotomized behavior of prices, characterized by a much greater upward than downward flexibility, that partly explains the persistence of high rates of price inflation during periods of slack in aggregate demand.

One final point must be made about the limitations of monetary policy in controlling output. We noted above that in the long run—a length of time we expect in this context to be at least two or three years—the aggregate supply curve may be vertical. This condition follows from the gradual adjustment of labor markets to changes in the general price level. And if the AS curve is vertical, then monetary policy cannot possibly further increase real output. Ultimately, all that an expansion of the supply of money can accomplish is to stimulate aggregate demand. That stimulus will increase the output of goods and services only so long as business costs do not rise proportionally with prices, i.e., only so long as labor does not demand proportional wage adjustments.

In the long run, that situation cannot be expected to persist, and monetary policy will succeed mainly in driving up prices. So if we wish to design a successful policy for expanding output and employment, we realistically can expect monetary policy to play only a temporizing role. The supply of money is a powerful stabilization weapon. But it can neither produce nor substitute for a healthy economy.

REVIEW QUESTIONS

1. If there should occur a 10 percent rise in prices during the course of a year, and if wages also rose by 10 percent (assuming no change in the productivity of labor), what would happen to the demand for labor? The supply of labor? Total supply of output in the economy?

2. If prices were to rise by 10 percent but all *nominal* incomes were constant (implying that real output falls by the same percentage), what would happen to the market for money balances? The markets for expenditure on goods and services? Total demand for goods and services in the economy?

3. How does the effect on interest rates of an expansionary monetary policy differ from the effects produced by expansionary fiscal policy? What accounts for this different pattern?

4. Trace through the chain of events generated by a contractionary monetary policy designed to reduce price inflation, noting the effects on real output, prices, and interest rates. Are these effects merely the mirror images of expansionary impacts?

SUGGESTED FURTHER READING

Miller, Roger Leroy and Raburn M. Williams. *Unemployment and Inflation.* St. Paul: West Publishing Co., 1974.

Samuelson, Paul A. and Robert M. Solow. "Analytical Aspects of Anti-Inflation Policy," *American Economic Review* 50, May 1960.

APPENDIX: A MODEL OF GENERAL EQUILIBRIUM

The supply of goods and services is a considerably more complex process than the demand for them; a complete mathematical explanation of this process would require more extensive tools than the linear algebra to which we have promised the reader to limit ourselves.[1] This appendix provides an introduction to the subject by simplifying the production process down to a few linear equations.

An aggregate production function is inherently nonlinear; labor, land, and capital are combined (not added together) to produce outputs. The most commonly applied forms show output as an increasing function of the various inputs, but with diminishing marginal returns as any single input is increased by itself. If we hold capital and land usage constant, allowing only labor employment (N) to vary, we can approximate a production function for the U.S. economy as follows:

$$Y = \$106.12 \text{ billion} + (\$10.83 \text{ billion}) N - (\$.0115 \text{ billion}) N^2 \quad (1)$$

Note that this last term captures the diminution of returns to labor as N (the number of workers) increases.[2]

The demand for labor may be derived directly from the production function, provided we are willing to make one more assumption: that employers will in equilibrium be willing to hire workers up to the point where the marginal worker is being paid exactly the value of the product which his employment makes possible. We have observed that in 1970, some 79 million workers were hired; from equation (1) we can calculate the potential output from that volume of employment at \$890 billion (cf. Figure 10–1). Now suppose that 80 million workers had been hired instead. Our

---

[1] Interested readers may wish to consult a more advanced text such as R. G. D. Allen, *Macro-Economic Theory: A Mathematical Treatment* (New York: St. Martin's Press, 1968). See especially Chapter 3, "The Technology of the Economy."

[2] This equation is a linearization of the function $Y = \$27$ billion $(N^{.8})$; the two give approximately equivalent results for the range of values observed in 1970. The nonlinear equation is a "Cobb-Douglas" production function in which only one factor of production (labor) is allowed to vary; see Allen, *Macro-Economic Theory*, pp. 49–52. The linearization is by a mathematical technique known as "Taylor's series." See R. G. D. Allen, *Mathematical Analysis for Economists* (New York: St. Martin's Press, 1938).

production function tells us—as we urge the reader to calculate—that output would have risen to $899 billion. That amounts to $9 billion of output from 1 million workers, so the wage rate should settle around $9,000 per year. By making a series of similar calculations,[3] we can derive a relationship between the wage rate (in real terms: W/P) and the quantity of labor which can profitably be employed at that real wage:[4]

$$\frac{W}{P} = \$10,831 - \$23 \cdot N \tag{2}$$

For example, when 79 million workers are employed, equation (2) tells us that the average annual real wage rate should approach $9,014.

We may complete this supply model by hypothesizing that the supply of labor is related positively to the level of real wages offered by employers; and that—at least in the short run—higher prices at a given level of real wages (i.e., proportional increases in money wages and in the price level) will lure additional workers into the labor market. This last hypothesis is equivalent to an assumption of "money illusion" in the market.

$$N = 48.9 + .002 \frac{W}{P} + 12P \tag{3}$$

Equations (1), (2), and (3) may be solved together for the aggregate supply curve as described in this chapter. Combining equations (2) and (3),

$$N = 48.9 + .002 \, (10,831 - 23 \, N).$$

Collecting terms and solving for equilibrium employment:

---

[3] Some calculus is required to derive this result properly. The production function is $Y = 27 \cdot (N^{.8})$. Differentiating with respect to N gives the marginal productivity of labor: $dY/dN = 21.6 \cdot (N^{-.2})$. The assumption that workers are paid the value of their marginal product implies that $dY/dN = W/P$. Linearizing this result at the values observed in 1970 gives our equation (2).

[4] N here is measured in millions of workers; the wage rate W is measured in dollars per year.

$$N = 67.46 + 11.47\,P. \tag{4}$$

Then combining equations (1) and (4),

$$Y = 106.12 + 10.83(67.46 + 11.47P) - .0115(67.46 + 11.47P)^2.$$

Collecting terms and rounding the coefficients,

$$Y = \$784.4 \text{ billion} + (\$106.5 \text{ billion})\,P - (\$1.5 \text{ billion})P^2 \tag{5}$$

Equation (5) is the aggregate supply (AS) curve derived in this chapter.

Note that it is a short-run relationship, both because all factors of production other than labor are held constant but also because laborers are presumed to be subject to money illusion. In the long run, prices are likely to drop out of equation (3) and therefore out of (4) and (5) as well. That modification produces the vertical long-run supply curve (Figure 10–9). The curve also will shift outward with increases in the supplies of any factor of production.

The aggregate demand curve is derived from the EE and ME curves described in the Appendixes to Chapters 8 and 9. But recall that in Chapter 9 we simplified the ME curve by suppressing the price level in the money demand function. The following linearized approximation to that function incorporates prices directly (cf. equation 1, Appendix to Chapter 9):

$$M^d = -\$56 \text{ billion} + (\$178 \text{ billion})P + .2Y - (\$10 \text{ billion})i. \tag{6}$$

Using equation (6), the ME curve becomes (cf. equation 4, Appendix to Chapter 9)

$$Y = 50B - \$2{,}600 \text{ billion} - (\$890 \text{ billion})P + (\$60 \text{ billion})i. \tag{7}$$

Note that the ME curve shifts when the price level changes. When this curve is combined with the EE curve

$$Y = \$300 \text{ billion} + 3G - (\$10 \text{ billion})i, \tag{8}$$

a solution for income may be obtained in exactly the same way as in the last Appendix (cf. equation 7, Appendix to Chapter 9):

$$Y = 2.57G + 7.14B - (\$127.1 \text{ billion})P - \$114.3 \text{ billion}. \qquad (9)$$

Equation (9) is the aggregate demand (*AD*) curve described in this chapter. It may be combined with the *AS* curve (equation 5) to solve simultaneously for the equilibrium price level and real income.

The multipliers for government spending (*G*) and the monetary base (*B*) appear to have the same values here that we derived before we introduced variations in the price level (equation 7, Appendix to Chapter 9). But observe that any increases in *P* resulting from increases in *G* or *B* will reduce the rise in real income (*Y*). This reduction becomes apparent when we combine equation 5 (*AS*) with equation 9 (*AD*). First computing a linear approximation to the *AS* curve (for $P \cong 1$),

$$Y = 784.4 + 105P. \qquad (5)$$

Solving (5) for *P*,

$$P = \frac{1}{105} Y - \frac{784.4}{105},$$

and plugging this result into equation (9),

$$Y = 2.57G + 7.14B - 127.1 \left(\frac{1}{105} Y - \frac{784.4}{105} \right) - 114.3.$$

Collecting terms,

$$2.21Y = 2.57G + 7.14B + 835.2.$$

Solving for *Y*,

$$Y = 1.12G + 3.23B + \$377.9 \text{ billion}. \qquad (10)$$

This final equation is a general equilibrium equation which may be used to calculate the points of intersection between the *AS* and *AD* curves for various values of *G* and *B*. As suggested in the final section of this chapter, the ability of monetary or fiscal policy to affect real output is not inconsiderable; but, as one can now see by comparing equations (9) and (10), this power is substantially weakened by the inflationary consequences of expansionary policies.

chapter 11

Money and International Finance: The Balance of Payments

11.1 INTRODUCTION

The preceding three chapters have presented a simplified but rather comprehensive set of relationships describing the behavior of the economy under the difficult conditions of the 1970 recession. These relationships can readily be adapted to the description of other—perhaps even more difficult—circumstances such as the inflation of 1973–74. But one phenomenon which cannot be dealt with through this model, because we have so far suppressed it, is that of imbalances in international payments. In practice, international trade and international investment of various types constitute an important economic activity and one which can be influenced by monetary policy more readily than by most other means available to governments. Consequently, monetary policy has a major responsibility in modern economies to keep the financing of international activity in balance; to keep international monetary flows from upsetting the course of domestic economic activity. We shall see in Part Four the ways in which monetary policy accomplishes that task. In this chapter and the next, we set forth a basic framework for viewing international financial relationships.

The recession of 1970, with its rising unemployment and

falling production rates, was clearly the most serious macro-economic problem in the United States that year. But at the same time, we faced an unprecedentedly large outflow of dollars from this country. Through a combination of ordinary business activity and speculation that the dollar was an over-priced currency,[1] foreigners and Americans alike attempted to increase their holdings of other currencies on an enormous scale. Somebody had to end up owning the dollars so disposed of, and the principal bag-holders were the major foreign central banks, who were willing to hold them in order to keep the world economy functioning smoothly. Altogether, about $8 billion flowed out of the United States in 1970. As we explain in more detail below, this massive outflow could not be allowed to continue; there were vague but real limits to the quantity of American money that foreign governments would be prepared to accumulate, and we simply did not have assets of sufficient value to buy them back. So the Federal Reserve had to find some way to reverse the outflow, at the same time that it was worrying about getting out of the trough of the domestic recession.

As may be evident already from this brief introduction, international finance is a highly complex and technical subject, albeit a fascinating topic to anyone attracted to monetary economics. It is not possible for us to deal with its details here.[2] But the essential elements of international finance—the pieces necessary for an understanding of the conduct of monetary policy—are rather simple and straightforward. Unfortunately, the model used above to describe the domestic economy cannot be applied directly to international finance,

---

[1] In the context of international finance, the word *currency* is used to refer to a national unit of account or to assets denominated in it.

[2] Readers wishing a more detailed introduction to international finance should refer to: Robert M. Stern, *The Balance of Payments* (Chicago: Aldine Publishing Company, 1973) and Robert A. Mundell, *International Economics* (New York: The Macmillan Company, 1968).

because now we have to examine purely financial transactions—the exchange of ownership of existing assets—in addition to the production and sale of new goods and services. So a special framework has been developed for summarizing international transactions, known as the "balance of payments accounts" for a country.

11.2 THE BALANCE OF PAYMENTS ACCOUNTS

The balance of payments accounts are a record of all transactions involving an exchange of money between residents of one country (say, the United States) and those of other countries (generally referred to as "the rest of the world"). Each transaction is, in principle, recorded twice: the outflow of dollars (perhaps in payment for a purchase of foreign-made goods) as a minus, and the corresponding inflow (or reflow) of dollars as a plus (as, for example, when the foreign exporter deposits his check in an American bank). So when we add up all the international transactions of dollars over any period of time, the net sum has to be zero by definition. The essence of the accounting technique is to separate transactions into categories. Then by adding up part but not all of these categories, we can derive subtotals that will give us useful information about the development of international economic relationships and about the actual or potential values of various national currencies.

The complete balance of payments accounts for the United States, which are published by the Department of Commerce every three months, recognize more than 30 different kinds of transactions. But we can consolidate most of them, leaving three basic categories: transactions involving currently produced goods and services, other private transactions, and official settlements of imbalances in the first two categories. This simple structure is outlined in Table 11–1.

TABLE 11–1

Structure of the Balance of Payments Accounts

I.	Exchange of goods and services:		
	a.	Exports.....................................	$+a$
	b.	Imports.....................................	$-b$
	c.	Current-account balance......................	$a - b = c$
II.	Private capital flows:		
	d.	Capital inflows (borrowing and investment capital from abroad).........................	$+d$
	e.	Capital outflows (loans to foreigners and foreign investments).........................	$-e$
	f.	Balance of official settlements.................	$c + d - e = f$
III.	Official settlements:		
	g.	Sales of official assets........................	$+g$
	h.	Liability financing (official borrowing from foreign governments and central banks)...	$+h$
			$f + g + h = 0$

11.2.1 The Current Account

The exchange of *goods* across national borders is commonly known as international trade. Companies or individual residents of one country export goods to foreign countries and import other goods from abroad. The difference between the values of exports and imports of goods is called the trade balance and is considered in most countries to be a basic indicator of the competitiveness of the country's economy in international trade.

Services transactions include such items as tourist expenditures in foreign countries and income from foreign investments. Thus when a European family travels in the United States, its expenditures constitute an inflow of dollars, with effects on the balance of payments which are the same as if we had exported goods to Europe. If foreigners own shares of stock in American companies, then the payment of dividends to those foreigners must be recorded in the same manner as an import of goods: it involves a direct payment of dollars to a foreign resident; it generates an outflow of dollars; and it enters the accounts as a minus. So for our purposes, we can lump together these invisible or services transactions and commercial trade in goods; together, they are equivalent to the concept of goods and services which we have used in describing the national income accounts.

The current-account balance (exports less imports) corresponds to the value of net exports described in Chapter 8. The current-account balance is therefore of direct importance to the domestic economy because it is a component of the net national product. A positive (surplus) balance on the current account is a source of income to the country's residents; a deficit is a drain on income. (Note, however, that it is current dollar rather than real flows that are relevant to international finance.) In terms of our model of the economy, changes in the current account balance directly affect the expenditure equilibrium (EE) and aggregate demand (AD) curves. Suppose that there is an increase in foreign demand for goods produced in the United States; the increase in exports raises aggregate demand in the United States in exactly the same manner as an autonomous rise in business investment or in government spending. The EE curve shifts to the right, as does the AD curve. With no change in monetary or fiscal policy, output, prices, and interest rates will all have a tendency to rise (Figure 11–1).

In some countries, swings in the value of the current account balance can be a major source of instability in the economy. These so-called open economies, such as the Scandinavian and some European countries, generally do large volumes of foreign trade relative to their total economic activity. If they are not careful to minimize fluctuations in trade or to offset changes in the current-account balance through appropriate monetary or fiscal policies, they may be subjected to recurring inflationary or recessionary pressures. An increase in exports could force up aggregate demand for goods and services when the economy is already near full

FIGURE 11–1

The Effect of an Increase in Net Foreign Demand (net exports)

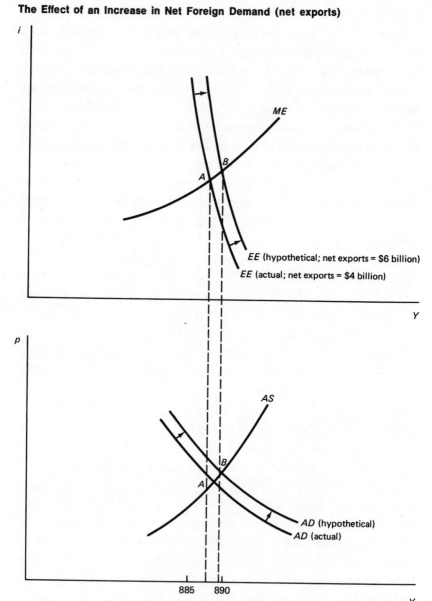

employment and generate an increase in the price level. Under these circumstances, a country may be described as "importing" inflation. Similarly, a decrease in exports could bring unemployment to an economy just as readily as would a drop in government spending. But this source of instability is not particularly important for the United States most of the time. In 1970, only $4 billion of our $890 billion of net national product was from net exports, and the net balance rarely changes by more than $2 billion or $3 billion from one year to the next.

11.2.2 The Capital Account

The capital account of the balance of payments includes a wide variety of types of private capital flows. We might usefully examine three broad categories. First, there is *direct* investment, which is similar in concept to but not quite the same as what is called fixed investment in the domestic accounts. It includes construction or purchases of business firms or of business plant or equipment in foreign countries. When a U.S. company forms a foreign branch or builds a foreign factory, or when a foreigner buys an American factory, that is direct investment. The first example would be recorded as an outflow of dollars (minus), and the second as an inflow (plus). These direct investments are long term in nature and are determined primarily by long-term factors such as labor costs, marketing prospects, and tax laws. The net flow of direct investment does not change dramatically in the short run and in any case cannot be altered very much by monetary policy.

A second category of capital flow consists of long-term *portfolio* transactions, mainly purchases of foreign corporate stocks[3] and of bonds issued by corporations or governments

---

[3] Purchases of large blocks of stocks—sufficient to provide control of ownership in a company—are treated as direct investment. Smaller purchases are regarded as portfolio transactions.

in foreign countries. The effects of these flows of money on the balance of payments are exactly the same as the effects from direct investment. But portfolio transactions are more influenced by relative interest rates. A German or Japanese resident, for example, may decide to purchase American government bonds instead of the securities issued by his own government if their yields are higher. So even though long-term interest rates are relatively sluggish,[4] there is some scope for monetary policy to be used to affect the net flow of dollars through bond and stock purchases.

The most important part of the capital account from the viewpoint of monetary policy is the flow of short-term capital. This item includes bank loans to foreigners, deposits in foreign banks, and short-term securities (i.e., securities maturing in one year or less, such as treasury bills). The net flow of funds of this type responds quickly and strongly to changes in relative interest rates. There are many very large banks and corporations today which regularly do business in several countries. These multinational companies have to maintain bank deposits and other liquid assets in each of a number of currencies, so that they can make payments easily throughout the world. But they also have wide scope for varying the proportions of their liquid assets which they hold in New York or London or Tokyo. By keeping track of the interest rates available on assets in each of the large financial centers and shifting their funds accordingly, they can try to increase their total earnings.

In the open and internationally volatile economic world of the 1970s, the volume of funds that can be shifted across national borders in search of higher interest rates and greater profits is enormous and potentially destabilizing even to an economy the size of the United States. Multinational corporations control trillions of dollars of assets, hundreds of billions

---

[4] See Chapter 16, section 16.4.1.

of which are held in liquid and readily transferable forms. The Federal Reserve and other central banks can influence the placement of these funds through their ability to influence short-term interest rates. But it is important to note that central banks may often find that international capital movements interfere with their domestic policy objectives. Suppose that the Federal Reserve wishes to expand the supply of money in order to stimulate spending and incomes. The M^s curve and the ME curve both shift to the right, and interest rates fall. American and foreign companies and individuals now will have an incentive to sell these assets with the falling yields and perhaps buy higher yielding securities in other countries. If the Federal Reserve is concerned about this outflow of dollars (and we shall see in Chapter 12 what some of the costs to the economy might be), it will have to find some way to resolve the conflict between its domestic and international goals.

11.2.3 Official Settlements

Official settlements are transactions among governments or central banks which are designed to settle imbalances arising from foreign trade or from private capital flows. If Americans were to buy more goods (and services) abroad than foreigners were to buy here, so that our current-account balance were negative; and if this imbalance were not offset by flows of capital into the United States; then foreigners would be accumulating dollars. Individuals and companies abroad usually prefer to hold their own national currencies, so they ultimately exchange the excess dollars at their central bank for the local currency. The dollars then would become official "reserve assets" of that central bank and "official liabilities" of the United States.

There exists a highly complex set of institutional arrangements to handle these official accounts, and we have more to say about them in the next chapter. But the essential element of the process is that the Federal Reserve (acting as the agent of the U.S. government) can settle its accounts in one of two ways, as illustrated above in Table 11-1. When foreign central banks accumulate dollars, they can present them to the Federal Reserve for redemption in exchange for some agreed official asset. Historically, the most commonly used asset for this purpose was gold. But recently, and especially since the early 1960s, accounts have been settled more often in bank balances (demand deposit accounts). If France were to accumulate dollar balances and present them to the Federal Reserve for redemption, we would be able to pay with deposit balances denominated in French francs, British pounds, or some other widely accepted currency instead of gold. This practice has greatly facilitated the settlement of international accounts during the period of rapid growth in world trade since the end of World War II.

A second method, which has become the dominant means of settlement for the United States since 1970, is known as liability financing. This term refers to the practice of arranging for the foreign central bank to let us owe it the funds at some agreed interest rate instead of redeeming the dollars immediately. The foreign central bank simply exchanges its dollar holdings for a special bond issued by the U.S. Treasury. The United States thereby preserves its own assets intact, while the foreign central bank obtains an income-producing asset.

11.3 THE BALANCE OF OFFICIAL SETTLEMENTS

The first two general categories of international transactions—sales of goods and services, and private capital flows—represent all the exchanges of dollars between residents of the United States and residents of other countries. If we add up all such exchanges, we obtain an estimate of the *net* inflow or outflow of dollars during some specific period of time. Then by adding up the official settlements, we can see how this inflow or outflow was financed by the governments involved. Because of the double-entry book-keeping used in these accounts, the settlements must be ex-actly the same amount, but with the opposite sign, as the net flow through the first two categories. If foreigners accumu-late dollars and turn them in to their central bank rather than hold them, then the amount turned in is the same amount that has to be settled in one of the two ways just described. Similarly, if Americans accumulate foreign currencies or de-posits and exchange them at the Federal Reserve banks (through their own commercial banks) for dollars, then that amount of dollars will be settled in some way between the Federal Reserve and foreign central banks.

One of the most revealing ways of analyzing the flow of international payments is to examine what is called the balance of official settlements. We can measure this balance either by adding up the actual settlements or by adding up the transactions in the first two categories (see Table 11–1).[5] In effect, we draw a line between current-account and pri-vate capital flows (above the line) and official settlements (below the line). The sum of all the transactions above the line (which equals the sum below the line) is then called the balance of official settlements. It is this balance which is generally referred to in the financial press as the balance of payments.[6] When the sum is positive, the country is said to

---

[5] In practice, there are many transactions which the Commerce Department is unable to record. In order to make the accounts add up properly, the capital ac-count includes an item called "errors and omissions." Normally, this balancing item is relatively small and can be ignored for most practical purposes. But when the residents of a country are making large transfers of funds to buy foreign short-term securities and the like, a major part of the transfers may be unrecorded. In 1971, almost half of the net short-term capital outflow from the United States (over $10 billion) showed up in "errors and omissions."

[6] There are, however, many other ways of separating transactions, many other points at which one could draw the line. For a review of the various measures of the balance of payments, see Stern, *Balance of Payments*, Chap. 1.

have a surplus on its balance of payments. A negative figure reveals a deficit.

The reason for distinguishing official settlements from other types of international transactions is that an increase in official liabilities or a decrease in official assets is regarded as a fundamentally different kind of plus in the accounts from an increase in private liabilities or a decrease in private assets. The private inflows are presumed to arise because foreigners want to hold more dollars or Americans want to hold a larger portion of their assets at home rather than abroad. But inflows of dollars through official settlements arise because foreigners or Americans do not want to hold dollars. Thus the balance of official settlements is an attempt to measure the extent of the imbalance of private transactions among residents of different countries.

11.4 THE U.S. BALANCE OF PAYMENTS

As shown in Figure 11–2, the relative stability exhibited in the balance of payments for the United States throughout the 1960s has been shattered in the 1970s. In the first eight years, 1960–67, the United States enjoyed a small but predictable surplus in its trade and services accounts, the size of the surplus varying only between $1.8 billion (in 1960) and $5.8 billion (in 1964). The inflow of dollars from this source enabled us to engage in highly profitable direct investment projects around the world and to help finance foreign investment in various ways through short- and long-term security purchases. Each year, this investment activity, representing an outflow of dollars on the capital account, exceeded the inflow through the current account. But this excess resulted at least partly because foreign governments found it to their advantage to increase their official holdings of dollars, so they were willing to add these dollars to their official assets. We thus registered deficits in the official settlements

FIGURE 11–2

U.S. Balance of Payments, 1960–73

$ Billion

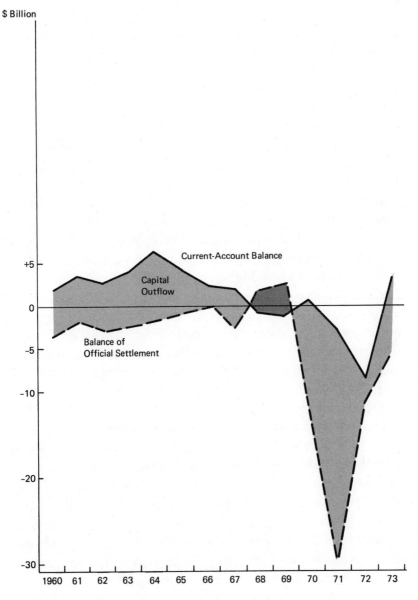

balance every year without encountering serious financing problems.

The next two years, 1968–69, were characterized by a complete reversal of the traditional pattern. Now we had a deficit in the current account but a sizeable net *inflow* of capital, mostly in very short-term forms. We actually registered surpluses in our official settlements in each of those two years, the first surpluses we had had in more than a decade. These surpluses, however, were mainly the result of innovative efforts by U.S. banks to attract foreign capital in the face of a restrictive U.S. monetary policy,[7] and did not reflect any underlying strength in our foreign competitive position.

Then in 1970 the problem worsened dramatically, and we have not yet fully recovered (as of mid-1974). Short-term interest rates fell sharply in the United States that year, providing encouragement to banks, companies, and individuals in this country to buy higher yielding foreign securities. The Federal Reserve, as we have noted throughout these past few chapters, was trying to combat a serious drop in spending and income by making money more freely available at lower interest rates. But the current account of the balance of payments was not strong enough to offset the ensuing capital outflows, and the official settlements balance swung into an unprecedentedly large deficit.

One problem with balance of payments deficits is that they feed on themselves. When the 1970 deficit was followed by a further weakening of the trade balance in early 1971, the market began to feel more and more that the value of the dollar relative to other currencies was bound to fall. At that point, the desire to get rid of dollars in favor of currencies expected to rise in value (most notably German marks) became overwhelming. For the whole year 1971, we had the largest current-account deficit in our history (just over $3 billion), and an almost unbelievable $30 billion deficit on

[7] This innovation, known as the Euro-dollar market, is discussed in section 11.5.3.

official settlements. Since then, matters have improved somewhat, largely because of actions taken by the United States and other governments to improve our competitive position. But the dollar clearly is no longer the darling currency it once was. Essentially, we failed from 1964 through 1972 to promote export growth sufficiently to keep pace with the rapid growth in our imports of goods and services from other countries (notice the downward trend in the current account during those years, in Figure 11–2). Eventually investors decided that other currencies were better values, and the desire to hold dollars virtually vanished.

11.5 SOME SAMPLE TYPES OF INTERNATIONAL TRANSACTIONS

One feature of international transactions which is not brought out very clearly in the summary balance of payments accounts is the interlinkage among entries in the various items. It might appear that imports of goods and inflows of capital are unrelated, whereas in fact they are intimately bound together. A few examples may illustrate this point.

11.5.1 Merchandise Exports

Suppose that a British retailer imports $100,000 worth of ballpoint pens from an American manufacturer for resale in England. This transaction is fairly straightforward and is not much different from the sale of a similar amount of pens to a New York buyer. But there are some complications regarding the method of payment. The British firm probably does most of its business in England, and it therefore is likely to keep its own cash balances in the English currency, known as the pound sterling or simply the pound (£). That is, the company maintains a checking account at a London bank, the balance in which is specified in terms of pounds. But the American company may well require payment in terms of dollars, since that is the most convenient form of cash in this country (have you ever tried to buy lunch in Chicago with an English pound note?). So the British buyer has to exchange pounds for dollars before he can pay for the pens.

The simplest way to make this exchange is to use the London bank as an intermediary. The major banks in each country's principal financial centers—London, New York, Paris, Frankfurt—keep portions of their assets in foreign currency balances. Thus a London bank will have a checking account at a New York bank, and vice versa. Each such bank knows at any time what the going price is for each foreign currency in terms of the domestic currency, a price that is known as an *exchange rate* between the two currencies.[8] If the price of a dollar in London happens to be 40 pence (0.40 pounds), then the importer can request his banker to write a check to the American company for $100,000 and to deduct £40,000 from his account.

This transaction by itself generates a surplus in the U.S. *trade* balance, but it has no immediate effect on the balance of payments. There is an inflow of dollars through the current account, but there is a simultaneous outflow of what we have called short-term capital; the form of this outflow is initially just a reduction in foreign-owned U.S. bank accounts:

New York Banks		London Bank	
	Deposit account of American exporter + $100,000 Deposit account of London bank −$100,000	Deposit in N.Y. bank −$100,000	Deposit of British company − £40,000

U.S. Balance of Payments

Exports...........................	+$100,000
Current-account balance..............	+$100,000
Short-term capital (liabilities to foreigners).......................	− 100,000
Balance of official settlements.........	—

[8] Exchange rates are discussed more fully in Chapter 12.

There may now occur a secondary transaction affecting the balance of payments. Recall that the London bank has depleted its holdings of dollars (i.e., has run down the balance in its New York bank account) by $100,000. If the bank wants to replenish its balance, it will have to buy the dollars somewhere. There are two possibilities. If it can find another bank or a dealer in foreign currencies willing to reduce its dollar balances at the going price, then the two parties can just work out a sale. The ownership of dollars will change, but there will still be no net change in the voluntary ownership of dollars by foreigners and no effect on the U.S. balance of payments. The second alternative is that the British central bank, the Bank of England, may step in to sell dollars to the London bank, particularly if the latter has trouble finding the dollars in the open market. In that case, the U.S. *official* liabilities will fall. The Bank of England will decrease its deposit account at the Federal Reserve Bank of New York, the London bank will replenish its own dollar balance, and the United States will have a surplus in the balance of payments as well as in the balance of trade.

An important side effect of this surplus is that it directly increases bank reserves in the United States (and decreases assets in the other country). Unless the Federal Reserve takes offsetting action such as an open market sale of securities, there will follow an expansion of the supply of money. Imbalances in international payments constitute one of the major short-run determinants of changes in bank reserves which have to be monitored and countered by the Federal Reserve.[9]

Federal Reserve Bank		Bank of England
	Deposits of foreign central banks −$100,000 Reserve deposits +$100,000	Deposit in Federal Reserve Bank −$100,000° * $1 = £0.40.	Deposits of banks − £ 40,000

[9] See Chapter 5 for a more thorough discussion of this point.

New York Banks		London Banks	
Reserves +$100,000	Deposit account of American ex- porter +$100,000	Deposits at Bank of England − £ 40,000	Deposit account of importer − £ 40,000

U.S. Balance of Payments

Exports........................... +$100,000
Current-account balance.............. +$100,000
Private capital accounts..............   —
Balance of official settlements......... +$100,000
Official liabilities....................   − 100,000

11.5.2 Merchandise Imports

Suppose, as a second example, that an American retailing chain buys $100,000 worth of German cameras for resale in the United States. The company pays for the cameras in dollars by writing a check on the New York bank. Now the alert reader will spot an asymmetry between this case and the previous one. Most international trade, as implied in the first example, is settled in the domestic currency of the seller (the exporter). The major exception concerns the dollar, which, because it is such a widely circulated and internationally accepted medium of exchange, is often (certainly not always, but often) used for payment to sellers in other countries.[10] Furthermore, it is not unreasonable for us to assume that the German company is willing to accept and hold onto the dollars, because it may be doing a large volume of business here and probably maintains a bank account of its own in New York. So the German exporter simply deposits the dollar check in his account. There is thus a current-

---

[10] On occasion dollars may even be used in payment between two parties neither of which is located in the United States. For example, a Brazilian company selling coffee in Japan may be quite happy to receive payment in dollars (which it can readily use in payment for other international transactions) rather than in Japanese yen (which the Brazilian company does not want because yen are less readily negotiable) or in Brazilian cruzeiros (which the Japanese importer may find expensive to acquire in Japan).

account outflow (an import) and a short-term capital inflow, with no effect on the balance of payments.

New York Banks

	Deposit account of American importer −$100,000
	Deposit account of German exporter +$100,000

U.S. Balance of Payments

Exports............................	—
Imports............................	+$100,000
Current account balance.............	−$100,000
Short-term capital..................	+ 100,000
Balance of official settlements.........	—

Up to this point, the import is exactly the mirror image of the export. But the significance of the central role of the dollar in international finance is that the process is now more likely to stop right here; that is, trade deficits for the United States are quite likely to lead to voluntary capital inflows if foreigners are willing to hold the dollars they receive. In fact, foreign ownership of dollars has increased at least tenfold in the past ten years. On the other hand, deficits of other countries (which correspond to surpluses here) are less likely to induce American firms to hold correspondingly higher quantities of foreign currencies.

11.5.3 Pure Capital Flows

Not all international capital flows are associated with the exchange of goods and services. In fact, a major portion of such flows arises because individuals and companies with liquid assets can find higher interest rates, dividends, or other income in countries other than their own. Suppose, for example, that the financial officer of a Dutch oil company is looking for a 90-day asset with a high yield in order to gener-

ate some profit on a short-term excess cash position of, say,
250,000 Dutch guilders. He might find that excellent returns
are being offered on certificates of deposit (CDs) denominated in dollars and issued by banks in New York. Even if
the company's assets are all in Dutch guilders and other
European currencies, the officer can still buy the dollar assets.
He requests his Amsterdam banker to write a draft (a check)
in dollars and to deduct the corresponding amount of guilders from his account. If the price of a dollar in Amsterdam is
2½ guilders, then the company can buy a $100,000 CD.
The transactions will be as follows:

New York Banks		Amsterdam Bank	
	Deposits of Dutch banks −$100,000 Deposit (CDs) of Dutch company +$100,000	Deposit in New York bank −$100,000	Deposit account of Dutch company −250,000 guilders

So far, there are no balance of payments effects at all. The
Dutch bank has given up dollar assets, and the Dutch company has taken them over. But now the bank may wish to
restore its original holdings of dollars. As before, this process
may continue within the private markets for foreign currencies, in which case ownership of the same amount of dollars
just keeps changing hands. But if the Dutch central bank
(the Netherlands Bank) helps to supply the dollars, then the
official accounts will be directly affected. The final impact on
the balance of payments will then be a surplus, with no
change at all in the current or trade account.

Federal Reserve Bank		Netherlands Bank	
	Deposit of foreign central banks −$100,000 Bank reserve deposits +$100,000	Deposit at New York Federal Reserve Bank −$100,000	Deposit account of banks −250,000 guilders

New York Banks		Amsterdam Banks	
Reserves +$100,000	Deposits (CDs) +$100,000	Deposit at central bank −250,000 guilders	Deposit −250,000 guilders

U.S. Balance of Payments

Private capital...................... +$100,000
Balance of official settlements......... +$100,000
Official liabilities.................... − 100,000

One problem with the type of capital inflow just described is that it is a complex process for the foreign company, which has to acquire dollars and then hold its assets in a distant bank. In response to the demand for a simpler and more efficient system of international transfers of short-term funds, there has emerged a market structure known as the Euro-currency market. This system, of which the Euro-*dollar* market is by far the largest part, consists of bank deposits and loans which are denominated in a currency other than the domestic currency where the deposit or loan is made. Euro-dollar deposits are bank deposits in Europe or elsewhere in the world (but not in the United States) which are denominated in dollars. These deposits typically are interest-bearing with yields very close to those available on CDs in New York. In fact, many of the largest banks participating in the Euro-dollar market are branch offices of major American banks.

The Euro-dollar market greatly facilitates the type of transaction just described. Now the Dutch company calls the Amsterdam branch of a New York bank and inquires about interest rates on large, 90-day Euro-dollar deposits. If the rate is favorable, an ordinary check on the Amsterdam bank payable to the American bank will complete the transfer of funds from guilders into dollars. The Dutch company obtains an asset (the Euro-dollar deposit) redeemable in

Amsterdam rather than in New York, so that it has much less
inconvenience to overcome than in the preceding (CD) case.

So long as the Amsterdam office of the New York bank
holds its assets in Europe (perhaps by making loans of dollars to European companies), there will be no direct capital
inflow to the United States. But one important use of the
Euro-dollar market is for the European branches of American
banks to channel deposit funds back to their home offices. In
our example, the Amsterdam branch has a new deposit of
$100,000. Typically it has no reserve requirement on that
deposit, since it is not a regular part of the Dutch banking
system. So it can transfer the whole amount to the United
States by lending the funds to the home office. The balance
of payments effects now are the same as if the Dutch company had bought a certificate of deposit in New York.

New York Bank		Amsterdam Branch of New York Bank	
Reserves +$100,000	Liabilities to foreign branches +$100,000	Loans to home office +$100,000	Euro-dollar deposits +$100,000

Amsterdam Bank	
Deposits at central bank −250,000 guilders	Deposits −250,000 guilders

11.6 CONCLUSIONS: EQUILIBRIUM IN THE BALANCE OF PAYMENTS

The balance of payments accounts are structured so that
the actual values of inflows and outflows will have to be
equal over any period of time. But there is no guarantee that
equilibrium will necessarily be attained at all times, in the
sense that the quantities of dollars which foreigners desire
to add to their assets would be exactly equal to the quantity
which American residents would be willing to supply. If this
distinction sounds familiar, that is because it is completely

analogous to the distinction between actual equality of saving and investment flows and equilibrium between planned values.[11] Saving and investment are defined in the national income accounts so as to be identically equal. But the desired values of those categories are independently determined and will be equal only at an equilibrium value of income. If necessary, incomes will change in order to bring about such an equality.

The equilibrating mechanism for inflows and outflows of currencies is the price (the exchange rate) which is offered in the market for foreign currencies (the foreign exchange market). If foreigners desire to hold more dollars than is supplied freely by U.S. residents who are purchasing other currencies, then one of two things must happen. Either the U.S. government, through the Federal Reserve System, will have to supply the extra dollars by purchasing foreign currencies (thus adding to our official reserve assets and creating a surplus in the balance of payments); or the price of dollars will have to rise in the marketplace in order to restore equilibrium. But the existence of this choice raises some fundamental questions. First, just how is the price of the dollar determined?[12] And second, what are the considerations on which governments decide whether to let their currency values be determined in the marketplace or to intervene through official settlements? These issues are our central concern in the next chapter.

REVIEW QUESTIONS

1. When the Soviet Union buys wheat from American exporters and borrows the necessary funds from a New York bank to make the

---

[11] See Chapter 8, section 8.3.

[12] Caution! The price of the dollar in the market for foreign currencies is quite different from, and should not be confused with, the value of the dollar in purchasing domestic goods and services. The latter has to do with the general level of prices; the current subject is the foreign exchange rate of the dollar.

payment, what effects are there on the U.S.'s current balance, capital account, and balance of payments? When the loan eventually is repaid (say, in the following year), what effects will there be in that time period?

2. When the price of oil was raised by foreign producers, how would the major components of the U.S. balance of payments have been affected under each of the following assumptions: (*a*) the oil exporters spent all of the increased proceeds on American goods; (*b*) the oil exporters placed all of the increased proceeds in U.S. Treasury securities; and (*c*) the oil exporters placed all of the increased proceeds in Swiss bank accounts, and the Swiss central bank ultimately presented the accumulated dollars to the Federal Reserve Bank of New York for conversion into Swiss francs?

3. What effects would each of the transactions described above have had on the stock of money and the level of interest rates in the United States? (Hint: Work out the effects of each part of the transactions on the balance sheets of *all* of the parties involved, and then add up the total effects.)

SUGGESTED FURTHER READING

Department of Commerce. *Survey of Current Business*. Washington, D.C., monthly (balance of payments statistics and explanatory articles appear at three-month intervals).

Report of the Review Committee for Balance of Payments Statistics. *The Balance of Payments Statistics of the United States: A Review and Appraisal*. Bureau of the Budget. Washington, D.C.: April 1965.

Stern, Robert M. *The Balance of Payments: Theory and Economic Policy*, new ed. Chicago: Aldine, 1973.

chapter 12

Money and International Finance: Exchange Rates

12.1   INTRODUCTION

Money is a national phenomenon. Like the flag and the uniform of the soldier, it symbolizes and identifies its country. The monetary unit in the United States is the dollar, a word which perhaps even more clearly than the phrase "stars and stripes" is unfortunately the overseas trademark of American culture. The unit of account in the United Kingdom is the pound sterling (£). In France it is the franc, in West Germany the deutschemark (German mark), in Russia the ruble. Within each country, prices of goods and services are quoted in terms of this domestic unit of account, and the residents of the country tend to think of relative values in terms of that accounting unit. Correspondingly, the medium of exchange is unique to each country. The supply of dollars is controlled by the Federal Reserve System; the supply of pounds by the Bank of England. As a rule, those currencies are used in exchange only in the countries where they are issued. It is this strongly nationalistic and segmented nature of money that leads to the importance of international finance; if goods and services are to be traded across national boundaries, then some means must be found for linking together the national monetary systems into an international payments mechanism.

12.2 EXCHANGE RATES AND THE MARKET FOR CURRENCIES

The means for linking together national units of account is the exchange rate: the price of one currency expressed in terms of another. Exchange rates provide the missing piece in the puzzle of prices quoted in foreign countries. For example, the price of a hotel room in the London Hilton could be quoted at £15 per night, while the price of a similar room at the New York Hilton might be $30. These prices are precise enough to an Englishman from Manchester planning a trip to London or to a Philadelphian preparing to spend a weekend in New York. But by themselves they are useless to the American flying to London or the Englishman about to sail to New York. These travelers normally carry money expressed in their own currency units, and they are accustomed to thinking in those units. So the American will have to know exactly how many pounds sterling he can buy with his dollars, and the Englishman will want to know the price of dollars in pounds. In other words, they both have to know the exchange rate between pounds and dollars in order to translate the foreign price into terms meaningful to them.

Now it happens that since 1967 the pound has been selling at prices generally close to $2.40. This exchange rate implies simply that most of the time Americans have had to pay around $2.40 for each pound they have wanted to buy, while in Britain one has had to pay about 42 pence (0.42 pounds) for each dollar($1/2.40 \simeq 0.42$). At that price, the Englishman knows that his hotel room in New York will cost him twelve pounds fifty. Our Philadelphian going to London can calculate the cost of his hotel accommodations at $36 per day.

12.2.1 The Foreign Exchange Market

Just as the exchange rate is the link between units of account, there exists a foreign exchange *market* which connects the various media of exchange. It obviously would not help very much for there to be exchange rates if there were no system for buying and selling foreign currencies; indeed, the existence of exchange rates implies the existence of such a market.

The foreign exchange market consists of groups of banks and specialized dealers in the major financial centers around the world. Whenever anyone wants to buy foreign currency, he can go directly to any bank. If he goes to a smaller bank which cannot afford to keep foreign currencies on hand and does not maintain bank deposits in foreign countries, the bank will function as an intermediary by acquiring the funds from a larger bank which does deal in foreign exchange. Those banks in turn acquire balances of various currencies by buying them from people and corporations wanting to sell them. And there are times, as we noted in Chapter 11, when the national *central* banks will step in to help supply or absorb particular currencies in order to stabilize exchange rates. We therefore can think of the foreign exchange market as consisting primarily of the major private banks in each country, backed up by the central banks which *intervene* in the market from time to time.

12.2.2 Demand and Supply for Foreign Currencies

Prices in the markets for foreign exchange are determined by the forces of supply and demand in exactly the same way as domestic prices of goods and services. But there are some unusual wrinkles in this market which we should keep in mind. First, we are dealing with two units of account in each transaction, so that we have to be careful about how we quote prices. By the dollar exchange rate, we shall mean the amount of a foreign currency which $1 will buy. An increase or appreciation in the dollar exchange rate (also called a "revaluation") therefore implies that the value of the dollar in foreign trade and finance has gone up; a decrease (called a "depreciation" or "devaluation")[1] implies a drop in foreign purchasing power. There are in practice as many as 100 dollar exchange rates, one against each different currency unit.[2] The dollar exchange rate against the pound, then, would be about 42 pence. Similarly, the pound exchange rate against the dollar would be $2.40. An increase in the dollar exchange rate to 50 pence would imply a decrease in the pound rate to $2.00. For convenience, we shall use the dollar as our basic unit of account and shall quote exchange rates wherever possible in terms of dollar rates.

An interesting implication of this duality of exchange rates is that a demand for one currency requires that there be a supply of equal value of some other currency. If dollars and pounds were the only currencies being traded, then dollars would be supplied in search of pounds, and pounds would be supplied in search of dollars. And a final wrinkle is that the demand for currencies is at least partly a *derived* demand. People demand dollars not because they enjoy having them rather than some other currency but because they are planning to buy goods from American companies and will have to pay in dollars. An export of American goods implies that foreigners are buying dollars in order to buy our goods. An inflow of capital implies that foreigners are buying dollars to buy our assets. Similarly, when we import goods or travel abroad, we normally must first acquire foreign currencies. An outflow of capital also requires a prior purchase in the foreign exchange market.

Like that of any other good, the quantity of dollars which

---

[1] Normally the terms devaluation and revaluation are applied to changes in official parities; appreciation or depreciation refer more generally to exchange rate movements.

[2] It also is possible to calculate an *effective* exchange rate. The effective dollar exchange rate would be an index number expressing a weighted average value of the dollar against all other major currencies. When no single foreign currency is mentioned, we shall have in mind this sort of exchange rate.

will be demanded and supplied in the foreign exchange market will be a function of its price. A rise in the dollar exchange rate will increase the supply and decrease the demand for dollars. But the linkages by which this process works are somewhat more involved than for most other markets, thanks to the wrinkles we have just described. For the sake of simplicity, let us momentarily assume away international capital movements. Then all transactions in foreign exchange markets will be associated directly with trade in goods and services. In fact, under that assumption, there would be an exact correspondence between our exports and the demand for dollars, on the one hand, and our imports and the supply of dollars, on the other.

Suppose, on that assumption, that the exchange rate between British pounds and the U.S. dollar is initially 40 pence per dollar ($2.50 per pound sterling) and that at that rate corporations and individuals in the United States desire to import $476 million of British goods. They first must buy £190 million (i.e., $476 million × 0.40) through their banks, since the British exporters will demand payment in their own domestic currency.[3] We therefore can say, on the basis of this information, that at a dollar exchange rate of 40 pence there exists a demand for £190 million and a supply of $476 million.

What would happen to these quantities demanded and supplied if the exchange rate were higher, say 44 pence ($2.27 per pound sterling)? It would now be cheaper to buy British goods in the United States. A £1,000 English automobile which had sold here for $2,500 could now be offered for $2,270. Americans then would normally buy a larger

---

[3] In practice, companies may be able to bypass the foreign exchange market by settling all transactions in dollars; in effect, by making the dollar into an international currency. See Chapter 11, section 11.3.3 for a description of this practice.

quantity of them. However, there is no reason a priori for us to expect the dollar value of purchases of British goods to rise, because the amount spent on each purchase will be smaller. In technical terms, the result depends on the price elasticity of the demand for imported goods. An elasticity greater than unity would imply that a 10 percent price cut (from the rise in the value of the dollar) would induce an increase in the volume of purchases by more than 10 percent. In that case, the supply of dollars in foreign exchange markets would rise in response to a rise in the dollar exchange rate. A less-than-unitary elasticity would produce the opposite result. In practice, there is no reason to expect one result or the other to hold in all or even most circumstances, though in the very short run (the time period within a few months of a change in the exchange rate) elasticities may be small. In the absence of clear evidence, we shall here assume that all price elasticities are around unity.

In this case the change in the dollar exchange rate does not affect the supply of dollars to the foreign exchange market. If the prices of imported goods fall 10 percent, we just buy 10 percent more goods and spend the same amount of dollars. Nonetheless, our demand for pounds (the foreign currency) does rise, since the price of British goods in pounds is assumed not to change. These effects are shown in Table 12–1 and are illustrated in Figure 12–1.

At the same time, the change in the dollar exchange rate also affects the demand for dollars. Just as it is cheaper for Americans to buy British goods, it is correspondingly more expensive for the English to buy American goods. If General Motors is to get the same return in dollars for the car it was selling in the United Kingdom at £1,000, it will now have to raise the price to £1,100. If we again assume unitary price elasticity of demand, British customers will reduce their purchases of our goods (and consequently their purchases of dollars) by approximately 10 percent. But regardless of the

TABLE 12–1

Supplies and Demands for Currencies

£/$	(millions) U.S. Imports (supply of $)		U.K. Exports (demand for £)	$/£	(millions) U.K. Imports (supply of £)		U.S. Exports (demand for $)
0.40	×	$476	= £190	2.50	×	£200	= $500
0.42		476	200	2.38		200	476
0.44		476	209	2.27		200	454

exact elasticity, the demand for dollars should vary inversely with the price of the dollar in the foreign exchange market (Figure 12–1).

12.2.3 Determination of Exchange Rates

Prices in the foreign exchange market are set directly by the banks and other dealers who make up the market. These dealers are operating continuously on both sides of the market, buying and selling dollars and buying and selling German marks every day. They profit from the activity by charging slightly higher prices when they sell than those at which they buy. Their objective, then, is not to accumulate or to get rid of their holdings of currencies but rather to stabilize their portfolios in order to minimize the cost of doing business. If they initially set the price for dollars too high, they will find the incoming supply to be greater than the demand; in their own interest, they will cut the price. In this way, equilibrium is reached in the foreign exchange market. According to the diagram, the exchange rate between the pound and the dollar should settle around 42 pence per dollar ($2.38 per pound sterling). A rate of 44 pence to the dollar would be too high and would cause dollars to accumulate at the banks; a price of 40 pence would generate an accumulation of British pounds.

The foreign exchange market is one which tends to be

FIGURE 12–1

Equilibrium in the Foreign Exchange Market

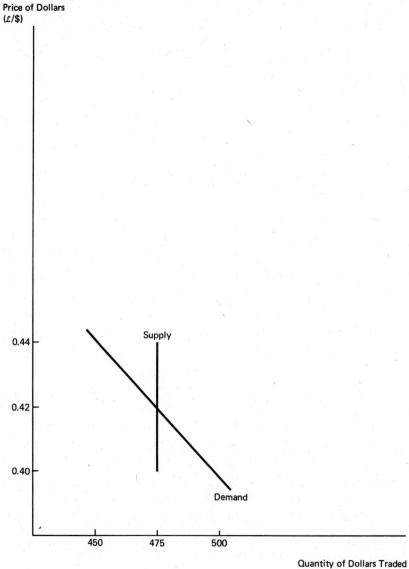

Price of Dollars
(£/$)

Supply

0.44

0.42

0.40

Demand

450   475   500

Quantity of Dollars Traded
(millions)

equilibrated very quickly. There are a large number of companies, banks, and individuals who keep track of movements in exchange rates on a daily and even hourly basis. If the price of dollars in Frankfurt is lower than it is in Paris at 10:00 in the morning, traders will quickly swarm to buy dollars in Frankfurt and sell them in Paris. The gap will be closed long before lunch.

Exchange rates nonetheless are often volatile, shifting much more than could be explained by changes in the underlying demands for imports from the countries involved. The actual course for the pound exchange rate against the dollar in 1973 is shown in Figure 12–2. During that time, trade between the United States and Great Britain was fairly stable and generally followed the patterns of earlier years. And yet the exchange rate fluctuated substantially throughout the year, falling by 9 percent between January and early July, and rising by more than 12 percent by the end of the year.[4] The reason for this discrepancy is that the demand and supply curves for each currency are affected by several factors, of which the requirements of foreign trade are important but not controlling.

One major influence on relative currency demands is the rate of interest prevailing in each country. As we noted earlier in our discussion of international capital flows, investors—particularly large multinational companies—will respond to disparities among yields on similar assets in various countries by shifting their funds in the direction of the higher rates. These shifts require currency purchases in the foreign exchange market and cause the demand and supply curves to shift. In 1973, for example, interest rates in London on bank time deposits and other highly liquid assets were generally

---

[4] One of the authors of this book retains painful memories of that episode of fluctuating exchange rates. Living in London but receiving his income in dollars from January through June, he saw the purchasing power of his salary decline by 9 percent in just six months.

FIGURE 12–2

Exchange Rate between Dollars and Pounds Sterling, 1973 (weekly)

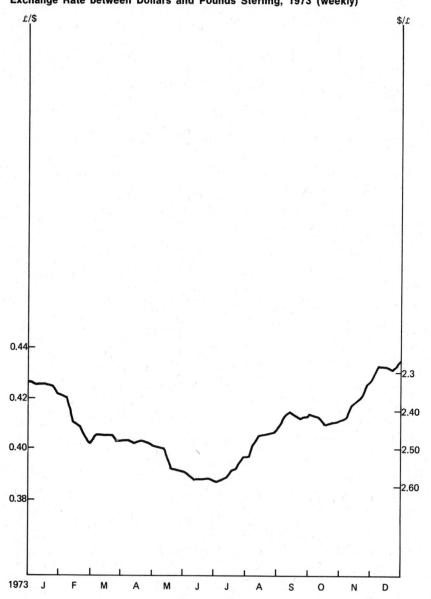

well above those on similar assets in New York, though U.S. rates did catch up partially around mid-year. The relatively high British rates probably contributed to the downward pressure on the dollar early in the year, and the later rise in U.S. rates certainly helped turn the picture around in the second half.

Countries with interest rates that are high relative to those of other countries, therefore, may expect to see their currencies increase in value, given the other influences on exchange rates. In terms of our diagram, a rise in U.S. interest rates would increase the demand for dollars by foreigners and simultaneously decrease the supply of dollars by Americans who would otherwise be buying foreign assets. Both shifts operate to drive up the exchange rate of the dollar (Figure 12–3).

A final market influence on exchange rates is the powerful role of expectations. To a great degree in the short run, exchange rates rise or fall because they are *expected* to rise or fall. Any news that leads investors and currency traders to believe that a particular currency is soon going to increase in value will quickly induce a shift into that currency and out of others. Consequently, its price will rise. Eventually, if the news that generated the shifts proves to be untrue or of feeble effect, the market participants probably will go back to their former preferences. The demand and supply curves will shift back, and the former alignment of exchange rates will be approximately restored. The extent of this type of purely speculative activity is practically impossible to identify, but it is generally regarded as the main explanation of most exchange-rate movements which cannot reasonably be attributed to foreign trade developments or to changes in relative interest rates. It certainly was an important factor behind the gyrations in the pound/dollar rate shown in Figure 12–2.

In summary, exchange rates are determined by the equi-

FIGURE 12–3

Effect of a Rise in U.S. Interest Rates on the Value of the Dollar

Exchange Rate
(£/$)

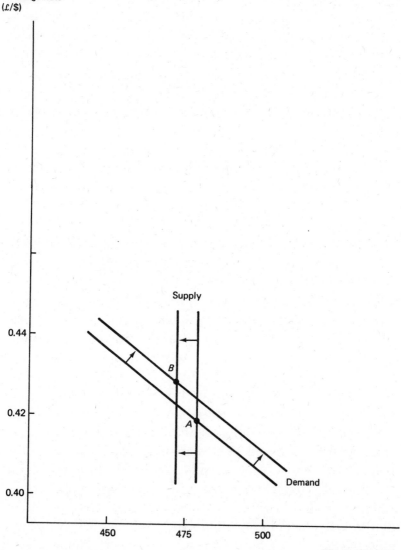

Quantity Traded
(millions of dollars)

libration of the demand for and supply of each currency in the foreign exchange market. These demands and supplies in turn are influenced by three major market factors. First, currency demands arise as a derived demand related to foreign trade; purchases of a country's goods and services by non-residents require that the buyers first purchase the appropriate currency. Second, currency demands may arise because investors wish to purchase assets denominated in foreign currencies. And probably the most important determinant of such activity is the international pattern of interest rates. High interest rates attract inflows of capital and generate demands for the country's currency. Third, currency demands may be purely speculative as investors attempt to acquire currencies which are likely to rise in value. Whenever exchange rates suddenly become unstable, this type of speculation is probably the culprit; during more normal times, speculative activity serves merely to accelerate exchange rate changes which would occur anyway.

12.3 EFFECTS OF EXCHANGE RATE CHANGES

The market forces described in the previous section are not the only determinants of exchange rates. Governments and central banks also take an interest in the foreign exchange market and often directly intervene in the market by buying or selling currencies in order to influence the prevailing rates. What may seem odd at first is that sometimes a central bank may intervene in support of its own currency in order to prop up its value, and at other times it may intervene in order to *prevent* the exchange rate from rising. If we wish to understand the role of monetary policy in the foreign exchange market, we must first examine the economic and political effects of increases and decreases in the foreign exchange rates.

12.3.1 The Trade Balance

The most important effects are those on the balance of foreign trade in goods and services. These effects, however, are often capricious and perverse. Suppose that the United States has a deficit in its current account which it would like to eliminate. A possible solution is to allow the dollar's exchange rate to fall (i.e., to devalue). That fall will make foreign goods more expensive, and the quantity of imports should therefore decline. At the same time, foreigners will be able to acquire dollars, and thereby our goods, more cheaply; so the quantity of exports should rise. Without question, the real value of the trade balance will rise.

The value of the trade balance in dollars, however, is the value which is relevant for currency flows. And here the effects are much less certain. The devaluation will induce us to buy fewer imported goods, but we shall have to pay more dollars to get them. If our price elasticity of demand for imported goods is low enough (less than unity in the simplest case), the dollar value of our imports will actually rise. And if the foreign price elasticity of demand for our goods is also very low, imports could rise by more than exports; in that case, the dollar value of the trade balance would decrease rather than increase as expected.[5]

The practical implication of this possibility is that exchange rate changes may take a long time to bring about the desired effects on the current-account balance. Short-run price elasticities are always smaller than long-run elasticities because consumers take time to adjust spending patterns fully when

---

[5] In a simple model, one can show that the perverse effect will occur whenever the sum of the two elasticities—our demand for imports and foreign demand for our exports—is less than unity. But in practice this rule, known as the "Marshall-Lerner" condition after the economists who first explained it, is subject to considerable modification. For a more complete explanation, see Charles P. Kindleberger, *International Economics*, 5th ed. (Richard D. Irwin, Inc., Homewood, Ill.: 1973).

prices change. Furthermore, exchange rate movements may not be fully passed on to consumers in the short run, particularly when price decreases would be required. Devaluations thus are unlikely to discourage imports very quickly (people keep on buying the more expensive products, at least for a while), nor are they very quick in encouraging exports (exporters may not proportionally reduce their foreign-currency prices). In the longer run, however, devaluations should improve the trade balance.

A good example of this process is provided by the devaluation of the dollar in December 1971. As is shown in Figure 11–2 (Chapter 11), this devaluation was followed by a sharp deterioration of an already weak current account for the year 1972. But by the following year, a dramatic turnaround had occurred. The United States had greatly improved its international competitive position by making its currency about 10 percent less expensive to acquire and by making it correspondingly more expensive for Americans to buy foreign currencies. But a year or so was required before that improved position could be translated into a higher net sales balance vis-à-vis the rest of the world.

12.3.2   The Terms of Trade

Lest we get too involved in our concern over the balance of trade, we should remember that the exchange rate also governs our ability to buy goods and services from foreigners. A rise in the exchange rate has the very beneficial effect of reducing the cost of acquiring foreign currencies and—indirectly—of acquiring imported goods. Foreign travel becomes less expensive and a lot more fun. It is only a slight oversimplification to conclude that devaluations are good for business and for increasing income levels, but that revaluations are good for consumers and for getting the most mileage out of a given income.

12.3.3   Inflation

Because of the asymmetry of price changes—increases meeting less resistance than decreases—exchange rate movements may have a generally inflationary bias. As described in the last few paragraphs, devaluations should in theory increase import prices, while revaluations should correspondingly decrease them. Since every devaluation of one currency implies an equal revaluation of another, there is no necessary impact on the total world price level. One country's inflation could in theory be matched by another country's deflation. But the world does not operate quite so smoothly. Exporters in the devaluing country are less likely to cut prices than importers are to raise prices. For example, when the Italian lira falls in value relative to the German mark, all of the major German automobile manufacturers are going to try to maintain their auto prices at their initial levels *in marks*. The prices in terms of lira thus will have to rise. At the same time, the Italian companies will be able to continue to sell cars in Germany at close to the original prices, pocketing the higher receipts of lira as additional profits.[6] Some price cuts may occur, but the inflationary effects will be pretty predictable.

12.3.4   Interest Rates

There is no clear relationship between observed movements in exchange rates and the pattern of interest rates. What can be important, however, is the effect on interest rates of exchange rates which the market believes to be out of balance. If the dollar were considered to be too high and therefore likely to fall, investors would normally start to sell dollar assets in favor of other currencies. By selling, for example, U.S. government bonds, they would tend to drive up interest rates on those assets. By purchasing similar bonds in another

---

[6] There are limits to this rip-off. If a large enough discrepancy arises between the prices of the same Italian car in Turin and in Munich, people living in Munich can always buy lira themselves and go to Turin to pick up their cars.

country, they would exert some downward pressure on rates in that market. It therefore is of some advantage to central banks if exchange rates freely and quickly adjust to any changes in supply or demand. For exchange rates to be out of equilibrium will interfere with the efforts of the Federal Reserve or the Bank of England to stabilize and control their own interest rates independently of international economic developments. Correlatively, central bankers who wish to use monetary policy to influence exchange rates would be very lucky indeed if the effects of that policy on interest rates were consistent with the effects they would have desired for purely internal purposes such as encouraging business investment spending.

12.3.5 Politics

There is no small degree of chauvinism at work in the management of exchange rates by governments. Declines in exchange rates often have been viewed politically as indicative of national defeat, of a failure to keep pace with the rest of the world. In a sense, of course, this view is well based. Persistent declines often are the result of a slow rate of productivity growth or a high rate of price inflation, either of which would imply a decline in the country's ability to compete in the international trading of goods and services. On the other hand, the ensuing devaluation of the exchange rate is an integral part of the cure for that problem. Imports become more expensive, exports become cheaper to foreigners. Eventually, the suffering country will again become a formidable competitor if its exchange rate falls far enough. Pride in this case does not precede but prevents the fall.

12.4 FIXED EXCHANGE RATES

There are advantages, then, to devaluations under some circumstances and to revaluations under others. But the exchange rate for a single currency is not determined in a vacuum; as we have noted above, every devaluation is mirrored in a revaluation of one or more other currencies. Governments which would like to engineer their exchange rates upward or downward have to rely on the cooperation of their foreign counterparts. If every government were to attempt to devalue (or to revalue) simultaneously, there could be no net gain at all. To avoid this sort of unproductive and even destructive competition, governments have for centuries tried to establish rules for fixing exchange rates through international agreements.

12.4.1   The Gold Standard

In Chapter 3, we discussed a number of types of monetary systems, one of which we called a controlled commodity money. The characteristics of this system are that (1) the unit of account is defined in terms of a commodity the supply of which is fixed or is at least stable, and (2) the government is able to fix the price of the commodity in terms of the unit of account by operating a minting service.[7] There are advantages and disadvantages to such a system for domestic purposes, as described in Chapter 3. But now we can note an interesting by-product of the controlled commodity money from the viewpoint of international finance: it provides an automatic mechanism for fixing exchange rates. All that is necessary is that each national government define its own currency in terms of some single commodity. Then once we know all of these commodity prices, we can readily calculate all of the exchange rates between currencies.

This type of system was widely used throughout the world from roughly 1870 to 1914. The commodity was gold, and the system was known as the international gold standard. During

----

[7] See Chapter 3, section 3.2.2.

the period after 1900 the U.S. government defined the dollar as 23.29 grains of gold (there are 480 grains in one troy ounce) and freely bought and sold gold at that price ($20.67 per ounce, plus or minus a fraction to cover transaction costs).[8] On the other side of the Atlantic, the British government defined the pound sterling as 112.86 grains of gold and freely bought and sold gold at £4.25 per ounce. The exchange rate between dollars and pounds was firmly fixed by these practices at £1 = $4.86. The international gold standard was in fact an international monetary system.

Under this international monetary system, countries whose currencies were undervalued would accumulate gold at the expense of those with overvalued currencies. For example, if coal were available from both American and British firms at a price ratio of less than $4.86 = £1, then customers around the world (assuming that the price difference were substantial enough to overcome differences in shipping and other expenses) would buy American rather than British coal; the pound would be overvalued, given the official exchange rate of $4.86. British customers buying American coal would have to supply gold to the American government in the process of buying the cheap dollars.

There existed a self-correcting mechanism within the gold standard which prevented one country from accumulating gold without limit. Gold was not only the international unit of account; it was also the domestic medium of exchange. Before 1933 the gold flowing into the United States, for example, was not hoarded by the government; the Treasury merely minted gold into coins. Instead, the gold receipts were income to the companies selling coal (in our example) and were directly added to the publicly held money supply. Prices would rise in the surplus country (the United States) both directly

---

[8] The dollar was devalued by President Franklin Roosevelt in January 1934. The dollar was redefined as 13.71 grains of gold, making the price of an ounce of gold $35. That price was maintained until December 1971 (see section 12.4.2).

(through the increased foreign demand for exported products) and indirectly (through the increase in the quantity of money). Simultaneously prices would fall in the deficit country (England). Over time, these price and income effects would eliminate the competitive differences among countries.

This so-called *specie-flow* mechanism did not always work perfectly.[9] Governments sometimes intervened to neutralize the effects of gold flows on the money stock; (in a curious premonition of modern argot, governments which neutralized gold flows by hoarding or dishoarding gold stocks were said to be "not following the rules of the game"). Furthermore, prices sometimes took a long time to adjust. As we have seen in the past few chapters, it would be a bit naive to suppose that there exists a simple fixed relationship between the stock of money and the level of prices. Nonetheless, the system did provide some means of adjustment so that countries were able to achieve a high degree of stability in exchange rates over a long period of time.[10]

12.4.2   The International Monetary Fund

The international monetary system was severely strained by the world depression of the 1930s and the world war of the early 1940s. During that time, some countries attempted to adhere to fixed exchange rates under the old gold standard while others gave up and allowed exchange rates to float. By the time these upheavals had run their course, it had become obvious to all but the staunchest diehards that a system of greater flexibility than the gold standard was required. Such a system was worked out and agreed upon at an international

---

[9] The term *specie* refers to a commodity which also functions as money. The specie-flow mechanism was first described by David Hume in his exposition of the quantity theory of money (see Chapter 6, section 6.6).

[10] For a good discussion of monetary policy under the gold standard, see: Arthur I. Bloomfield, *Monetary Policy under the International Gold Standard, 1880–1914*, Federal Reserve Bank of New York, October 1959.

conference held at Bretton Woods, New Hampshire, in July 1944.[11] The new system, known as the International Monetary Fund (IMF), worked very much like the gold standard except that the specie-flow mechanism was scrapped in favor of a system of control of international reserve balances. The IMF thus made neutralization of gold flows respectable and greatly enlarged the scope for the discretionary use of domestic monetary policy.

The essence of the IMF system was for each member country to set a fixed price for its currency in terms of dollars, and for the U.S. government to set a price for dollars in terms of gold. The only difference between this practice and the former policy of each country directly setting a gold exchange rate was computational convenience, but it did have the psychological advantage of recognizing explicitly that a strong key currency such as the dollar was a more important source of stability than was any linkage to gold.

Every government participating in the IMF maintained a stock of internationally acceptable reserve assets which it could exchange against its own currency in order to stabilize exchange rates close to the official peg. One of these assets was gold, the same commodity that had served as the basis for the old system. But because the inflexibility of gold had proved to be dangerous to dynamic economies, fiat currencies now were seen as an essential supplementary reserve asset. The reserve assets of the United States would now include British pounds, French francs, and the currencies of the other major countries, in addition to its stock of gold. For other countries the U.S. dollar would be a key reserve asset. Increases in the demand for dollars by foreigners would be a source of foreign currencies for the U.S. government; decreases in demand would be offset by sales of these cur-

---

[11] Only 30 of the 44 countries represented at the Bretton Woods meeting decided to become members of the IMF in time for its inception in December 1945. But by 1973, a total of 125 countries had joined.

rencies from our accumulated stocks. In this manner, each government could peg the price of its currency in foreign exchange markets.

The Bretton Woods agreements also assigned each country a line of credit (called "drawing rights") at the IMF. Under these rules, the member governments deposited an agreed amount of gold with the fund; the United States, for example, initially deposited close to $700 million.[12] The total line of credit was equal to four times the gold deposit. The country in effect exchanged part of its own gold stock for a (larger) asset in the form of the right to borrow foreign currencies from the IMF, while at the same time recognizing a contingent liability for foreign governments to borrow our currency from the IMF.[13] The total drawing right was then split into a *right* to borrow sums up to the value of our gold deposit (this slice of the drawing right being called the "gold tranche") and a *privilege* to borrow above that limit up to the total quota (the remainder being the "credit tranche").

This borrowing facility was a timid first step in the direction of the establishment of a true international credit money standard. It has been supplemented since 1970 by *special drawing rights,* called SDRs. The rights and privileges of borrowing from the IMF still are limited by strictly defined quotas. But the SDR quota is a borrowing right in addition to the country's gold tranche, so these drawing rights are a *pure* credit money for international exchange. They circulate only among central banks: should the Bank of England wish to exchange part of its dollar account at the Federal Reserve

---

[12] The U.S. gold deposit subsequently has been increased or revalued on several occasions. As of the end of 1973, we had deposited $2 billion of gold with the IMF.

[13] This practice is often described by reference to a "quota," of which 25 percent is paid in gold and the rest in the country's currency. The reference is misleading in that no payment of currency is actually made. When a foreign government borrows dollars from the IMF, it obtains a deposit balance (denominated in dollars) with the Federal Reserve Bank of New York. The top 75 percent of our quota is a recognition of the right of foreign governments to make these drawings.

Bank of New York for pounds sterling, the Fed could use its allocation of SDRs to settle the claim. The balance sheet effects might be as follows:

Federal Reserve Bank of New York

SDR account —	Foreign deposits —

Bank of England

Deposits at Fed —	
Credit balance at IMF +	

The reserve-asset scheme of the International Monetary Fund worked extremely well under most circumstances from the end of World War II until 1971. In a few circumstances, it exhibited dinosaurian rigidities which ultimately fossilized the whole system. The great advantage of the Bretton Woods rules was that they permitted a country to eliminate cyclical or seasonal fluctuations from its exchange rate. The resulting stability may have been a factor in the enormous growth in world trade that characterized the postwar economy. The great disadvantage of the rules was that they blinded governments to the development of *trends* in exchange rates. A country whose exchange rate was in fundamental disequilibrium could be seduced into defending that rate instead of letting it move to a more appropriate level.

One of the worst examples of this failing occurred in 1967. The exchange rate between the dollar and pounds sterling had been pegged at $2.80 for almost 20 years, but the British government had encountered increasing difficulties defending that rate. Relatively low productivity growth in England had made many British goods too expensive to compete in world markets, while imports became increasingly attractive to British firms and consumers. The trade balance and the capital account both had been in deficit most of the time since the late 1950s.

The theory outlined in this chapter would indicate a devaluation to have been in order under these circumstances. Instead, the United Kingdom attempted to maintain the $2.80 parity by deflating economic demand; by reducing consumer income and expenditures to slow the growth of imports and by reducing inflationary pressures in order to make British goods more competitive. By late 1967, however, it became apparent that this policy was not successfully eliminating the chronic balance of payments deficits. After generating a serious recession and paying out billions of dollars worth of international reserve assets in support of the exchange rate, the government announced a devaluation to $2.40 in November 1967. Our hindsight clearly suggests that if the exchange rate had to be changed it should have been changed much earlier; the costs of trying to peg an exchange rate above its equilibrium level are enormous. But the Bretton Woods rules strongly encouraged countries to avoid exchange rate movements and prevented a timely adjustment.

The final blow to the system fell in 1971. In that year, some $30 billion of capital funds were shifted out of the United States in a wave of speculation against the value of the dollar in world trade (see Chapter 11, section 11.4). A readjustment of exchange rates was in order, but the IMF system did not provide a simple method for devaluing the dollar. Our exchange rate, unlike those of the other member countries, was pegged to a fixed gold price ($35 per ounce) rather than to another currency. We could devalue either by raising the price of gold or by persuading other countries to revalue their exchange rates vis-à-vis the dollar. The diplomatic route was unsuccessful in 1971, partly because the dollar was overvalued relative to a wide range of currencies. The U.S. government also resisted the gold-price remedy, on the grounds that a higher price could reestablish gold as the primary reserve asset for international settlements. We preferred that the reserve structure remain flexible and continue to be based on national currencies rather than gold, and we were engaged in a fundamental dispute with a number of other countries—notably France—on that score.

The Bretton Woods rules collapsed on August 15, 1971. That evening, President Nixon announced that the U.S. government would no longer convert dollar claims into gold. The dollar would still be priced at $35 per ounce of gold, but the official price would now have no practical significance. This major event forced a complete reevaluation of exchange rate agreements among governments, because it put all of the burden of any realignment on countries other than the United States. An overvalued dollar would cause dollar balances to accumulate at foreign central banks, which could either accept those balances or revalue their own currencies (i.e., adjust downward the prices at which they were willing to buy foreign currencies).

The next 18 months witnessed a series of attempts to reform the rules so as to make possible a resumption of convertibility of dollars into gold and to establish a realistic and workable set of newly fixed exchange rates. The IMF member governments met at the Smithsonian Institution in Washington, D.C., in December 1971 and agreed on an interim set of exchange rates which effectively devalued the dollar by about 10 percent from its old level. These new rates lasted little longer than a year; by March 1973 the foreign exchange markets had lost confidence in the fixed values, and companies and individuals were shifting vast sums out of weak currencies—again including the dollar. This time the major central banks just gave up, agreeing no longer to peg exchange rates at fixed values.

12.5 FLOATING EXCHANGE RATES

Since March 1973 most of the world's major currencies have been *floating;* that is, their values have been determined

in private markets for foreign exchange without overt interference from central banks. The system has not been a clean
float, however; central banks still intervene in foreign exchange markets so as to manage rate movements. Ideally, a
managed float permits exchange rates to float toward equilibrium values while the central bank offsets temporary disturbances and prevents sudden or large movements that
might induce destabilizing speculative pressures. Though the
degree of success with this strategy has varied over the first
year of its operation, the long-run outlook for managed floating appears to be favorable. Its advantages were spotlighted
by the oil crisis of late 1973 and 1974, when many industrial-
ized economies suddenly faced an unprecedented downward
shift in nominal trade balances because of increases in the
cost of imported fuels. The managed-float strategy provided
the means for orderly adjustment of exchange rates under
exactly the sort of circumstance that would have incapac-
itated the Bretton Woods system.

The IMF still plays a central role in the functioning of the
managed float. Gold is not at present used by central banks
for international settlements, partly because the free market
price has risen far above the official price (now $42.22). For-
eign currency reserves and IMF drawing rights, however,
still form the basic set of international reserve assets.

The IMF reserve-asset system, however, is of meager proportions in comparison to the volumes of assets held by large
multinational companies. For this reason, liability financing
of the sort described in Chapter 11 (section 11.2.3) has
evolved into an important supplement to asset financing,
especially for the United States. As Figure 12–4 reveals, the
huge payments deficits experienced by the United States
since 1970 have not been financed to any great extent by sales
of our official assets. In fact, we started 1970 with less than
$17 billion of reserve assets (Table 12–2), so we could not
have begun to stabilize our exchange rate with that portfolio

FIGURE 12–4

Financing the Balance of Payments, 1960–73

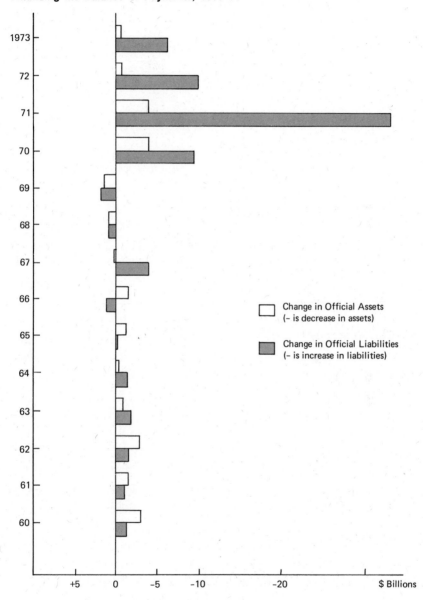

TABLE 12–2

U.S. Reserve Assets (end of year)

	($ millions)	
	1969	*1973*
Gold stock....................	$11,859	$11,652
Foreign currencies..............	2,781	8
IMF gold tranche..............	2,324	552
SDRs........................	—	2,166
Total Assets...........	$16,964	$14,378

as our only weapon. As foreign central banks accumulate dollar balances, they may exchange them for marketable or special nonmarketable U.S. treasury securities. They still are left holding dollars, but they at least have an interest-earning asset guaranteed by the U.S. government. They also may simply buy CDs, Euro-dollar deposits, or other financial assets denominated in dollars. At the end of 1973, U.S. liabilities to foreign official institutions totaled almost $67 billion, up from less than $16 billion at the end of 1969. This solution is not completely satisfactory to all of our often-reluctant creditors, but it is for the moment an essential element to the imperfect but evolving world of international payments.

Another major supplement to our reserve assets is a network of so-called *swap lines* among central banks. The Federal Reserve System has formal agreements with 15 other central banks and international agencies under which a central bank wishing to intervene in support of its exchange rate may borrow foreign currencies from another participating institution. For example, during February and March of 1974, the Federal Reserve Bank of New York sold about $225 million of German marks in exchange for dollars, thereby propping the demand for dollars in foreign exchange markets. We did not own these marks; we acquired them from the Deutsche Bundesbank (the German central bank) by swapping them for dollars. The Bundesbank obtained a dollar balance at the Fed, the Federal Reserve directly pulled $225 million of reserves out of the banking system, and the supply of marks to the German economy correspondingly rose. These reciprocal currency arrangements currently total about $20 billion; under normal circumstances, drawings against these swap lines will be a small fraction of the total.

12.6 CONCLUSIONS: THE INTERNATIONAL ROLE OF MONETARY POLICY

These past two chapters suggest a number of linkages between monetary policy and international payments. The demand for imported goods is causally related to total income in the economy. Foreign demand for our goods and services will be affected by the rate of inflation here relative to that in other countries. Capital flows are strongly influenced by relative interest rates. All of these variables are determined partly by monetary policy actions.

The nature of these linkages is such that monetary policy has a greater impact on the balance of international payments than other methods of demand management. A contractionary monetary action—say, a reduction in the availability of bank reserves—will tend to reduce aggregate demand and inflationary pressures and also will push interest rates upward. (The *ME* curve shifts to the left and induces a movement to the left along the *EE* curve.) That policy will thereby attack a balance of payments deficit on a broad front by increasing the trade and capital-account balances simultaneously. By contrast, a decrease in government spending would reduce aggregate demand but normally would result in *lower* interest rates. (The *EE* curve shifts to the left and induces a movement along the *ME* curve.) This form of contraction should increase the trade balance but could have a perverse impact on the capital account. The direction of the net impact on the balance of payments cannot be predicted.

Monetary policy therefore can play an important role in influencing the balance of international payments. On the other hand, both government and academic economists often argue that the United States should not be greatly concerned with international payments and should concentrate instead on our domestic problems such as inflation and unemployment. International trade is small relative to our total output and expenditure, so why should we let it dominate the formulation of policy? A fast answer to this objection is that stability of exchange rates is important to the growth of world trade and benefits the rest of the world as well as ourselves. The United States is the world's largest economy, and we have obligations to those who trade with us to exercise responsibility in the management of our economy and our currency. A more complete answer must also be slower than that, for the issue hinges on the relationships between international and domestic objectives and the relationships among the various policy instruments which are available. Those relationships are the subject of Part Four of this book.

REVIEW QUESTIONS

1. What are some of the likely causes of the rise in the value of the dollar relative to pounds sterling in the second half of 1973?

2. What groups in the United States probably gained from that rise in the exchange rate? Which groups probably lost income or market value of assets? Was the rise "good" for the country? Explain.

3. What are the similarities and differences between the international adjustment mechanisms under the gold exchange standard and the International Monetary Fund?

4. The United States in 1973 faced a rising rate of inflation and a surplus in its balance of payments. The contractionary monetary policy then put into effect as an anti-inflationary measure also had effects on the balance of payments. Would you expect the effect to be to reduce or to increase the surplus? Explain.

SUGGESTED FURTHER READING

Bloomfield, Arthur I. *Monetary Policy under the International Gold Standard, 1880–1914.* Federal Reserve Bank of New York, October 1959.

Kindleberger, Charles P. *International Economics,* 5th ed. Homewood, Ill.: Richard D. Irwin, Inc., 1973.

Triffin, Robert. *Gold and the Dollar Crisis.* New Haven, Conn.: Yale University Press, 1960.

part four

The Conduct of Monetary Policy

chapter 13

The Goals of Monetary Policy

13.1 INTRODUCTION: THE BUSINESS OF STABILIZATION POLICIES

Our economy does not always properly behave. Unemployment, inflation, balance of payments disturbances, and inequities of income distribution are not so much news as they are the common stuff of existence. But they are not so common as they once were, partly because we are beginning to understand the causes of such disturbances, and we are learning how to intervene constructively. All industrial countries now recognize that central governments must help to regulate the course of economic growth in order to minimize fluctuations and relieve economic disturbances. The carrying out of that task is known broadly as *stabilization policy*.

There are many forms of stabilization policy in use today, but we can usefully divide them into four categories. First is a set of policies designed to increase or decrease the effective aggregate demand in an economy by altering either government expenditures or tax rates. In terms of our macroeconomic model, these policies are designed to shift the aggregate demand curve through shifts in the *EE* relation. For

example, an increase in government spending should cause
both income and interest rates to rise; the *EE* curve and the
aggregate demand curve should shift to the right. An increase
in tax rates causes spending to fall, and the curves shift to the
left. These actions are known as fiscal policy.

The second group of policies involves management of the
public debt. Because fiscal policy actions often result in the
government spending greater sums than it receives in tax
revenues, we are endowed with a large and growing government debt in the form of bonds and other interest-bearing
securities. In the United States, the Treasury is responsible
for deciding what kinds of securities to issue, on what terms,
and at what times. These decisions are called *debt management* policies.

Sometimes it is or seems necessary to try to deal with the
problem of inflation directly. Fiscal policy can attack inflation
only indirectly, by reducing aggregate demand and, in many
cases, reducing employment. A seemingly more attractive
proposal for curbing inflation is, as the argument goes, "to
control prices by controlling prices." Such programs as the
wage-price control systems used in the United States from
1971 to 1974 are known collectively as *incomes policies.*

Finally, we come to *monetary policies,* which are our main
and immediate concern. We may define monetary policy as
the process whereby the monetary authority attempts to
achieve a desired set of economic goals by controlling either
the money supply, the cost and availability of credit, or the
allocation of credit to its various uses. The monetary authority in most countries is usually a central bank such as our
Federal Reserve System, but national treasuries or ministries
of finance may exercise and on occasion have exercised monetary authority as well. We showed in Chapter 5 how the
United States Treasury, for example, could affect reserves
and thus the total supply of money by issuing new or repay-
ing old debt, by changing the location of its deposit balances
between the commercial banks and the central bank, or by

buying or selling gold and foreign currencies. The coordination of treasury and central bank action is thus a prerequisite for rational monetary planning.

If monetary policy is a species of stabilization policy, then stabilization policy may be regarded as a genus of general economic planning. And crucial to the success of any kind of economic plan is a set of clearly defined and articulated objectives or goals and an empirically validated theory of how these goals can be implemented. The range of goals or objectives is restricted by the ways in which specific actions by the monetary authority can be expected to influence economic activity. In previous chapters we explored how changes in the supply of money can affect output and prices. The way in which we view the "transmission mechanism"—the channels through which monetary policy can be expected to work —defines a set of realizable macroeconomic goals, those goals or objectives that can be affected by monetary policy action.

The conduct of monetary policy can be understood best, we think, within a broad planning framework consisting of instruments, targets, and goals. Policy instruments refer to the tools directly available for exercising monetary management such as open market operations, reserve requirements, and the discount rate. Goals are the ultimate objectives or ends for which monetary planning is undertaken. Price stability, high employment, economic growth, and avoidance of disturbances in the balance of international payments have been a few of the more widely accepted of the macropolicy goals. Presumably, when the central bank increases its discount rate we ought to be able to estimate the impact on a set of ultimate goals. As we shall see, however, it is sometimes preferable to identify an intermediate target or targets through which a change in a policy instrument transmits the impact of monetary policy to the goal variables. Interest rates, both long and short term, and the money supply are examples of such intermediate targets.

Monetary decision making, therefore, may be viewed

ideally as a process of establishing certain desirable and achievable goal objectives, devising appropriate targets for influencing these goals, and employing the relevant instruments of policy to affect desired levels of the intermediate targets. That is not to say that all monetary policy formulation conforms to this ideal but only that analysis of actual policy decisions requires a standard of performance by which the success or failure of monetary policy can be evaluated.

13.2 MONETARY POLICY IN THE UNITED STATES: WHO MAKES THE DECISIONS?

Monetary policy decision making in the United States is not a model of either administrative simplicity or rational calculation. At the center of the U.S. system of monetary control is a unique financial institution—unique in its organizational structure and unique in its relationship to the government. Everywhere else in the world the apparatus of monetary control is centralized in an institution with a readily identifiable name; for example, the Bank of England, the Bank of France, the Bank of Italy. Furthermore, the activities of these central banks generally are closely controlled by each country's government. Not so in the United States. As described in Chapter 1, our central banking machinery is the Federal Reserve System linked together and controlled by a Board of Governors which acts independently of the executive branch of the government. Monetary policy decision making is neither the responsibility of the president nor that of the Congress.

13.2.1 The Federal Open Market Committee (FOMC)

The locus of power resides in a committee of 12, known since 1935 as the Federal Open Market Committee. The FOMC includes the seven members of the Board of Governors and an additional five members who are presidents of regional Federal Reserve banks. The chairman of the FOMC is the chairman of the Board of Governors who is appointed by the president to serve a four-year term. The vice chairman is always the president of the Federal Reserve Bank of New York. The other four positions on the FOMC are rotated annually among the remaining 11 Federal Reserve bank presidents. All Reserve bank presidents normally attend the monthly meetings of the FOMC, but only the five official members have the right to cast votes.

The control machinery is also unique because of the different manner in which members of the FOMC are selected. The seven members of the Board of Governors are appointed by the president with the approval of the Senate to serve 14-year staggered terms. Reserve bank presidents, on the other hand, are elected by the nine-member Board of Directors of each Federal Reserve bank with the approval of the Board of Governors. The president of each Federal Reserve bank is responsible to his Board of Directors and ultimately to the Board of Governors in Washington, D.C. His appointment is removed from the direct influence of any elected government official. In this manner, monetary decision making in the United States has by legislative fiat been isolated from the threat of intervention by either the Congress or the president in day-to-day operating strategy. The alleged advantage of this independent monetary authority is that it minimizes interference for purely partisan or political purposes with the monetary policy process. But the isolation of monetary policy from the machinery of political control can have serious disadvantages as well, and we shall have more to say on this subject later in the discussion.

13.2.2 Monetary Politics: The Constituency of the Federal Reserve

Ideally monetary policy should have a set of clearly defined goals with definite priorities attached. It should be logically consistent and easily monitored. The framework of policy decisions should be fully specified including the channels through which monetary policy is supposed to exert an impact on the real economy. Simply put, monetary policy ought to be rational. Unfortunately, the annals of monetary policy do not conform very closely to that ideal. Central bankers have not made and do not make decisions in a social or historical vacuum. The decisions which they make are no better than the best knowledge available to them—no better than the tools at their disposal—no better than their collective administrative competence. And, not least important, their decisions can be no better than their collective persuasive skills to carry public opinion along with them at crucial decision-making points.

The administration of monetary policy is in part a species of politics, by which we mean the art of winning approval for decisions taken in matters tinged with the public interest. Monetary politics is a subtle art. The public in most countries, including the United States, tends to regard central bank policy as remote and technically complex, best left to the experts and to those specifically charged with overseeing monetary policy. But at times, particularly in periods of rising interest rates or acute inflation, the public has been known to register rather powerful protests through the government, the press, and the medium of television.

The central banker's constituency is normally rather narrowly circumscribed. Among the general public, the influence of two groups stands out: the commercial banks who are members of the Federal Reserve System and the community of large business corporations which own a major share of the country's financial assets. Both groups are highly articulate, they maintain well-financed and skillful lobbyists in Washington, and they will not hesitate to reveal their views on matters of monetary policy. In addition, the member banks are in a uniquely advantageous position to influence policy because of the organizational structure of the System. The nine-member Board of Directors of each Federal Reserve bank is drawn one third from the banking profession and one third from the rest of the business community, and the commercial banks themselves elect each of these six directors. Only the remaining third of the directors are representatives of the public at large and are appointed by the Board of Governors. The Board of Directors of each Federal Reserve bank then must elect the bank's president who in turn will serve as a member of the principal policy-making body, the FOMC. There thus is ample opportunity for both business and banking interests to be heard at all levels of the decision-making process.

The rest of the public affects the policy-making process primarily through the Congress and the executive branch of the government, including the President. There are three pivotal points at which these governmental branches contribute to the policy-making process. The first and the most important is through the initiation and enactment of legislation defining the goals of policy and changing the structure and organization of the Federal Reserve System. Congress frequently has made significant amendments to the Federal Reserve Act since its initial passage in 1913; and we shall shortly have a good deal to say about the impact on monetary policy of the employment act passed by Congress shortly after World War II. A second governmental role is through the selection of the key personnel—primarily the seven governors of the Federal Reserve System—who are the ultimate decision makers. And the third influence is that of persuasion by the president and by certain powerful and often well-informed legislators. An example of the latter is Senator William Proxmire (Democrat from Wisconsin) who as chairman of the Joint Economic Committee has held frequent public hearings during which Federal Reserve officials present testimony and are subjected to questioning on the conduct of monetary policy. Thus the Federal Reserve tempers its independence in day-to-day operations with a continuing attentiveness to public views of the national interest.

One other point that should be made about the climate in which monetary policy is made concerns the growing importance of the role played by professional economists. Until the 1960s, the Board of Governors was dominated by bankers, businessmen, and lawyers, men who had to learn central banking by on-the-job training. The role of the professional economist was restricted mainly to description and analysis of monetary conditions and to what may be the most unenviable task of all: rationalizing the decisions taken by others. But in recent years a number of economists have been appointed to the board and have made important contributions to the formulation of policy. Most notable among these is the current chairman, Arthur F. Burns. Dr. Burns is a gentle-looking, white-haired, pipe-smoking man who gained an outstanding reputation as an academic economist and as an expert on aggregate business cycles before becoming first an economic adviser to Presidents Eisenhower and Nixon and then, in 1970, chairman of the Federal Reserve Board. And as of January 1974, three other members of the board are professional economists.

13.2.3 The Chairman

Even given these various kinds of political or professional input to the policy-making process, the fact remains and must be asserted that the formulation of monetary policy is a centralized and concentrated power and responsibility. The principal decision maker as well as the principal spokesman is the chairman of the Board of Governors and of the FOMC. The extent of his power and influence cannot be underestimated. Sherman Maisel, a former member of the Federal Reserve Board, has conjectured in his memoirs that the chairman himself held roughly 45 percent of the monetary power exercised within the Federal Reserve System between 1965 and 1973. The remaining amount he apportioned as follows: the staff of the Federal Reserve Board and the FOMC, 25 percent; the other governors, 20 percent; and the Federal Reserve banks, 10 percent.[1] Estimates of the degree of monetary power exercised by the chairman will differ, of course, among the different interpreters of monetary policy, but there will be little disagreement that the chairman exercises the most monetary power.

13.3 FORMULATING POLICY GOALS

The aims and objectives of monetary policy have not always been the same as they are today. The goals of policy have changed with our increased knowledge of how the economy works and with our increased sensitivity to the quality of economic performance. Prior to World War I, the United States did not have a central bank or a well-defined monetary policy in the form now familiar to us. The only goal accepted during that era which we could call monetary in nature was the maintenance of international exchange rates through a smoothly functioning gold standard. This system, as operated by the U.S. Treasury as well as by the central banks which were already established in Europe, was simply a form of controlled commodity money as described in Chapter 3. As our earlier discussion revealed, the only control in such a system is over the price of the country's currency in terms of the chosen commodity (gold). The size of the money supply, the prices of goods and services in terms of currency (dollars), and the level of income and output in the economy are determined by economic rather than policy factors. In other words, monetary policy during that period of our his-

---

[1] Sherman Maisel, *Managing the Dollar* (New York: Norton, 1973), p. 110.

tory was directed only toward international stability; the domestic economy was supposed to take care of itself.[2]

When Congress established the Federal Reserve System in 1913, it had not formulated the goal of preventing monetary forces from disrupting the pace of domestic economic activity. Prior to that time, there had been numerous occasions when shortages of money, sometimes caused by nothing more than unusually heavy seasonal demands for bank loans (for example, because of late crop harvests), caused severe financial disturbances including the failure of both banking and other business firms. The Federal Reserve Act recognized the elimination of such disruptions as a legitimate monetary policy goal. Only much later did the Federal Reserve become ambitious enough to try to guide and govern the level of economic activity.

During the 1920s, the avoidance of wide swings in the price level began to emerge as a goal of Federal Reserve policy, though only in a vague and usually secondary manner.[3] Before we could develop the type of extensive monetary management in use throughout the world today, an unfortunate catalyst was required: the lengthy period of severe unemployment which so thoroughly and devastatingly characterized the 1930s. The experience of that decade finally convinced a large segment of public opinion that deliberate policies should be adopted by governments and by central banks to eliminate the evils of involuntary idleness. What emerged in the United States as well as in various European countries was legislation committing governments to the maintenance of high levels of employment and to stability of

---

[2] For an account of how the gold standard worked in practice, see Arthur I. Bloomfield, *Monetary Policy under the International Gold Standard, 1880–1914*, Federal Reserve Bank of New York, October 1959.

[3] One of the authors has fully described this period of Federal Reserve policy making: Elmus R. Wicker, *Federal Reserve Monetary Policy, 1917–1933* (New York: Random House, 1966).

general price levels. The act passed by Congress—the Employment Act of 1946—is one of the most important pieces of economic legislation ever enacted in this country, because it has so greatly widened our conception of government responsibility for economic stability.

The Employment Act of 1946 stated that the federal government has the responsibility for keeping unemployment low. The act declared that "it is the continuing policy and responsibility of the federal government to use all practicable means to promote maximum employment, production, and purchasing power." In the final conference stage of the bill the word *maximum* was substituted for both *high* and *full* employment. No mutually satisfactory definition could be found for full employment, and hence it was dropped. The word *maximum* apparently was meant to give more flexibility to the policy makers in the determination of an employment criterion.

The employment act did not distinguish between the separate roles of monetary and fiscal policy in achieving economic stability. It made no provision for insuring the coordination of Federal Reserve actions and the tax and expenditure policies of the Treasury. Responsibility was given to the president to design appropriate policies but within the existing framework of an independent central bank. The 1946 act also failed to define an unequivocal set of macroeconomic goals and objectives. Nor did it attempt to specify target levels of the desired goals; that is, the act did not set a target for the behavior of the price level or the unemployment rate.

Since there was no machinery other than voluntary cooperation to guarantee the coordination of monetary and fiscal policy, the task of identifying specific monetary goals and assessing their priority devolved upon the Federal Reserve. The employment act had set the general guidelines, but the implementation rested with the Federal Reserve System.

13.3.1   The Goal of Full Employment

Americans are no longer haunted, as our fathers were, by
the vision of massive unemployment. It has been 40 years
since we last saw the depressing spectacle of an idled industrial economy, and most of us have long since concluded
that we shall never see it again. So today when we discuss
the importance of full employment as a policy goal, our meaning is somewhat different from that of our fathers and grand-
fathers. It is the 6 percent unemployment rate which we fear,
not the 25 percent rate.

But that is not to diminish the importance of full employment. In 1971 (a year of 6 percent unemployment), more
than 5 million people in the United States were without jobs
and looking for work in an average week. If that figure could
have been reduced even to 3 million unemployed (a rate of
about 3.4 percent of the labor force), an additional $20 bil-
lion or more worth of goods and services could have been
produced, sold, and consumed in the United States that year.
And 2 million more people would have been earning a living.
So it is not surprising to find that the Federal Reserve is concerned with helping to achieve low rates of unemployment.

In the light of these obvious evils of unemployment, it may
seem somewhat surprising that the achievement of full employment is seldom considered to be the top-priority goal of
monetary and other stabilization policies in the United States.
There are several reasons for this indifference, some of which
are more defensible than others. The most compelling argument is that there may not be very much that monetary policy
can do about unemployment, and the Federal Reserve therefore should concentrate on more soluble problems. Whether
we should accept such an argument depends basically on
whether the unemployment is caused by structural deficiencies in the economy—such as by shortages of basic materials
required for production of goods or by shifts either in the

types of goods desired by consumers or in the techniques used for producing goods, either of which could temporarily generate unemployment among workers whose skills are no longer in demand—or whether it is caused by a general cutback in the demand for and the production of goods and services. Only in the latter case would an expansionary monetary policy be able to do much good. When unemployment rose in 1970, both structural and demand-reducing forces were at work. In addition to the overall slowdown in economic activity that year, we were faced with large numbers of army veterans returning from Vietnam, virtually all of whom had to find new jobs. And certain areas of the country, especially Los Angeles and Seattle, faced particularly acute problems because of the reductions in the federal government's aerospace programs. It would obviously have been futile to expect monetary policies to solve these problems.

The second excuse is that no one knows what an appropriate goal is for unemployment. The only acceptable value in the long run is zero; why should an economy fail to provide jobs for those who seek them? But for any realistic span of time, that goal is impossible to achieve. There will always be some amount of *frictional* unemployment, as people who lose jobs are in the process of finding new ones or as people who enter the labor force for the first time (for example, students or army veterans) look for appropriate work. In an economy as complex as that of the United States, there is bound to be a certain amount of *structural* unemployment, since people without jobs will not necessarily have the skills desired by employers looking for workers.

In recent years, apologists for the acceptance of unemployment have offered the concept of *demographic* unemployment as an additional problem. During the 1960s, the labor force increasingly comprised both women and youth, groups with traditionally higher unemployment rates than have been enjoyed by mature men. It is argued by many that the employment of heads of household is a greater economic priority than the hiring of women and teen-agers. In any case, the presence of these latter groups in the labor force—given the resistance to them among employers—certainly makes more difficult the achievement of a given overall rate of unemployment. One recent study concludes that if a given level of aggregate demand would have reduced the unemployment rate to 4 percent in 1960, it would reduce it only to 4.6 percent today. Should we therefore accept this higher figure as our goal for the unemployment rate?

A third problem with using unemployment as a goal variable for monetary policy is that the standard indexes tell us more about the performance of the economy relative to its potential than they tell us about the amount of hardship associated with the lack of employment. The most closely watched statistic is the ratio of people looking for jobs but unable to find acceptable employment, to the total labor force (those employed plus the unemployed as just defined). It tells us nothing about the length of time people have been unemployed, and it tells us nothing about the extent of dilettantism among the unemployed. Surely someone who has been looking for a job for six months is in a more difficult position than someone who lost his job last week; but should we regard the $60,000-per-year executive who is holding out for a better offer as being in the same category as the $8,000 laid-off factory worker who has found no openings at all? These are difficult issues. Nonetheless, changes in the standard unemployment rate generally are in the same direction as more sophisticated measures of duration or type of unemployment. These complexities need not deter policy makers from seeking to increase employment opportunities.

In practice, unemployment serves more as a constraint on monetary policy than as a goal. It is rare that the Federal Reserve will seek actively to achieve a given value of employment for the economy. But it is equally rare that officials will take any major restrictive action without first considering the adverse impacts that their decisions could have on employment opportunities.

13.3.2   The Goal of Price Stability

High on the priority list of monetary policy objectives is the avoidance of wide swings in the general level of prices. Throughout most of the history of the Federal Reserve System, the major problem with the price level has been that it tends to rise more rapidly than most people would like, that is, we have suffered from inflation of prices. During the depression years of the 1930s, there occurred a serious deflation of prices which, even apart from the unemployment which accompanied it, was just as serious an economic distortion as the now more familiar inflation. In fact, most of the discussion of inflation presented here applies to deflation as well, except that in some cases the gainers and losers are reversed.[4]

Inflation is a different type of problem from unemployment. The loss of jobs represents an actual decline in output and in income for the whole economy; we produce less than we are capable of. Inflation may represent only a redistribution of income among people and among groups of people in the economy. It is an evil mainly because this redistribution is arbitrary and capricious and usually hurts most those groups which are least able to protect their own interests.

Who is hurt by inflation? Most obviously, anyone whose income is entirely fixed in terms of dollars will suffer a loss of real income when prices rise. But we should be careful in defining who those people are likely to be. Economists used to be fond of using pensioners—retired people living on pensions and social security payments—as the archetype of this category of inflation losers. But it is becoming more and more

---

[4] The reader would be advised to test his understanding of inflation by working out the implications of deflation for each group discussed below.

common for pension payments to rise with price levels, so long as the value of the pension fund's assets also rises; and social security benefits now regularly rise to keep pace with inflation. So, although pensioners clearly do worse than most other groups during inflationary periods, the gap is less wide than a casual examination might lead us to believe.

There is no evidence that the poor are systematically hurt by inflation. That proposition would imply that, as a result of inflation, the real incomes of, say, the bottom fifth of the income distribution would either fall or would rise less rapidly than the real incomes of those at the top of the pile. But the evidence suggests that inflation is neutral in its effects on the overall distribution of income. Why? Partly because of the adjustment of public assistance levels to rising costs; partly because inflation normally is a consequence of very high levels of economic activity, so that many poor individuals who might otherwise not find enough work will be more fully employed.

Wages and salaries tend to rise more rapidly than corporate profits during inflationary years, contrary to commonly held views. It is the worker, not the company, who benefits from the tight labor markets that accompany high demand and rising prices. When prices (and costs) stabilize, corporations gradually regain their share of total income. But not all workers are able to partake in the inflationary feast; non-unionized workers, especially if their skills are not particularly scarce, will find it very difficult to secure wage increases that keep pace with the rising cost of living.

One dislocation caused by inflation is potentially quite serious for the overall economy. Part of our national income comes from the sale of goods abroad, and our ability to make such sales depends partly on our being able to charge prices which are competitive in world markets. If we run our own prices up faster than other countries, then the value of our currency will have to fall relative to those others. But the real problem occurs when we try to fix (or peg) our exchange rate under these circumstances: we then succeed only in pricing ourselves out of the market altogether. In that case, the real value of total national income is reduced.

The list of arbitrary effects is endless. Farmers often see the prices which they have to pay for materials and labor rising more rapidly than the prices they receive in the marketplace. Home-owners usually discover that the cost of maintaining a house, including property taxes, goes up faster than the value of the house. Bond prices and often corporate stock prices fall whenever prices rise faster than investors had anticipated, simply because anyone buying financial assets will demand a higher dollar return when he expects that the dollar value of the asset will decline. Thus people who already owned such assets will lose. On the other hand, anyone who is in debt is likely to gain, because the real value of the dollars he has to pay back will be reduced by inflation.

An analysis of the incidence of inflation couched primarily in terms of various economic groupings: wage earners, business managers, debtors, creditors, pensioners, and so on is correct as far as it goes. But it does not go far enough. Individuals are not likely to fall into only one of these socio-economic groupings. Wage earners, for example, may also own government securities, possess a mortgage, or hold savings accounts at local banks or savings and loan associations. To describe correctly the effects of inflation on households we require both an income statement and a balance sheet for each household. The income statement is not sufficient. Nor is the balance sheet. We need to scrutinize carefully the total impact of inflation on the distribution of income and wealth.

It is indeed surprising how little empirically validated knowledge we have about the actual impact of inflation on the distribution of income and wealth. But the prospects for the near future are encouraging as more and more economists attempt to fill the various lacunae.

Inflation, unlike unemployment, is therefore not an un-mixed evil. Some people gain from it while others lose. We could eliminate most of its evils simply by denominating all contracts in real rather than nominal terms; then everyone would be protected from a loss of real income or a loss of the real value of financial assets as a consequence of changes in general price levels. Such a scheme would have to include complete flexibility of international exchange rates, so that the prices of one country could not get out of line with those of its trading partners. But until we can achieve complete flexibility, inflation will remain a problem with which monetary policy will have to be concerned. It certainly is not the menace which popular fears often make it out to be, but it is a pattern we would be better off without.

13.3.3 The Goal of Exchange Rate Stability

In addition to domestic stabilization objectives such as high employment or price stability, monetary policy may be guided by balance of payments considerations. The goal of stability in a country's international payments is in practice a more critical goal for European central banks than it is for the United States, because our economy is relatively insulated from international pressures. Nonetheless, there have been occasions during which Federal Reserve officials have con-centrated heavily on international problems, virtually to the exclusion of domestic goals. And as world trade grows during the 1970s, it is likely that the accompanying problems will continue to preoccupy policy makers.

The most common form for an international goal of mon-etary policy is the achievement of a given value for the coun-try's exchange rate. Until 1971, the United States and virtually all of the countries with which we conducted trade and other economic transactions were committed by formal agreements to maintaining a fixed set of relative currency values.[5] Whenever it became clear that the value of the dollar was out of line vis-à-vis one or more other currencies, some sort of remedial action had to be taken by one or both countries or else the fixed-rate agreement had to be changed.

Monetary policy has always been a leading candidate for the job of keeping exchange rates in line because it has a strong impact on all the variables which in turn influence the exchange rate. A low rate of domestic inflation helps to keep our prices competitive in world markets. High interest rates help to attract funds from abroad. Monetary policy could even be used to create unemployment in order to make it more difficult for American residents to buy imported as well as domestically produced goods, though we would hope that such proposals would not be taken seriously.

It is not immediately obvious that the maintenance of fixed exchange rates is a desirable goal for monetary policy. There are advantages: companies engaged in international trade can have a high degree of certainty about foreign prices and foreign demand for goods, and much of the uncertainty in planning foreign travel can be eliminated if relative currency values are fixed over time. A country whose exchange rate falls in value will be faced with higher costs in buying foreign goods; a country whose exchange rate rises in value will find it more difficult to sell goods in foreign markets. Exchange rate stability can avoid these disruptions.

But stability is by no means an unmixed blessing. The biggest problem is that governments are likely to kid themselves in deciding how much their currencies are worth. When central banks finally gave up trying to support fixed parities in early 1973, so that exchange rates could be determined in a relatively unregulated market, businessmen, bankers, and other traders collectively decided by their actions that the

---

[5] See Chapter 12.

dollar was worth somewhat less than governments had previously agreed. By early 1974, it cost $.37 to buy one German
mark, compared to $.28 three years earlier. The Japanese yen
similarly had risen in price from $.28 per 100 to $.34 per 100.
In maintaining the lower prices of these currencies (i.e., the
higher prices for the dollar), the Federal Reserve—along
with the central banks of Germany and Japan—had essentially created an artificial demand for dollars above the natural demand from businesses and individuals. The Bank of
Japan and the Deutsche Bundesbank both had been willing
to create additional money of their own (more yen and more
marks) in order to buy up dollars and thereby to support the
value of the dollar. Eventually they became tired of expanding the supplies of their currencies and of accumulating dollars. But even though the fixed-rate system now has been
replaced by floating exchange rates, the management of exchange rates to maintain orderly market conditions remains
an active goal for U.S. monetary policy.

13.3.4 Other Policy Goals

There are other goals which seem sometimes to be important to Federal Reserve officials but which over the long run
do not carry the same weight in policy decisions as those we
have discussed already. One is the prevention of financial
panics. This goal in fact was the raison d'être for the establishment of the Federal Reserve System, as we saw earlier in
this chapter. Today it takes over only rarely. It took over in
the fall of 1966 when a shortage of funds was threatening the
collapse of a number of banks and savings and loan associations. It took over in the summer of 1970 when the bankruptcy of the Penn Central Railroad left creditors holding
hundreds of millions of dollars of practically worthless assets
and left other lenders wondering about the value of their own
assets; a panic could have ruined scores of large banks and

other businesses by choking off vital sources of financing. It took over again in 1974 when the largest bank failure in the history of the United States (the Franklyn National Bank) could have pushed the country to the brink of financial collapse had the Fed failed to react quickly.[6] The prevention of such panics had to become the first priority of the Federal Reserve.

A variant of this goal is that of maintaining stability in financial markets and particularly in the market for federal government securities. Whenever the U.S. Treasury is bringing out a new issue of securities or is replacing (refinancing) a maturing issue, the Federal Reserve usually avoids making policy changes or otherwise confusing potential buyers of the new issue. This policy of caution is known as "even keeling."

The final goal is one which has been of minimal significance in the past but which later editions of this book may have to display more prominently: the allocation of credit to uses which are deemed to be socially desirable. Banks are naturally inclined to favor borrowers who offer the highest long-run return on their loans. These borrowers usually are corporations which not only can afford to pay competitive interest rates but which are large and stable enough to provide the bank with a steady source of income over the years. The portion of bank loans going to small businesses and individuals tends to fall whenever lendable bank funds get scarce. The brunt of restrictive monetary policies thus falls on home buyers, consumers, and people trying to organize new or small businesses. In a number of countries, including most European countries and Japan, the central banks have imposed direct controls to prevent banks from making too extensive a reallocation of assets toward corporate borrowers.

---

[6] The Federal Reserve Bank of New York made huge loans—up to $1.7 billion —to Franklin National for five months in 1974, until the FDIC arranged for the sale of the bank to a consortium of European banks which could assume its debts and keep it operating.

13.4   THE COMPATIBILITY OF THE VARIOUS GOALS

How compatible are the various policy goals? The mere fact that we may desire zero price inflation, zero unemployment, and a constant international exchange rate, for example, does not imply that these goals are simultaneously attainable. We must beware of confusing the real world with our conceptions of what constitutes the ideal. Like Voltaire's Dr. Pangloss we would like the best in the best of all possible worlds. Nevertheless, what we can reasonably expect must be tempered by the theoretical and empirical relationships which exist among inflation, unemployment, and balance of payments equilibrium.

Economists still differ about the meaning to be attached to the inverse relationship between inflation and unemployment which has been so persistently observed in the United States and other countries. As we saw in Chapter 10, it may be difficult to push up output by monetary or fiscal policies alone for more than two or three years, no matter how much inflation we are willing to tolerate. Thus the two goals of full employment and price stability may be compatible in the long run, provided we take a realistic view of what it is possible to achieve on either front. Excess zeal in driving down either the inflation rate or the unemployment rate will inevitably make the other goal more difficult to achieve. And certainly in the short run (that is, taking a two- or three-year horizon for formulating stabilization policy), the two goals will be highly incompatible. The Federal Reserve can move the economy up or down the aggregate supply curve depending on its objectives, but it has little power to shift the curve.

International and domestic stability need not be incompatible, but occasions arise when they are; 1970 provides a recent example. The economy was in a recession, and domestic stability called most clearly for an expansionary monetary policy. But the country also was facing an outflow of dollars to foreign countries, partly because higher interest rates were available in those other countries, and partly because of substantial speculation that the dollar was overvalued relative to a number of major currencies. International payments stability thus seemed to call for a contractionary U.S. monetary policy, in order to drive up our interest rates and to restore confidence in the dollar's value. Given that dilemma, the Federal Reserve opted for expansion, but the international goal served to place limits on the degree of the Fed's actions.

How should the Federal Reserve resolve conflicts among policy goals when they arise? Unfortunately, this question remains one of the great unresolved issues about monetary policy. As we have shown throughout this chapter, we know very little about the welfare economics of unemployment or inflation, about who is harmed or by how much. Improving our factual knowledge of the benefits and costs of inflation and unemployment should make the selection of the desired goal variable more rational. Ultimately, however, the decision about priorities and weights to be assigned to goal variables is a value judgment. But whose value judgment? Whose weights? The president's? Congress'? The Federal Reserve's?

Since Congress has refused to rank the various goal objectives, Reserve officials have, by default, filled the vacuum. And they have been extremely reluctant to reveal publicly their own relative preferences. Open market directives do sometimes contain qualitative statements about the increasing or diminishing importance the FOMC attaches to a particular goal variable. But neither the directives nor the official FOMC minutes reveal the existence of quantitative targets for the goal variables. There is no mention of a desired goal objective stated either in terms of the unemployment percentage or the behavior of any one of various price indexes—the consumer price index, the wholesale price index, or the GNP deflator. The dimensions of the goal variables invariably have been qualitative and not quantitative.

Various attempts have been made by economists to discover by empirical analysis the implicit weights the Federal Reserve has attached to different goal objectives. Their results generally suggest that the objective of high employment predominated mainly during the 1952–61 period. Price stability has been of secondary importance, and the balance of international payments has exercised only negligible influence.[7] Nonetheless, there clearly have been times when these latter goals and especially inflation have stood in the center of the stage.

We now can see that there are a number of problems with the current policy of allowing the Federal Reserve to determine goal priorities for monetary policy. One is that the policy places a great deal of power in the hands of a small number of men with little direct responsibility to the electorate; when policy goals conflict, the public has little to say about the priorities to be assigned. Another problem is that the Federal Reserve traditionally has been reluctant to specify its own objectives; it is difficult for outsiders, even congressional committees, to offer constructive criticism of policies whose substance must be viewed through the smoke from a placidly puffed pipe.

A somewhat radical alternative to the present system would be to shift the responsibility for monetary policy from the Federal Reserve either to Congress or to the president. In particular, since the Employment Act of 1946 states that the president has the duty to coordinate stabilization policy, there is ample reason for making him responsible for monetary policy formulation. If he must share the blame, then it is arguable that he ought to share more of the responsibility. The president would determine the relative importance of the goals to be pursued at any particular time. If the public

---

[7] See, for example, William Dewald and Harry G. Johnson, "An Objective Analysis of the Objectives of American Monetary Policy, 1952–1961," *Banking and Monetary Studies,* edited by Deane Carson (Homewood, Illinois: Richard D. Irwin, Inc., 1963).

were dissatisfied, it could seek recourse to the electoral process. But it is not obvious that this change would significantly improve public accountability. After all, the preferences of the Federal Reserve surely have been influenced by its perception of public opinion. The major pitfall is that the president might be more likely than the politically insulated Federal Reserve Board to be motivated on occasion by purely partisan considerations.

REVIEW QUESTIONS

1. Define instruments, targets, and goals and explain their functions in the formulation of monetary policy.
2. Who are the monetary decision makers in the United States? To what extent are they accountable to the public?
3. What possible reforms of the control of monetary policy are suggested by the discussion in this chapter?
4. How is the burden of unemployment and inflation measured?
5. Are the goals of monetary policy always compatible with one another? Explain.

SUGGESTED FURTHER READING

Dewald, William and Harry G. Johnson. "An Objective Analysis of the Objectives of American Monetary Policy, 1952–1961," *Banking and Monetary Studies.* Edited by Deane Carson. Homewood, Ill.: Richard D. Irwin, Inc., 1963.

Maisel, Sherman. *Managing the Dollar.* New York: W. W. Norton, 1973.

Wicker, Elmus R. *Federal Reserve Monetary Policy, 1917–1933.* New York: Random House, 1966.

chapter 14

Instruments of Monetary Policy: The Big Three

14.1 INTRODUCTION

Monetary policy would still be a relatively easy game to play if it required only the articulation of goals. Even if there are many goals, some of which may conflict, it is still always possible to choose. As, for example, in 1974. The economy was slowing down, but prices not only were rising but were actually accelerating. Tough choices had to be made, but the Federal Reserve Board made them: inflation, it said, was the moment's greater evil. But then came another set of choices to be made, for the objective of fighting inflation could be implemented in a variety of ways.

The officials of the Federal Reserve have available not just one policy instrument but a whole kit of tools with different functions. Some of these tools have been introduced to us already (see Chapter 4): open market operations, to control the supply of reserves available to banks; the discount rate, to control the cost of borrowing; and required reserve ratios, to limit the volume of bank deposits. These three instruments are the most important for monetary policy as practiced in the United States. The others may appropriately be characterized as supplementary, and we shall reserve them for the next chapter.

All of the policy instruments described in these two chapters are designed to enable the Federal Reserve to control the *supply* of money in various ways. In terms of the model of the economy developed in earlier chapters the Fed uses its policy instruments to shift the supply schedule for money and thereby to shift the *ME* (monetary equilibrium) schedule. In time, we can then observe effects on the stock of money and on various interest rates, and ultimately on prices and incomes. The exact workings of that process are very complex and depend on the choice of instruments, so we shall reserve that discussion for Chapter 16. What is necessary now is for us to see just how all these instruments work and how they differ from one another.

14.2 OPEN MARKET OPERATIONS

The basic mechanism for control of the money supply schedule in the United States is open market operations, which are defined as purchases and sales of assets by the Federal Reserve System in the open or secondary market. The assets traded are mainly the securities issued by the federal government, and the secondary market for those securities consists of about 25 large dealers, the majority of which are departments or divisions of private banks. In other words, the Federal Reserve System does not, as a rule, buy securities directly from the federal government (i.e., the Treasury); it buys existing securities from (and sells them to) private dealers. As we described in Chapter 4, the Fed pays for securities by crediting the selling bank's reserve-deposit account balance. Thus purchases of securities by the Fed directly increase the supply of bank reserves; sales of securities directly decrease reserve balances. Thus the whole money-supply schedule is shifted systematically by open market operations.

Open market operations are by far the most important instrument available to the Fed. Purchases or sales are conducted every day, and the volume of operations often totals hundreds of millions of dollars in a single day, perhaps 2 or 3 billion in a month. At the end of each week, the Fed releases information on the volume of operations conducted during the week, in a statement like the one shown for the week following Christmas of 1973 (Table 14–1). To read total (net) transactions from this statement, examine the second column (changes from the previous week). There, we find that the Fed bought or sold three major types of securities during the week: U.S. government securities, federal agency obligations, and bankers' acceptances.[1] Some of these securities were "bought outright," while others were purchased for temporary usage, under agreements that the dealer buy them back at a specified time and price (known as "repurchase agreements" or "RPs"). Total open market operations in the week shown amounted to a net increase in Fed holdings of $705 million.

U.S. government securities—			+684
Bought outright	+	879	
Held under repurchase agreement	−	195	
Federal agency obligations—			+ 80
Bought outright	+	117	
Held under repurchase agreement	−	37	
Acceptances—			− 59
Bought outright	+	9	
Held under repurchase agreement	−	68	
Net increase through open market operations:			+705

But we have to be careful in using information about the volume of open market operations. The direct impact of operations in the week shown was to increase bank reserves by $705 million, which by itself is an enormous increase for one week and would represent an aggressively expansionary monetary policy. But much of the activity in the Fed's open

---

[1] See section 14.2.3 for a description of these assets.

TABLE 14–1

The Federal Reserve Weekly Statement of Factors Affecting Bank Reserves*

	Averages of Daily Figures (in millions of dollars)	
	Week Ended January 2, 1974	Change from Previous Week
Reserve bank credit:		
U.S. government securities—		
Bought outright—system account.................	78,323	+879
Held under repurchase agreements.................	502	−195
Federal agency obligations—		
Bought outright...............................	1,915	+117
Held under repurchase agreements................	111	− 37
Acceptances—		
Bought outright...............................	69	+ 9
Held under repurchase agreements................	93	− 68
Loans—		
Total member bank borrowing...................	1,210	+168
Includes seasonal borrowing of:.................	31	− 4
Float...	3,865	−832
Other Federal Reserve assets.....................	1,201	− 28
Total Reserve bank credit.....................	87,289	+ 13
Gold stock......................................	11,567	—
Special drawing rights certif. acct.................	400	—
Treasury currency outstanding.....................	8,676	+ 4
	107,932	+ 18
Currency in circulation...........................	72,471	+238
Treasury cash holdings...........................	333	+ 5
Treasury deposits with Federal Reserve banks...........	2,254	+ 26
Foreign deposits with Federal Reserve banks...........	331	−200
Other deposits with Federal Reserve banks.............	976	+282
Other Federal Reserve liabilities and capital............	2,969	− 78
	79,334	+273
Member bank reserves:		
With Federal Reserve banks.....................	28,598	−256
Currency and coin...............................	6,780	+272
Total reserves held...........................	35,445	− 1
Required reserves...............................	35,249	+300
Excess reserves.................................	196	−301

* The average of total reserves of member banks decreased slightly in the statement week (December 26, 1973 through January 2, 1974) to $35,445 million. Required reserves and member bank borrowings at Federal Reserve banks increased while excess reserves declined.

A decline in float and increases in currency in circulation and other deposits with Federal Reserve Banks were the major factors absorbing reserves in the latest statement week. Partially offsetting these reserve drains were declines in foreign deposits with Federal Reserve banks and other Federal Reserve liabilities and capital. In addition, System Open Market operations provided $705 million reserves net, on a weekly average basis through outright purchases of Treasury bills and repurchase agreements.

market account is what may be termed *defensive* in nature.[2] It is designed merely to prevent undesired changes in bank reserves resulting from changes in the other sources and uses of reserves. The major short-run culprit here is Federal Reserve float,[3] which, in our sample week, fell by $832 million!

So the Fed was not really on the offensive at all that week; it was just trying to cope with the vagaries of check collection that inevitably occur during the annual Christmas crunch. Without a large volume of defensive open market operations, bank reserve positions would be highly volatile and unstable. Preventing such seasonal and even random crises remains a major operating objective of the Fed. In fact, one empirical study of open market operations from 1930 to 1968 suggested that approximately 80 to 85 percent of total operations were defensive. The authors concluded that the dynamic element was effectively zero for all but five of the annual periods examined.[4] If correct, their study appears to imply that the Fed was not using open market operations vigorously in the pursuit of purely countercyclical monetary goals. And it certainly is indicative of the great quantitative importance of defensive reactions in determining the volume of open market operations.

For these reasons, the Federal Open Market Committee cannot specify its policy objectives in terms of a volume of securities to buy or sell. It cannot say, "We want to increase bank reserves by $300 million this month, so we shall instruct the account manager to buy $300 million of securities." There

[2] The term *defensive* was first applied in this context by the distinguished former manager of the System's open market account, Robert V. Roosa, in *Federal Reserve Operations in the Money and Government Securities Markets,* Federal Reserve Bank of New York, July 1956.

The term is contrasted to *dynamic* operations, those which are designed to alter the volume of reserves to further policy objectives.

[3] See Chapter 5, section 5.2.4 for a description of Federal Reserve float.

[4] Vittorio Bonomo and Charles Schotta, "A Spectral Analysis of Post-Accord Open Market Operations," *American Economic Review* 49 (March 1969), pp. 50–61.

are too many other factors to take into account, some of which—such as float—are difficult to predict or to measure from day to day. So it is necessary for the committee to work out some rules or procedures under which it will operate.

14.2.1 Determining the Appropriate Volume of Open Market Operations

Open market operations are conducted by a department of the Federal Reserve Bank of New York known as the "trading desk" or as "the Desk." The Desk is run by a vice president of the bank known as the manager of the open market account or as the account manager. He attends the monthly meetings of the FOMC in Washington, where he receives instructions on how to manage the account until the next meeting. These instructions are generally pretty specific, but the account manager has to have a wide scope for conducting defensive operations, the necessary volume of which the committee cannot foresee. So the FOMC tends to work in terms of guides, which serve as signaling devices to warn the account manager when he should buy or sell securities.

An abbreviated version of the FOMC policy directive is released to the public about three months after each meeting (the delay being thought necessary to prevent speculators from attempting to profit from the information). A copy of a recent directive is shown below. Notice that there is no mention about recommended volume of purchases or sales, but only a set of instructions as to short-term and longer-term objectives. The key items here are the desired values of the Federal funds rate and of the growth rate of the money supply. We can only speculate as to how these guidelines were decided, but the process normally goes something like this. Before the FOMC meets, its staff produces a detailed description of the current course of the economy (spending, output, prices, interest rates, international exchange rates, and so on)

The Committee agreed that the economic situation and outlook called for moderate growth in monetary aggregates over the longer run, including a slightly higher rate of growth in M_1 [the money supply] than contemplated earlier. Taking account of the staff analysis, the Committee concluded that growth in M_1 . . . over the January–February period at annual rates . . . of 3 to 6 percent . . . would be consistent with its longer–run objectives for the monetary aggregates. The members . . . decided that in the period until the next meeting the weekly average Federal funds rate might be permitted to vary in an orderly fashion from as low as 8¾ percent to as high as 10 percent, if necessary, in the course of operations [the rate was around 9¾ percent at the time of this meeting]. It was understood that a slight easing in reserve and money market conditions would be sought promptly, provided that the data becoming available later in the week of the meeting did not suggest that the monetary aggregates were growing rapidly.

Source: Excerpt from the "Domestic policy directive" of the FOMC for the meeting held on January 21–22, 1974.

and a projection of how it is expected to develop if monetary policy is conducted in the same manner as in recent weeks. The committee then decides whether it is satisfied with the course of events and, if not, what it might be able to do about it. At this particular meeting in January 1974, it decided that it should make bank reserves more freely available in order to stimulate bank lending and thus total spending. But by how much? Would purchases of $5 million do the job, or of $500 million?

The volume question cannot be answered precisely, so the FOMC decides first on an intermediate target (3 to 6 percent annual growth in the money supply) which, on the basis of projections by staff economists, it believes to be consistent with its goals. And then, again relying heavily on its professional staff, the FOMC works out a short-term operating guide. Simply put, the FOMC is saying to the account manager, "Go back to the Desk and buy enough securities to drive down short-term interest rates; see if you can get the Federal funds rate, for example, down to around $8\frac{3}{4}$ percent. But if it looks as if bank lending or the money supply is growing too fast, then back off a bit."

In fact, these objectives were effectively met over the succeeding four weeks. Whenever the supply of bank reserves threatened to fall because of a change in one or more of the other sources of reserves, the Desk bought securities; whenever technical factors seemed to be pushing up reserve balances temporarily, sales of assets by the Federal Reserve pulled funds out of the banking system. And gradually, the Desk managed to supply enough extra reserves that banks no longer had to bid so aggressively to acquire additional balances elsewhere. By the time the FOMC met again in late February, the Desk had bought almost $1.3 billion (net) of various types of assets, and the Federal funds rate had dropped below 9 percent, almost to the bottom of the range specified in the policy directive.[5] But that, of course, was only the short-term objective of the expansionary policy; in the next chapter we are going to take a closer look at the longer-term effects, on money supply growth, longer term interest rates, and ultimately on output and prices.

14.2.2   Determining the Types of Assets to Buy

The manager of the Federal Reserve's open market account has to decide not only the volume of assets to buy but also the types of assets. Potentially there are a large number of factors which he has to consider in this latter choice. Suppose, for example, that he were given the authority (which he does not now have) to buy and sell shares of stock in private companies. The effect on bank reserves would be the same as if he bought or sold U.S. government bonds. When he bought, say, $5 million worth of stock in General Motors, the seller of the shares would be able to deposit the payment in his bank account, and the bank would thereby gain $5 million in reserves. The problem, aside from the important political one of choosing which companies should be favored, is that no corporation, not even General Motors or IBM, has enough outstanding stock held by a wide enough ownership to be able to absorb regular trading by the Federal Reserve to the tune of millions of dollars every week.

Stock prices could become much more volatile than they are now if they were subject to regular intervention by the Federal Reserve in pursuit of its policy objectives. So the first rule of the game is that the Desk must confine itself to assets for which there is a very large and very active secondary market and for which political considerations are minimal.

---

[5] Reserve balances of member banks actually declined during the four-week period, as a result of decreases in float and increases in treasury deposits at Federal Reserve banks. But a sharp drop in treasury deposits at *member* banks allowed a bigger portion of reserves to support private deposits; hence there was a net expansionary effect.

14.2.3   The Money Market

The only assets which meet this criterion fully enough for everyday use are those which are regularly traded in what is called the "money market." This phrase refers to the activity of traders (principally banks) who are continually exchanging money for short-term securities and short-term securities for money. It thus is quite distinct from, though institutionally related to, what we have called the market for money balances in earlier chapters (referring to the total supply and demand for money in the economy). The money market, unlike the stock market, has no fixed address. But the central core of the market in the United States is in New York City, still the hub of financial, if not nonfinancial, business activity.

The purpose of the money market is to provide an efficient means by which portfolio managers of banks, other financial institutions, and nonfinancial businesses can satisfy their requirements for liquidity. If commercial banks, for example, desire to expand loans, they may dispose of securities which they own; if there exists a large and smoothly operating market for such securities, then the banker knows that he can obtain quickly a good price for them. Similarly, corporations with short-term excess cash balances on hand can purchase money-market securities in order to earn some interest income, secure in the knowledge that the corporation can readily resell the securities on any business day if it becomes necessary to replenish the cash box.

There are a wide variety of assets traded in the domestic U.S. money market. The principal ones include:[6]

1.   Short-term securities issued by the Treasury, mainly in the form of treasury bills.
2.   Commercial paper—short-term IOUs of leading fi-

---

[6] For a more detailed explanation of the money market, see Jimmie R. Monhollon, ed., "Instruments of the Money Market," Federal Reserve Bank of Richmond, 1970.

nance companies, bank holding companies, and a few nonfinancial corporations, all borrowing directly from ultimate lenders (mostly from one another) rather than through the intermediation of ordinary bank loans; these IOUs are freely negotiable in the money market.

3. Bankers' acceptances—also IOUs of corporations, normally issued by importers to finance specific shipments of goods in international trade and then sold (discounted) by the exporter to banks which endorse ("accept") them and resell them as their own obligations in the money market.[7]

4. Bank certificates of deposit(CDs)—the large (it takes an ante of at least $100,000 to buy into this game) negotiable time deposits issued by banks to large corporations at interest rates usually above those available to smaller savers.

5. Federal funds—reserve deposit balances of commercial banks which are lent from one bank to another on an overnight basis.

6. Longer term government securities, including those issued by the Treasury, by agencies of the federal government such as the Federal Housing Administration, and by state and local governments, but to a lesser extent.

The trading desk of the Federal Reserve is a major day-to-day participant in this money market in its conduct of open market operations. But it does not deal in all of the assets described above. Some are unacceptable because they are assets or liabilities of private business corporations (commercial paper, CDs), some because they are the Fed's own liabilities

---

[7] Thus when someone buys an acceptance, he is in effect lending money to a bank, which lends it to an exporter, who lends it to an importer to pay for the goods. Each lender, of course, takes his own cut.

(Federal funds). The Desk does deal to some extent in bankers' acceptances, agency securities, and long-term treasury securities, mainly in order to bolster the markets for those particular issues; the markets are too thin to sustain regular intervention by the Fed.[8] So the only part of the money market in which the Desk can operate continually, buying and selling large amounts every day, is that for short-run government securities and particularly for treasury bills. How big is it? As of January 1974, there were more than $11 billion of treasury bills outstanding, and average daily trading amounted to more than $2 billion, of which the Fed probably accounted for about $300 million.

14.2.4 The Bills Only Doctrine

The extreme example of limiting open market operations came in the period from 1951 to 1960. For those years, the FOMC adopted a policy of confining open market operations largely, though not entirely, to securities with a maturity of less than one year, mainly treasury bills. The rationale for this policy at the time was an expressed desire to minimize the effects on interest rates of official intervention in the money market. That is, the objective of the committee at that time was to control the volume of bank reserves with as little impact as possible on specific interest rates. Furthermore, intervention in the comparatively small long-term market would in its opinion have created intolerable uncertainty for government security dealers and would have created special problems about the smooth functioning of the government securities market. Allegedly, dealers would have refused to "make markets" or deal effectively in longer-term securities if there had been added uncertainty about when and to what extent the trading desk would intervene. To avoid any mal-

---

[8] A market is characterized as "thin" when there are so few offers to purchase or to sell that a large order can cause wide fluctuations in price.

functioning of the government securities market, the FOMC decided to confine open market operations to "bills only."

Although open market transactions are no longer confined to bills only, the overwhelming volume of open market operations is still in the maturity range of less than one year. Table 14–2 shows open market transactions by maturity for January

TABLE 14–2

Open Market Transactions* by Maturity, January 1974 (millions)

Type of Security	Gross Purchases	Gross Sales
Bills...................................	$1,340	$335†
Others maturing within 1 year.............	9	0
Maturities of 1 to 5 years.................	93	0
Maturities of 5 to 10 years................	77	0
Maturities of 10 years or more.............	0	0
	$1,519	$335

* Data include only outright purchases and sales; maturity information is unavailable for repurchase agreements.
† Excludes redemptions; most bills acquired by the Fed in the open market are held until they mature. In January 1974, redemptions totaled $1,402 million.

1974. The table reveals quite clearly that purchases and sales of treasury bills still constitute the principal form of open market transaction.

14.2.5 Foreign Currencies

One other type of asset with which the Federal Reserve occasionally conducts open market operations is foreign currencies. This type of operation is not designed so much to affect the volume of bank reserves (though it does have the same impact on reserves as any other open market operation) as to influence the foreign exchange rates of the dollar. If, for example, the major New York banks find that the demand for British pounds sterling increases, reducing their own holdings of pounds (either in cash or in deposit balances at British banks); then they will raise the selling price of pounds and thereby cut the dollar exchange rate against pounds. To prevent this drop, the Federal Reserve can intervene by selling pound deposits to the banks. For this purpose, the Federal Reserve Bank of New York has an account at the Bank of England. By writing a draft on this account in favor of a New York bank in the manner described above in Chapter 12, the Fed helps to support the exchange value of the dollar. The transaction also constitutes an open market sale and directly reduces bank reserves.

14.3   THE DISCOUNT WINDOW

Of the Big Three tools of monetary policy, the one most closely monitored by the financial press is the discount rate. No other action by the Federal Reserve System receives half the amount of publicity accorded to this instrument, partly because it is used only infrequently. As shown in Figure 14–1, there were only ten changes in the discount rate during the whole decade up to the end of 1970. There were a flurry of changes (eight in all) in the next several months, none at all in 1972, seven more in the early months of 1973, and then only one more in the following year. With such long periods of dormancy, the changes have tended to produce dramatic effects out of all proportion to the significance of the event. Increases in the rate, for example, are often interpreted to mean that the Federal Reserve is attempting to tighten credit; interest rates are going to rise; the money supply is going to decrease; business and mortgage loans will be more difficult to obtain; and short-term inflows of foreign capital will be encouraged.

The financial markets and the press attribute these seemingly magical powers to the discount rate in the face of what is usually a bland announcement by the Fed (see example below) to the effect that the increase is merely intended to

FIGURE 14–1

The Discount Rate, 1961–74

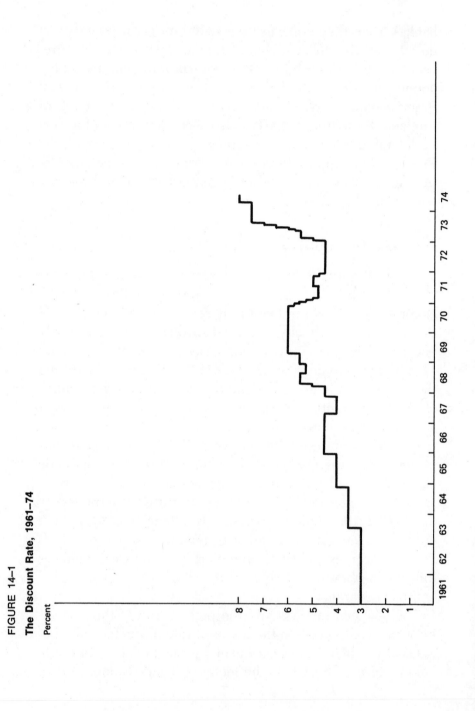

keep the discount rate in line with other short-term interest rates. In truth, the discount rate is more powerful an instrument than a casual reading of the typical announcement would suggest but not quite so potent as one might think from reading the above list of interpretations. It is necessary, then, for us to understand just how this instrument works in practice.

Announcement: Change in Discount Rate

The Board of Governors on August 13, 1973, approved actions by the directors of the Federal Reserve banks of New York, Philadelphia, Cleveland, Richmond, Chicago, St. Louis, Minneapolis, Kansas City, Dallas, and San Francisco increasing the discount rate of those banks from 7 percent to 7½ percent, effective August 14. The Board subsequently approved a similar increase for the Federal Reserve banks at Atlanta, effective August 16, and Boston, effective August 23, at which time the rate was 7½ percent at all Reserve banks.

The action was taken in recognition of increases that have already occurred in other short-term interest rates and is intended to bring the discount rate—which is the rate charged member banks for borrowings from their district Federal Reserve banks—into better alignment with short-term rates generally.

14.3.1   What Discounting Is

The discount rate is the rate at which a member bank can borrow from its district Federal Reserve bank. These loans, which are made by the individual Reserve banks under rules (Regulation A) established by the Board of Governors, are usually collateralled by U.S. government securities.[9] The rules specify that under most circumstances the use of the "discount window" (Federal Reserve jargon for the borrowing facility) is a privilege rather than a right of membership. The only formal exception is a borrowing right which was recently established (April 1973) for certain small banks which have pronounced seasonal imbalances between deposit and loan fluctuations and which do not have a reasonably reliable access to the national money markets. (See Table 14–1.)

For example, a bank with a primarily agricultural clientele might face dwindling deposit and expanding loan volume every spring and summer (the planting and growing seasons) and be flush with funds in the fall (after the harvest). The bank could establish a seasonal line of credit with its Federal Reserve bank in order to get through the summer without having to deny loan requests to local farmers. The total amount of funds available through this special window is, however, relatively small (in the first year of operation, borrowings for the whole country averaged $72 million, peaking at $185 million in late August).

Ordinarily the Federal Reserve expects its member banks not to look to the discount window for additional resources with which to expand their banking operations. The purpose of the window is to provide the banks with the means to meet temporary and unexpected deficiencies in reserve balances. It is, of course, difficult for the Fed to determine the motiva-

---

[9] In the earlier years of the system, borrowings by member banks were usually secured by "eligible paper": short-term loans of the member bank to business customers. This practice of temporarily reselling loans to the Federal Reserve banks was then known as "rediscounting," and the discount rate was called the "rediscount" rate, a term which one still occasionally encounters.

tion of bankers who borrow, so it has to exercise fairly close scrutiny over the administration of the window. Each Federal Reserve bank keeps track of the amounts and frequency of each member bank's borrowing, and it discourages borrowing in successive weeks.[10] In addition, each Federal Reserve bank may try to discourage overall borrowing, to limit the total amount of funds made available through the discount window, especially during periods when the Board of Governors and the FOMC are pursuing a restrictive monetary policy.

The discount window is therefore a temporary source of funds for banks with reserve deficiencies. But it is not the only or even the most important source. Quantitatively, the dominant means by which banks meet reserve deficiencies is the Federal funds market, which we met earlier in our discussion of the "money market." Suppose that one member bank has a reserve deficiency, but that another—perhaps in another part of the country—has a surplus. The simplest way to adjust these imbalances is for the surplus bank to lend its excess to the deficient bank for a day or two. That way the surplus bank has an extremely liquid outlet for its excess balance (which after all, may last only for a few days), and the deficit bank avoids having to go to the Fed, hat in hand, to ask for a loan. At times the desire to avoid the discount window can be so great that banks will borrow in the "Fed funds market" (more jargon) even though the prevailing rate there is well above the discount rate. Why? Simply because the Fed does view the discount window as a privilege to be used infrequently and not abused. The Federal funds market consequently has grown into a highly efficient market in which several billion dollars of one-day interbank loans are made every day.[11]

---

[10] Each member bank is permitted to average its reserve balances over a full week in meeting its legal requirement. See section 14.4.1.

[11] In order to learn more than you care to know about the Federal funds market, see James M. Boughton, *Monetary Policy and the Federal Funds Market* (Durham, N.C.: Duke University Press, 1972).

Two other substitutes to the discount window are available to banks with reserve deficiencies,[12] but both are viewed with less enthusiasm by bankers in most circumstances. One is to sell securities from the bank's asset portfolio. Banks usually own some highly liquid money-market assets (treasury bills, commercial paper, acceptances, even negotiable CDs issued by other banks) specifically for this purpose. The only problem is that sales of these liquid assets[13] are only a stopgap measure; once they run out, the bank will have to find other sources.

As a last resort, banks can always refuse to make additional loans and could even reduce total loans by not renewing or replacing maturing notes. But loans are the arteries that pump profits into the bank, and the manager who values his business life will avoid constricting or hardening them more than he must. In general, the bank is faced with a classic problem of economic choice in its struggle to meet its legal reserve requirement. It has to find the option—whether it be the discount window, the Federal funds market, sales of liquid assets, or a cutback in lending—which minimizes the total cost of adjusting its balance sheet. But it is a subjective choice, because the total cost includes a strong nonpecuniary element. Many banks completely avoid ever using the discount window, in the hope of improving or retaining a good working relationship with the ever-watchful Fed, even though the window often is nominally the cheapest option available.

---

[12] An additional alternative would be to increase total deposits by somehow inducing the public to shift out of currency into deposits; this normally is not a viable option for curing short-term deficiencies at individual banks. The larger banks may be able to attract some net new balances through the Euro-dollar market; see Chapter 11, section 11.5.3.

[13] Liquid assets held for the purpose of having something convenient to sell in order to meet reserve requirements are sometimes called "secondary reserves." One must carefully distinguish them, however, from actual reserve balances.

14.3.2 The Discount Rate

The rate charged for loans at the discount window is formally set by vote of the nine-person board of directors of each Federal Reserve bank, subject to approval by the Board of Governors. But that description belies the true power of the board in Washington. The directors in each of the 12 districts recognize that the market for bank loans is national and is not segmented along district boundaries; they thus cannot responsibly set their own discount rate independently from the national pattern. Each district therefore looks to the board for guidance as well as official approval. The result is that except for adjustment periods of one or two weeks whenever the rate is being changed, there exists a single national discount rate and not 12 district rates.

How shall we interpret changes in the discount rate? The rate per se gives us little information about what its impact will be on the amount of borrowing by member banks from the Federal Reserve. The incentive to borrow will depend upon the level of the discount rate compared to open market rates. Suppose, for example, that during a period of economic expansion the Federal funds rate and the treasury bill rate rise but the Federal Reserve declines to change the discount rate. The relative cost of borrowing from the Federal Reserve will therefore decline and thus stimulate the amount of member bank borrowing. A policy of keeping the discount rate unchanged under these circumstances would be expansionary in the sense that the volume of borrowed reserves and hence of the net monetary base would increase. Similarly, an increase in the discount rate relative to open market rates should be contractionary. In interpreting the behavior of the discount rate, it is important to remember that looking at the rate alone does not give sufficient knowledge to warrant inferences about policy intent or consequences.

Reserve officials have, however, occasionally in the past used a change in the rate to signal a major shift in monetary policy—from ease to restraint or vice versa. On these occasions they preferred to use a change in the rate rather than a formal public announcement as the primary method of communication of information about the intent and direction of monetary policy.

The discount rate is often set below the rates available on other short-term credit instruments. There thus will be a profit incentive for member banks to borrow from their Federal Reserve bank and then to use these additional funds to increase loans. As we have seen, the Federal Reserve casts a heavy frown on this application of entrepreneurial free enterprise. It would seem to be easier for them to set the discount rate high enough to eliminate the profit incentive, rather than to resort to the obviously imperfect and arbitrary device of rationing credit. But now we are back to those ambiguous and noncommittal announcements put out by the Fed when it changes the rate. The Federal Reserve System is under constant political pressure from Congress to hold rates down as much as possible. And the board is keenly aware of the debilitating impact of high rates on total economic activity for the reasons set out in Chapters 8 through 10. These considerations make it desirable to try to conduct policy in such a way that monetary restriction is accompanied by at least a show of limiting the rise in rates.

The idea is to force banks to reduce lending, to make a smaller volume of funds available to the public, while at the same time persuading banks to hold down interest rates. By keeping the discount rate below other interest rates during periods of tightening, the Fed can apply this psychological pressure on banks. When the rates get too far out of line, the Fed then will often raise the discount rate but will accompany the increase with an announcement designed to dissuade banks from using the occasion as an excuse for raising their own lending rates. The discount rate may be a fairly powerful policy instrument, not because of its direct impact on the cost of borrowing at the window but because of its psychological impact on the setting of other market rates of interest. Its effects are inherently short run because they generate a disequilibrium, for example by keeping interest rates below competitive levels. Eventually, the psychological effects will wear off.

14.4 RESERVE REQUIREMENTS

The last of the Big Three policy instruments is the power to change reserve requirements. Of all available instruments, this one is potentially the most powerful, but it also is the most neglected. Federal Reserve officials tend to view it as a blunt instrument, suitable only for major policy shifts and not for regular use. It is possible, though, that reserve requirements will emerge as a more flexible instrument in the 1970s. In contrast to the 1960s, there now are so many different categories of reserve requirements that a change in any one of them would have a comfortably small impact on the total dollar volume of required reserves. Furthermore, the Federal Reserve has begun to employ marginal (see Chapter 15) in addition to regular reserve requirements, again increasing the scope for making subtle policy changes.

14.4.1 Reserve Requirements and the Money Supply

The basic role of reserve requirements was described in Chapter 4, when we analyzed the fundamentals of the supply of bank deposits. The equilibrium supply of demand deposits (D^s) is summarized by equation 4.15 (Chapter 4, section 4):

$$D^s = \frac{1}{q_D} \cdot B_n$$

where B_n is the net monetary base and q_D is the required reserve ratio against demand deposits. With a given monetary base, the Board of Governors can readily constrict the supply of demand deposits and hence the money stock by raising the required reserve ratio (q_D). To encourage banks to expand deposits without making additional reserves available through open market operations, they can simply cut q_D, increasing the ratio of D^s to the net monetary base.

The net base, B_n, is also affected by changes in reserve requirements, as is revealed in our equation 4.22 (Chapter 4, section 4.5.2).

$$B_n = B - K_p - q_T \cdot T - ER^d$$

Thus an increase in the required reserve ratio on time deposits (q_T) will require a greater portion of available reserves to be absorbed by the banks' outstanding stock of time deposits (T) and will reduce the quantity of reserves available to support demand deposits or other uses of reserves.[14]

This simple money-supply model understates the richness of the current institutional framework in which reserve requirements are determined. In the first place, changes in a bank's deposit volume do not lead immediately to changes in its reserve requirement. Banks are permitted to average their holdings of reserves over a seven-day period ending each Wednesday; there is no penalty for being deficient early in the computation period so long as it is made up by Wednesday. Even then, the Fed will waive the penalty if the shortage is no greater than 2 percent of the requirement and if it is made up by an equal excess in the following week. Furthermore, the bank's legal requirement is not based on its *current* deposit liabilities but upon those it held two weeks earlier. When we take all of these factors into consideration, we see that an increase in deposits has no effect on required reserves

---

[14] Recall that B is the total base, K_p is currency held by the public, and ER^d is the demand by banks for excess reserves.

for at least two weeks, and the lag can stretch to three weeks for relatively small increases.

A second complication is that the Federal Reserve's requirements apply only to member banks and to those nonmembers that are headquartered in states that impose reserve ratios matching those of the Fed. Perhaps 10 to 20 percent of total bank deposits in the United States will be unaffected by changes in Federal Reserve requirements.[15]

The most important complication, however, is the variety of ratios set by the Fed. As Table 14–3 shows, there are not

TABLE 14–3

Regular Reserve Requirements in Effect in January 1974

Category	Requirement
Net demand deposits:*	
First $2 million at each bank	8%
Next $8 million ($2 to $10 million)	10½
$10 to $100 million	12½
$100 to $400 million	13½
Over $400 million	18
Time deposits:	
Savings	3
First $5 million of other time deposits	3
Over $5 million	5

* Net demand deposits are defined as gross demand deposits minus cash items in the process of collection and demand balances due from domestic banks.

two required reserve ratios (q_D and q_T) but eight: five against demand deposits, depending on the total size of the bank's demand deposit business, and three against time deposits. To see how this system works, consider a bank with $50 million of demand deposits, $20 million of savings deposits (regular passbook accounts, plus Christmas clubs and the like), and $30 million of other time deposits (special pass-

---

[15] Approximately 25 percent of total bank deposits are held by nonmember banks; about half of the states match Federal Reserve requirements for the nonmember banks within their borders.

books, small nonnegotiable certificates, and perhaps some large negotiable CDs). What are its reserve requirements? Against demand deposits, it has to hold

a.   8 percent against its first $2 million of deposits, or $160,000;
b.   10½ percent against the next $8 million, or $840,000; and
c.   12½ percent against the other $40 million, or $5,000,000;

for a total reserve requirement of $6 million, which is 12 percent of total demand deposits. By averaging these requirements over all member banks, we could obtain a figure for q_D.

The bank's requirement against its time deposits would be

a.   3 percent against its savings accounts ($20 million), or $600,000;
b.   3 percent against the first $5 million of its other time deposits, or $150,000; and
c.   5 percent against the rest ($25 million), or $1,250,000;

for a total requirement of $2 million, which is 4 percent of total time deposits. If this bank were typical, q_T would thus be 0.04, and q_D would be 0.12.

If the whole scale of reserve requirements on demand deposits were now shifted upward by even half of 1 percentage point, this bank would have a rather large adjustment to make in its portfolio of assets. Where it had been required to set aside $5,000,000, it would now have to produce an extra $250,000 in one of the ways we described in the previous section (borrow at the discount window or in the Federal funds market, or sell other assets to raise cash). In the process, the bank would have to raise its lending rates in order to cover its higher costs. It probably would have to dispose of a part of its holdings of interest-bearing securities. And eventually its volume of lending would have to fall. In this manner the increase in reserve requirements would contract the volume of bank credit and, along with it, the stock of money and total bank deposits.

14.4.2 The Adjustment Problem

The question arises, however, as to whether these adjustments can be made smoothly by the banks without putting excessive strain on loan and security markets. Large banks with relatively liquid asset portfolios and with the means to raise funds in the Euro-dollar, Federal funds, and commercial paper markets would have little trouble meeting the additional requirement. Smaller banks would be more likely to grumble a lot. And all banks would suffer some loss of profitability, since the Federal Reserve does not pay interest on funds deposited with it.

One solution to this adjustment problem would be to change reserve requirements in smaller steps. But the Federal Reserve generally does not make changes of less than 0.5 percentage point, perhaps in recognition of the bookkeeping problems that frequent changes or odd-fractioned requirements could bring to small computerless banks. After all, membership in the Federal Reserve System is still not compulsory; an ill-tempered banker can always opt out in favor of state-chartered nonmember status.

This possibility is in fact not one that the Federal Reserve can afford to regard casually. In 1972, for example, five banks with deposits of $100 million or more chose to withdraw from the System. And of 212 new commercial banks receiving charters, only 13 elected Federal Reserve membership. As nonmember banks, the others also are subject to a form of reserve requirement, imposed by the state that charters them. In most states, the percentages are comparable to or even higher than those set by the Federal Reserve; only in a few are they lower. In any case, the *form* of the requirement tends to be less burdensome for nonmembers. Whereas member banks are permitted to count only vault cash and deposits at Federal Reserve banks, nonmembers may include demand balances at other commercial banks. These balances are held by members and nonmembers alike for ordinary business purposes: for banking services provided by the depository bank (called a "correspondent" bank). Furthermore, nonmember banks in some states can even count a part of their interest-bearing assets—such as treasury bills—in meeting their legal reserve requirements.

There thus is a profit incentive for banks to withdraw from the System, which the Fed must hope to offset by its own ability to provide services—and prestige—to the member bank. Any increase in reserve requirements helps to tip the balance against the Federal Reserve. Decreases obviously work favorably for bank profits. But reserve requirements would quickly become an instrument of license rather than of monetary policy if they could be adjusted only in the direction of zero.

A second solution is to change only one or two requirements. But this option has been fully viable only since 1972. Before November of that year, reserve requirements were much less varied. Banks were divided into two categories: reserve city banks and country banks.[16] Until 1968, any bank within each category had the same fixed reserve requirement on all of its demand deposits, with higher percentages applying to reserve city than to country banks. From 1968 through

---

[16] The criteria for these classifications were somewhat complex in practice, but the basic definition of a reserve city was one in which a Federal Reserve bank or branch office was located. Before 1962, there were even "central" reserve cities, defined rather arbitrarily as consisting of New York and Chicago, for the purpose of extracting even higher reserve requirements out of banks so placed. The reserve city classification is still in use, but its only practical bearing on reserve requirements is through the legal limits on the percentages which the Fed may impose. Under the Federal Reserve act as presently amended, requirements on the demand deposits of reserve city banks [now defined simply as any bank with $400 million or more in demand deposits] may be varied between 10 percent and 22 percent. For other banks, the limits are 7 percent and 14 percent. Time deposit limits are uniformly fixed, with a minimum of 3 percent and a maximum of 10 percent.

1972, an extra one half of 1 percent of deposits was required as a reserve on all demand deposits over $5 million at any bank. These requirements are summarized in Table 14–4.

Then in 1972 came the proliferation of categories for reserve requirements which we saw in Table 14–3. Under this new system, it is possible for the Board of Governors to change requirements so as to affect only the very largest banks (giants with $400 million or more in demand deposits) or only those with $100 million or more, and so on. Thus reserve requirements could be used as a flexible instrument of monetary policy without generating the readjustment traumas of a more generalized change.

14.5 CONCLUSIONS

We now have been introduced to the three basic instruments of monetary policy: open market operations, changes in the discount rate, and changes in reserve requirements. Each has its own comparative advantages, and each plays a unique role in the Federal Reserve's attempts to control the flow and the cost of money and credit to the economy. Yet it is equally clear that open market operations are the dominant instrument, by far the one most often used by the Fed. Having seen the characteristics of each of the others, we should now be able to see the rationality behind this dominance.

Perhaps the most striking characteristic of open market purchases and sales of securities is that they can be used continuously and in whatever amounts the Federal Open Market Committee desires. In a word, this instrument can be used with far more *flexibility* than is possible with any other instrument. Second, open market operations can be carried out discretely and quietly, with little or no psychological or expectational impacts on other buyers and sellers in the market. In a phrase, there are *no announcement effects* from

TABLE 14–4

The Evolution of Regular Reserve Requirements (percent), 1962–72

Effective Date	Net Demand Deposits				Time Deposits	
	Reserve City Banks		Country Banks			
			16½	12	Savings*	Other
November 1962	16½		12		4	
July 1966	16½		12		4	5
September 1966	16½		12		4	6
March 1967	16½		12		3	6
	First $5 million	Over $5 million	First $5 million	Over $5 million		
January 1968	16½	17	12	12½	3	6
April 1969	17	17½	12½	13	3	6
October 1970 (Until November 1972)	17	17½	12½	13	3	5

* Including the first $5 million of deposits in the other category. The latter comprises certificates of deposits, special passbook accounts, and the like.

these operations, a characteristic which is usually but not always an advantage. And third, security operations take effect with a relatively short time lag (for reasons we shall examine in the next chapter). They are *quick* and *effective*.

The other instruments have advantages which make them useful for specific occasions but not for general purposes. Reserve requirement changes are the most *powerful* instrument; they are the atomic bomb of the monetary arsenal. Until the recent development of these requirements, they were too powerful for all but the rarest occasions. The other major characteristic of reserve requirements is more of a practical advantage: their impact is *geographically diffused.* In contrast to open market operations, which directly affect only a group of 25 or so banks and other dealers in New York City, changes in reserve requirements affect all banks of a given size with equal force. The *quickness* of their impact can therefore be even greater than that of open market operations.

The discount rate is useful mainly for its *psychological impact.* When the Federal Reserve System feels it necessary to emphasize a change in the direction of policy or when it wishes to persuade banks to hold down lending rates at times when credit availability is being squeezed by a tightening of monetary policy, the discount rate comes to the fore. But this rate has little real impact on bank costs, so its effects tend to wear off quickly.

There are times when the policy objective is to control the *uses* of bank credit and other financing as well as the total volume and cost of funds. At such times, these general policy instruments may need reinforcement. It is to these supplementary tools that we now turn our attention.

REVIEW QUESTIONS

1. Suppose that you are the manager of the Open Market Account and that the FOMC has instructed you to try to increase the money supply at an annual rate of 5 percent. What actions will you take between now and the next meeting of the committee? How will you know whether you are on course?
2. Does the "bills only" doctrine limit the account manager's ability to control the money supply?
3. What determines the amount of member bank borrowing from Federal Reserve banks?
4. Should control over reserve requirements by the Federal Reserve Board be extended to include nonmember banks?
5. Under what circumstances would a change in reserve requirements be preferable to open market operations or changes in the discount rate?

SUGGESTED FURTHER READING

Boughton, James. *Monetary Policy and the Federal Funds Market.* Durham, N.C.: Duke University Press, 1972.

Roosa, Robert V. *Federal Reserve Operations in the Money and Government Securities Market.* Federal Reserve Bank of New York, July 1956.

Young, Ralph A. *Instruments of Monetary Policy in the United States.* Washington, D.C.: International Monetary Fund, 1974.

chapter 15

Instruments of Monetary Policy: The Supplementary Tools

15.1 INTRODUCTION

If one's only interest in monetary policy were to understand the means by which the Federal Reserve controls the
flow of credit to the economy in order to keep unemployment
and inflation from getting out of hand, then a knowledge of
the three major instruments described in Chapter 14 would
be quite sufficient. But the story of monetary control does
not end there for three reasons. First, at least one of the
three major instruments—reserve requirements—has not
been used frequently in its traditional form. It has been expanded in recent years to include a system of marginal requirements, which we examine in a later section.

Second, the Federal Reserve often has had more specific
policy objectives than simply to control the aggregate level
of economic activity; hence the necessity for selective policy
instruments. Open market operations, the discount rate, and
regular reserve requirements are *general* instruments of
monetary policy. They exert their principal influence by
affecting the supply of and the demand for bank reserves.
Banks thus are induced or forced to adjust their asset port-

folios, altering the volume of bank credit and the stock of money in the process. An important characteristic which these three instruments have in common is that they do not directly determine the *allocation* of credit and money to various sectors of the economy. Their use is confined largely to influencing the aggregate level of expenditure and income in the economy but not its distribution. The latter is left to the marketplace. The amount of credit flowing to consumers to finance the building and purchase of homes or automobiles, the amount available for helping people to buy shares on the stock market or for supporting business investment projects; these allocations will be determined primarily by relative prices which reflect the strength of demands and supplies in the separate credit markets. The purpose of the selective instruments described in this chapter is to enable the Federal Reserve to intervene in these markets and to alter the prevailing relative costs and prices.

The third point is that the Big Three policy instruments affect the money supply only by providing economic incentives to banks which operate in the context of a competitive market system. But the assumption of relatively free competition does not apply very rigorously to the U.S. banking system, and it applies even less rigorously to most other countries. Central banks therefore sometimes resort to direct controls over bank behavior.

15.2 MARGINAL RESERVE REQUIREMENTS

As we saw in the last chapter, the Federal Reserve has chosen to make very little use of its power to change reserve requirements on bank deposits. There are a number of reasons for this reluctance. One of the most serious problems with changes in reserve requirements is that they alter the profitability of each bank's total asset portfolio and thus may be highly disruptive. A second problem, which is partially solved by the development of multiple categories of requirements, is that changes affect too large a volume of reserves to be applicable to any but the most severe policy shifts. Both of these difficulties may be minimized by the introduction of *marginal* reserve requirements.

Marginal requirements have been employed by European central banks for many years, but have been used in the United States only since 1969. To see how this system works, let us return to our example of the previous chapter. We have a hypothetical bank with $50 million of demand and another $50 million of time deposits, against which it holds $6 million and $2 million in reserve balances, respectively. A one-half point increase in all regular reserve requirements would force the bank to raise an additional $500,000 in reserves (.005 × $100 million).

Now suppose that the Board of Governors imposes a marginal reserve requirement. It keeps all of the regular requirements at their present levels, but decrees that any *additional* deposits will be subject to the regular requirement plus, say, a 3 percent marginal requirement. There is no immediate impact on the bank's requirements, and no portfolio realignment is called for. But the bank will be partially discouraged from expanding its scale of operation; for every extra $10,000 of deposits which it takes in, it will have to hold $300 more than it would have otherwise in the sterile form of reserves. The reserve against $10,000 of regular time deposits for example would thus be $800 instead of $500.

Marginal requirements can be a useful supplementary instrument when the Fed is primarily interested in curbing the growth of the money supply and bank lending, rather than actually trying to induce a contraction. Since reduced growth has become the primary target of policy in the 1970s, marginal requirements may have a beneficial role to play. But they have another application which makes them an even greater part of the mix of policy instruments. We refer

to the use of marginal reserves against selected classes of
bank liabilities.

15.2.1   Marginal Reserve Requirements as a Selective Control

The Federal Reserve has applied marginal reserve requirements, at various times between 1969 and 1974, against three
types of bank liabilities: Euro-dollar borrowings, borrowings
from domestic bank-affiliated companies, and negotiable certificates of deposit (CDs). The rationale for this selection is
twofold. First, these liabilities are the primary means by
which large banks attract additional loanable funds during
periods when the Federal Reserve is pursuing a restrictive
monetary policy. Second, there may at times be reasons to
discourage the use of these particular channels because of
their disruptive effects on the rest of the economy.

Perhaps the clearest example of the effectiveness of this
instrument is afforded by the Euro-dollar market. In 1969,
the Federal Reserve was trying to restrict the growth of
the money supply, primarily in order to reduce inflationary
pressures in the economy. The Fed had used open market
operations to reduce the growth of bank reserves and had
increased reserve requirements on all classes of demand deposits. These contractionary policies pushed interest rates
sharply upward, but the Fed refused to allow commercial
banks to raise rates on time and savings deposits.[1] These deposits became less and less attractive to savers as the year
progressed, and the differential between deposit rates and
yields on treasury bills and deposits in other financial institutions widened. The resulting outflow of funds from banks
furthered the Federal Reserve contractionary objectives.

But commercial banks, especially the large money-market
banks, were neither helpless nor passive in the face of this

---

[1] See section 15.3 for a discussion of ceilings on deposit rates.

disintermediation of funds. The most serious outflow from the viewpoint of the large banker was a runoff of large CDs. Corporations which had purchased, say, 90-day negotiable certificates early in the year at a 6 percent interest rate were not about to renew them when they matured in the middle of the year, when rates of 7 percent or even 8 percent—rates the banks were forbidden from paying—were available on other assets. What to do about it? Well, the banks worked out an ingenious though rather circuitous system. The corporation would take its $100,000, or whatever amount it had invested in CDs, and deposit it in a foreign branch of the American bank. The foreign branch, operating outside the legal reach of the Fed, could pay whatever interest rates it chose. The head office of the bank, back in New York, Chicago, or San Francisco, then would simply borrow the same amount of money from its foreign office. The only difference so far as the corporation was concerned was that it owned an asset called a Euro-dollar deposit rather than a CD. So during 1969, the volume of negotiable CDs shrank from $24 billion to under $11 billion, while there was a corresponding growth in U.S. banks' liabilities to their foreign branches.

The Federal Reserve could do nothing about the high interest rates being offered overseas. But they became highly concerned over the existence of a major loophole in their system of reserve requirements. For at that time, liabilities other than deposits were not subject to any requirements at all. Therefore, the banks were not only retaining their initial level of total liabilities by shifting them out of CDs and into Euro-dollar liabilities, they were actually gaining loanable funds in the process.

A simple solution would have been to impose a reserve requirement on Euro-dollar liabilities at least equal to that imposed on CDs (5 percent). But the Fed had been presented with a fait accompli. To have imposed a 5 percent reserve requirement on over $14 billion of liabilities, most of which were held at a very few large banks, would have been the blow of a bigger stick than the Fed was willing to wield. The time for the idea of marginal requirements had arrived.

Effective in October 1969, the Board of Governors established a 10 percent reserve requirement on increases in Euro-dollar borrowing (and on the sale of assets by member banks to their foreign branches) above the amounts then outstanding. The market was not impaired, but the massive circular flow of funds was brought to a halt. Since 1969, the marginal requirement has been varied between 8 percent and 20 percent in order to control the inflow of foreign funds to the U.S. banking system. The higher requirements effectively prevent U.S. banks' branches from offering competitive interest rates to European or other foreign depositors in order to induce short-term capital inflows to this country.

Starting in the late 1960s, many of the largest banks formed holding companies, parent corporations which owned not only the bank but such nonbanking operations as insurance companies, finance (small personal loan) companies, travel agencies, and so on.[2] These holding companies were then able to raise funds in ways closed to the banks themselves. The finance companies, for example, could directly tap the commercial paper market, borrowing from corporations at terms more favorable to the corporation than those prevailing in the CD and other deposit markets. The bank could then borrow these funds from the finance company by channeling them through the parent corporation, the holding company. The higher interest cost of these funds would be compensated by the fact of their being completely free of reserve requirements. By 1973, the Board of Governors had closed most such loopholes through the imposition of marginal reserve requirements.

Even though the Board of Governors has not yet used

---

[2] Activities of these so-called one-bank holding companies have been controlled by the Federal Reserve only since 1971.

marginal reserve requirements in a general way to control overall deposit growth, it has made frequent changes in the regulations in recent years both to tighten loopholes and to restrict or encourage the use of certain channels by which banks raise funds. Table 15–1 shows the variety of applications for marginal requirements in 1973.

These applications are clearly limited, and there remains wide scope for increasing the role of marginal and other selective reserve requirements. One proposal which Andrew Brimmer made on several occasions when he was a member of the Board of Governors is to impose reserve requirements on selected categories of bank assets as well as on liabilities. Then if the Board of Governors wished to encourage bank lending to homebuilders and to discourage lending to large corporations, they could simply shift the mix of asset-reserve requirements in favor of the former. One of the main problems with this proposal is that of political control. Who would determine the priorities? The Board of Governors operates largely outside the political system, and Congress might be reluctant to turn over to it a power as sensitive as this one. Direct congressional intervention, however, could be even more readily abused.

TABLE 15–1

Changes in Marginal Reserve Requirements, 1973

June 21.	Requirements on Euro-dollar liabilities reduced, from 20 percent to 8 percent.
June 21.	A similar 8 percent requirement imposed on the growth of negotiable CDs and on some liabilities to bank affiliates (i.e., loans to the banks from other companies controlled by the same holding company).
July 12.	The 8 percent requirement extended to cover various liabilities to affiliates which had escaped the earlier regulations.
August 29.	The 8 percent requirement extended to cover large nonnegotiable CDs.
October 4.	Marginal requirements on all the above liabilities *except* Euro-dollars raised to 11 percent.
December 27.	All requirements dropped back to 8 percent.

15.2.2   Some Problems and Recommendations

The present system of reserve requirements, with its multi-
plicity of regular and marginal requirements, has distinct
disadvantages to counter its beneficial flexibility. In particular, the control of the money stock is now much more complicated a task than it otherwise would be. Whenever the public
shifts its deposit balances from one bank to another or from
one type of deposit to another, the amount of money and the
amount of bank lending which can be supported by a given
volume of reserves will change. In terms of our model of the
money supply process, both q_D and q_T become variables
which the Federal Reserve cannot fully control because they
depend on individual choices as well as on official policy
actions.

The issue may reasonably be posed as to whether changes
in reserve requirements should remain in the Federal Reserve's tool kit at all. To be a useful instrument this multi-
plicity and flexibility seems essential. And even so, changes in
requirements still affect bank profitability in a capricious
manner. Furthermore, there is little that reserve-requirement
changes can achieve that cannot be accomplished through a
sufficient volume of open market operations. The latter alters
the supply of reserves; the former alters the supply of deposits supportable by a given supply of reserves; the effect
is the same. But the reserve requirement tool is not completely useless. It can be effective in discouraging activity in
specific sectors, such as the Euro-dollar market. More generally and perhaps more importantly, it helps to take pressure
off open market operations when the Fed is making large
shifts in policy. It helps to minimize the extent of intervention in the bond market and thereby may contribute to
money market stability. In short, whereas open market
operations are clearly the best instrument for day-to-day
defensive policy actions, reserve requirement changes are a

helpful supplement when dynamic policies are being pursued.

An oft-voiced recommendation for overcoming many of the objections to reserve requirement changes is for the Federal Reserve to completely standardize requirements on all deposits and nondeposit liabilities and to pay interest to member banks on their reserve deposits at a rate competitive with, say, treasury bill rates. This proposal would eliminate the profit problem, reduce the money-stock control problem, and simplify calculations sufficiently to render feasible the possibility of making small fractional changes in the level of requirements. But the introduction of interest payments on reserves would present the banks with a windfall that would meet with congressional disapproval.

A less far-reaching proposal with a greater chance of success in the political marketplace is to require all banks to join the Federal Reserve System. Some problems would of course remain. But the Board of Governors would at least be able to conduct monetary policy without having to worry at every turn whether they might be tromping too hard on a few bankers' toes.

15.3   CEILINGS ON INTEREST RATES

For more than 40 years, the Federal Reserve has attempted to prevent the large banks from outbidding everyone else for deposit funds. Until the early 1930s, banks were permitted to pay whatever interest rates they were able to offer on deposits, both demand and time. But the fear developed in Congress and at the Board of Governors that the large New York banks were able to afford higher rates than their smaller competitors and that a reallocation of funds from country to city might ensue. To limit this opportunity, Congress passed two major reforms: the banking acts of 1933 and 1935 (the same acts which established federal deposit insurance). These acts prohibited the payment of interest on demand deposits and empowered the Federal Reserve Board and the newly created Federal Deposit Insurance Corporation (FDIC) to impose ceilings on rates payable on time and savings deposits at member and insured nonmember commercial banks.[3]

Interest rate ceilings have been administered by the Federal Reserve under a set of rules known simply as Regulation Q. It has proved to be a difficult regulation to administer; one which, used unwisely, can aggravate the very problems it was designed to solve. So long as the only real competition for funds was among the commercial banks themselves, Regulation Q worked fairly well. Everyone lived under the same set of rules. But the structure and even the nature of the banking system changed dramatically during the 1960s, in ways that undid the utility of Regulation Q.

One major development was the increasing willingness of the public to shift its savings deposits out of banks and into savings and loan associations or mutual savings banks whenever these so-called thrift institutions offered higher interest rates. Witness the disruption of 1966, the year of the Great Credit Crunch. To combat what was then an emerging inflationary pressure in the economy, the Federal Reserve shifted to a contractionary policy, reducing the growth of the money supply and driving interest rates upward. The Fed kept the screws on the Regulation Q ceilings, so that banks were prohibited from raising deposit rates to attract additional funds. The thrift or savings institutions, however, were free to raise their rates, and many of them did.

The most dramatic developments came in the volatile California financial markets, where a group of very large savings and loan associations not only raised their deposit

---

[3] Under the terms of the act, all member banks were required to be insured by the FDIC, and nonmembers had the option to subscribe. The FDIC acts as a regulatory agency over insured nonmembers.

rates (technically called "dividends" but practically the same as deposit rates in the minds of most savers) well above the rates offered by commercial banks, but also began to solicit mailed-in funds nationally through clip-out coupon advertisements in newspapers and magazines. The banks could not meet the competition because of Regulation Q. Furthermore, few savings and loans could meet it either. Under the laws by which thrift institutions are chartered, they must hold most of their assets in the form of real estate loans (mortgages). In return, they receive favorable tax treatment. But mortgages are long-term commitments. When interest rates rise, it is only the *new* mortgages on which these lenders can raise rates. On the bulk of their assets, they are locked in to a fixed interest-rate income. The larger institutions may be able to sell large blocks of their old mortgages to secondary lenders, taking a loss but freeing assets to make new loans at higher rates. Hence a severe reallocation of funds occurred in 1966, crunching the commercial banks and small thrift institutions alike.

In September of 1966, Congress passed new legislation empowering the appropriate regulatory agencies to extend the maximum-rate rules to cover thrift institutions as well as commercial banks. But the financial system reacted like a good yeast dough: pushed down and flattened, it rose again in a different shape. The banks had already in the early 1960s developed the negotiable CD as an instrument for tapping the cash boxes of corporate treasuries. Through 1966, the ceilings applicable to CDs were higher than on savings deposits, high enough that rates were competitive and attractive to corporations. So the money-market banks had some protection against the outflow of funds in 1966.

As we saw in our discussion of marginal reserve requirements, the banking system was again squeezed by rising interest rates in 1969. This time, rates on commercial paper,

treasury bills, and other nonbanking, short-term borrowing
instruments rose above the ceiling rates applicable even to
CDs. Again the large banks beat the system, first by developing the Euro-dollar market and then by tapping the commercial paper market through holding companies (see section
15.2.1). By 1973, the Fed had completely given up on this
particular application of Regulation Q. Since then, the maximum rates have been suspended on large CDs (see Table
15–2).

TABLE 15–2

**Regulation Q: Maximum Rates Payable by Banks (as of
January 1974)**

Type of Deposit	Maximum Rate
Savings deposits	5%
Other time deposits, in amounts of:	
Less than $100,000, with maturities of:	
30–89 days	5
90 days to 1 year	5½
1–2½ years	6
2½ years or more	6½
4 years or more in denominations of $1,000 or more	7¼
$100,000 or more (whether negotiable or not)	No ceiling

What remains of Regulation Q is a limitation on the rates
which banks and thrift institutions can pay to small savers.
Because of market imperfections such as the federal government's required minimum purchase of $10,000 for treasury
bills, and because of a lack of information to small savers,
this group is discriminated against by the present rules. The
argument in favor of their retention is that the possibility
remains for large institutions to outbid smaller competitors
and for banks to outbid thrift institutions in attracting funds.
But it no longer is applicable as an instrument of monetary
policy in the manner in which it was used in 1966 and 1969.

15.4 MARGIN REQUIREMENTS ON STOCK MARKET LOANS

One of the earliest and most often used selective-control instruments is the margin requirement, a limitation on the loan-to-value ratio for loans secured by corporate stocks. To see the rationale for this rule, consider the following examples.

Suppose that you were interested in buying 100 shares of stock in the Ford Motor Company and that the stock were selling at $30 per share at the time of your purchase. You could of course pay your broker in cash, writing a check for $3,000. But you might wish instead to borrow part of the funds, perhaps directly from the broker. In this example, he might require a 70 percent down payment; you would pay him $2,100 and sign a note for the other $900 at some specified rate of interest.

The significance of having a percentage *margin* on such loans is that the amount that you can borrow from the broker or other lender will vary with the selling price of the stock. Shares which are listed on the major stock exchanges and are widely traded may also vary substantially in price. When the price drops, so does the value of the collateral (the shares of stock) which is providing the broker security against his loan to you. So the broker can be protected against price fluctuations by requiring that you pay off part of your loan whenever prices fall. Algebraically, if the unpaid principal on your loan is L and the value of the collateral is C, then the margin is

$$\text{Margin} = 1 - \frac{L}{C}.$$

The requirement of a 70 percent margin therefore implies that you can borrow only up to 30 percent of the current market value of the stock.

Suppose that, in our example, the price of Ford Motor

stock were to drop to $25 per share. To maintain the 70 per-
cent margin, you would have to reduce the value of your
loan to $750 (30 percent of $2,500) by paying the lender
another $150. Conversely, if the price were to rise, the lender
would normally be willing to lend you more money against
the value of the shares.

Now notice the effect of operating on a very small margin.
Suppose that the broker required only a 10 percent payment,
loaning you $2,700 secured by 100 shares of stock. When the
price drops to $25 per share, you must reduce your loan to
$2,250 by paying off $450 immediately. (Lenders refer to
this requirement as a "margin call.") The smaller margin
therefore enables purchasers to borrow larger sums and to
buy greater quantities of stock. But it also implies that any
drop in stock prices will force larger cash loan repayments.
And if a borrower is unable to raise the cash to meet the
margin call, then the loan is foreclosed, and he loses his investment. In short, he is wiped out.

When the stock market crashed in 1929, there were no
legal limitations on the use of stocks as loan collateral at
brokers, banks, or other institutions. Thirty percent or even
smaller margins were common. The decline in stock prices
quickly became ruinous for a great many people who could
not meet their margin calls. Furthermore, the decline became
cumulative as people were forced to sell other stocks in an
effort to raise the necessary payments. To limit the possibility
of a repetition of this greatest of financial disasters, the Federal Reserve imposed in 1937 a set of legal *margin requirements* on banks and other major lenders (not to be confused
in any way with the completely different animal "marginal
reserve requirements").

Margin requirements have been used by the Federal Reserve since 1945 as a flexible instrument to limit the extension
of bank credit for purchases of common stock. When the
Fed is pursuing a generally restrictive policy, it may wish to

reduce so far as possible the effects on loans to such vulnerable sectors as home builders and new or small businesses. One way to further that objective is to reduce stock market loans by raising margin requirements.

The more basic reason for varying margin requirements, however, is to control the purchase of stocks on credit. During periods of high rates of aggregate demand—periods when the Federal Reserve is likely to be pursuing a restrictive policy in order to reduce inflationary pressures—it is often, though by no means always, the case that stock prices are rising. This phenomenon, combined with that of rapidly growing personal income, may encourage speculation in the stock market. Again there may be a rationale for raising legal margin requirements as a supplement to the generally tight monetary policy.

The actual changes in margin requirements since 1937 are summarized in Figure 15–1. Most of the time, requirements have been either 70 percent or higher—when stock prices have been climbing rapidly or the Fed was operating a tight monetary policy or both—or else around 50 percent, during stock market slumps. Unfortunately, it is not at all clear that these variations have been successful either in reducing speculation in stocks or in diverting bank loans toward borrowers favored by the Federal Reserve. A reasonably high margin requirement, say 60 percent, is definitely beneficial in helping to prevent the worst abuses of the 1929 financial debacle. Whether variation in requirements around that level is worthwhile is less well established.

15.5 CONSUMER CREDIT CONTROLS

It is possible to control other types of lending in the same manner as stock market loans by employing the equivalent of margin requirements on various types of collateral. In addition, regulations may be issued to limit the maximum

FIGURE 15–1
Margin Requirements, 1937–74

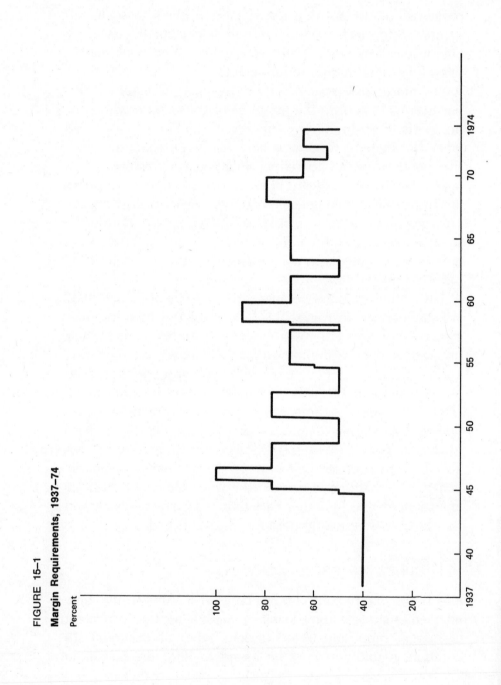

repayment periods for specific kinds of loans. This latter practice would increase the size of each monthly payment and make it more difficult for relatively less affluent borrowers to meet the requirements. Rules of this sort would have little effect on corporate borrowers, so in practice they have been confined to the control of consumer loans.

There are a variety of reasons for resorting to control of consumer credit, even though the Fed normally would have little reason to discourage consumer expenditure as such. Interest rates on consumer loans are restricted in many states, under what are still called usury laws even in an age of federal "truth in lending" statutes. Interest rates therefore may be immobilized as a rationer of consumer credit in periods of general economic expansion. Direct controls could provide some assistance. A more regularly invoked argument is that consumer demand may have to be curtailed in wartime in order to release resources for military production and prevent precipitous increases in consumer prices. This argument carried particular weight in the 1940s, when the Federal Reserve had committed itself to a policy of pegging interest rates on government bonds at a very low level, severely constraining the applications of the general instruments of monetary policy.[4]

During and immediately after World War II, the Federal Reserve attempted to control the extension of consumer credit—loans secured by automobiles or other durable consumer goods—through the regulation both of minimum down payments and maximum repayment periods. Control then was temporarily suspended but was reinstated during the Korean War (1950–52) and was extended to include real estate credit (mortgage loans). Since that time, however,

---

[4] For a history of this period of monetary policy, through the 1940s and up to the Treasury–Federal Reserve "accord" of 1951, see Milton Friedman and Anna Schwartz, *A Monetary History of the United States 1867–1960* (Princeton, N.J.: Princeton University Press, 1963).

even during the inflationary years of the Vietnam War, the
Federal Reserve has avoided the reimposition of these regulations.

These rules did not work in quite the same way as margin
requirements in the following sense. Consumer goods, unlike
stocks, are expected to decline steadily in value (i.e., to depreciate). The borrower, instead of having an open-ended
loan on which he may have to meet margin calls, has a fixed-
maturity loan on which he must meet regular payments.
Hence the concept of margin requirements is replaced by
that of the minimum initial payment as a percentage only of
the initial purchase price of the good to be used as collateral.

15.6 MORAL SUASION

Another selective control sometimes used by the Federal
Reserve is known by the slyly misleading title, *moral suasion.*
It is a common instrument available to all administrators
whether they be politicians, civil servants, business managers,
or teachers. Anyone exercising leadership expects to get at
least part of his or her job accomplished by the gentler arts of
persuasion and moral force without resort to regulations,
rules, or commands. The Federal Reserve is no exception. On
specific occasions Reserve officials have requested that member banks voluntarily curtail the volume of business lending.
The Federal Reserve thus hoped to achieve its policy objectives in part by the cooperation of the member banks without
having to rely solely on the other available policy instruments.

The only two occasions in recent years when the Fed has
resorted to this Big Brother technique[5] have been in 1966
and 1973, when they sent the letters reproduced in Figure
15–2. On the first occasion, many banks had been selling
their holdings of securities issued by state and local govern-

---

[5] For a good criticism of the practice, see Edward Kane, "The Central Bank
as Big Brother," *Journal of Money, Credit, and Banking* 5, November 1973.

FIGURE 15–2

Moral Suasion

I. Excerpts from the letter dated September 1, 1966, sent by each Federal Reserve bank president to all the member banks in his district:

It is the view of the Federal Reserve System that orderly bank credit expansion is appropriate in today's economy. However, . . . the aggregate total of credit-financed business spending has tended towards unsustainable levels and has added appreciably to inflationary pressures. Furthermore, such exceedingly rapid business loan expansion is being financed in part by liquidation of other assets [especially municipal securities] . . . in ways that could contribute to disorderly conditions in other credit markets. . . . Hence, the System believes that a greater share of member bank adjustments should take the form of moderation in the rate of expansion of loans, and particularly business loans.

Accordingly, this objective will be kept in mind by the Federal Reserve Banks in their extension of credit to member banks through the discount window. Member banks will be expected to cooperate . . . .

II. Excerpts from the letter dated April 6, 1973, from the chairman of the Board of Governors to all banks with $100 million or more in deposits:

I am writing to you about a matter of concern to all members of the Board—the heavy volume of bank loan commitments to commercial and industrial companies and financial institutions. . . . There is no question as to the legitimacy of—and the need for—bank loan commitments. . . . It is the intention of the Federal bank supervisors that this practice continue, but that it be based on careful judgment, in the interests of a sound banking system and healthy economic expansion. . . .

Each bank should maintain a record of the aggregate volume of its commitments to lend . . . periodically make a careful judgment as to the potential volume of takedowns of these commitments . . . [and] . . . give adequate consideration as to how it would obtain the funds . . . .

Federal bank examiners will henceforth ask the management of each bank they examine to demonstrate that it is giving adequate attention to the above principles. . . .

---

ments (municipals) in order to make business loans. The Fed became concerned about the effect of this runoff on the ability of municipal governments to raise funds. Lacking direct controls, they decided to try persuasion, coupled with a hint that a bank's ability to borrow at the discount window might be made contingent on its cooperation.

On the more recent occasion, the problem was potentially more serious. Corporate borrowers had been making increasing use of "lines of credit" and other forms of loan commitments at banks, arrangements under which the bank would agree to make loans in the future in return for the payment of fees or the placement in the bank of demand balances by the corporation. In the early months of 1973, the combination of a restrictive monetary policy and heavy corporate demand for bank loans led to an unusually heavy drawing on these lines of credit. The Federal Reserve became concerned that the existence of credit lines on that scale would (1) limit their own ability to control the growth of bank credit and (2) possibly even limit the ability of the banks themselves to control their asset structure. The impending decline in liquidity throughout the economy could have generated serious financial problems. As a warning to the banks, the Fed again applied persuasion, this time coupled with the threat of tighter examination practice.

On both occasions, moral suasion proved to be at least a partial and temporary success. Nonetheless, its use stirred up sufficient confusion and resentment among bankers that its long-run effects may have been negative. Would a banker now think twice before buying a municipal security that he might later be dissuaded from selling? Would he perhaps be induced to develop less open, less readily measurable means of protecting his relationships with his major corporate customers? Considerations such as these are bound to relegate moral suasion to the category of an emergency rather than an everyday instrument of control.

15.7   DIRECT CONTROLS

Another last-ditch policy measure is in theory the epitome of simplicity. If the objective of the central bank is to limit the amount of lending by commercial banks, it may resort to ceilings and just tell the bankers that they cannot make any loans beyond some specified maximum limit. The Federal Reserve does not have and has not sought such sweeping powers, but it did for about eight years (December 1965 through January 1974) operate a program of direct controls on foreign lending by banks and other financial institutions. This program was known as the Voluntary Foreign Credit Restraint (VFCR) program, but it was not, except at the outset, truly voluntary. Banks were assigned ceilings on lending and other credits to foreigners, the ceilings being based on the amounts outstanding in some base period. For example, by the end of 1966, banks were expected to show foreign credits of not more than 109 percent of the value held at the end of 1964.

The purpose of the VFCR program was twofold. It was instituted at a time when monetary policy was moving toward restriction but when interest rates in the United States were still significantly below those prevailing in other countries. There was heavy demand for loans at U.S. financial institutions by foreigners trying to take advantage of these low rates. Growth in these loans was further squeezing the amount of funds available to domestic corporations and other borrowers. The Federal Reserve could have made enough bank reserves available to satisfy both domestic and foreign borrowers, but it judged that that policy would have implied a greater growth in total bank credit and in the money supply than was deemed desirable. To prevent the given degree of monetary restriction from contracting domestic loans excessively, the VFCR program was devised.

Secondly, the program was designed to limit the deterioration in the U.S. balance of international payments which was then emerging. Loans to foreigners are an outflow of capital and show up as a minus figure in the balance of payments accounts (see Chapter 11, section 11.2.2). If the foreign borrowers then convert their dollars into their own domestic currencies, the outflow will lead to a deterioration in the official reserve position of the U.S. government. The market solution to this threat would be to allow our own interest rates to rise at least as high as those abroad, eliminating the incentive for foreigners to borrow here. It was in fact to obviate the need for a rise in interest rates that the government proposed the introduction of direct controls on bank lending.

Other countries have made wider and more prolonged use of direct controls. Throughout Europe (except in West Germany) and in Japan, the central banks have for many years imposed ceilings on bank lending, both specifically (to limit loans to consumers or foreigners) and generally (to limit total growth in bank loans). However, it often is difficult to distinguish the application of this type of instrument from the other tools described in this chapter. The central bank must establish some form of sanction or penalty for banks which violate the regulations. In some cases (including the VFCR program and the ceilings imposed by the Bank of Japan), no formal sanctions have been used; then the instrument becomes almost indistinguishable from moral suasion. The Bank of England has applied a scheme of graduated penalty reserve requirements to banks whose growth exceeds specified limits; these rules could well be classified as a severe form of marginal reserve requirements. Thus the purest form of direct control is confined to countries such as the socialist bloc of Eastern Europe, where the banking system is an arm of the central government and is assigned lending targets as part of a more general economic plan.

15.8 CONCLUSIONS

We now have examined a wide variety of available instruments of monetary policy, each with its own peculiarities and each designed in some way to help to achieve one or more of the goals described in the opening chapter to this Part. There remains one major issue on this topic: the way in which instrumental changes are transmitted to the goal variables. We know, of course, how the basic process works. The central bank generates a shift in the relations affecting the supply of money. The market for money balances is thrown out of equilibrium, and both interest rates and the money-stock change as the banks and the public adjust their portfolios of assets. The demand for goods and services eventually must respond; and incomes, prices, and output follow suit.

The mechanics of this process are still hidden in a black box which we have not yet opened. How important are interest rates compared to changes in the availability of money and credit in transmitting policy changes? Which interest rates are most important? Why do some policy changes take effect only after a very slow adjustment? Which categories of expenditure—business investment, housing construction, government spending, and so on—are affected most strongly by changes in monetary policy? These are some of the questions that the central banker or the economic analyst must answer in order to know exactly how and when monetary actions should be taken.

REVIEW QUESTIONS

1. It is sometimes said that the Federal Reserve System has responsibility for determining the *volume* of credit and that the *allocation* of credit should be left to the market. Evaluate the merits of that argument.
2. What is the distinction between money and credit?

3. Does Regulation Q contribute to economic instability? What would be the consequences if ceiling rates were abandoned?
4. What is the rationale for the regulations on the minimum down payment required for the purchase of stock exchange securities?
5. Under what circumstances is "jaw-boning" or the use of moral suasion likely to be effective?
6. What are the advantages and disadvantages of imposing reserve requirements on selected *assets* of commercial banks?

SUGGESTED FURTHER READING

Haywood, Charles F. *Regulation Q and Monetary Policy.* Association of Reserve City Bankers, 1971.

Hodgman, Donald R. *National Monetary Policies and International Monetary Cooperation.* Boston: Little, Brown and Company, 1974.

Kane, Edward J. "The Central Bank as Big Brother," *Journal of Money, Credit and Banking* 5. November 1973.

Young, Ralph A. "The Supplementary Instruments." *Instruments of Monetary Policy in the United States.* Washington, D.C.: International Monetary Fund, 1974; Chap. 6.

chapter 16

The Transmission of Monetary Policy

There is many a slip
'Twixt the Fed and its goals
And a poorly helmed ship
Could end up on the shoals.

Ancient proverb

16.1 INTRODUCTION

In the spring of 1974, the Federal Open Market Committee (FOMC) agreed that it should return to a restrictive monetary policy in order to further its goal of reducing the rate of price inflation. Its chosen spearhead was the open market portfolio: the FOMC decided to provide bank reserves at a slower pace. In April, as a supplementary measure, the Board of Governors approved increases in the discount rate to the all-time record level of 8 percent.

Having taken these actions, no one in the Federal Reserve System expected the inflation rate to fall immediately. For there is no simple formula connecting the price level to the Federal Reserve's security portfolio or to the discount rate. Instead, policy actions launch a sequence of events which only gradually ripple outward through the economy and eventually influence the motion of prices, payments, and employment.

The processes by which actions on policy instruments work through the economy to reach the goal variables are known collectively as the *transmission* process for monetary policy. It is tempting to draw an analogy between this process and the transmission mechanism in an automobile. Indeed, they do serve the same purposes: in an automobile, to transmit the power of the engine to the wheels; in the financial system, to transmit the powers of the Fed to the pace of real economic activity. Unlike the former, the latter is not a straightforward mechanical process. When the Federal Reserve changes gears, it is likely to hear a lot of groaning, wheezing, and grinding before very much happens at the other end of the chain. In fact, at times the nature of the slippages—lags, unpredictable shifts in aggregate demand or supply conditions—becomes a more important consideration in the formulation of monetary policy than the nature of the known linkages.[1]

The basic structure of the transmission process has four components: instruments, proximate targets, intermediate targets, and goals. These components are linked together in a causal chain such that instrumental changes directly influence the values of the proximate targets, which then directly influence the intermediate targets and thence the goal variables.

Instruments → Proximate targets → Intermediate targets → Goals.

We already have seen the beginning and the end of this chain (in Chapters 14 and 15): before we can make an overall assessment of the process, we must examine its interior links. In so doing, we shall concentrate on the transmission of open market operations, which are both the most important tool and the one generating the most complex process of adjustment in the economy.

16.2   THE PROXIMATE TARGETS

The proximate targets are those variables which are closely connected to open market operations and which the manager

---

[1] See Chapter 17 for a fuller statement of this point.

of the open market account at the Federal Reserve Bank of New York can watch on a daily or weekly basis to monitor the impact of purchases or sales. These variables in fact are the basis for the short-run formulation of open market operations, as we described in Chapter 14 (section 14.2.1). When the FOMC meets each month, it specifies target ranges for these variables to be maintained throughout the period until the next meeting of the committee.

There are two categories of proximate targets: short-term interest rates and related aggregates. Specifically, these targets include the following.

1. The monetary base—Total bank reserves plus currency in circulation.
2. The "unborrowed" base—The total base less reserves borrowed by member banks.
3. Reserves to support private deposits (RPDs)—Total bank reserves less those absorbed by interbank deposits or by deposits of the federal government.
4. Free reserves—Excess reserves less reserves borrowed by member banks.
5. Interest rates on treasury bills.
6. Interest rates on interbank loans in the Federal funds market.

As we saw in our examination of the money supply process, it is necessary for the Federal Reserve to control the supply of reserves and currency if it wishes to control the supply of money. But the theory is simpler than the practice. One problem is that the monetary base may not be completely controllable over short periods of time largely because member-bank borrowing could increase and thereby offset the effects of open market sales of securities. To the extent that the borrowing is merely a temporary effort by the banks to ride out the adjustment period without having to sell assets before they mature or to refuse loans to regular customers, the data on the total monetary base may be misleading during the initial weeks of a restrictive policy. So, both because the total base is difficult to control precisely and because it is not the most meaningful reserve aggregate, the FOMC may wish to pay more attention to the unborrowed portion of the base.

Since 1972 the FOMC has employed a reserve aggregate called RPDs: reserves to support private deposits. The rationale for the use of this aggregate is that changes in the volume of deposits placed in banks by other banks or of deposits of the U.S. government may not affect economic activity to the same extent as "private" deposits. A typical situation regularly facing the Fed occurs whenever corporate or individual tax payments shift deposits from private accounts to government accounts in commercial banks. The supply of reserves is unchanged, but the availability of funds to the private sector is diminished. By using RPD's as the short-run operating target, the manager of the open market account can accommodate this shift by supplying enough extra reserves to offset it. Total bank reserves will rise, while reserves available to support private deposits will be unchanged. When the government later spends the accumulated funds, drawing down its own deposit accounts and replenishing those of the private sector, the Fed's account manager will have to take defensive action to reduce total reserves again.

The use of RPDs does not solve all of the FOMC's operational problems. By ignoring changes in public holdings of currency, it may reduce the Fed's control over the stock of money. By lumping together borrowed and unborrowed reserves, it could lead to more erratic behavior in bank deposits in the short run. The experiment is still too young to permit a clear evaluation of these problems.

Another proximate target of open market policy which was used during the 1950s and 1960s is the level of *free* reserves (excess reserves — borrowed reserves). Presumably an increase in free reserves would supply the banks with greater liquidity; they could therefore be expected to adjust their portfolios by making more loans. A decrease in free reserves similarly signaled an impending contraction. The difficulty with setting a free reserve target is that the banks' demand for free reserves—the amount of free reserves which banks *want* to hold—is not constant; it varies with interest rates, bank expectations about changes in Federal Reserve policy, and other economic information. Furthermore, an expansionary policy might well develop with no increase at all in free reserves, so long as banks adjust their portfolios to absorb new reserves at the same rate at which the Federal Reserve supplies them. Changes in free reserves often do supply useful information about the course of policy, but they are not predictable enough to serve as a primary proximate target.

In addition to the reserve targets, the Federal Reserve closely watches movements in sensitive short-term interest rates. Open-market operations are conducted primarily through purchases and sales of treasury bills, so it is reasonable to suppose that the prices of these assets should be an important proximate target. Ceteris paribus, whenever the Federal Reserve purchases treasury bills—thereby adding to the total demand for these securities—the prices charged by the dealers in the market should rise and the percentage yields should correspondingly fall. Changes in bill rates clearly are one of the most direct and immediate consequences of open market operations, though on a daily basis purchases or sales by the Fed may have little or no effect on the rate.

The difficulty with reliance on bill rates as a proximate target is that nonmonetary considerations also influence movements in the bill rate and thereby cloud their role in the transmission process. During that tight-money episode in early 1974, for example, treasury bill rates rose by only a small margin at a time when other short-term interest rates were rising rapidly to all-time record levels. Banks were willing to buy and to hold treasury bills yielding 8 percent even though such close substitutes as commercial paper and acceptances were yielding 10 percent to 11 percent. Treasury bills play a unique role in the banks' asset structure, because they can be used as collateral for loans from the Federal Reserve System or through the Federal funds market. When monetary policy tightens, banks may become even more dependent on their holdings of bills as their borrowing requirements increase. Bill prices therefore hold up (keeping interest rates stable) much better than those of other money-market assets during periods of monetary restriction.

Gradually, treasury bill rates have been supplanted by Federal funds rates as a proximate policy target. A tightening of monetary policy, by reducing the availability of bank reserves, will force banks to scramble for funds. And the first line of defense today for large and small banks alike will be the Federal funds market, the market for overnight interbank loans. Small banks which had been net suppliers (i.e., lenders) of funds will become less willing to offer reserves at the same time that large banks are increasing their demands. The extremely short-term nature of this market and its great sensitivity to the relative supplies and demands for bank reserves make its prevailing interest rates an ideal indicator of changes in the pressure on the reserve market. Since 1972, the Federal funds rate and RPDs have served as principal proximate targets of open market policy. Their movements over the past few years are shown in Figure 16–1.

It is always precarious to infer the direction of monetary policy from the behavior of a few variables, particularly when—as was the case on several occasions during the period shown in the chart—the information is contradictory. So the labeling of "restrictive" and "easy" periods is more of a broad description of the course of monetary policy than a specific characterization of the movements of the proximate target variables.

In the first year or so shown in Figure 16–1 (up to Febru-

FIGURE 16-1

Behavior of RPDs and the Federal Funds Rate, 1969–74

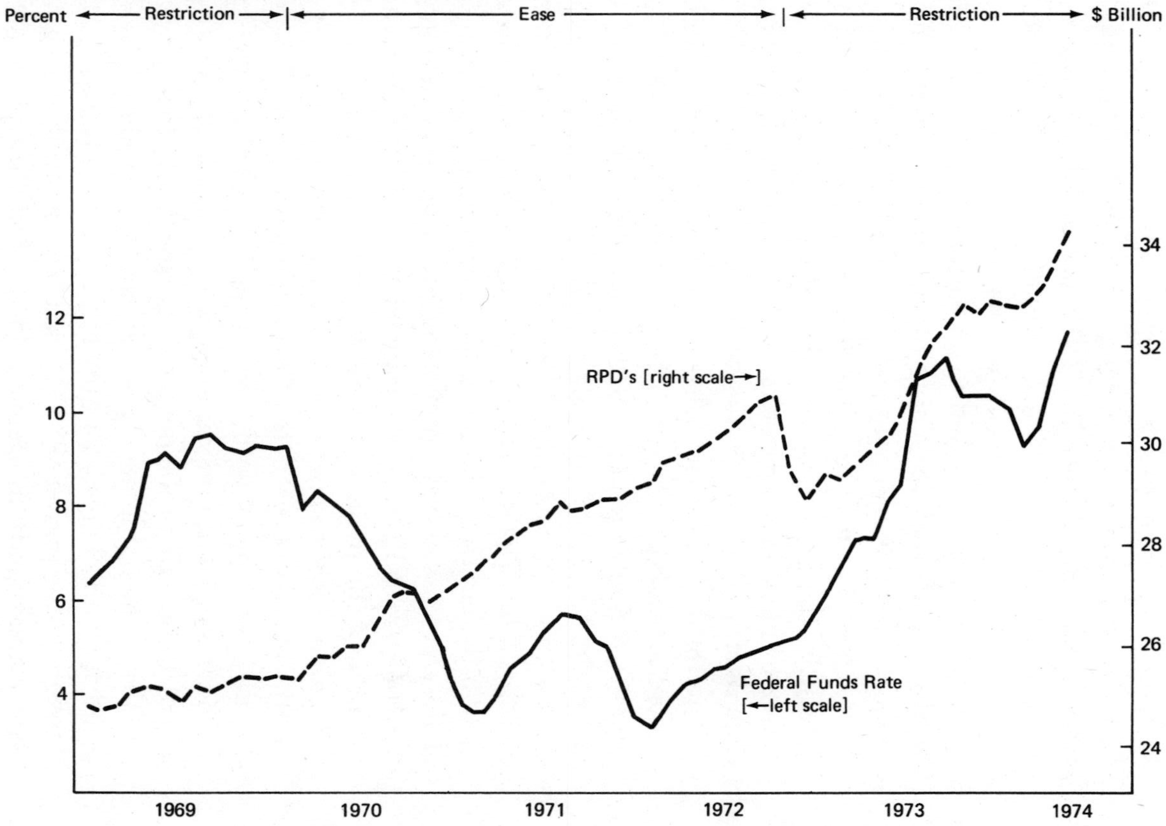

ary 1970) the Federal Reserve followed a policy which had a restrictive effect on the markets for bank reserves. The Federal funds rate rose to 9 percent and remained at that high level for almost a year. Meanwhile, the FOMC supplied reserve balances at a trickle. The stock of RPDs grew at an average rate of $43 million per month, for a percentage increase of just over 2 percent per year.

When the System shifted to an easier policy in early 1970 in response to the weakening of economic activity, one of the first effects was a sharp drop in the Federal funds rate. Over the next year, it fell steadily to near $3\frac{1}{2}$ percent. Simultaneously, the growth of available bank reserves accelerated to a pace in excess of 8 percent (about $175 million increase each month).

The third major policy phase shown in the figure exhibits a more ambiguous pattern. The Fed apparently shifted to a restrictive policy in late 1972, in an effort to control the mounting inflationary pressures in the economy. The initial impact on RPDs was quite dramatic: a $2 billion drop in two months. The Federal funds rate began to creep upward, though by less than one might have expected, given the size of the decrease in reserve availability. But from the beginning of 1973, RPD growth resumed the pace it had attained throughout the preceding period of monetary ease. The only immediate indication that a restrictive policy was in effect was the persistent rise in the Federal funds rate, which was in double figures most of the time after July 1973.

These apparently contradictory developments spotlight one of the major problems faced by the Federal Reserve in the short-run implementation of monetary policy. The demand for bank loans was growing at extremely rapid rates throughout the period 1973–74, first because of the growth in aggregate expenditure demand in the first three quarters of 1973, and thereafter because of the effects of price inflation on the dollar volume of business spending and borrowing requirements. As a result of this unusual growth in demand, the same growth in reserves which would have been expansionary in more normal times was now restrictive in its effects. The degree of restriction was difficult to judge until the whole transmission process had time to work. Is was thus necessary for the Federal Reserve to watch as many variables as possible.

16.3   THE INTERMEDIATE TARGETS

There remains a long road between the proximate targets and the goal variables; between, for example, a change in the supply of bank reserves and a change in the rate of unemployment. We traveled a theoretical version of this road in our study of money and the economy (Part Three). The increase in reserve availability provides banks with funds which they can use to purchase earning assets such as loans and securities. At the same time, the drop in interest rates will encourage businesses and consumers to increase spending. The increase in demand deposits desired by the public increases the required reserves of the banking system, eventually restoring equilibrium to the banks' balance sheets. The higher level of total spending increases aggregate income, output, employment, and prices.

While this whole process is going on, the Federal Reserve has to have some means of assuring that its policies are putting the economy on course, some means of observing whether the increase in reserves or the drop in short-term interest rates is approximately of the right amount to increase output and employment without an excessive rise in prices. And this is where the intermediate targets come in. These targets are financial variables which are linked both to the proximate targets and to the goal variables and which provide the Federal Reserve with significant landmarks as it watches the effects of its policies travel through the economy.

There are a large number of variables which either have been used by the Federal Reserve or have been suggested by kibitzers as intermediate targets. Three may be isolated as of particular importance:

1. Yields on corporate and government bonds.
2. The stock of money.
3. The stock of bank credit.

Corporate bond yields are important because they are one of the most important channels through which financial conditions affect real economic activity. Recall that the *EE* curve (expenditure equilibrium) in our graphic model of the economy reveals that desired total expenditure is causally related to interest rates, primarily through the dependence of investment spending on the cost of financing. Since much of business investment is financed through the issuance of bonds, the yields on those securities can be used as a good proxy for the actual cost of raising funds, which may also depend on factors such as the ability of corporations to generate internal cash flow from sales, the condition of the markets for corporate stock, and the like. As a first approximation, then, the Federal Reserve may conclude that a drop in corporate bond yields will be followed by a rise in business investment and in aggregate national income.

The role of interest rates in transmitting monetary policy actions is in practice much more complicated than this first approximation would suggest. There are a large number of interest rates in our economy; they do not always move together, and each rate has an impact on some specific sector of economic activity. Furthermore, it takes a substantial passage of time for the effects of interest rate changes to work through the economy. Meanwhile, the changes in the flow of economic activity are likely to feed back to the financial markets and affect interest rates. Thus an expansionary monetary policy may produce either falling interest rates (as the basic model would suggest) or rising interest rates (if the economy expands rapidly and pulls interest rates upward). These complications are important enough to occupy our attention for much of the remainder of this chapter.

So the search continues for a variable which gives more intelligible information to the FOMC and the account manager about the intermediate effects of monetary policy. Generally, the remaining candidates may be described as *monetary aggregates*. Regardless of what is happening to interest rates, one may argue, increases in the money stock are expansionary, while decreases are contractionary. But the truth of this proposition may be questioned on at least two grounds. First, we live in a growing economy. Some growth in the money stock may be necessary just to keep up with population and production increases, and it is the growth beyond that rate which is expansionary. It is not contraction but slow growth in the stock of money that is indicative of monetary restriction. Before the money stock can serve as a useful intermediate target, we must be able to estimate the slope of this break-even trend line.

Second, the demand for money associated with a given level of real economic activity may not be stable. We saw in Chapter 7 that the demand for money depends on interest rates and perhaps on inflationary expectations, as well as on income. Ideally, we need to know whether the growth in the stock of money is in line with these fluctuations in money demands.

What these two qualifications imply is that the true measure of the intermediate impact of monetary policy is the existence of an excess supply of money (in the expansionary case) or of an excess demand (equals insufficient supply to meet the demand; this indicating monetary contraction). Subject to the qualifications already raised, changes in interest rates play a useful role in measuring these disequilibrium situations.

The third intermediate target is another type of monetary aggregate, along with the stock of money: the outstanding volume of bank credit. This variable consists of all of the loans made by banks, plus the securities and other earning assets which they hold.[2] As an indicator or as an intermediate target of monetary policy, it is subject to the same difficulties just described for the money stock. But it has the advantage of being a more inclusive variable. For example, suppose that the public were to shift its preference for assets away from demand deposits in favor of time deposits. The asset demand for money would fall, as would the supply of money. Should we describe this circumstance as contractionary? The banks have the same lending capacity as before and even more, since the reserve required against time deposits is lower than that for demand deposits. So by watching bank credit rather than the stock of money, we could better gauge the true market condition.

Whether in other circumstances bank credit is more useful than the money stock is an empirical issue which we shall examine in the next chapter. But perhaps we have said enough already to convey the impression that the search for a single variable which can serve either the Federal Reserve System or the outside observer as a single intermediate target or indicator is even less likely to succeed than the perennial exploration of Loch Ness. While we have a right to feel disappointed, we should not be surprised. We live in a complex world and should not waste our time on one-dimensional explanations of it. We have seen that open market operations simultaneously alter both the supply of reserves and the rates of interest in the money market. These changes then are transmitted to the volume of bank credit, the stock of money,

---

[2] The Federal Reserve is able to collect data on bank credit only at intervals of several months and with substantial delay. But it does regularly monitor what it calls the bank credit proxy. Based on the idea that the growth in bank assets can be approximated by the growth in liabilities, this variable consists of total bank deposits plus a part of their borrowings.

and other rates of interest. What we must have in order to complete this puzzle is a more detailed awareness of the channels through which all these financial variables affect real economic activity.

The extent to which the Federal Reserve has actually used intermediate rather than proximate targets as guides for the conduct of open market operations has varied over time. During the 1960s the instructions to the FOMC account manager were geared primarily to short-term interest rates, and there was no deliberate strategy to control any particular monetary or reserve aggregate. However, in January 1970 the FOMC made a dramatic shift of emphasis in policy making by setting targets for quarterly growth rates of the money supply. This was alleged to be the first time that the Open Market Committee had specifically adopted a monetary aggregate as a target. It would no longer be possible to characterize FOMC policy as tight or easy solely on the basis of movements in the Federal funds rate and other proximate targets. The consequence of this new emphasis on the quarterly growth rate in the stock of money was revealed, however, more by the relative stability in the growth of reserves (see the pattern for RPDs in Figure 16–1) than in monetary growth. The latter proved harder to stabilize:

Quarter	Growth in Money (seasonally adjusted annual rate)
1970–	
1	5.9%
2	6.2
3	7.6
4	3.8
1971–	
1	8.9
2	9.0
3	3.3
4	1.9
1972–	
1	9.0
2	6.2
3	8.7
4	9.9

Since early 1972 the Federal Reserve has set target ranges for RPDs as well as for the money stock. However, the specified ranges have not been inflexible targets. Movements of the Federal funds rate also have been a constraining influence. The account manager may move outside the targeted range when and if the Federal funds rate moves more widely than had been anticipated by the committee. Thus the shift to a more restrictive policy in late 1972 is not revealed by the behavior of the growth rate of RPDs; beginning in 1973, the RPD growth rate was even more rapid than it had been during the preceding period of monetary ease. And the money stock grew at a 7 percent annual rate compared with a 7½ percent growth rate during the earlier easy period.

Looking at these diverse developments, one might reasonably ask: Was the FOMC pursuing a policy of ease or restraint in 1973? The RPD and the money stock growth rates indicated relative ease; the Federal funds rate indicated restraint. Which leaves us with the same problem we faced when we examined the proximate targets alone. How do we measure the thrust of FOMC policy when the behavior of various targets give inconsistent readings? The answer again depends partly upon how we view the channels for the transmission of monetary policy.

16.4 TRANSMISSION OF POLICY VIA INTEREST RATES

One of the most important channels through which monetary actions are transmitted is the level of interest rates. As we shall describe in some detail momentarily, lending rates and bond yields affect business investment, house building, international capital flows, and even some government expenditures. But these disparate categories of spending are not all affected by the same interest rates: home builders care little about corporate bond yields so long as mortgage rates do not change along with them. Furthermore, the Federal

Reserve's control is not equal over all interest rates; certainly the account manager has a bigger clout on treasury bill rates than on rates in the markets for state and local government securities. In the one, he is the largest single participant; in the other, he is merely an interested bystander.

Overall, there are three facets to the role of interest rates in the transmission process. First, changes in the rates closely controlled by the Federal Reserve (the proximate targets) must ripple outward to affect the whole structure of interest rates. Second, these various rates must then affect desired spending and portfolio allocations in order to alter the total flow of income and output. And third, changes in aggregate income—especially insofar as they alter the rate of price inflation—will further change the prevailing levels of interest rates. An expansionary policy which initially drives down interest rates in order to stimulate total spending may, if it is successful enough, ultimately cause interest rates to be *higher* than their initial level. But before we tackle that complication, let us examine the first two aspects.

16.4.1   The Structure of Interest Rates

If all financial assets were perfect substitutes for all investors, then all interest rates would be the same—a tautology, but a useful starting point for uncovering the reasons for differences among rates. When the manager of the Desk at the Federal Reserve Bank of New York buys treasury bills, he has to induce someone (probably a bank) to sell them. Prices rise, and yields fall. If the seller is indifferent as to whether he holds bills or some other money-market asset such as commercial paper, and if interest rates on commercial paper and treasury bills initially are equal, then he probably will use the proceeds from the sale to buy commercial paper. This increase in the demand for paper will drive down yields in that market as well. Sellers of commercial paper then may well shift into still other markets: acceptances, CDs, Euro-dollars, government or corporate bonds. Gradually, interest rates all will be brought back toward equality, but at a lower level.

In practice, investors are not completely indifferent among assets to hold. We already have mentioned the special role of treasury bills in the banking system. When the Federal Reserve buys a larger quantity of bills, banks may make a special effort to maintain their initial holdings by buying more bills from other institutions or from individuals. Thus the drop in interest rates may not be completely transmitted to other financial markets. Nonetheless, there generally is sufficient substitutability among the various assets of the money market that all of these rates tend to move up and down at the same time; not in lockstep, but at least sufficiently together to appear to be marching to the same drum (Figure 16–2).

The pattern begins to break up a bit when we examine interest rates on assets with significantly different maturities. Suppose we look at the market for securities issued by the U.S. Treasury. At any point in time, there are 70 or more different outstanding treasury securities, some maturing (i.e., redeemable at par value at the Treasury) in a few days, some maturing in 20 years or more. Aside from maturity, there really are very few differences among these assets. Their technical characteristics differ. For example, treasury bills (the shortest maturities) carry no explicit interest payments and sell at discounts to provide income to the buyer. Long-term bonds offer periodic interest (coupon) payments. But all of these securities are the legal obligations of the U.S. Treasury; their similarities far outweigh their differences. And yet, the percentage yields on these various securities, calculated as yields to maturity, may differ by several percentage points. Sometimes it is the long-term assets which have the highest yields, sometimes the shortest. To explain the nature of these complex relationships, economists have

FIGURE 16–2

Interest Rates on Money-Market Assets, 1969–74

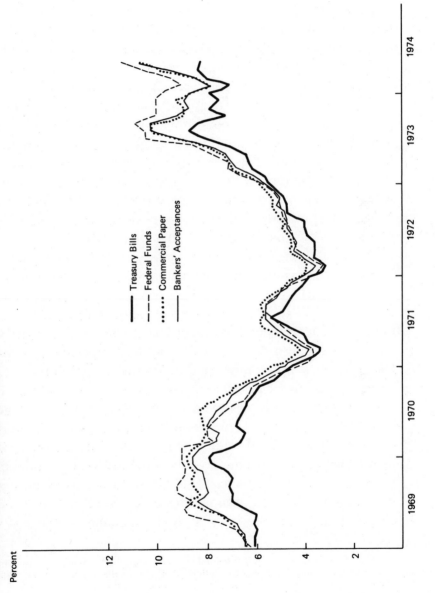

developed a theory of what is called the *term structure* of interest rates.[3]

There are three basic elements to modern theories of the term structure of interest rates. First, investors in financial assets appear to have a preference for liquidity: they tend to be relatively more concerned about preserving the resale value of their assets (capital risk) than they are about assuring that they will get a steady interest income over a long period (income risk). Second, investors are likely to choose among similar assets of different maturities partly on the basis of what they expect to happen to interest rates as well as what interest rates are currently. And third, many investors will have strong preferences for assets of a specific maturity (known as preferred habitats), even if the yields on those assets are somewhat below available alternatives.

Consider, then, the decision regularly faced by the financial managers of corporations which frequently have large sums of assets to invest in bonds and other securities. Setting aside for the moment the issue of whether they will buy corporate, municipal government, foreign, or U.S. government securities, we might suppose that they have somehow decided on the last. Further suppose now that all 70-odd available treasury issues are selling at prices such that, if they were held until they mature, they would yield exactly the same percentage return, say 5 percent. Which one should they buy? By purchasing a 10-year bond rather than a 90-day bill, the buyer is assured a 5 percent income over the whole 10-year period. On the other hand, if the buyer should wish to sell the bond before it matures (i.e., any time during the next ten years), he cannot be sure of the price it will command in the open

---

[3] The discussion here is not intended to offer a complete theory of the term structure. For a more detailed theoretical analysis, see Friedrich A. Lutz, *The Theory of Interest*, Part Four (Dordrecht: D. Reidel, 1968) Translated from the German by Claus Wittich.

market. It could be higher (if interest rates generally fall); it could be lower (if interest rates go up).

In the absence of any sort of expectation about whether future interest rates will be higher or lower than at the present moment, our financial officer may well decide to buy the short-term asset (the bill) rather than the bond. In so doing, the officer increases the risk that interest income will vary over the next few years. But the buyer reduces the risk of having to take a capital loss by selling the bond before it matures. This preference for liquidity is simply a milder manifestation of the behavior that generates the asset demand for money (Chapter 7).

If investors generally behave in this manner—avoiding capital risks at the expense of income risks—then on average over time long-term interest rates will have to be higher than short-term rates. If they were all equal as in our example, investors would opt out of the long-term assets in favor of shorter maturities to reduce capital risk. These shifts would tend to drive down short-term interest rates while pushing up long-term yields.

Occasionally, securities buyers develop strong expectations that interest rates are going to change in one direction or the other, usually the other. That is, the expectations factor—at least in recent years—has most prominently come into force at times when interest rates have been unusually high by historical standards. As we described in Chapter 7, investors appear to have a vague sense of what constitutes a normal level for interest rates. When rates rise above that general range, the market will expect them to fall again. Therefore, times of high interest rates are times to buy long-term securities. If securities maturing in one year are selling at prices low enough to yield 9 percent while ten-year bonds are yielding only 7 percent, many well-informed people will still buy the ten-year bonds. Then they are assured of a 7 percent return for the full ten years. If interest rates generally fall to, say, 5 percent after a year or two, the purchasers of the high-flying one-year assets will be out eating lunch at MacDonald's.

Periods of high interest rates are therefore times when long-term interest rates are likely to be at or below the level of short-term rates. As is indicated by Figure 16–3, whenever interest rates on government securities maturing in one year have risen above 6 percent in the last five years, they also have risen above the yields available on bonds with ten years or more of remaining life. Otherwise, the short rates have been below the long.

A major consequence of these relationships for the conduct of monetary policy is that long-term rates are much more inert than are short-term rates. But it is the long-term rates which, as we shall see in the next section, are the most important influences on real economic activity. The ability to move money-market rates quickly and effectively does not imply the ability to push around the real economy.

Another factor limiting the ability of monetary policy actions to alter the whole range of interest rates is the existence of preferred habitats for a large part of securities buyers. Commercial banks, for example, have a strong preference for highly liquid short-term assets because of the extremely short maturities on their liabilities. Life insurance companies are major purchasers of long-term securities, again to match the very long-term nature of their liabilities. For insurance companies to purchase short-term assets would greatly increase the turnover rate of their portfolio and correspondingly increase their transactions costs. As a general rule, investors are able to minimize transactions costs, income risk, and capital risk simultaneously by buying assets the remaining life of which corresponds approximately to the period over which the investor's funds are available. There is, therefore, a segmented market for securities. Investors who deal only in long-

FIGURE 16–3

The Term Structure of Yields on U.S. Treasury Bonds

Percent

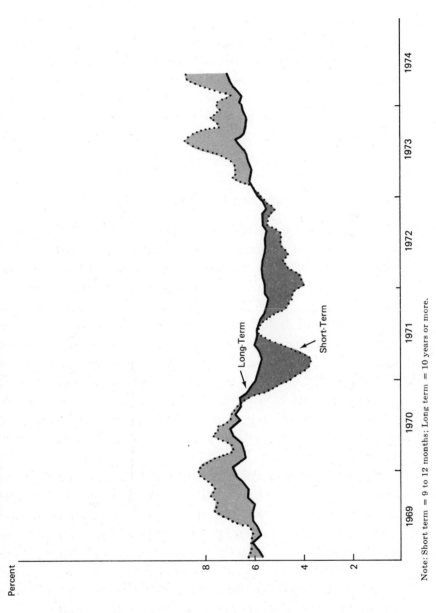

Note: Short term = 9 to 12 months; Long term = 10 years or more.

term assets will not react to short-term rates until the differences between short and long yields become substantial.

Nonetheless, the Federal Reserve does rely on a transmission mechanism in which it confines open market operations largely to money-market assets and relies on the securities market to adjust other interest rates. The account manager must sometimes feel as if he is kicking a dead elephant. But it must be said that the market, kicked hard enough and long enough, does eventually begin to shuffle along.

16.4.2 Interest Rates and Economic Activity

It would be rather idle of us to worry about the behavior of long-term interest rates if we could not demonstrate that they were important in influencing the course of the economy. In fact, a large number of studies by economists over the years have examined the relationships between specific interest rates and such items as housing construction, consumer purchases of durable goods, business expenditures on plant and equipment, state and local government projects, and international transfers of capital. The general conclusions to emerge from these studies are that interest rates are significant, that the most important rates usually are long-term yields, and that the effects often take quite a long time to work.

For two decades until around 1960, the prevailing view among economists who had studied the behavior of *business fixed investment* (i.e., purchases of new equipment and plants) was that this category of expenditure was not significantly affected by changes in interest rates. Business managers were thought to take a view of the profitability of fixed investments which depended on expected sales and profits but not much on the cost of financing the project. This view was a gloomy one from the vantage of monetary policy, because it implied that only very large movements in interest rates could alter the pace of real business investment. Since 1960, more sophisticated statistical techniques have been brought to bear on this issue, and most of the new evidence has suggested a stronger linkage.[4]

An economist named Dale Jorgenson summarized in 1971 the diverse findings of research by various investigators into the role of interest rates in affecting fixed investment expenditure, breaking the results down by industry within the manufacturing sector of the economy.[5] The results were partly ambiguous: in two studies, the interest rate on corporate bonds was significant in at least half of the 13 industries examined; in two others, interest rates played a barely significant role. Other studies, especially more recent ones, generally support the view that changes in corporate bond rates (shown in Figure 16–4) are an important determinant of fixed investment. For example, a study conducted by one of the authors of this book concludes that a 1 percentage point rise in the corporate bond rate maintained for the year would produce a drop of nearly $5 billion in real fixed investment. The same policy pursued for five years would generate a huge $22 billion drop, mostly through cutbacks in the manufacturing sector.

Empirical studies of residential construction uniformly show that interest rates charged for new mortgage loans (Figure 16–4) are an important determinant of expenditures on new housing. Our own study referred to above found that a one-point rise in mortgage rates would drive down housing

---

[4] The main technological advance has been the development of methodology for estimating complex distributed lag relationships. We now know that the effect of interest rates on investment are spread out over time (see Chapter 17, section 17.3); pre-1960 studies had no way to measure that effect accurately. A brief but highly technical explanation of methods for estimating distributed lags is contained in Zvi Griliches, "Distributed Lags: A Survey," *Econometrica* 35, January 1967.

[5] Dale W. Jorgenson, "Econometric Studies of Investment Behavior: A Survey," *Journal of Economic Literature* 9, December 1971.

FIGURE 16–4

Long-Term Interest Rates, 1969–74

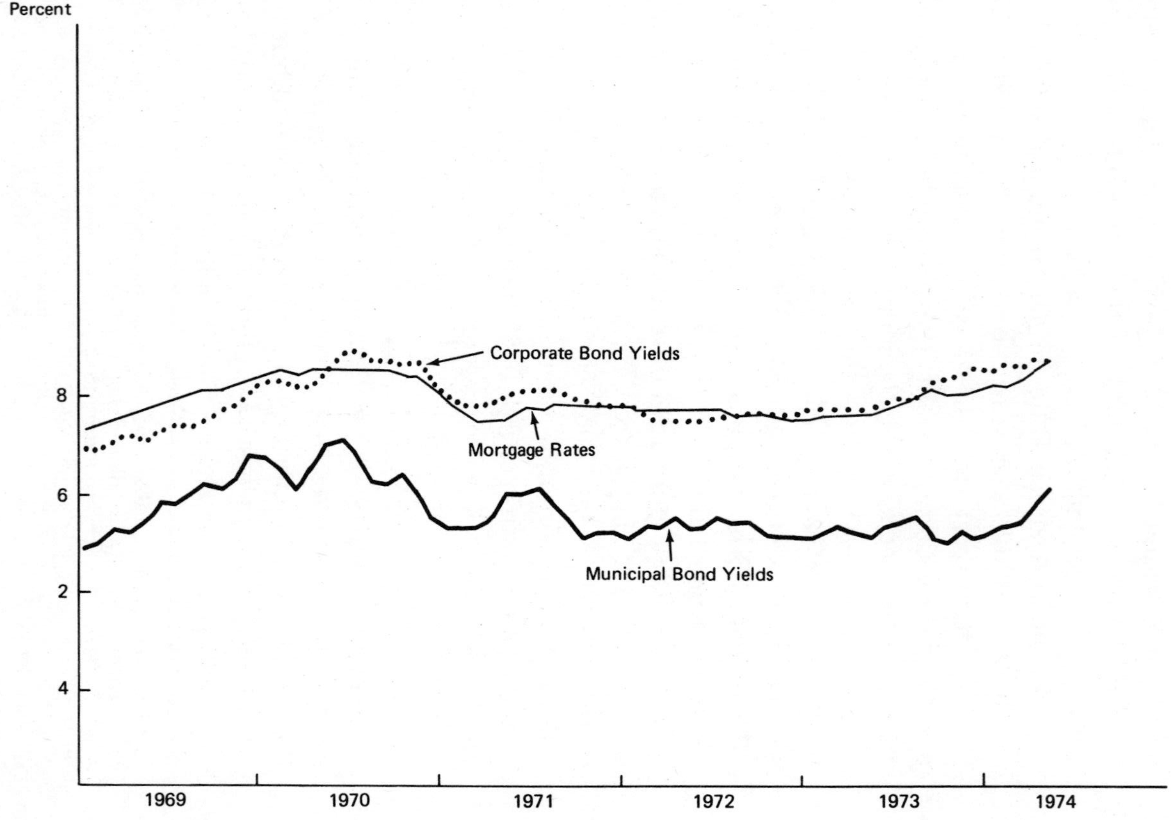

Percent

Corporate Bond Yields

Mortgage Rates

Municipal Bond Yields

1969   1970   1971   1972   1973   1974

construction by about $3½ billion within a year or so. Similar conclusions have been reached by most other investigators.[6]

The great importance of mortgage rates should not be surprising, for interest costs are a crucial element in people's ability to afford new homes. The system used in the United States (though not in many other countries, such as England) is for mortgage rates to be fixed over the whole life of the loan, which might last up to 20 or 30 years. Suppose, then, that a blue-collar worker has managed to save up $5,000 to make a down payment on a $25,000 house. He plans to borrow the other $20,000 on a 25-year mortgage. If the interest rate on mortgages is 6 percent, his monthly payment will be approximately $125. But if mortgage rates were 8 percent instead, his payments would be $155 per month. This extra $30 per month could be a strong deterrent to many potential buyers.

In the absence of government intervention and protection, a major part of the burden of any tightening of monetary policy would fall on the housing market. Most mortgages are made by "thrift" institutions (see Chapter 15, section 15.3) rather than by commercial banks. When interest rates rise, these institutions cannot afford to compete in attracting savings because most of their assets are locked into long-term mortgage loans made in earlier periods when rates were much lower. When the interest rate ceilings set under Regulation Q come into effect, the ability of thrift institutions to compete is worsened still further. Funds then flow out from them into more profitable assets such as government and corporate notes and bonds. This loss of deposits, referred to as *disintermediation,* makes it difficult or impossible for savings and loan associations or mutual savings banks to extend additional credit for mortgages.

---

[6] See, for example, R. Bruce Ricks, ed., *National Housing Models,* (Lexington, Mass.: Lexington Books, 1973).

To limit the disruptive effects from this particular channel of monetary policy transmission, the federal government has established several agencies to support the housing market. There is the Federal National Mortgage Association (known whimsically as "Fannie Mae"), now privately owned but functioning as a federal agency; the Government National Mortgage Association ("Ginnie Mae," we're embarrassed to report), which operates as part of the Department of Housing and Urban Development; and the Federal Home Loan Mortgage Corporation (are you ready for "Freddie Mac"?), a subsidiary of the Federal Home Loan Bank System.[7] Each of these agencies is authorized to purchase mortgage loans from thrift institutions, thereby freeing the funds of those institutions for additional lending. Funds for this secondary mortgage market are provided partly from direct federal subsidies and partly from the sale of bonds by the agencies in the open market. This latter device is a means for tapping the bond market to channel funds into housing construction as a supplement to the direct deposit of savings funds in thrift institutions. The net effect of these various programs is to neutralize a large part of the impact of restrictive monetary policies on mortgage interest rates and on housing expenditures. Nonetheless, the housing market still bears a significant part of the transmission burden.

The evidence is less overwhelming on the interest rate effects on consumer spending or on state and local government projects. Interest rates which banks and other lenders charge on consumer loans (loans secured by durable goods such as automobiles, boats, television sets) do not exhibit the same sensitivity to business conditions as do bond yields or even mortgage rates. Tight-money periods, when

---

[7] These programs supplement the work of two other government agencies —the Federal Housing Administration and the Veteran's Administration—which help to support the housing market by assuming all or part of the risk on loans for low-cost housing (loans which may be insured by the F.H.A.) or loans to military veterans (loans which may be guaranteed by the VA).

banks might be eager to raise rates on consumer loans, are also periods when major retailers are willing to accept lower profit margins on their own loans to customers in order to move the merchandise. So the rates stay flat. Furthermore, changes in the rates offered to savers tend to influence the form in which savings are held rather than the amounts saved (see Chapter 8, section 8.1.3). For example, a rise in rates paid on savings deposits may induce people to place more funds in savings accounts but have little impact on spending decisions. Consumer spending certainly is affected by monetary policy, but through channels other than interest rates.[8]

There is good reason to think that high interest rates would have a strong impact on the expenditure plans of state or local governments. A major part of such spending is on long-term investment projects: the construction of schools, hospitals, highways. These projects must be financed by some means other than taxation in order to avoid concentrating the burden of the cost. The usual practice is for the governmental unit to float a bond issue backed either by its general taxing power (ordinary municipal securities) or by the expected revenue from the project (in the case of toll roads, sewage treatment plants, and the like; these municipal securities being known as revenue bonds). When interest rates rise, the high cost of bond financing may well lead governments to decide that the time is not ripe to initiate new programs. And in some states, this reluctance may be imposed through the existence of legislative ceilings on payable rates.

This argument is not without empirical support. Economists studying the restrictive policy periods of the 1950s concluded that investment expenditures by municipal governments fell by about 5 percent as a consequence of rising interest rates. But these cutbacks tended to be postponements rather than cancellations, and the overall pattern of govern-

---

[8] See section 16.5.

mental spending does not appear to have been greatly affected. One reason for this insensitivity may be the absence of
a profit incentive in governmental planning. Another may be
the nature of the market for municipal bonds. The income
from these securities is exempt from federal income taxation
to enable state and local governments to sell them at lower
interest rates (see Figure 16–4). Financing costs therefore are
not likely to be a major factor in the planning of state and
local budgets, even when the overall level of rates is high.
With the one major exception of the 1966 credit crunch (see
Chapter 15, section 15.3), this market has not borne much of
the cost of high interest rate policies.

Most of the effects of changes in interest rates on domestic
spending are thus confined to business fixed investment (via
corporate bond yields) and to housing (via mortgage rates).
Bank lending or deposit rates have little direct impact, though
they are important links in the policy chain. But there is another area of economic activity where short-term rates rise to
the fore: international trade and payments. As we described
in Chapter 11, changes in interest rates in one country relative to those prevailing elsewhere in the world will induce
investors to shift at least part of their portfolio of assets to
that country. The practical importance of this principle can
be substantial whenever countries pursue different monetary
policies.

A good example of the effects of international interest differentials is provided by the abortive attempt by the Federal
Reserve to ease conditions in U.S. money markets between
December 1973 and February 1974. Most of the other major
industrial countries were at the time pursuing highly restrictive policies, and this disparity opened some wide differentials between interest rates here and abroad (Figure 16–5).
Suddenly there was every reason to borrow and no reason to
lend in the United States. European companies and even gov-

FIGURE 16–5

Money-Market Rates Internationally, December 1973–May 1974

Percent

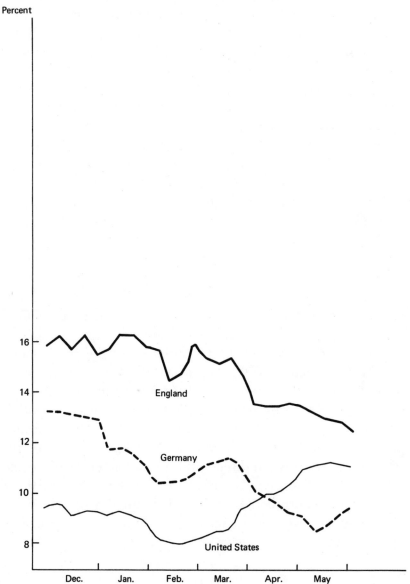

ernments—all of which had to borrow substantial amounts just then because of the dramatic increase in oil prices decreed by Arab producers—discovered that they could borrow much more cheaply in New York than in London, Frankfurt, or Tokyo.[9] American banks had to step up their borrowings in the Euro-dollar market to acquire more funds; even so, the Federal Reserve had to supply enormous quantities of reserves to the banks in order to enable them to meet the demand for loans without increasing interest rates beyond the relatively low levels then desired by the Fed. By the end of February, the System had given up. It had become apparent that the combination of domestic and foreign loan demand had to be constrained by higher interest rates if any hope of controlling the price level were to be retained. The FOMC then shifted to the contractionary policy with which we introduced this chapter.

This international link in the transmission chain is more often a nuisance than a help to the Federal Reserve. We have just seen an example where an attempt to ease monetary policy was effectively thwarted; the table was set for a family banquet, and the whole world came in for the feast. Conversely, a restrictive policy might be upset by the willingness of foreign lenders to supply funds to American companies at the higher U.S. rates. The irony is that this offset to policy effectiveness may work more quickly and surely than the processes through which interests rates influence domestic spending in the desired direction. International capital movements respond to money-market rates, the short-term rates most closely controlled by the Fed. Estimates of the exact size of the response cover a wide range of numbers, but a one-point rise in the U.S. treasury bill rate is capable of pulling at

---

[9] The *ability* of foreigners to borrow in the United States also was increased at the same time through the termination at the end of January 1974 of both the interest equalization tax on foreign securities and the Voluntary Foreign Credit Restraint program (see Chapter 15, section 15.7).

least $1 billion into the United States within a few months.[10]

The Federal Reserve has at times tried to neutralize this offset by playing with the term structure of interest rates. The most famous such episode was a policy known as "operation twist," which was in effect from 1961 through 1964.[11] The overall policy goal was to stimulate real investment and thence employment and simultaneously to improve our sagging balance of international payments by encouraging inflows of foreign capital. The corresponding intermediate targets were to lower long-term bond yields (to stimulate investment) and to *increase* money-market rates (to encourage capital inflows)—easier planned than executed.

The policy required a combination of instruments, the essence of which was to support the bond market through long-term open market purchases while depressing the bill market through short-term open market sales. This policy of buying long-term and selling short-term would then have twisted the term structure in the desired direction. To some extent, the operation succeeded. Economists have estimated that bill rates may have been as much as a half point higher, relative to bond rates, than they would have been under a single-instrument policy. And a more vigorous twisting might have produced more visible results. But clearly there are limits to this type of intervention in the marketplace. When the Federal Reserve shifts the composition of its portfolio in order to drive up short rates relative to long, the rest of the market will rush in to buy up the increasingly attractive short maturities. Success therefore depends on the segmentation of the bond markets by maturities. As we have seen (section 16.4.1), some compartmentation does exist, but it can easily

---

[10] None of the work on this complex topic is very good, but less unsatisfactory than most is William Branson and Raymond Hill, *Capital Movements in the OECD Area*, OECD, December 1971.

[11] See Burton G. Malkiel, *The Term Structure of Interest Rates* (Princeton, N.J.:Princeton University Press, 1966), Chap. 8.

be bridged by wide enough differentials among relative yields.

16.4.3   Economic Activity and Interest Rates

The relationship between interest rates and the flow of real economic activity is not one of simple unilateral causation. There also exists an important degree of feedback. When, for example, the Federal Reserve pursues an expansionary policy for a long enough period, the ensuing drop first in money-market rates and then in bond yields and mortgage rates will produce increases in expenditure and in national income. These increases will then restore at least part of the initial pressure in financial markets. The transactions demand for money will rise along with income; the quantity of money available to satisfy preexisting demands will be reduced, and interest rates will have to rise. In terms of our model, we can think of the full transmission process up to this point as consisting first of a shift in the ME curve (see Figure 16–6) which produces a large drop in interest rates (movement from A to B in the diagram); then of an adjustment process in which the economy moves along the new monetary equilibrium curve toward point C. This process is based on the assumption that the money market adjusts more rapidly than the expenditure market, that interest rates are more flexible than either the output or the prices of new goods and services. Interest rates thus bear most of the initial adjustment to policy changes and only gradually are pulled back up toward a new equilibrium level. The expected path of interest rates over time then might look like the curve shown in the right-hand panel of Figure 16–6. The length of time required for this adjustment is shown rather arbitrarily as one year; the actual time will depend greatly on which interest rate we consider.[12]

---

[12] These lags are discussed more fully in Chapter 17, section 17.3.

FIGURE 16–6

The Adjustment of Interest Rates

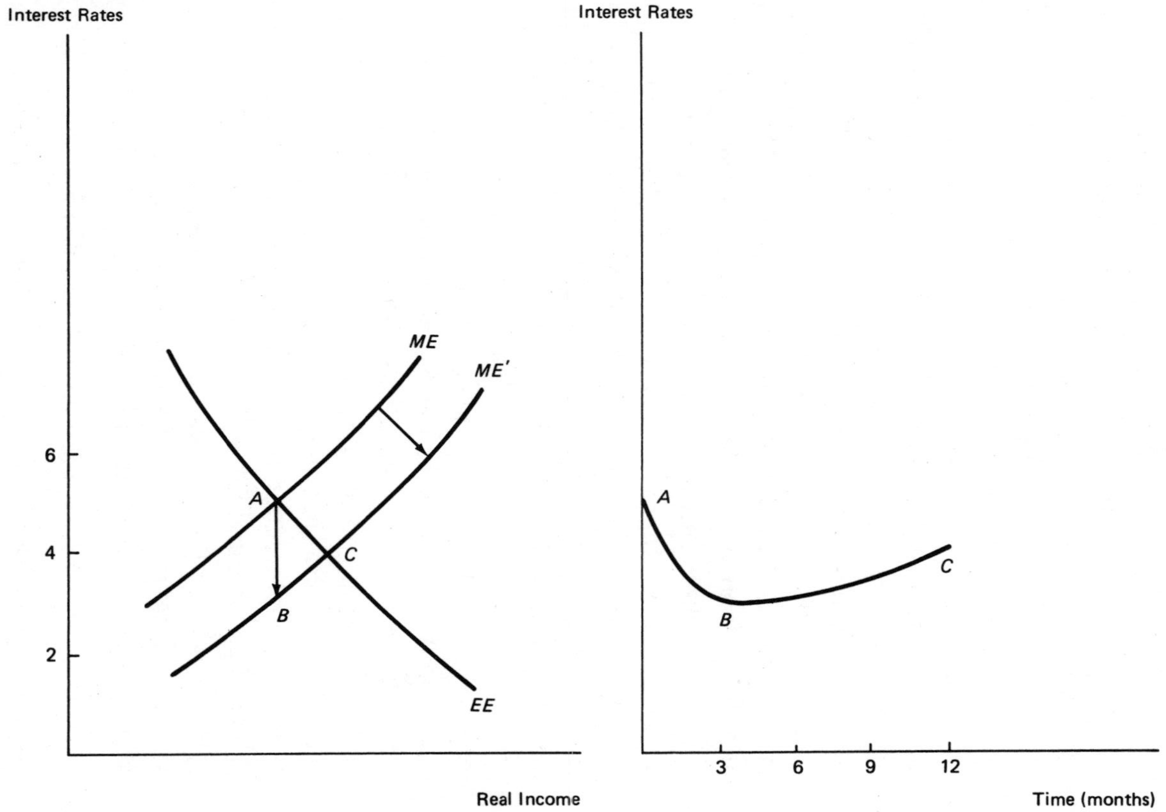

The adjustment process is not over, however, if the monetary expansion is strong enough to have an inflationary effect on the economy. The rise in income and expenditure is not likely to take the form exclusively of output increases. And the closer the economy gets to its capacity, the steeper will be the aggregate supply curve (see Chapter 10), and the greater will be the impact on price inflation. Furthermore, when business people read of the monetary expansion and see that prices are beginning to rise (or that the rate of inflation is beginning to accelerate), they will come to expect some inflation in the future as well.

The importance of this expectation of inflation is that it may induce a shift in the expenditure curve (EE). Business managers who expect to be able to raise the prices they charge for their future output may become more willing to undertake investment expenditures now. The future price rise would raise the nominal rate of return on their present investment outlays, and they therefore would be willing, ceteris paribus, to pay higher rates of interest to acquire funds for the purpose. This linkage is not rigid and cannot be expressed by a mathematical equation.[13]

It could even work in the opposite direction, because no corporation can know in advance the extent to which it can successfully pass on cost increases in the form of higher prices without discouraging demand for its own product. But if business people generally see inflation as a phenomenon in which their nominal rates of return will increase, then at any given level of interest rates they will undertake a larger real volume of investment expenditures. The inflationary monetary policy will shift not only the ME curve but the EE curve

---

[13] Some economists have argued that real investment expenditure should be causally related to a real interest rate—the nominal rate of interest *minus* the rate of inflation expected by investors—rather than to the nominal rate alone. The empirical evidence accumulated to date is still ambiguous as to the validity of that hypothesis.

as well. Interest rates will be pulled up still further (point D, Figure 16–7).

If the effect of inflationary expectations on interest rates is strong enough, the ultimate effect of an expansionary monetary policy could be to raise interest rates rather than to reduce them. As we read the evidence, however, this tertiary effect does not appear to have been that powerful in any observed episode of expansionary U.S. monetary policy; all of our periods of high interest rates have followed directly from shifts toward contraction.

But one need not take an extreme view in order to judge correctly that a widespread expectation of inflation will push interest rates higher than they otherwise would have been. Seen purely from a financial view, it is apparent that most lenders and savers will demand higher returns to compensate for the expected loss of purchasing power by the time they regain their funds. Borrowers may be willing to meet these demands if they share the expectation of being able to repay in cheaper dollars. The net effect of these shifts in view probably is to increase interest rates eventually by one fourth to one half of a percentage point for every 1 percent expected rise in the level of prices.

16.5 TRANSMISSION OF POLICY VIA THE STOCK OF MONEY

Our topic in this part of the book is monetary policy, and it would seem from that title alone that the stock of money should be an integral part of the subject. And indeed it is, but less in the process of policy transmission than in ways we examined elsewhere in the book. When the Federal Reserve employs open market security purchases for expansionary policies, it sets in motion the adjustment process which already has been described fairly completely with no reference

FIGURE 16–7

The Adjustment of Interest Rates, with Inflationary Expectations

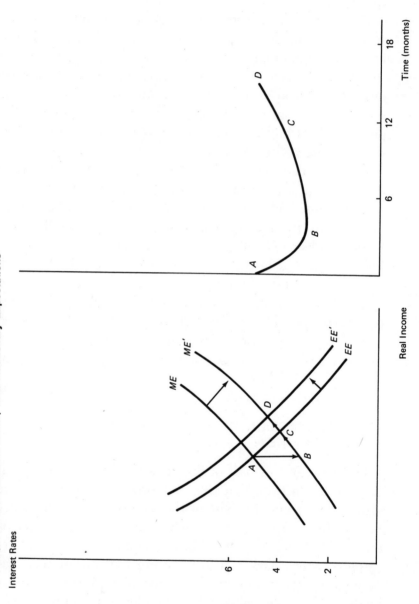

at all to the stock of money. Reserves expand, inducing banks to make more loans; interest rates fall to encourage loan demand; spending in various sectors is stimulated. As a by-product, people generally end up holding a larger quantity of money balances.

The expansionary impact on money balances is, to be sure, an important part of the adjustment of the economy to the new situation. Banks cannot make additional loans unless businesses and individuals can first be persuaded that they will be made better off by borrowing, which is to say that they must be induced to acquire and spend money balances. As economic activity picks up, people *demand* more money, which is then made available by banks through their lending function. When the additional quantities which banks are willing to supply match the rise in balances desired by the public, the adjustment comes to an end. So in a very real sense, the increase in the stock of money—though it must occur in order to restore equilibrium—may not be part of the basic transmission mechanism at all. For it appears to be the demand for money associated with the rise in spending and incomes which pulls up the supply of money.

Nonetheless, there are ways in which the money stock helps to transmit policy actions to economic activity. And the evidence suggests (see Chapter 17, section 17.2) that these processes are significant enough that changes in the money stock will precede changes in national income by several months. For one, the direct impact of monetary expansion on the economy is partly to encourage the purchase of financial assets, such as corporate stocks, rather than additional spending. Some spending occurs immediately, but time is required for the resulting rise in incomes to lead to further rounds of income creation; meanwhile, money balances, along with other liquid assets, may accumulate. It is difficult to measure this part of the chain; economists differ in their estimates of its importance.

Of a greater practical import is the role of the money stock in transmitting policies which accompany and accommodate *fiscal* actions. Suppose, for example, that the Treasury undertakes an expansionary fiscal policy involving additional spending financed by borrowing (issuing bonds) and that the Federal Reserve decides to support this policy by buying an equivalent amount of existing bonds. This one-two punch is the modern equivalent of the old-fashioned government printing press. The Treasury creates incomes at the same time that the Federal Reserve creates the money balances to pay them, just as if the Treasury itself had printed up new dollar bills and passed them out at the pay window. The supply of money rises, providing both the means and the incentive for additional spending. The transmission chain for the combined policy (in which the monetary role is called with deceptive benignity an "accommodative" policy) clearly runs through the stock of money.

A third linkage via the money stock brings in consumer spending more directly than any of the processes examined above. Once an expansionary policy succeeds in producing new money balances, then the total wealth of consumers (and of businesses) increases. The economy as a whole has a greater value of assets without an offsetting rise in debt liabilities.[14] Thus the desires of individuals to save out of any given level of income will be diminished; the average propensity to consume (the APC) will rise.

This increase in consumers' willingness to spend when they have a bigger nest of eggs in the bank gives an extra boost to the effect of monetary policy on the economy. It is not, however, the biggest booster in town. If we may be so brash as to refer again to our own estimates,[15] it appears that a $1 billion increase in the supply of money will induce less

---

[14] The issue of whether the increase in banking liabilities in the form of deposits constitutes a sufficient offset to nullify this wealth effect involves theoretical difficulties beyond the scope of the present discussion.

[15] See section 16.4.2.

than $100 million of consumer spending through this wealth effect. And even that estimate requires the assumption that the increase in the supply of money does not drive up the price level. Surely if everyone had 10 percent more money than last year but all prices also were 10 percent higher, we would be clever enough not to think we were any better off. So it is the value of *real money balances*—the money stock held by consumers, divided by an index of the prices they pay—that matters here.

We have seen in Chapter 10 that monetary expansion normally will result partly in price inflation and partly in a rise in output, the mix depending on the degree of slack left in the economy. If there is enough slack for monetary policy to push up the flow of output, this success will be enhanced by the real balance effect. It cannot work by itself.

In sum, the role of the money stock in the transmission chain is less important than one might have deduced intuitively. It is supplementary, less a link than a reinforcement to other linkages. But before we relegate money to the footnotes in our memories, we should consider another use for it, a use for which it is all but indispensable: as a target for the account manager and as an indicator of the direction of policy. It may be the great irony of monetary policy as practiced in this country that the variable which matters most in the transmission of policy—the level of interest rates—is useless and misleading as an indicator; while another variable which for the most part just trails along at the end of the chain—the stock of money—is the best indicator of where and how fast the chain is going. It is by no means always true that the acceleration of monetary growth is indicative of a more expansionary policy or that contraction will be accompanied by a slower growth rate. But most would agree that these signals are more reliable than those emitted by the rate of interest.[16]

---

[16] See Chapter 17, section 17.4.1, for a further explanation of this relationship.

16.6   CONCLUSIONS

This chapter has examined the central elements of the transmission process for monetary policy, concentrating on the effects of open market operations and focusing particularly on expansionary actions. It is easy enough, and a highly recommended exercise for the reader, to work out the corollary processes for contractionary policies; they are not mirror images of those we have seen here, but they are closely related. In either direction, changes in the Federal Reserve's security portfolio affect (1) bank reserves and interest rates on money-market assets (the proximate targets), which in turn affect (2) the stock of money and longer term interest rates (the intermediate targets); these then influence (3) spending decisions, purchases of assets, and international capital movements and thereby output, the price level, employment, and the balance of international payments (the goals).

The other instruments of monetary policy produce simpler and in some cases different transmission processes. The repercussions from changes in required reserve ratios are almost identical to those from open market operations; after all, they are very similar instruments. Discount rate changes differ in that they engender an immediate shock wave of changes in other rates; the effects are transmitted more quickly but may die out before they reach their goals. But the biggest differences are between the Big Three and the other, more selective, instruments. The latter—margin requirements and other controls on credit terms, interest rate ceilings, moral suasion—do much of their work through the forced rationing of credit. If Regulation Q prevents thrift institutions from bidding for deposit funds, then mortgage credit will have to be rationed. If banks are required to demand more corporate stock as collateral against loans, then a smaller amount of funds will go into the purchase of stocks. These rationing devices therefore constitute a third channel in addition to interest rates and the supply of money for the transmission of policy decisions.

REVIEW QUESTIONS

1. Distinguish between proximate and intermediate targets. Of what use is this distinction for policy formulation?
2. What does it mean to say that monetary policy works through the mechanism of changes in interest rates? Does this statement imply that interest-rate stability is a good target for monetary policy?
3. Can the Fed control interest rates? Explain.
4. What would happen to the rate of interest on long-term government securities if the Treasury were to add substantially to the supply by increasing the size of the national debt?
5. Why is the volume of construction of new housing so sensitive to monetary policy?
6. What is operation twist? How is it supposed to work?
7. Under what circumstances could the purchase of a substantial amount of securities by the FOMC lead to higher interest rates?

SUGGESTED FURTHER READING

Board of Governors of the Federal Reserve System. *Open Market Policies and Operating Procedures: Staff Studies,* July 1971.

Jorgenson, Dale W. "Econometric Studies of Investment Behavior: A Survey," *Journal of Economic Literature* 9, December 1971.

OECD Monetary Studies Series. *Monetary Policy in the United States,* 1974.

Ricks, R. Bruce (ed.). *National Housing Models,* Lexington, Mass.: Lexington Books, 1973.

chapter 17

The Role of Monetary Policy

17.1 INTRODUCTION

Monetary policy is a powerful weapon in the war against unemployment and inflation. Like all big guns, it has a greater potential for evil than for good. Managed well, it can help a sound economy to stay on course; managed badly, it can wreck the most deliberate plans, the most deserving hopes.

This final chapter is an appraisal of American monetary policy as a means of stabilizing our economy. We have seen that "money matters," that the ease or tightness of monetary policy can be an important factor in determining output, employment, and the level of prices. But we cannot leave the reader with the impression, into which our preoccupation with money might lead him, that monetary policy is the only or even necessarily the best weapon of stabilization. Nor can we conclude without a further examination of the evidence that monetary policy has in fact helped to stabilize the economy. We have had recessions; we have had inflations. Have monetary forces contributed to these disturbances? And if, as one must surely think inevitable, we find some faults in the course of this survey, we could not earn our supper without explaining their causes and offering some suggested remedies.

462

17.2   HAS MONETARY POLICY BEEN STABILIZING?

The importance of money in the economy may reveal itself in two quite different ways: as a powerful independent destabilizing force, upsetting the smooth course of events, or as an effective tool for promoting stability when there occur other disturbances essentially of a nonmonetary origin. Our model of the economy developed in Part Three unfortunately makes clear that monetary policy can upset the economy. Changes in the supply or demand for money can shift the ME schedule, pushing the economy away from a stable equilibrium point. We can infer that continued expansion of the money supply after high employment levels have been reached will generate price inflation; contraction of the money supply can cause bottlenecks, shortages, and unemployment of resources.

Monetary policy is not, however, the only source of instability. The worst culprits probably have been the capriciousness of the budgetary planning by the federal government and of the capital investment plans of private businesses. These plans cause the EE schedule to slide back and forth, generating not only disequilibrium but marketplace havoc as well. It then becomes the task of monetary policy to offset and compensate for these nonmonetary disturbances.

17.2.1   Some Historical Evidence

Monetary history is replete with episodes in which monetary policy has been a potent source of economic instability: the great influx of precious metals into Europe following the conquest of the New World in the 16th and 17th centuries, the full-steam paper-money printing presses of Germany in the 1920s, the policies of the Federal Reserve System to contract the money supply in the early 1930s and then to peg bond prices through massive open market purchases in the forties. Wherever we find the worst examples of inflation or depression in the history of the modern world, we are likely to discover a poorly planned or poorly executed monetary policy.

The 60 years that have passed in the United States since the establishment of the Federal Reserve System in 1914 have been years neither of uninterrupted progress nor of complete economic stability. One major problem to which monetary policy clearly is related is price inflation, of which we have experienced four major episodes. But each of these periods has been characterized by war, the anticipation of war, and the aftermath of war (Table 17–1).

TABLE 17–1

Major Inflationary Periods

Duration of Inflation	Associated with	Annual Growth Rates	
		Wholesale Prices*	Stock of Money†
1914–20...........	World War I	15%	13%
1940–48...........	World War II	9	12
1950–51...........	Korean War	8	5
1965–73‡.........	Vietnam War	4	6

  * Compounded annual rate of change, calculated from annual data except in 1914–20 (monthly, from Friedman and Schwartz).
  † Compounded annual rate of change, calculated from yearend data. Money defined to include time deposits in 1914–20.
  ‡ This inflation is continuing as of 1974. The much higher inflation rates of 1974 appear now to be the beginning of a separate period.
  Source: *Economic Reports of the President* (Washington, D.C.: U.S. Government Printing Office); Milton Friedman and Anna J. Schwartz, *A Monetary History of the United States* (Princeton: Princeton University Press, 1963).

War inevitably entails very substantial increases in government expenditures and cutbacks in the availability of consumer and industrial goods. Armies of former civilians must be mobilized and paid. Factories must be converted to the production of munitions and other military hardware. With no knowledge of monetary policy, a simpleton can see that the conduct of war will drive up the prices of goods.

But the government must finance these expenditures in

some manner: by raising taxes, by borrowing from the public or from the banking system, or by printing fiat paper money. The least inflationary method is that of raising taxes: money balances are taken from the public, transferred to the government, and disbursed back to the public through military purchases and payroll. Some inflation still results from reduced supplies of goods and from the efforts of consumers to maintain present living standards by reducing the amounts they save. But this policy minimizes the rightward drift of the *EE* curve associated with the rise in government spending, and it involves no change in monetary policy and thus no shift in the *ME* curve.

Congress has been extremely reluctant to finance the wars of the 20th century by raising taxes. With the exception of the Korean War period the growth of federal government tax receipts has fallen far short of expenditure increases during these conflicts. The tax rates which would have been required in order to balance the projected budgets have been feared as exhorbitant, disruptive to incentives for consumers and workers, and definitely not conducive to the self-preservation of congressmen.

Fortunately, this reluctance to tax has not led us to the printing press. The U.S. government pays for its expenditures by checks drawn on demand deposit accounts at the Federal Reserve banks, and the law does not provide a means to write up these accounts except by making deposits.[1] So we have been forced to rely on the middle road: the government has had to borrow a substantial portion of the funds required for war.

It is at this point that monetary policy has contributed to the situation by accommodating the government's borrowing requirements. The clearest example of this type of policy is

---

[1] The only exception is that the Treasury may borrow up to $5 billion directly from the Federal Reserve System; this provision is intended to ease seasonal cash-flow pressures and not to provide a permanent source of treasury financing.

that of the inflationary forties. The Federal Reserve pursued a policy from 1942 to 1951 under which it stood ready to purchase whatever quantity of treasury securities necessary to keep the long-term rate from rising above $2\frac{1}{2}$ percent and the bill rate from rising above three eighths of 1 percent. The implication of this strategy was that any increase in government debt not readily purchased by the private sectors of the economy would be financed ultimately by the Federal Reserve. During those ten years, the Fed actually purchased about 10 percent of the more than $200 billion increase in the federal debt. This accommodative policy, which was repeated in modified forms during each of our other wars in this century, therefore was in fact an aggressively expansionary monetary action that contributed to the wartime inflation.

It is important to note that the initiator of these major inflations has been a *fiscal* policy of increased spending without compensating increased taxation. The central bank has been in each case presented with a Hobson's choice: accommodate the military program by monetary expansion or force the Treasury to raise funds by borrowing from the private sectors of the economy. The latter option would be viable only if the Treasury were willing to finance the war at rising interest rates. Congress simply refused to raise taxes sufficiently.

Depression also has hit the United States, three times since the establishment of the Federal Reserve System. These depressions, in each of which the unemployment rate exceeded 10 percent of the civilian labor force, occurred in 1920–21, 1929–33, and 1937–38. Throughout the 1920–21 depression, the Federal Reserve discouraged bank lending and monetary expansion by maintaining the same high rediscount rate that it had set before the end of the preceding inflationary boom. By June 1921, the money supply had declined 9 percent and wholesale prices had fallen to 56 percent of the level reached in May of the previous year. The Federal Reserve had not yet discovered open market operations as a policy instrument;

more seriously, Reserve officials still believed that the process of contraction—or liquidation, as it was then called—was a form of blood-letting to which we had to submit before the economy could recover its strength. They had no real comprehension of the harmful effects of a deliberate policy of price deflation. Undoubtedly the Fed's failure either to reduce the discount rate or to reduce the $2.5 billion of expensive borrowed reserves through open market security purchases contributed to the severity of the 1920–21 depression.

During the Great Depression, the one in capital letters, which lasted from 1929 to 1933, the Federal Reserve pursued a policy of what a later generation would have called benign neglect. Following the 1929 collapse of stock prices, the general public as well as the money market grew to fear the onset of a complete failure of the financial system. Withdrawals of bank deposits forced a severe contraction of bank lending which the Federal Reserve failed to offset through open market purchases to supply reserve balances. Widespread bank failures were the result; more than 9,000 banks closed their doors during this period. By permitting these banks to fail, the Fed gave its indirect blessing to a decline in the money supply of more than 30 percent. This decline and the insolvency of so many banks spread fear and uncertainty throughout the financial system, disrupted the normal processes of financial intermediation, and reduced the efficiency of the capital market. We do not believe that monetary policies alone caused the initial downturn, though a case can be made for that view. The excessive and unbalanced expansion of economic demand in the late twenties was a problem that went well beyond the normal consequences of easy money. A fiscal policy that focused narrowly on budget balancing was a major contributor to our difficulties. But faulty monetary policy certainly aggravated and prolonged the depression.

Another good example of how monetary policy contributed to generating a depression came in 1937–38, when the slow recovery from the miseries of 1933 was sharply reversed. In the course of 1936–37, the Federal Reserve Board *doubled* reserve requirements in an attempt to offset substantial inflows of gold resulting from political uncertainties in Europe following the rise of Adolph Hitler in Germany. But the policy sledge-hammered a still weak economy and buttressed a contractionary fiscal policy. The rate of growth of the money stock was reduced, long-term interest rates rose sharply, and havoc hit the bond market. Aggregate demand fell, and depression set in.

Each of these acts of omission or commission contributed to the seriousness of the economic slowdowns. Whether monetary policy can be said to have *caused* any of the three interwar depressions is a controversy historians are still attempting to untangle. But there is no doubt that in each case monetary policy produced serious destabilizing effects and that the downward movement of output and employment was aggravated by these errors.

The Federal Reserve does seem to have learned from its mistakes. Monetary policy has improved greatly since the end of World War II, and there have been no major depressions. There have, however, been recessions[2] in which national output has declined by as much as 3 percent and the unemployment rate has risen as high as 6 to 8 percent. The frequency of these recessions is depressing by itself (Table 17–2); in each of these episodes, as with the more serious interwar depressions, we can find contributory failures of monetary policy.

The record of U.S. economic performance during the past quarter century, characterized by these six recessions and three periods of significant price inflation, is far from satisfactory even if on balance it is superior to that of earlier years. The improvement can be attributed in part to progress in

---

[2] See Chapter 8, section 8.2.

TABLE 17–2

Recessions since World War II

Recession Period	Decline in Real GNP (peak to trough)		Peak Monthly Unemployment Rate (percent)
	(billions of 1958 dollars)	(percent of peak value)	
1948–49.............	−$ 6.2	1.9	7.9
1953–54.............	4.3	1.0	6.1
1957–58.............	17.7	3.9	7.5
1960–61.............	7.6	1.6	7.1
1969–70.............	9.9	1.4	6.1
1974–?.............	23.0*	2.7	6.5†

* As of the third quarter of 1974.
† As of November 1974.
Source: *Business Conditions Digest*, Department of Commerce.

Federal Reserve understanding of its responsibilities and of the instruments available to it. In part it can be attributed to the greater general stability of the economic environment in which the central bank must function. Our wars have placed smaller drains on our resources, and business and consumer confidence have been subjected to smaller shocks than formerly. And in any case, there clearly is ample room in which to improve the skill with which stabilization tools are utilized by both the fiscal and the monetary authorities.

17.2.2 Some Econometric Evidence

To untangle the relative importance of monetary policy and other factors as determinants of aggregate demand requires a more powerful methodology than that of simply reviewing observed historical facts. As helpful as the facts are by themselves, they are rich, complex, and ambiguous enough to deserve a formal econometric analysis.[3] And in fact, econ-

---

[3] Econometrics is the science of applying statistical methods to test mathematical representations of economic relationships. For a good introduction, see Edward J. Kane, *Economic Statistics and Econometrics* (New York: Harper & Row, 1968).

omists have conducted a large number of statistical experiments over the past 20 years—ever since large electronic computers have been available to do the work—in an attempt to answer the fundamental questions about the role of monetary policy.

There are two types of econometric tests of the linkages between monetary variables and aggregate demand. The simpler kind is to measure directly the statistical relationship between variables which policy makers can control (exogenous variables) and those which they can only influence indirectly (endogenous). Our model of the economy revealed two particularly important exogenous policy instruments: the monetary base, as one measure of monetary policy actions; and the amount of spending by the federal government, as one measure of fiscal policy actions. So a very elementary test can be made by a regression[4] of aggregate demand (nominal value of national product, either net or gross) on the monetary base and government spending. This type of test is known as a *reduced form*, because it reduces a large number of complex economic relationships into a single equation.

The other method is to estimate a *structural form* economic model. Recall that our simplified model consists of a set of functional or structural relationships: a consumption function, an investment function, a money demand function, and so on. A complete econometric model measures each of these relationships on the basis of observed data. We start with the raw numbers: for example, the value of total consumer spending and the value of disposable personal income in each quarter for 25 years. We then hypothesize that a certain form of relationship exists between them: when income rises, consumers will spend more. Next we test these hypotheses through regression analysis; we thereby determine how much additional consumption occurred in an average quarter for

---

[4] A regression is a statistical estimation of an assumed relationship between two or more variables.

each increment to disposable income. And finally, we can fit all these estimated functional relationships together to find out how a shock to the system will work its way through the economy, just as in Part Three we fit together the various graphs to get a qualitative impression of how, say, a shift in the money supply curve will disturb the equilibrium position of all the other relationships in the economy. This technique of feeding in a new value for one or more exogenous policy variables and measuring the impact on all of the model's endogenous variables is known as a *policy simulation* of the economy.

The most carefully conducted reduced form experiments on the U.S. economy were designed and run by two economists from the research department of the Federal Reserve Bank of St. Louis on the basis of quarterly data for the period 1952–68.[5] They—and subsequently some of their critics within the Federal Reserve System—tried a number of different specifications for their tests and obtained a variety of results. Perhaps the most interesting are those which correspond closely to what many economists would consider the true theoretical structure of the economy. In these tests, the exogenous instrument of monetary policy is the unborrowed component of the monetary base, and the instruments of fiscal policy are the levels of spending and receipts in the federal government budget which would be obtained if the economy were fully employed. Nominal gross national product was regressed against these three variables simultaneously.[6]

The results of that test are striking in that they suggest that monetary policy—but not fiscal policy—has a powerful effect

---

[5] Leonall Andersen and Jerry Jordan, "Monetary and Fiscal Actions: A Test of Their Relative Importance in Economic Stabilization," Federal Reserve Bank of St. Louis *Review* 50, November 1968.

[6] This version of the test was run by Frank deLeeuw and John Kalchbrenner of the Federal Reserve Board's staff in a comment on the Andersen–Jordan article; Federal Reserve Bank of St. Louis *Review* 51, April 1969.

on nominal GNP. An increase of $1 billion in the unborrowed component of the monetary base is calculated to drive up aggregate demand by more than $12 billion over a two-year period.[7] An increase in federal expenditures of the same magnitude produces an anemic $600 million response, and a comparable tax cut has an even smaller effect. Almost half of the variation of GNP around its growth trend is unexplained by the test and is presumed to result from a variety of unspecified nonpolicy influences. These results obviously conflict with the interpretation of the historical evidence presented above, and they have generated a substantial controversy ever since they were first published.

There are three major problems with the St. Louis results and with reduced-form estimates in general. One is that they are highly sensitive to the exact specification of the exogenous variables. When the unborrowed monetary base is replaced by the supply of money, the apparent potency of monetary policy is greatly increased, simply because the latter estimates pick up the influence of changes in GNP on the stock of money as well as the influence of money on GNP. Since this "reverse causation" is less pronounced for the more closely controlled monetary base, the corresponding multipliers also are smaller.[8] But economists do not agree as to which of all possible measures of the monetary base is really best, so the interpretation of the results remains ambiguous.

A second problem is that reduced-form estimates suffer from all the diseases of simplistic analyses of complex problems. There are far more exogenous influences on GNP than anyone could fit into a single equation; whichever are se-

---

[7] To be precise, suppose that the monetary base had been $1 billion higher than its actual value for just one quarter during the period examined. The statistical estimate is that a total of $12 billion more income would have resulted and that this effect would have been spread out over two years. We examine the reasons for the delay in the next section (17.3).

[8] This sensitivity causes some intricate complications. When, for example, one measures *monetary* policy by unborrowed reserves rather than by the unborrowed monetary base, the *fiscal* policy multipliers increase several fold.

lected will inevitably pick up a part of these other factors as well. If the Federal Reserve happened to increase the availability of bank reserves in the same calendar quarter that a drought in the Soviet Union increased foreign demand for our wheat crop, the estimated equation would erroneously attribute most of the rise in GNP that quarter to monetary policy.

The third problem, which may be the most serious in this context, is that reduced-form tests measure only the effects which have in fact occurred in the past, not the impact that could have been achieved by different policies. Fiscal policy probably fares badly in this test because it has been *applied* badly over the past two decades. Federal spending often has been increased when the economy already is picking up steam (as in the mid-1960s); its impact on total spending is inevitably much smaller at such times than it would be during a slump because the government expenditures will tend to crowd out private spending to some extent.[9] It therefore is not surprising that little statistical relationship has been found in regressions of GNP on actual federal spending.

Large-scale structural models attempt to meet these problems head-on. Modern structural models usually contain more than 100 separate equations, each one estimating a specific functional relationship. Simulations with these models permit the economist to estimate the effects that could have resulted had the Federal Reserve followed a different policy from that actually pursued. It is less important to be able to determine before we begin whether the unborrowed monetary base is "more exogenous" than the money supply, since we are con-

---

[9] For an introduction to this crowding out effect, see R. W. Spencer and W. P. Yohe, "The 'Crowding Out' of Private Expenditures by Fiscal Actions," *Federal Reserve Bank of St. Louis Review* 52, October 1970, pp. 12–24. For an analysis of the ineffectiveness of fiscal policy and its relationship to reduced-form statistical tests, see George M. von Furstenberg and James M. Boughton, "Stabilization Goals and the Appropriateness of Fiscal Policy during the Eisenhower and Kennedy-Johnson Administrations," *Public Finance Quarterly* 1 (January 1973): 5–28.

structing a hypothetical policy of our own. We can hold constant all the myriad of other exogenous forces that appear in the model. And even if monetary or fiscal policies have been bungled in the past, we still have a chance to find out whether they might be effective if applied differently in the future.

One highly regarded and particularly detailed simulation of monetary and other policy influences on GNP was performed by economists from the staff of the Federal Reserve Board, using a model constructed by the board's staff and by a number of university economists.[10] This quasi-structural model, which contains a total of more than 100 equations, is based on the type of theoretical model described throughout Part Three of this book.

The simulations performed with the Board model[11] include tests of both monetary and fiscal instruments, each of which individually is assumed to follow a different time path from the one actually observed, over a period of several years. What if the supply of reserves through open market operations had been consistently higher than it actually was? What if the government had hired additional workers? What if personal income tax rates had been lower, so that smaller tax revenues would be collected at a given level of income?

The money multipliers derived from these simulations differ little from those calculated directly from the St. Louis

---

[10] See Frank deLeeuw and Edward M. Gramlich, "The Channels of Monetary Policy," *Federal Reserve Bulletin* 55 (June 1969), pp. 472–91.

[11] Anyone rummaging through the professional literature on this topic will find references to the "Board" model under a variety of names in addition to the clean and simple one which we have chosen. It originally was constructed by a team from the Federal Reserve Board and from the Massachusetts Institute of Technology, and it sometimes is called the Board-MIT or FRB-MIT model. Later, a group from the University of Pennsylvania came aboard; FRB-MIT-PENN was a tiresome appellation, so the FMP model was born. Our own favorite is the MAD model, after three of the principal model-builders: Franco Modigliani of MIT, Albert Ando of Pennsylvania, and Frank deLeeuw of the Federal Reserve Board.

reduced-form equations. A $1 billion rise in unborrowed reserves would gradually drive up the nominal value of GNP; after two years, total income would be about $15 billion higher than in the absence of the policy shift (compared to $12 billion, as reported above). But the effects of *fiscal* policies now are estimated to be strong as well. A $1 billion rise in the real value of federal wage payments would, according to the Board simulations, produce close to $3 billion of new GNP after two years; thus a $1 billion open market operation and a $5 billion per year federal wage payment are roughly comparable expansionary policies. Similar impacts also follow from a tax cut of 4 percentage points (i.e., a reduction in federal tax revenues of about $9 billion per year at the initial level of income).

Most of the available econometric evidence, like the raw historical evidence, clearly indicates the importance of monetary policy as a determinant of aggregate demand. The evidence from structural models suggests with equal force that shifts in government spending have a powerful impact on the economy. All of which implies that monetary policy plays a crucial and very delicate role in the economy. The worst policy errors of the past, such as the doubling of reserve requirements in 1936–37, demonstrate the independently destabilizing force of monetary policy. All of our major inflationary periods of the 20th century demonstrate the consequences of a passive and accommodative monetary policy when fiscal policy is playing the role of destabilizer. Somewhere between these extremes must lie a design for the conduct of monetary policy that would enable this loaded gun to serve us better on the side of economic stability; the improved record of the past 25 years indeed offers some grounds for optimism. But can we ever hope for perfection, for a policy strategy that can fine-tune the economy well enough to eliminate both recession and inflation? Or are the problems too severe and too complex?

17.3   MONETARY POLICY LAGS

One major barrier to policy effectiveness which is unlikely ever to be completely breached is the existence of long lags in the execution and transmission of policy actions. It is not sufficient that an open market security operation affect aggregate expenditures. It is not even sufficient that the Federal Reserve always take the right amount of action in the right direction. Equally important is the timing with which expenditures are affected by the policy actions.

Countercyclical monetary action normally requires the Federal Reserve to attempt to induce additional expenditures during recessionary periods and to curtail demand during inflationary booms. They can try, and they do try, to foresee the need for evasive maneuvers to head off the income cycle. Nonetheless, the more quickly the System can induce or curtail expenditures, the more effective will countercyclical policies be. The longer the delay, the greater is the risk that the effect will be nugatory or even perverse.

17.3.1   Types of Lags

Monetary policy lags are the result of two quite different processes, known as the *inside* lag and the *outside* lag. The first delay involves (1) the recognition by Federal Reserve System officials that the time for action has arrived and (2) the actual undertaking of the policy action. The inside lag thus consists of the time between the true need for countercyclical action and the observed change in the policy instrument.

The main reason that the inside lag presents problems for the Federal Reserve is that economic turning points usually are characterized by conflicting information. The beginning months of a recession may still exhibit quite a bit of price inflation, stable rates of unemployment, strong demand for money and for bank loans; throughout the country, stocks of unsold inventories may be piling up even though only a few major sectors of the economy are experiencing a true slump in demand. As the various pieces of data begin to filter in to the FOMC, the committee members will begin to debate whether expansionary action is required. Months could slip by before a consensus evolves that the economy is in trouble.

Improvements in the forecasting ability of the staff economists of the FOMC are bound to shorten the inside lag. Conceivably, this component of the lag could even be negative if the staff were able to predict the onset of recession or excessive growth far enough in advance. But good forecasting is not enough. The execution of a countercyclical policy, particularly one based on prediction rather than hard data, is an administrative process requiring discretion and leadership. The decision makers of the Federal Reserve must have the courage to act decisively and must know when to be steadfast in the conduct of unpopular policies. Either inadequate knowledge of the economy or weak leadership can contribute to the lengthening of the inside lag of monetary policy.

The outside lag consists of the time between a change in an instrument of policy and the consequent change in the goal variables. It differs from the inside lag in two ways. First, it results from economic rather than political processes. If it takes an instrumental action a long time to affect the rate of unemployment, it is not the fault of the decision maker; it is a natural consequence of the way our economy is organized. Second, the outside lag is distributed over time, whereas the inside lag is a discrete interval. A change in the discount rate may have some immediate effect on bank lending and even on total spending in the economy. But its total impact will be spread out, perhaps over a very long stretch of time. We therefore have to measure the outside lag in terms of a maximum impact or in terms of the time required for half of the full impact to occur, or some other summary datum. It would not help us to look for the total length of the lag, and in any case we probably would grow old while we waited.

The outside lag in turn has a number of components, corresponding to the various stages of the transmission chain. First, there may occur a delay, usually very short, between a change in a policy instrument and the effect on the proximate targets. In the case of open market operations, this *reserve-market lag* should be nonexistent; the purchase of a treasury bill by the Federal Reserve immediately creates bank reserves and drives down the market yields on bills. Selective instruments such as Regulation Q ceilings or moral suasion could involve longer initial response times. And sometimes the Federal Reserve may impose an initial lag in order to soften the impact of the policy shift. Whenever reserve requirements are raised, the System normally conducts expansionary open market operations for a week or two, giving the banks time to adjust their portfolios gradually.

The further we get from the source, the longer become the lags in response. The next component is that between the proximate and intermediate targets, which we may call the *credit-market lag*. A change in bank reserve availability may directly and immediately change the stock of money, but only to the extent that the Fed buys assets from the nonbank public; only as banks react by purchasing earning assets and making loans to their customers will the monetary aggregates respond fully to the policy action. Depending on circumstances, this adjustment process could take quite a while. Certainly if the Federal Reserve were to make available additional reserves at a time when banks already were flush and loan demand was weak, we should not expect a very quick or very large response in the stock of money or bank credit.

Another part of this slice of the lag is the delay between changes in short-term money-market rates and long-term bond yields. We saw in Chapter 16 that the term structure of interest rates does not offer the Federal Reserve a very stable channel through which to transmit policy actions. Only when short-term rates stay above or below their former levels for some length of time will investors begin to arbitrage among different maturities to any great extent. If the FOMC were able to alter quickly the markets' expectations about the future course of short-term rates, they could shorten this part of the lag quite a bit. But most of the time, the money market initially views rate changes as temporary, and the bond markets are unmoved.

The longest lags occur at the end of the chain, between the intermediate targets and the goal variables: the *product-market lag*. As we showed in the last chapter, monetary policy works largely through its influence on the capital expenditures of businesses and consumers for housing, factories, capital equipment, and the like. All of these expenditures take time to plan and carry through. It was not only Rome which was not built in a day; neither was Barkley dam nor the Fairless steel works.

When, for example, a corporation constructs a new plant, it goes through several stages before it turns on the conveyer belts. First, it decides to go ahead with the project on the basis of its own estimates about the future course of the economy and the expected costs of raising the funds. Note that a substantial change in interest rates may be necessary before monetary policy can significantly affect business expectations about future financing costs; meanwhile, corporate planning goes on as before. The second stage is to appropriate the funds and let the contracts for construction, a process which normally takes several months. And finally, the actual investment expenditures are spread out over the whole construction period. The resulting lag between an initial change in long-term bond yields or other measures of the cost or availability of credit (the intermediate targets) and the actual flow of investment expenditure can be very long indeed.

17.3.2 The Length of the Lags

As this review suggests, most of the lag in the effects of monetary policy is concentrated in the response of output, income, and prices to changes in monetary variables; the part we have called the product-market lag. Even in the 1950s, the Federal Reserve had the ability to forecast turning points in economic activity well enough to render minimal the inside lag.[12] With the advent of large-scale econometric forecasting models, there no longer is any serious excuse not to act promptly in advance of the development of instability in the economy. If the goal is to reduce inflation, we usually can see it coming before it hits us, and the Fed can begin to restrict monetary growth. If the goal is to maintain full employment, the System should be able to forecast the approach of recessionary pressures and head them off by encouraging the expansion of money and credit. What may induce an inside lag of up to several months, however, is a situation in which inflation and recession both charge the forecasters at the same time, short-circuiting the will to act in either direction. Nonetheless, the bulk of the evidence now available does not point to a significant inside lag for most Federal Reserve policy decisions.

The credit-market lag is less subject to influence by improvements in the conduct of policy, since it results primarily from delays in the adjustment of commercial bank asset portfolios to changes in the availability of reserves. But bankers also are becoming more sophisticated. During the 1950s, it may have taken as long as a year for the bulk of the effect of changes in the monetary base to be reflected in the stock of money held by the public. Since that time, banks have reduced their average holdings of excess reserves practically

---

[12] See Karl Brunner and Allan Meltzer, *The Federal Reserve's Attachment to the Free Reserve Concept.* Report prepared for the subcommittee on Domestic Finance of the Committee on Banking and Currency, U.S. House of Representatives, 1964.

out of existence; they have developed efficient markets (chiefly, the Federal funds market; see Chapter 14, section 14.3.1) for transferring reserve balances from areas with little loan demand to those with high demand; and the larger banks are able to examine their portfolios of loans, securities, and reserves every day and, with the aid of their computers, to determine very quickly the adjustments necessary to increase their profits. Consequently, changes in the availability of reserves are rapidly transmitted through the financial markets, and the stock of money responds accordingly. This part of the lag probably now averages no longer than two or three months.[13]

One of the longest sources of the monetary policy lag is the time required for completion of business investment projects, for the various reasons described above. Thomas Mayer, an economist from the University of California, once estimated average lags of 6 months from the time investment plans initially are drawn to the placement of the first orders for construction; 2 more months to the actual start of construction; and 15 additional months until the completion of the project.[14] Furthermore, a substantial length of time may be required for changes in the cost or availability of funds for financing these projects to affect the initial plans. So the potential exists for a product-market lag averaging more than two years.

To measure the total product-market lag requires either a full-scale model of the economy, in order to include all of the possible effects of monetary policy on spending and income, or a reduced-form equation which includes lagged values of policy instruments as determining variables. The two studies referred to earlier in this chapter therefore can provide us not

---

[13] See Richard G. Davis, "How Much Does Money Matter? A Look at Some Recent Evidence," Federal Reserve Bank of New York *Monthly Review* 51 (June 1969), pp. 119–31.

[14] Thomas Mayer, "Plant and Equipment Lead Times," *Journal of Business*, April 1960.

only with estimates of the size of the impact of monetary policy on income but also of the time required for the effect to be felt.

The reduced-form tests reveal a quick initial impact from monetary policy actions which builds up gradually over a two-year period. Of the total $12 billion response in GNP, the bulk occurs between 6 and 15 months after the open market operation; about half is completed within one year, and all of the impact that can be measured by this technique is felt within two years.[15] This response lag is not trivial, because it requires monetary policy decisions to be made several months in advance of the desired maximum impact. But it is quite a bit shorter than we might have been led to believe by examining the individual elements of the total lag.

The simulations performed with the Board model show somewhat longer lags; the effects of open market operations on GNP actually continue to accumulate for three full years, to a maximum of more than $20 billion. Less than $1 billion appears in the first quarter, and about $6½ billion (32 percent) after one year. The biggest increases in GNP show up between 9 and 18 months after the policy action.

There is no question that a significant lag exists in the effects of monetary policy. Experiments with a structural model are more likely to reveal the full extent of the lag than are the reduced-form tests because the large models directly incorporate all of the individual parts of the lag while the single-equation tests must rely on rather arbitrary statistical techniques for estimating a general lag structure. But even the simplest techniques often show lagged responses that are both long and variable. Milton Friedman several years ago compared the timing of peaks and troughs in the rate of

---

[15] The original equations estimated by Andersen and Jordan had computed lags only of one year; the later estimates by deLeeuw and Kalchbrenner lengthened the lag to two years. The immediate impact of open market operations as calculated by deLeeuw and Kalchbrenner is actually negative, an apparent statistical anomaly.

change in the money stock with peaks and troughs in general business activity.[16] The monetary peaks, he found, preceded the business peaks by a minimum of 6 months and a maximum of 29 months. Comparing troughs, the lags ranged from 4 to 22 months. Taking all of this information into account, it appears reasonable to conclude that the biggest impacts of monetary policy actions on incomes will usually occur between half a year and 1½ years later.

17.4   RULES FOR THE CONDUCT OF POLICY

The Fed faces an almost Herculean assignment. It has an interest in achieving several difficult and important goals, including the avoidance both of recessions and inflations; for tools, it must rely largely on its control over the cost and availability of reserves to commercial banks; and consequently, uncertainty and delay stand between any actions it takes and the results it expects. It therefore is not surprising that the System has had only mixed success over the years in achieving economic stability. The answer to the question we posed a few pages back—can we ever hope for perfection?—is beginning to answer itself.

Some economists—we encounter again the name of Milton Friedman—have responded to the difficulty of this task by urging circumscription of the role of monetary policy.[17] It is possible that a rule or a set of rules for the behavior of the stock of money, the level of interest rates, or some other variable would produce better economic performance than the discretionary countercyclical actions now taken by the Board of Governors and the Federal Open Market Committee. Before we judge this recommendation, we should examine the possibilities a bit more closely.

---

[16] Milton Friedman, "The Lag in Effect of Monetary Policy," *Journal of Political Economy*, October 1961.

[17] Milton Friedman, *A Program for Monetary Stability* (Bronx, N.Y.: Fordham University Press, 1959).

17.4.1   Interest Rates versus Aggregates Revisited

Most economists who recommend the imposition of rules for the conduct of monetary policy have in mind a fixed rate of growth for the stock of money. But it is no less plausible to envision a rule such as the one the Fed actually followed in the 1940s, viz pegging interest rates at a certain level. In fact, if the officials of the Federal Reserve had complete information about the economy and could describe it by a model like the one described in Part Three of this book, it would make no difference which rule were followed.

Figure 17–1 recalls the money and expenditure sectors of the model. By controlling the monetary base, the Federal Reserve controls both the stock of money and the level of interest rates simultaneously. Now if total desired expenditure is to grow at a steady rate over time, the expenditure-equilibrium (EE) curve will be shifting steadily to the right. The Federal Reserve can accommodate this growth either by buying enough securities in the open market to expand the supply of money at a steady rate or by buying enough to prevent the level of interest rates from rising. One policy implies the other, and the choice is a matter of taste. In either case the monetary equilibrium (ME) curve shifts to the right at the same pace as the EE curve.

The difficulty arises when we introduce some uncertainty into our model or when we allow for the influence of other exogenous forces. These equilibrium curves are useful constructs, but we should not pretend to be able to measure them precisely. The EE curve shows us the most likely value of income corresponding to each level of interest rates when the markets for expenditure on goods and services are in equilibrium. In practice, a drop in interest rates may produce a smaller than predicted increase in business investment if business managers think that the drop is merely temporary. A rise in consumers' marginal propensity to save will shift the

FIGURE 17-1

Equilibrium in the Money and Expenditure Markets

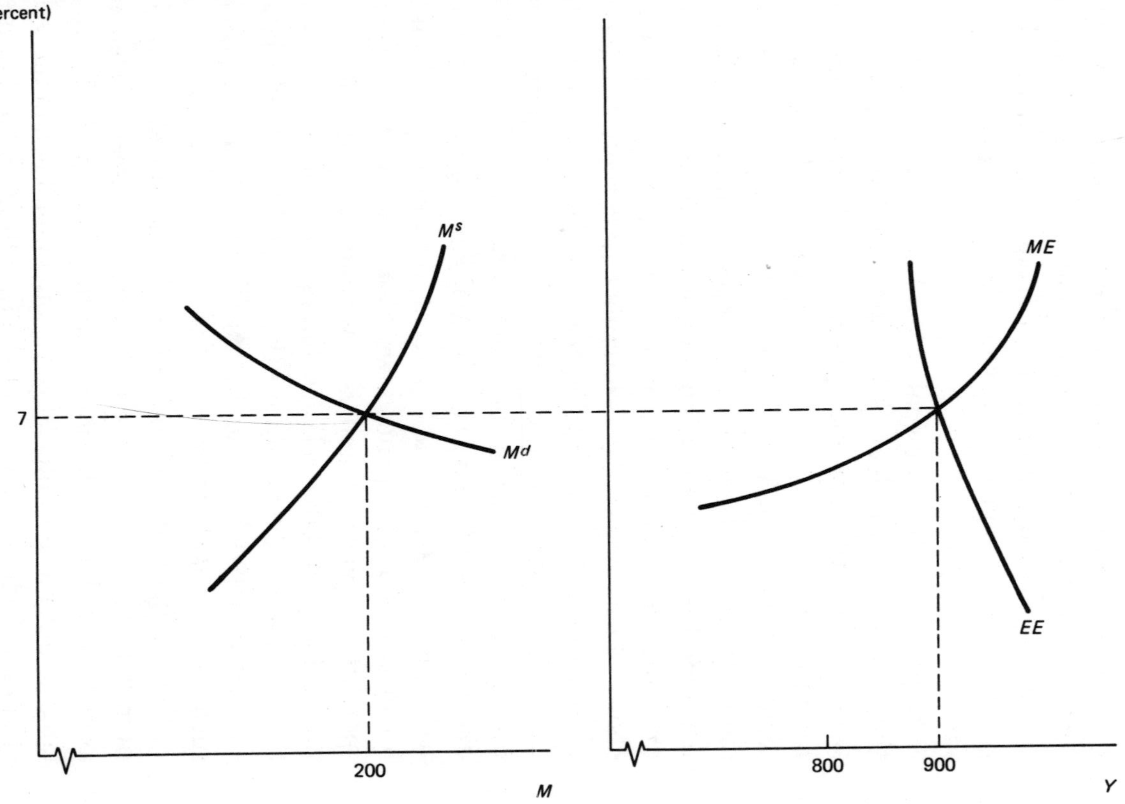

whole curve to the left. A tax cut will shift it to the right. Any factor that alters the consumption, investment, or government expenditure functions described in Chapter 8 will push the *EE* curve around. As these factors are not always predictable or even perceptible, the *EE* curve should actually be described as a range of values rather than a single line (Figure 17–2).

Suppose now that the goal of the Federal Reserve is to see the net national product (Y) at $900 billion. A lower value would imply excessive unemployment; a higher value would be impossible to achieve for long, since inflation of prices would eat away the income gains. There is no way to construct a policy that will guarantee success so long as the exact nature of the *EE* relationship is uncertain. The Fed can, however, minimize the degree of uncertainty by making a wise choice of rules regarding its intermediate targets. If it focuses on the stock of money, fixing the *ME* curve at the location shown in Figure 17–2, it can limit the range of possible values for income between the points labeled Y_1 and Y_2 in the diagram (points C and D on the *ME* curve). But if it should try to peg interest rates at 7 percent, the range of possibilities for income would expand down to Y_0 and up to Y_3 (corresponding to points A and B). A policy of pegging interest rates relies on a stable relationship between interest rates and the demand for expenditures; the less stable is that relationship (summarized by the *EE* curve), the less successful is such a policy likely to be.

The problem does not end here, for the monetary equilibrium curve may be subject to random or unseen movements as well. The demand for money in the economy is closely related to income and interest rates, but confidence in the value of money—which can be eroded either through bank or other corporate failures or through the onset of inflation—plays a role as well, one that is all but impossible to measure or predict. The supply of money is determined primarily by move-

FIGURE 17–2

Uncertainty in the Expenditure Market

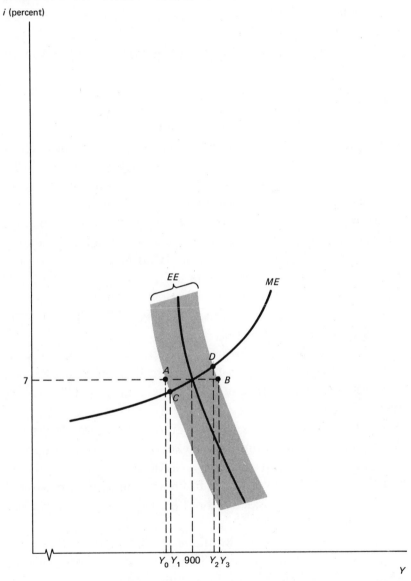

ments in the monetary base, but consumer and business preferences for time deposits—especially, in recent years, for high-yielding certificates of deposit—often influence and sometimes dominate changes in supply. So, as shown in Figure 17–3, the *ME* curve also should be represented as a range of values.

One can readily determine that uncertainty in the market for money balances has exactly the opposite effect on the choice of an intermediate-target rule as does uncertainty in the expenditure market. By attempting to control the money stock, the Federal Reserve can only limit the variation in income to the range from Y_4 to Y_5 (points E and F); by pegging the level of interest rates, it can—in the absence of uncertainty about the *EE* curve—also peg the level of income exactly at $900 billion. A policy of aiming for a fixed value of the stock of money, which in our dynamic economy implies a fixed rate of growth over time, relies on stable supply and demand functions for money. The less stable are those relationships (summarized by the *ME* curve), the less successful is such a policy likely to be.

If both sets of functions are known only approximately, as anyone who has ever tried to estimate them will attest, then it is not clear that *any* kind of rule will be beneficial to the performance of monetary policy. An eclectic approach in which the Fed keeps track of movements in interest rates and in the stock of money and tries to keep both within as narrow a range as possible may in this case be necessary in order to minimize undesired variations in income; in short, exactly the kind of policy pursued by the Federal Reserve in various ways since 1951.

The reader may well complain at this point that we are painting a gloomy picture. The present system, with its eclectic efforts to head off all manner of economic shocks, has failed to eliminate the cycle of recessions and inflations that have characterized our economy throughout its history;

FIGURE 17–3

Uncertainty in the Market for Money Balances

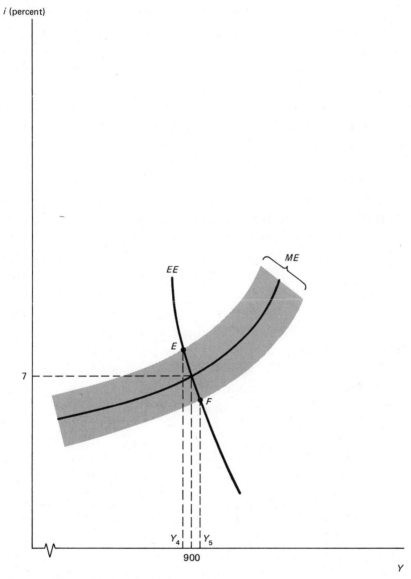

though it has succeeded in limiting both frequency and amplitudes. But we have painted in some clouds over the proposal to simplify procedures by imposing rules of conduct. We hasten to add that these clouds do not counsel acceptance of the status quo; they imply only that the evidence now available, as we read it, is inconclusive as to whether a fixed rate of growth in the money stock or a fixed level of interest rates or some other policy would be in any sense best. There is too much about the economy that we and you and the Fed do not yet know.

There is a sizeable group of economists who disagree with the conclusions which we have just drawn; economists who, like Milton Friedman, believe that the monetary relationships in the economy are stable enough to warrant a recommendation for steady monetary growth. We have tried to avoid labeling people in this book, out of a general distaste for the practice. But most of the economists to whom we now refer would not object to being called "monetarists," and many of them would not even object to being called "Friedmaniacs." They are, for economists, a remarkably homogeneous group. But there is one small point about which monetarists have a great deal of trouble agreeing among themselves. They all agree that money is important and that it is quite different from everything else, but they do not all agree on what it is.

17.4.2   The Definition of Money

In the beginning, we defined the word: *money* is any asset which is widely used in an economy as the means of payment. We further noted that the two assets which most closely meet this definition for the United States are currency and demand deposits, and we have worked with that concept throughout this book. But that practice varnishes over some troublesome issues in the application of monetary theory to real-world problems. If the Federal Reserve is to attempt to control the flow of economic activity through its influence on the stock of money, then economists have a responsibility to determine a precise definition of money which maximizes that control; the one we have chosen may or may not be optimal in that sense. If Congress is to pass laws regulating the activities of financial institutions, with an objective of stabilizing and securing the means of payment for the economy, then legislators must know which assets are widely used as media of exchange; there may be others than the ones on which we have concentrated our attention.

The Federal Reserve Board distinguishes three measures of the stock of money (Figure 17–4). The first (called M_1) corresponds to the definition used throughout this book. The second (M_2) is equal to M_1 plus "net" time deposits, i.e., total time deposits less negotiable certificates of deposit. The third (M_3) adds to M_2 the value of deposits at mutual savings banks and shares of savings and loan associations. And this list obviously is far from exhaustive.

There really are two issues at stake in this discussion. One is measurement: the choice of assets to put into the box called "money." The other is the definition of the box itself. But though this second issue has logical priority over the first (how can we fill up an undefined box?), it cannot be resolved without some reference to the properties of the specific assets waiting to go into it; hence the difficulty which economists face in agreeing on a single definition.

For example, suppose that we pursue the "medium of exchange" definition of money to its essence. Clearly, currency is the first asset to go into that box. But then someone hands us a $1,000 bill. Is this an asset which can be widely used in payment? Or is it a near-money asset, one that we should consider as monetary in nature but not actually money? Similar difficulties arise with demand deposits; checking account

FIGURE 17–4

Three Measures of the Money Stock, 1959–73

Billions of Dollars

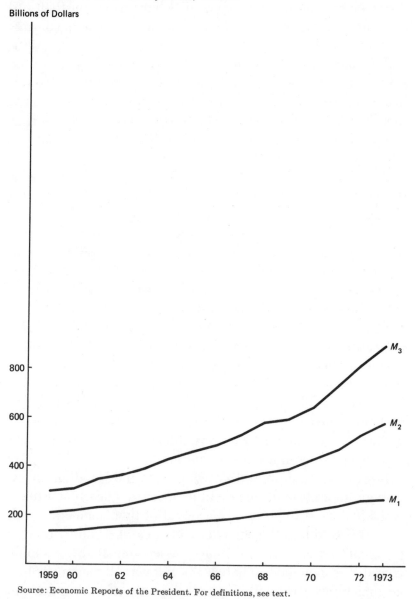

Source: Economic Reports of the President. For definitions, see text.

balances are readily transferable in some circumstances but not in others, notably where the owner of the account is not known to the person to whom he is making payment. And the issue becomes even more complex when we begin to consider other assets.

Travelers' checks are widely used as a medium of exchange, but they do not circulate at all: they are used once and then retired. When we try to include the outstanding stock of travelers' checks as part of the money stock, we can never tell how much room they take up in the box. Credit cards also are widely used. To the extent that the card-holder is able to postpone payments a month or so without incurring any additional liabilities, his line of credit constitutes an asset with all of the properties of money. But how are we to measure this value? It seems that we have defined a box of indeterminate dimensions.

The ambiguity of the medium-of-exchange definition has led some economists to define money as a store of value which is fixed in price in terms of the unit of account. A dollar of currency will always exchange for a dollar of anything. So will a dollar of checking account deposits. You would be very surprised indeed if tomorrow the price of a $1.00 Federal Reserve note were quoted at $.95 or you were told that your checking account could be drawn upon only at $.90 to the dollar. Similarly we expect a dollar of time deposit accounts (including negotiable certificates of deposit) or of savings and loan shares to exchange at par. Series E savings bonds, issued by the U.S. Treasury, can always be redeemed at a fixed and known price. So can travelers' checks and too many other assets to list here.

The definition of money as a fixed-price store of value does not resolve all of the problems raised by the medium-of-exchange definition, but it is less ambiguous. Its biggest failing is that it is such a broad and encompassing concept. As we noted at the outset of this discussion, money should be defined so as to be useful to us in solving real problems. For most problems related to monetary policy, a definition which is big enough to include all fixed-price assets is likely to be too big to wield.

Instead of treating the definition of money as a purely logical puzzle, we might think of it as an empirical problem the solution to which depends upon observation and experimentation. If we can first identify our objectives in defining money, then we can test for the measure of money which best serves our purposes. This approach begs the question of definition, replacing it with the simpler question of measurement; but even this simplification has not resolved the issue.

One empirical method for distinguishing money from other assets is to start with a basic measurement (usually currency plus demand deposits) and then to test whether adding or subtracting similar assets reduces the stability of the demand function for money. The researcher estimates statistical functions (regressions) of various measures of money on income and interest rates or on some similar set of variables, and then selects the measure which is best explained by this function. The difficulty is that the results depend sensitively on the form of the demand function chosen for the experiment; the tests to date have been inconclusive.

A closely related type of test is to correlate rates of change in various measures of the stock of money with the rate of change in GNP. If one is interested in locating a collection of assets the control of which will also result in control over GNP, this test will provide an initial basis for the choice. But the only conclusion to come out of this line of effort is that the relative correlation varies over time. Up to 1960, M_2 seems to have been more closely related to GNP than M_1; during the 1960s, the narrow measure performs better.[18] As interest

---

[18] See, for example, Karl Brunner and Allan H. Meltzer, "Predicting Velocity: Implications for Theory and Policy," *Journal of Finance*, May 1963; and George Kaufman, "More on an Empirical Definition of Money," *American Economic Review*, March 1969.

rates change, as the nature of the assets evolves, as people's understanding of alternatives improves, the relationships between these assets and spending also changes.

Two other types of empirical test have provided marginally clearer evidence in support of the limitation of money to currency plus demand deposits. One test is to compare the substitutability of demand and time deposits; what happens to the demand for demand deposits when the price of time deposits (the yield) varies?[19] Economist Edgar Feige of the University of Wisconsin concluded from extensive research that the substitutability of demand deposits and other liquid assets was relatively low.[20]

A final consideration, one which is of central importance for the formulation of monetary policy, is the controllability of whatever set of assets we choose. The evidence on this point, though scarce, gives a slight edge to the narrow definition (M_1). Allan Meltzer, a prominent monetarist, has correlated changes in two measures of the money stock—M_1 and M_2—with variables over which the Federal Reserve or the Treasury have a strong influence (the monetary base and the level of treasury deposits at commercial banks). He found that these variables accounted for a higher portion of variations in the narrower stock than in M_2 (85 percent against 75 percent).[21] Federal Reserve officials probably could control either measure fairly closely on a yearly or even quarterly basis if they were strongly interested in doing so. But they

---

[19] Substitutability may be measured by the "cross-elasticity of demand," which is defined as the percentage change in the demand for one good in response to a given percentage change in the price of another. A value of zero implies no substitutability; a value of minus infinity implies perfect substitutability (try changing the price of nickels and see what happens to the demand for dimes); a positive value normally implies that the two goods are complements rather than substitutes.

[20] See Edgar L. Feige, *The Demand for Liquid Assets: A Temporal Cross-Section Analysis* (Englewood Cliffs, N.J.: Prentice Hall, 1964). For a contrasting view, see Tong Hun Lee, "Substitutability of Non-bank Intermediary Liabilities for Money," *Journal of Finance*, September 1966.

[21] Allan Meltzer, "Controlling Money," *Federal Reserve Bank of St. Louis Review* (May 1969), pp. 18–19.

would have a slightly more difficult task by including time deposits in their target.

17.5 CONCLUSIONS

This final chapter has focused on some of the major problems facing the Federal Reserve System in the formulation and implementation of monetary policy. The multiple goals of those making policy decisions often conflict. The instruments must be used with sensitivity in order for the System to avoid disrupting the stability of the banking system or the flow of credit to sectors of the economy which are heavily dependent on credit. The transmission of policy actions is a long and uncertain process. We have seen that monetary policy has not always been applied wisely in our history, but that its performance has improved in recent years. We have analyzed some recommendations for further improvement but have been hesitant in passing them on without reservation.

We would not wish to leave the reader with the impression that these problems are so severe as to render monetary policy a dangerous or even an inadequate weapon. Monetary policy is an important stabilization tool, one which has played and will continue to play a critical role in both the stability and the growth of our economy. But the limitations of monetary policy must be stressed. It cannot solve all of the country's economic problems. It cannot substitute for and cannot alone produce good management, efficient technology, a strong labor force. But a poorly executed monetary policy can upset and could even destroy an otherwise sound economy, either by choking off the flow of credit and corroding confidence in the banking system or by flooding the economy with funds and corroding confidence in the value of money. A constructive monetary policy, in short, is a necessary but not a sufficient condition for economic health.

It also must be stressed that monetary policy is but one

weapon in the government arsenal. Fiscal policies, the decisions of the federal government regarding the level of spending and of taxation, are an equal partner with monetary policy in the control of aggregate demand. Efforts by the government or by private industry to improve productivity or to stimulate employment can supplement demand management by shifting the aggregate supply curve for the economy; these supply policies can help to reduce the inflationary costs of policies designed to raise employment by stimulating spending and incomes. Further support in that direction may be provided by "incomes" policies, whether in the form of direct controls over prices and wages or in the guise of governmental persuasion; to the extent that such policies could reduce the expectation of price inflation, they could lead to a further reduction of inflationary pressures. But if incomes policies are to be at all beneficial, they must be accompanied by monetary and fiscal policies which themselves are not contributing to inflationary pressures. The U.S. experience with price controls from 1971 through 1973 provides an example of the perverse results from applying controls when governmental policies are accelerating aggregate demand.

Though monetary policy must be applied cautiously, it cannot be applied according to a fixed dogma or an inflexible set of rules. The demand for money in the United States is an empirically stable phenomenon. The relationship between monetary growth and income growth can be predicted with greater accuracy than most other macroeconomic relationships, with the possible exception of the ratio of consumer saving to disposable income. It is also true that the rate of growth of the stock of money can be strongly influenced by Federal Reserve actions and that over sufficiently long periods of time (perhaps a year) monetary policy can be used to control the growth of money (or of M_2) rather closely. Within limits, the Federal Reserve could instead stabilize interest rates. But our economy still is not predictable enough to enable one to conclude that monetary stability will always lead to income stability. Countercyclical monetary policies may go wrong, but that is no reason to stop hoping that they may go right. We shall continue to search for rules that will aid the formulation of monetary policy. But no rules will ever substitute for the wisdom of men and women who know when to violate them.

REVIEW QUESTIONS

1. What is an "accommodative" monetary policy? Under what circumstances will it contribute to inflation?
2. On the basis of the econometric and historical evidence presented in this chapter, what policies would you have recommended to cure the recession of 1970? (Review Chapter 8 if necessary). How early should these policies have been adopted in order to avoid the recession completely?
4. Why is it important to define money specifically?

SUGGESTED FURTHER READING

Davis, Richard. "How Much Does Money Matter? A Look at Some Recent Evidence." Federal Reserve Bank of New York *Monthly Review* 51, June 1969.

Fisher, Gordon and David Sheppard. *Effects of Monetary Policy on the United States Economy: A Survey of Econometric Evidence.* OECD Economic Outlook: Occasional Studies, December 1972.

Friedman, Milton. *A Program for Monetary Stability.* Bronx, N.Y.: Fordham University Press, 1959.

Hamburger, Michael J. "The Lag in the Effect of Monetary Policy: A Survey of Recent Literature." Federal Reserve Bank of New York *Monthly Review* 53, December 1971.

Index

Index

This book is set in 12 and 10 point Caledonia, leaded 2 points. Part numbers are 24 point (small) Helvetica Medium and part titles are 24 point (small) Helvetica. Chapter numbers are 18 point Helvetica and chapter titles are 18 point Helvetica Medium. The size of the type page is 26 x 43½ picas.